1981

THE COLONIAL LEGACY

THE
COLONIAL LEGACY

VOLUME III

Historians of Nature
and Man's Nature

VOLUME IV

Early Nationalist Historians

Edited by
LAWRENCE H. LEDER

Harper & Row, Publishers
New York, Evanston, San Francisco, London

CONTENTS

VOLUME IV EARLY NATIONALIST HISTORIANS

Prefatory Note

The historians discussed in these two volumes—as well as in the two previous volumes, *The Loyalist Historians* and *Some Eighteenth-Century Commentators*—have been selected because they are representative figures and because of the importance of their works. No selection is foolproof, of course, and many will quarrel with the choices. However, the sum total of thirty essays, it is hoped, will provide the most complete discussion available of America's early historians.

volume III

Historians of Nature
and Man's Nature

1.

Historians of Nature and Man's Nature:
An Introduction

LAWRENCE H. LEDER

Eighteenth-century colonials, prior to their acrimonious debates with England, reflected their growing maturity in several ways as they transformed themselves from transplanted Europeans into Americans. They found themselves fascinated by the novelty of their surroundings, the indigenous populations they encountered, and their own conversion from Europeans into Americans. That their New World setting differed sharply from anything previously known to Europeans, that their indigenous neighbors offered a unique insight into sharply differing societies, that their own histories offered valuable contrasts between Old World degeneracy and New World virtues—all of these ideas provided colonial Americans with incentives for investigation, analysis, and explanation. The New World became, in effect, a laboratory for testing and elaborating the theories of the Enlightenment.

Activity in the field of natural history expanded in the eighteenth century far beyond the hesitant efforts of previous years. Much of this came about through the application of Isaac Newton's cosmology, which profoundly influenced all thought in this period. The concept of a harmonious, orderly, and rational universe boggled men's imaginations, especially as they considered its applications to their own immediate situations. Although Newton speculated about celestial phenomena, man's own terrestrial habitat seemed the most readily available and most practical laboratory for a study of the mechanistic universe. Man needed to investigate and understand the harmonious, orderly, and rational existence of the plants and animals which surrounded and sustained him, and of the diverse social, economic, and political institutions which he found among the native populations and which he himself constructed.

American activity in the field of natural history involved both professional scientists and amateurs. Professor John Winthrop of Harvard, Cadwallader Colden of New York, and Dr. Alexander Garden of Charleston, South Carolina, had all received some formal scientific training; John Bartram of Philadelphia, Cotton Mather of Massachusetts, and Benjamin Franklin represented self-trained scientists. Each made noteworthy contributions to expanding scientific knowledge, and each participated in the ever-widening international circle of investigators who dealt with natural history and who correlated American findings with those from other parts of the world. This international group included the English naturalist Peter Collinson, the Dutch botanist John Frederick Gronovious, and the Swedish classifier Carolus Linnaeus.

Americans had a most obvious advantage over natural historians in Europe—they lived in the midst of a unique laboratory. European scientists needed correspondents who could tap American resources, whether these involved plants and animals unique to the New World, native populations which had developed in isolation from European or Asian contacts, or simply an advantageous position from which to make readings on heavenly phenomena such as the transits of Venus in the 1760s. American scientific reports, therefore, took on an importance out of proportion to the number of Americans making them, or to the training they had received. Europeans eagerly received these reports because they provided the evidence necessary to test and expand the ideas promulgated by European theorists from the time of Copernicus to that of Newton himself.

Typical of those interested in American plants and animals was

Mark Catesby, an English naturalist who spent four years collecting, drawing, and analyzing specimens in the southern colonies and West Indies, and then devoted the balance of his career to the preparation and publication of his findings. His *Natural History* provided the basis, during the next half-century or more, for much work done by Europeans in the fields of botany and zoology, even though Catesby had not utilized the more modern Linnaean system of classification. He offered to those who came after him on-the-spot illustrations of different varieties of plants and animals. Europeans had no opportunity to examine these plants and animals in their natural habitats. They could only view preserved specimens which had lost their lifelike colors and which lacked their natural surroundings. Although the Europeans could classify the varieties more accurately, they often referred their readers to Catesby's illustrations for visual guidance. His work, therefore, became the common frame of reference for botanists and zoologists well into the nineteenth century.

Perhaps as fascinating to Americans and Europeans as were the New World's plants and animals were its indigenous inhabitants and especially the great variety of social, economic, and political forms taken by their civilizations. Not only did the North American Indians fascinate European settlers in the New World, they also presented them with serious problems ranging from international relations to economics. Indian attitudes toward different groups of Europeans certainly helped shape the course of settlement, and the natives' ability to satisfy the newcomers' greed for valuable furs sustained the colonies in their fledgling days.

The Iroquois of northern and western New York, one of the most formidable of the native populations encountered by European immigrants, clearly played a key role in shaping the French, Dutch, and later the English colonies. These Indians found their champion in Cadwallader Colden, a physician-politician who had his own reasons for writing the history of Anglo-Iroquois relations. However, he approached the indigenous people of his colony with an understanding appreciation of their civilization, and especially of their political prowess. He emphasized in his *History* those years before the whites fully undermined the original vitality of the Iroquois. Colden not only admired the political structure of this confederacy of five tribes (later to become six, after the Tuscarora joined the confederacy about 1722), but he also appreciated their artistic use of oratory to resolve their problems and to hold together their confederacy. To Colden, the Iroquois represented the noble savage at his best and worst, they epitomized humanity's nobility as well as its debasement, and they perhaps provided the closest parallel to the ancient Romans that he could find.

Many Iroquois customs seemed attractive to Colden. Their practice of adopting prisoners into the tribe in place of members slain in battle seemed remarkably civilized; yet they often exhibited barbaric cruelty toward their enemies, and they themselves bravely endured unspeakable tortures. Noted as fierce warriors, the Iroquois were often at their best as peacemakers, a process described in some detail by Colden. He admired their awareness of their own self-interest, which occasioned their shift from aggressive warfare for the protection of their fur-hunting territory in the seventeenth century to more peaceable means of accomplishing this same end in the eighteenth century. That these indigenous people survived the impact of increasing intrusions into their territory, of continuing warfare between rival European claimants for domination, and of an ecological disaster as their hunting grounds became decimated offered testimony to their resiliency. Colden's *History* served as a memorial to these Indians whose political system in some ways seemed as sophisticated as that of the Europeans, even though the Iroquois' material culture lagged far behind.

Still another native population found itself surrounded and finally inundated by European settlement. These were the Natchez Indians of the lower Mississippi Valley, whose civilization was probably even more sophisticated than that of the Iroquois. Indeed, that very sophistication may have accelerated their final extermination. Just as the Iroquois found their champion and chronicler in Colden, so the Natchez found their memorialist in Antoine Simon Le Page du Pratz, a French architect-engineer who became a concessionaire under the auspices of John Law's Company of the West and participated in the scheme to colonize Louisiana.

As a true child of the eighteenth century, Le Page du Pratz devoted considerable attention to the geography and to the plants and animals of the New World, as well as to its native inhabitants. He concerned himself with Louisiana's potential for settlement and its problems, and finally with the Natchez Indians whom he had come to know intimately and who so completely fascinated him. Le Page du Pratz gave considerable attention to the manners and customs of this strange people, to their origins, and to their relationships with the French intruders, which culminated in their rebellion, in 1729, and consequent destruction as an independent nation.

Le Page du Pratz's major contribution stemmed from his intimate knowledge of the ways and beliefs of the Natchez Indians. By accepting them as people having both merits and demerits rather than as objects for the solicitude of the European, Le Page du Pratz exhibited a rare sensitivity which enabled him to learn a good deal more about the Indians than most of his contemporaries. He recorded the lore of the Natchez concerning their origins, religion, ethics, and social organization, thereby providing a unique and detailed account. Le Page du Pratz, by going out of his way to understand those who differed from him, realized that the natives of North America, and particularly the Natchez, represented something far more significant than was realized by less patient and tolerant Europeans. Yet, when the Natchez put the ultimate question to Le Page du Pratz—when they asked him directly, "What do the French want of us?"—he could offer no real answer. In his inability to respond, Le Page du Pratz perhaps epitomized the tragedy of the collision between European and Indian civilizations in the New World.

A different segment of Indian civilization was depicted by James

Adair, an Englishman and trader among the southeastern tribes of the Chickasaw, Choctaw, Creek, Cherokee, and Catawba. His *History* offered still another tragic illustration of a native people enmeshed in the intrigues and battles between two conflicting European groups. Moreover, Adair provided some acrid comments on the qualities of leadership of his own people as compared to that of the Indians.

Indeed, Adair seems to have used his *History* as a device to criticize English policy and practices in dealing not just with the southeastern Indians, but also with the colonials, with those transplanted Englishmen and other Europeans who peopled Great Britain's mainland colonies. Although Adair, like Colden and Le Page du Pratz before him, understood the spirit of the American Indians with whom he dealt, and appreciated their unique qualities, he added one additional feature. Adair understood his own people—the Americans—and warned Englishmen of the dangers looming before them in the 1760s.

As the transplanted Europeans became Americans, by the mid-eighteenth century, they discovered a pride of nationalism which expressed itself in a variety of ways, including the writing of provincial histories. William Stith's *History of . . . Virginia* and William Smith's *History of . . . New York* both reflected the growing awareness on the part of colonial Americans that they differed somehow from Englishmen, and perhaps for the better. In addition, these historians suggested Americans' increasing concern over the growth of tyranny and authoritarianism and its implications. They had earlier taken over the Whig political ideology, lock, stock, and barrel, a fact which most Englishmen in authority failed to understand or appreciate. Indeed, Englishmen by and large remained unaware that Americans had changed and that consequently the empire had changed. The once small settlements on the Atlantic's western shore had burgeoned in size and taken on a vitality of their own, one which Great Britain found it increasingly difficult to direct, control, or restrict.

Little wonder, then, that Americans by the mid-eighteenth

century began to explore their own origins and background in the light of contemporary policy decisions. William Stith, a Virginia Anglican priest, emphasized his Virginia affiliations. His support came not from England, but from America. His family connections included Peyton Randolph and Richard Bland, not some distant English placeman, and he protested any interference with the authority exercised over Virginia, including its church, by Virginians. Indeed, his *History* pointed out the immediate parallels between Governor Robert Dinwiddie, Commissary John Blair, James I, and the Jacobites of 1745. Personal frustrations accentuated the parallelism for Stith as he found himself denied the offices he sought at the apex of his career.

Stith the historian, like Stith the priest, remained primarily a political figure. From the very beginning of his *History*, he took sides against James I, supporting Sir Walter Raleigh and Sir Edwin Sandys in their contests with the monarch. In a lengthy paragraph, Stith lauded the Virginia Company of London's decision, under Sandys' leadership, to establish "British Liberty" in the colony by authorizing a House of Burgesses. He viewed its creation as the prime example of enlightened leadership, as the key element differentiating English colonies from those of other nations. Liberty versus tyranny became Stith's theme, epitomized by the recurring contests between Sandys and the settlers on the one hand and the Crown and the old leadership of the Virginia Company on the other. From Stith's *History* emerged a state of mind which said as much, or perhaps more, about Virginia in the 1750s as it did about the colony in the 1620s. Criticism of James I implied a challenge to all monarchy, emphasis upon a local representative assembly implicitly challenged Parliament's forthcoming efforts to control the colonies, religious indifference suggested the newer standards of the eighteenth century. William Stith was truly a scion of the eighteenth century.

A contemporary historian, William Smith of New York, also reflected eighteenth-century Whiggism as he discussed more contemporary events. He, like Stith, criticized British misunderstanding and mismanagement; he compiled his *History of the Province of New York* in order to provide a true account of the colony's problems, and to overcome the false tales recounted by corrupt and incompetent governors to mislead imperial authorities.

New York's primary difficulty lay in the Anglo-French tension along the New York–Canadian border, and in the Indians' role in that conflict from Governor Thomas Dongan in the 1680s onward. Rather than relieve the colony, English authorities neglected its defense. They failed the colony in a number of ways, including the sending of either incompetent or corrupt governors, providing inadequate military forces, and requiring the colonists to bear the largest burden of self-defense, and by failing to understand New York's importance to the British Empire in terms of people, land, and trade.

Smith wanted Great Britain to take an active role in suppressing the French menace to the colonies, a menace felt most strongly by New York. Had he had the courage, Smith would have continued his original narrative beyond 1732 to include a bitter denunciation of James De Lancey who, he believed, had frustrated William Shirley's military efforts to defeat the French. However, his compatriot and colleague, William Livingston, accomplished that purpose when he anonymously published a biting criticism of the William Cosby and George Clarke administrations under the title *Review of the Military Operations.*

William Smith urged—indeed demanded—that British imperialism become militant and consequently triumphant in the contest with France. He took comfort in William Pitt's policies during the French and Indian War, he gloried in the dominance of the British Empire, and he bemoaned Britain's misuse of power in the years after 1763. As a Whig, Smith deplored the attacks by English authorities upon the rights and liberties of Englishmen in America, upon the constitutional system in which all Englishmen gloried, regardless of their domicile. However, he criticized British actions as a lawyer, not a revolutionary. When Americans began, by 1774, to separate from Britain, Smith lagged behind because he could not abandon his lifelong advocacy of empire.

Once the colonists had declared independence, Smith dwelled on the problem of how the empire had reached such a point of self-destruction. He found the culprits in politicians, both English and colonial, who befuddled the proper relationship between the two elements of the empire. British failure to understand the Americans, British views of colonials as inferiors rather than equal partners, and the connivance in these attitudes by a few American politicians who sold the birthright of their fellow colonials for their own advancement precluded putting the empire on a proper footing. First among these politicians, Smith insisted, was James De Lancey, who had sabotaged the first serious effort to reconstruct imperial relationships when he successfully opposed the Albany Plan of Union in 1754.

William Smith wrote a partisan political history of his colony, and in doing so he revealed a great deal about both its history and his own times. He opposed France, he fought against the Church of England, he defended the autonomy of the assembly—these were the hallmarks of colonial Whiggism. However, he also had ambitions which remained frustrated, and these, combined with his Whig principles, created a serious dilemma for Smith when the Americans declared independence. His ultimate decision to remain loyal to Crown and empire was incomprehensible to many of his contemporaries; to the modern student, it had a ring of final sincerity.

Eighteenth-century Americans had acquired new goals as the number of their colonies increased, as the size of their population grew, and as they converted themselves into Americans. Much of what occurred went unnoticed in England and, to some degree, in the colonies until mid-century. The writers discussed in the following pages, however selective the sampling, wrote histories of nature and man's nature, and thus reflected America's growing maturity.

2.

Mark Catesby's Natural History of Carolina

George Frederick Frick

Mark Catesby's *The Natural History of Carolina, Florida, and the Bahama Islands* must be accounted the most ambitious eighteenth-century effort to treat the plants and animals of any British mainland colony. By combining texts and plates, both of his own production, Catesby provided naturalists of two continents with a common frame of reference. The plates particularly, even with flaws made by Catesby as a self-taught artist, gave the work a value not shared by natural histories attached to "civil" histories and travelers' accounts, or even by floras which lacked illustration. Although Catesby was born, lived most of his life, and died in England, he spent years in the field in America and had seen and drawn many of his subjects in their natural habitats.

Mark Catesby was born in the Essex village of Castle Hedingham on March 24, 1682–83, the fifth son of John Catesby and Elizabeth Jekyll.[1] The Catesbys were an ancient gentry family of Northamptonshire and Rutland, with this particular branch descending from Sir John Catesby, a fifteenth-century judge of Common Pleas. More immediately, the naturalist's grandfather, also Mark, had followed the familiar pattern of younger sons by moving into the city of London and becoming an apprentice, eventually rising to the position of first warden of the Skinner's

---

1. See George F. Frick and Raymond P. Stearns, *Mark Catesby: The Colonial Audubon* (Urbana, Ill., 1961) for a discussion of his birth date (cited as Frick and Stearns). (All dates before 1752 are given in the Julian, Old Style, calendar.)

Company. John Catesby, his son, made the move back to Castle Hedingham and prospered in the practice of law in the nearby borough of Sudbury, Suffolk, which he served as town clerk and mayor, while he also acted as deputy steward to the earl of Suffolk. His wife, Elizabeth Jekyll, came from a prosperous family of Essex lawyers and antiquaries.[2]

Nothing certain is known of Mark Catesby's education, although his letters and writing indicate a fair mastery of English and at least some knowledge of Latin. He was not bred to a profession as were two of his elder brothers, both of whom were admitted to the Inner Temple. Catesby's uncle, Nicholas Jekyll, a lawyer with antiquarian and gardening interests, was particularly important to him. Through Jekyll, Catesby "Hapned to fall in the acquaintance" of John Ray, the principal naturalist of late seventeenth-century England, who lived in the parish of Black Notley, not far from Castle Hedingham. According to George Edwards, Catesby's friend and fellow ornithological illustrator, Ray "inspir'd Catesby with a geni[u]s for natural history." The Ray-Jekyll friendship also introduced Catesby to Samuel Dale, author of a famous *Pharmacologia* (London, 1693), who served Ray as friend and assistant, and who ultimately brought Catesby to the attention of a larger natural history circle by publicizing his collections in Virginia.[3]

"Virginia was the Place (I having Relations there) suited most with my Convenience to go," was Catesby's simple explanation of his first stay in America, which began in April 1712. His sister Elizabeth, the wife of Dr. William Cocke, preceded him to the New World. Dr. Cocke went to Williamsburg in the party of

2. Anthony R. Wagner, Pedigree of Catesby (photostat in Virginia Historical Society); Charles F. C. Sperling, *A Short History of Sudbury* (Sudbury, 1896), pp. 34, 78.

3. For possible sources of his education see Frick and Stearns, pp. 6–8; George Edwards to [Thomas Pennant], London, December 5, 1761, in George F. Frick, "Mark Catesby: The Discovery of a Naturalist," *Papers of the Bibliographical Society of America* 54 (1960): 173; George Symonds Boulger, "Samuel Dale," *Journal of Botany, British and Foreign* 21 (1883): 193; Charles E. Raven, *John Ray, Naturalist* (Cambridge, 1942), p. 61.

Lieutenant Governor Alexander Spottswood, and he prospered under Spottswood's patronage, first as secretary to the colony and later as a member of the council. Catesby had only meager expectations in England, since he had received a relatively small inheritance upon the death of his father in 1705. The Virginia connection must have given him hope for a new start.[4]

Catesby later remembered his stay in Virginia as being rather unproductive: "I chiefly gratified my Inclination in observing and admiring the various productions of those Countries . . . only sending from thence some dried Specimens of Plants and some of the most Specious in Tubs of Earth." He did begin observing and collecting almost immediately after his arrival. In May 1712, he spent more than three weeks with William Byrd II at Westover, during which time Byrd, an enthusiastic though sometimes gullible naturalist, introduced him to the natural products of the Chesapeake tidewater. Catesby, in turn, helped Byrd mend his garden. Later that year, Catesby joined Byrd on a visit to the Pamunkey Indian town on the Pamunkey River, a sojourn which may have given the recently-arrived East Anglian his first close view of American aborigines.[5]

As early as the fall of his first year in Virginia, Catesby began to collect seeds. Governor Spottswood sent a packet gathered by him to Henry Compton, bishop of London, a great patron of botany and planting. Catesby sent others to Samuel Dale and to his brother Jekyll Catesby at Castle Hedingham, while still more went to Thomas Fairchild, a nurseryman of Hoxton. Fairchild's seeds particularly helped to publicize Catesby's efforts, when accounts of

4. Mark Catesby, *The Natural History of Carolina, Florida, and the Bahama Islands*, 2 vols. (London, 1731–1747), 2: v (cited as *Carolina*); "The Cocke Family of Virginia," *Virginia Magazine of History and Biography* 5 (1897): 190; Louis B. Wright and Marion Tinling, eds., *The Secret Diary of William Byrd* (Richmond, 1941), p. 194; The Will of John Catesby, P.C.C. Gee, 4 (MS in Principal Probate Registry, London).

5. *Carolina*, 1: v; Wright and Tinling, eds., *Byrd Diary*, pp. 534–44, 585–92.

them were published by James Petiver, the almost compulsive promoter of natural history.[6]

Catesby did not spend all of his time in the Virginia tidewater. In 1714, he traveled up the James River "to that part of the Apalatchian mountains where the sources of that river rise." This trip, which apparently did not carry him and his companions beyond the Blue Ridge, would form the basis, long afterwards, of his description of the mountains in his *Natural History*. Again, in the same year, he made a voyage to Jamaica, apparently stopping in Bermuda along the way. These visits produced descriptions of "Cacao-Walks" in Jamaica, and of the plat palmetto . (*Sabal palmetto*) in Bermuda, and in shipments of Jamaican seeds to Samuel Dale.[7]

Even before Catesby's return from Virginia in the fall of 1719, Samuel Dale made his collections known to William Sherard. That gentleman, praised by Catesby as "one of [the] most celebrated Botanists of this Age," is now remembered largely for the Oxford professorship in botany founded by his bequest. Sherard had returned to England late in 1717 from the Levant, where he had made his fortune as consul to the English factory at Smyrna. He now engaged in a project to expand the *Pinax* of Gaspard Bauhin (Basel, 1671) and to replenish his own botanical collection, which had been neglected during his absence from England.[8]

6. Governor Spottswood to the bishop of London, November 16, 1713, in R. A. Brock, ed., *The Official Letters of Governor Alexander Spottswood*, 2 vols. (Richmond, Va., 1882–1885), 2: 44–45; Seeds from Virginia Sent by Mr. Catesby to Mr. Dale, Sloane MSS (British Museum), 3339, fols. 73b–75; James Petiver, "Botanicum hortense, IV," *Philosophical Transactions of the Royal Society* 39 (1715): 357–359, 362; see Raymond P. Stearns, "James Petiver," *Proceedings of the American Antiquarian Society*, n.s. 62 (1952): 243–265.

7. *Carolina*, 2: v, vi; 1: xli; 2: xxxi, Appendix, 6; Samuel Dale to William Sherard, Braintree, January 19, 1718/19, February 2, 1718/19, April 1, 1719, Dr. Sherard's Philosophical Letters (MSS in Library of the Royal Society), 2: no. 203, 204, 206a.

8. *Carolina*, 2: v; Sherard Letters, 2: 196, 198, 203, 206a, 211, 244; George Pasti, Jr., "Consul Sherard; Amateur Botanist" (Ph.D. diss., University of Illinois, 1950), passim.

While Dale first suggested that Catesby's collections in the New World merited support, Sherard took the lead in securing patrons for that effort, principally among his connections in the Royal Society. On October 20, 1720, Francis Nicholson, newly appointed governor of South Carolina, pledged to the Society's council to give an annual pension of twenty pounds to Catesby "to observe the Rarities of that Country." Besides Nicholson and Sherard, the principal subscribers to the project were Sir Hans Sloane, the great collector whose holdings would form the basis of the British Museum, and Charles Dubois, treasurer of the East India Company. Still another patron, James Brydges, first duke of Chandos, nearly lured Catesby to Africa in the employ of the Royal African Company, but this project fell through, and Catesby sailed for Carolina early in February 1722.[9]

Catesby arrived in Charles Town May 3, 1722, where Governor Nicholson, who had almost despaired of his coming, received him warmly. The governor's patronage gave Catesby access to the plantations of the leading families of the province. He set to work collecting in the low country and soon realized that his needs and the desires of his patrons did not always coincide. He complained to Sherard, "The more specimens I collect, the more time it takes and consequently prevents my collecting as I should." He solved some of his problems when, in the spring of 1723, he bought a "Negro Boy" to help him. At other times he "employ'd an Indian" to carry his box of paints, paper, and seeds. There were, nevertheless, other problems. Catesby was kept from the field for most of the fall of 1722 by an infection which required surgery. In that same September, a hurricane blew the seeds from the trees, so

9. Royal Society, Council Minutes (MS in the Library of the Royal Society), 2: 324; Sherard to Dr. Richard Richardson, November 12, 1720, in Dawson Turner, ed., *Extracts from the Literary and Scientific Correspondence of Richard Richardson* (Yarmouth, 1835), pp. 157–58; for Sloane, see Gavin R. de Beer, *Sir Hans Sloane and the British Museum* (London, 1953) and Eric St. John Brooks, *Sir Hans Sloane the Great Collector* (London, 1954); for Dubois, see *DNB*. The list of patrons is given in *Carolina*, 1: vi; Sherard to Richardson, January 27, 1721/22, MS Radcliffe Trust (Bodleian Library, Oxford), C. IV, fol. 57.

that all the efforts of Carolinians on his behalf proved unproductive.[10]

In the time he remained in Carolina (the "Florida" of the title would soon be the province of Georgia), Catesby attempted to cover both the low country and piedmont thoroughly. "My method is never to be twice in one place at the same season. For if in the spring I am in the low Country, in the Summer I am at the heads of Rivers, and the Next Summer in the low Countrys, so I visit the two different parts of the Country." Catesby seemed to have done most of his back-country collecting in the vicinity of Fort Moor, a frontier garrison on the Carolina side of the Savannah River, nearly opposite the future site of Augusta. He did propose a trip to the Cherokees, but apparently did not go as far west as their mountain country.[11]

By the late summer of 1724, Catesby believed that he had exhausted the possibilities for further profitable collection in Carolina, and proposed a trip to Mexico in the company of Thomas Cooper, a young Oxford graduate who practiced "physic" in Charles Town. Cooper would make astronomical observations, while Catesby would study natural history. Apparently neither Sherard nor Sloane gave any encouragement to their ambitious undertaking, and Catesby sailed instead for the Bahamas in January 1724/25.[12]

Catesby largely confined his efforts in the Bahamas to the collection and description of marine life because there were "but few Quadrupeds and Birds" to distract him, and because he believed, quite rightly, that few of the fishes had been described. Again, as

10. Catesby to Sherard, May 5, 1722 (the date is given as May 23, in *Carolina*, 1: vi), June 20, 1722, March 19, 1722/23, December 9, 1722, December 10, 1722, Sherard Letters, 2: no. 163, 164, 165, 166, 169; *Carolina*, 1: viii–ix.

11. Catesby to Sherard, January 16, 1724, Sherard Letters, 2: no. 174; see also 2: 169, 170, 171, 176, and Sloane MSS, 4047, fol. 147.

12. Joseph Foster, ed., *Alumni Oxonienses . . . 1715–1886* (Oxford, 1891), p. 325; Catesby to Sherard, Charles Town, August 16, 1724, Sherard Letters, 2: no. 178; Cooper to Sloane, Sloane MSS, 4047, fol. 229; and see Sherard Letters, 2: nos. 183 and 184.

in Carolina, he had the assistance of the colony's leading men, including Governor George Phenny, with whom he stayed, and Councillor William Spatches, whose plantings of logwood he studied. Even with local assistance, Catesby had a painful experience with the poisonous sap of the "Mancaneel Tree" (*Hippomane mancinella*), which was one of a number of Bahamian species he illustrated.[13]

This ended Catesby's field work. After he returned to London in 1726, he devoted most of the remainder of his life to producing the *Natural History of Carolina*. He lacked the means to hire professional artists, and he turned to Joseph Goupy, a French-born etcher and watercolorist, who taught him the rudiments of the craft. Catesby etched all but two of the two hundred twenty plates in the *Natural History*, and either colored or supervised the watercolor washes of all the copies finished during his lifetime.[14]

While his work proceeded, Catesby supported himself by assisting nurserymen—Thomas Fairchild in Hoxton, and then, after Fairchild's death in 1729, his successor, Stephen Bacon. Still later, he lived and worked in the establishment of Christopher Gray, in Fulham, and illustrated Gray's *Catalogue of Trees and Shrubs That Will Endure the Climate of England* (London, 1737). These activities supplied a partial livelihood while also providing him with fresh specimens of American plants. Similarly, Peter Collinson, the Quaker mercer and patron of American science who had already secured subscriptions for Catesby's American travels, lent him money without interest and supplied him with additional botanical materials from his garden at Peckham, in Surrey.[15]

As originally projected, the *Natural History* was to have two hundred plates and was to sell for twenty guineas. Catesby en-

13. *Carolina*, 1: x; 2: xxix, 86, 95, Appendix 10.
14. Ibid., 1: xi; G. D. Ehret supplied pls. 61 and 96 of vol. 2.
15. See Frick and Stearns, pp. 50–51; for Collinson, see N. G. Brett-James, *The Life of Peter Collinson* (London, [1925]). (The present author is preparing a new biography.)

hanced its sale and his income by disposing of sections of twenty plates, as they were completed, for two guineas each. His progress with the work can be traced by the fact that he displayed each section to the Royal Society. The proud author brought the first to their chambers in Crane Court on May 22, 1729; he brought them the fifth and last part of the first volume on November 23, 1732. The second volume took even longer; he did not show the tenth part (the last as originally planned) to the Society until December 15, 1743. The "Appendix" of twenty additional pages and plates, taken from specimens either sent by American correspondents or available in England, was not completed until the spring of 1747, when Peter Collinson advised Linnaeus, "Catesby's noble work is finished."[16] The noble work had taken more than two decades of Catesby's life—much more if one included his years in the field.

As work on the *Natural History* continued, Catesby took his place in the international freemasonry of natural history. At a time when much scientific interchange was carried on by letter, he corresponded with men of similar interests in Europe and America, and exchanged further intelligence through the much wider networks of correspondence maintained by his friends and patrons, Peter Collinson and Sir Hans Sloane. Catesby's limited means prevented him from acting as scientific middleman on as grand a scale as either Sloane or Collinson, but he still participated in one of the more fruitful botanical partnerships between Europe and America in his time. Many of the materials sent by John Clayton of Virginia to J. F. Gronovius, in The Netherlands, for inclusion in the *Flora Virginica* passed through his hands.[17] He

16. Catesby to John Bartram, London, May 20, 1740, in William Darlington, ed., *Memorials of John Bartram* (Philadelphia, 1849), pp. 319–20; Journal Book (MSS in Library of the Royal Society), 14: 336; 15: 190; 19: 130; James Edward Smith, ed., *Selections of the Correspondence of Linnaeus* (London, 1821), 1: 18 (hereafter cited as *Linaeus Correspondence*.)

17. *Flora Virginica*, ed. 1 (Leyden, 1739–43); Edmond and Dorothy S. Berkeley, *John Clayton* (Chapel Hill, N.C., 1963), pp. 58, 63–69; for a discussion of the natural history cycle, see Roy N. Lokken, "The Progress of Science in Early America," in Lawrence H. Leder, ed., *Dimensions of Change: Problems and Issues of Colonial American History* (Minneapolis, 1972), pp. 107–10.

thus had a part in the work which dated much of the botany in his own *Natural History* even as he published it.

Both Sloane and Collinson sponsored Catesby's election as Fellow of the Royal Society in April 1733. Catesby, who supported his membership in the Society by drawing cuts for its register book, was an active member at a time whem many fellows were not. He reviewed Reamur's *Histoire des insectes* and was asked to review the first edition of Linnaeus's *Systema naturae*, which he wisely refused to do because he lacked sufficient background in system.[18] Catesby contributed letters from a number of correspondents, including Johann Amman, professor of botany in St. Petersburg, whom he had known in London, and his old companion William Byrd. Similarly, he sponsored a number of candidates for fellowship in the Society, most notably his friend the cartographer, botanist, and sometime Virginian, John Mitchell, and Lieutenant General James Oglethorpe, the founder of Georgia. More significantly, Catesby read a number of papers before the Society. In May and June 1743, he read substantial parts of the introduction to the second volume of his *Natural History*, "An Account of Carolina and the Bahama Islands." Finally, in March 1746–47, Catesby gave the Society his major effort in ornithological speculation, "Of Birds of Passage," which was published in the *Philosophical Transactions* and, in an abbreviated version, in the *Gentleman's Magazine*. In it he denied that migrating birds flew to their retreats above the atmosphere and also the commonly-held belief that swallows hibernated in ponds of water. He attributed migration to natural causes: cold weather and a diminution of food supply. Even though his assumption that birds wintered as far south of the equator as they summered north of it marred the

18. Certificates (MSS in Library of the Royal Society), 1: 41; Journal Book (Royal Society), 15: 283; René A. F. de Reamur, *Memoirs pour servir a l'histoire des insectes* (Paris, 1734–42); Carolus Linnaeus, *Systema naturae* (Leyden, 1735); Journal Book (Royal Society), 16: 60, 219, 295, 345, 358, 391 and later.

paper, it was, in a sense, a worthy valedictory to his friends in Crane Court.[19]

Catesby's personal life is much less clear than is his public existence in the Royal Society. His friend Emanuel Mendez da Costa recalled that he was "tall, meagre, hard favoured, and [had] a sullen look" and that he "was extremely grave or sedate and of a silent disposition; but when he contracted a friendship was communicative and affable." Peter Kalm, the student of Linnaeus who spent an afternoon with Catesby and John Mitchell in the spring of 1748 as he prepared for his own trip to America, would have added that Catesby was "short sighted." He, nevertheless, found the old naturalist extremely affable. Catesby discoursed on a number of topics, including the baneful effect of punch in America, an effect which, according to the description, apparently resulted from lead poisoning.[20]

Catesby spent his last years in the parish of St. Luke's, Old Street. He was living there on October 2, 1747, when he married Elizabeth Rowland, a widow with a grown daughter, at the chapel of the Reverend Alexander Keith in Mayfair. Keith's weddings were fashionable but irregular, for he performed them without license or banns, and they had only common-law standing. At the time of Catesby's death two years later, he and Elizabeth had two children—Mark, who was about eight, and Ann. In all probability, then, the ceremony gave added solemnity to an existing union. Catesby's friend Thomas Knowlton, gardener to the earl of Burlington, visited him early in July 1749 and found that "poor Mr. Catesby's legs swell and he looks badly. Drs. [Richard] Meade

19. Journal Book (Royal Society), 15: 422; 16: 201–2; 18: 269; 19: 98–99, 101, 106, 130; Byrd to Catesby, Virginia, June 27, 1737, Letter Book (MSS in Library of the Royal Society), 24: 115–18; Certificates (Royal Society), 1: 372, 527; *Philosophical Transactions* 44, pt. 2 (1747): 435–44; *Gentleman's Magazine* 18 (1748): 447–48.

20. "Notices and Anecdotes of Literati . . . ," *Gentleman's Magazine* 82, pt. 1 (1812):. 206; Joseph Lucas, tr., *Kalm's Visit to England* (London, 1892), pp. 117–19.

and [Thomas] Stack said there were little hopes of him long on this side of the Grave." These opinions were premature, even though Catesby's dropsy may have been symptomatic of conditions which caused his death. While "Crossing the way" in Holborn with his son, he fell and never regained consciousness. Mark Catesby died on December 23, 1749, and was buried in St. Luke's churchyard.[21] As he left little else to his widow and children except the plates and unsold copies of his great work, Catesby's only legacy was, in a double sense, his *Natural History of Carolina, Florida, and the Bahama Islands.*

These two great folio volumes are important for their depiction of American plants and animals. Here Catesby was an innovator of some significance. He broke with the traditional zoological illustration which showed animals in stiff profile, a tradition maintained in a work almost contemporary with his, Eleazer Albin's *A Natural History of Birds* (London, 1731–1738). Catesby frequently showed his birds, which constituted his largest group of animals, in motion, in poses which displayed significant markings to greatest advantage. In his best pictures, of which the blue jay or the smooth-billed ani are good examples, Catesby conveyed a sense of power and motion even with stationary pose.[22]

Catesby broke with tradition, also, in drawing most of his birds and some other animals against botanical backgrounds which were usually ecologically correct, although occasionally a want of space forced him to combine species from different regions or marine and land products on a single plate. Here he developed a genre of bird art which John James Audubon would later use with greater skill and for greater fame.[23]

21. For Catesby's marriage, see Frick and Stearns, p. 46–47; Knowlton to Richard Richardson, July 18, 1749, MS Radcliffe Trust, C. XI, fol. 57; Elsa G. Allen, *History of American Ornithology before Audubon* (Philadelphia, 1951) argues otherwise as to Catesby's death, but see Frick and Stearns, pp. 48–51, and Frick, "Mark Catesby," BSA *Papers*, pp. 162–75.

22. *Carolina*, 1: 47; 2: Appendix, 3.

23. Robert H. Welker, *Birds and Men* (Cambridge, Mass., 1955), p. 13. Maria Sybella Merian had already used such backgrounds for insects.

In other respects, Catesby's lack of formal training and the problems involved in producing plates three thousand miles from their live originals created weaknesses in a work which called for scientific precision. Many of his animals are adequate in gross details but are deficient in those minor elements which might distinguish species or subspecies. Sometimes he combined closely-related animals, as he did with his whippoorwill. Catesby apparently had not sketched this elusive bird or its equally elusive relatives while in the New World. He used specimens sent from Virginia by John Clayton, whose description of the whippoorwill he quoted in his text. The figure, though, is largely that of the eastern nighthawk, and is the basis of the modern designation of that species, *Caprimulgus minor*.[24]

While Catesby based most of his plates upon the watercolor sketches he made in the field or upon materials supplied by his correspondents, occasionally he fleshed out his volumes with materials from other sources. He derived seven of his figures and part of an eighth from copies, in the possession of Sir Hans Sloane, of paintings made by John White on Raleigh's sixteenth-century Roanoke expeditions. At least two of these, "The Cat Fish" (*Haustor catus*) and the "Sucking-Fish" (*Remora remora*), are among the poorest of Catesby's fishes.[25]

Catesby's plants sometimes suffered from his want of technical skill, his insufficient attention to detail, and also, in a sense, from the time in which they were done. In none of them did he give adequate attention to the parts of the flower needed for the Linnaean system of sexual classification which was gaining adherents even as he published his *Natural History*. Catesby can hardly be faulted, however, for a failure to read the future. More to the point, Catesby failed to record other details accurately, as in

24. *Carolina*, 2: Appendix, 16; see W. L. McAtee, "Confusion of Eastern Caprimulgidae," *The Auk* (1948), p. 128–29.
25. *Carolina*, 2: 23, 26; See Paul Hulton and David B. Quinn, *The American Drawings of John White* (London and Chapel Hill, N.C., 1964), 1: 50–51.

the excessively stylized venation of his leaves. Even the matter of transferring drawings to copper plates caused problems. Catesby apparently etched his plates directly from the originals without reversing them, thereby creating a mirror image which reversed plant elements that twine in a given direction.[26]

The second volume of the *Natural History* had much more diverse contents than the first, which was largely confined to birds and plants.[27] It began with "A Map of Carolina, Florida, the Bahama Islands and Parts Adjacent," which fairly summarized English ideas about North American geography in the 1730s and early 1740s, and which was derived from one of the great "mother maps," Henry Popple's *Map of the British Empire in America with the French and Spanish Settlements Adjacent Thereto* (London, 1733).

Catesby's map was followed logically (when binders' tricks did not place it elsewhere) by an "Account of Carolina and the Bahama Islands," which briefly recounted the history, topography, geology, ethnology, botany, zoology, and agriculture of those areas. This section—an attempt at a unified natural history—offered a valuable but somewhat neglected source for information about the land and economies of the regions visited by their author. As was true with the plates, the "Account" contained both "old" and "new" materials. The old was certainly present in its organizational scheme, which consisted of the four elements; he only discussed, however, air, earth, and water for Carolina, air and earth for the Bahamas, omitting fire in both.

The sections "Of the Air" of Carolina and the Bahamas contained unquantitative observations of heats, frosts, and cataclysmic events such as hurricanes. As might be expected, Catesby was most concerned with the effects of climate on plants; he noted fig trees

26. This can be seen in a comparison of Catesby's "original" drawings in the Royal Library, Windsor, and at the Pierpont Morgan Library with published versions; see H. A. Allard, "The Direction of Twist of the Corolla in the Bud," *Castanea*, 8 (1947): 88–94.

27. The volumes are bound in many ways: assignment of the map and "Account" is based upon the time of completion.

growing on the Eastern Shore of Virginia and oranges in coastal Carolina which did not survive farther inland. It would seem from this section that Catesby knew that North America had far more severe weather than Europe in the same latitudes, even though he posited climatic uniformity by latitude in his "Of Birds of Passage."[28]

Catesby's materials on the soil and water of Carolina comprised most of his considerations of geology and related sciences. He defined the principal soil types of the region by designations in common use: the rich, swampy "Rice Land" and "Oak and Hickory Land" productive of the best grains, "Pine Barren. Land" good only for forest products, and unproductive "Shrubby Oak Land." Catesby dealt perceptively with the formation of land areas. He recognized the marine origin of the coastal plain and the sea's role in building and destroying the shore itself. Catesby also saw clearly the significance of the fall line zone and the differences of streams above and below their cataracts. These streams, which also built and destroyed land, were produced by rains that fell in higher lands and not, as some contemporaries believed, by water which some sort of subterranean recirculation system carried back to its mountain sources.[29]

In other areas, Catesby's ideas were much less modern. He believed in a literal biblical flood, as did many others of his time, following such seventeenth-century works as Thomas Burnet's *The Theory of the Earth* (London, 1684). Shells found underground in Virginia, some distance from the sea, convinced him that "There is no part of the Globe where the signs of a Deluge more evidently appears than in many Parts of the Northern Continent of America."[30]

Catesby derived his treatment of the Indians in large part (and with due credit) from the work of a Carolina predecessor, John

28. *Carolina*, 2: i–iii.
29. Ibid., pp. iii–vii; see F. D. Adams, *The Birth and Development of the Geological Sciences* (Baltimore, 1938), pp. 443–60.
30. *Carolina*, 2: vii.

Lawson's *The History of Carolina*.[31] As such, it contained no trace of the noble savage. Catesby's Indians, who fought wars for reasons which seemed irrational to a European, were not receptive to "true Religion and Virtue." Unfortunately, either out of prudery or from a fear of repeating apocrypha, Catesby omitted Lawson's "tedious Narratives" of Indian religion and of their burial and sexual practices. Convinced by maps in Sir Hans Sloane's collection, Catesby accepted the Asiatic origins of American aborigines. This perceptive, if not original, concept of a common source for all American tribes, along with his observations in Virginia and Carolina, led Catesby to doubt Spanish accounts of higher native cultures in Mexico and Peru.[32]

As a naturalist and gardener, Catesby concerned himself with the uses Indians made of plants for food and medicine, so that his treatment "Of the Agriculture of Carolina" coincided much more with his own interests. It included a description of the wasteful farming practices of the colonial South—of moving to new land upon exhaustion of the fertility of the old. This he explained in terms compatible with those of most modern economic historians: dearness of labor and cheapness of land. He based most of this section on his own careful observation, including in it his useful description of rail fences and "The Manner of Making Tar and Pitch." Other information came from American botanizing companions. Robert Johnson, several times governor of South Carolina, supplied materials on the history of rice cultivation, and William Byrd informed him of the kinds and uses of Indian corn.[33]

The "Account of Carolina" contained, in its section "Of Beasts," Catesby's nearest approach to a systematic classification of genera and species. His primary concern, as was that of many better-trained English contemporaries, was with species rather than genera, and in the main body of his work he had little inter-

31. Probably the second edition (London, 1714).
32. *Carolina*, 2: vii–xvi.
33. Ibid., pp. xvi–xxiv.

est in going beyond John Ray or, in the case of animals, Ray's friend and collaborator Francis Willughby. Here he divided American animals, excluding those introduced from Europe, into three categories: those of different genus from the Old World, those of the same genus but of different species, and those of the same genus and species. Catesby erred seriously, if conservatively, in relating American animals such as the bear to similar European species, an error which even Linnaeus frequently made, but which may account for the fact that Catesby did not draw many of them for his *Natural History of Carolina.*[34]

At least two of the remaining sections of the "Account of Carolina and the Bahama Islands" dealt with the fishes of Carolina and the marine environment of the Bahamas. Catesby related them to the most important division of animals illustrated in the second volume.[35] The introductory material contained Catesby's disapproving description of the slaughter of migrating sturgeon on the Savannah, along with recipes for pickling that fish and for making caviar. While the naturalist could not condone wanton killing, he remained utilitarian in purpose.

Catesby included a total of forty-six fishes, all save one of them American and most of them taken from Bahamian waters. He reproduced his fishes in flat profile, unlike most of his other animals. While some have praised them as superior to the birds of the *Natural History*, this is a doubtful judgment.[36] Alexander Garden, the leading Carolina naturalist of the late colonial period, who was usually scornful of Catesby's performance, came nearer the mark. He complained that his predecessor had failed to render the rays of the mullet's fins (*Querimana curema*) accurately and had omitted some fins altogether.

It is sufficiently evident that his sole object was to make showy figures of the productions of Nature, rather than give correct and accurate representations. This is rather to invent than to describe. It is indulg-

34. Ibid., pp. xxiv–xxxi.
35. Ibid., pp. xxxiii–xxxiv, xli–xliii.
36. See Welker, *Birds and Men*, p. 12.

ing the fancies of his own brain, instead of contemplating and observing the beautiful works of God.[37]

Some of Catesby's inaccuracies in rendering fishes probably resulted from the fact that his stay in the Bahamas was brief, and from the fact that his original sketches had lain too long before he etched them on copper plates. The problem was compounded by the fact that fishes change color rapidly after their removal from water. Catesby sought to solve this by painting them "at different times, having a succession of them procur'd while the former lost their colors." Sometimes, though, as in the case of his "great Hog-Fish" (*Lachnolaimus maximus*), he saw only the head and produced a fair figure of it. Despite all their deficiencies, only two of the forty-six fishes in the *Natural History* are unidentifiable, and these were copied from drawings in the collections of Sir Hans Sloane.[38]

Other than the zoophytes, plantlike creatures which Catesby, along with most of his contemporaries, considered as plants, his remaining plates of marine animals dealt with crabs and sea turtles. All of them are recognizable even though they lack artistic merit or sufficient scientific precision. In his discussion of turtles, Catesby dwelled, as he did with the fishes, on their economic importance for the Bahamas, particularly their use as food. Catesby noted that large numbers of green turtles were taken to Carolina, where they were considered a delicacy. He also gave a detailed account of the methods used by the Bahamians to capture these great marine reptiles.[39]

Catesby's largest group of reptiles was the snakes, to which he devoted a whole section of twenty plates. American snakes, particularly rattlesnakes, had long interested Englishmen on both sides of the Atlantic, and Catesby tried to deal critically with the large body of folklore which had developed around them. He,

37. Charles Town, January 2, 1760, in Smith, ed., *Linnaeus Correspondence*, 2: 300–306; see *Carolina*, 2: 6, fig. 2.
38. *Carolina*, 1: xi; 2: Appendix, 19; see Frick and Stearns, pp. 84–85.
39. *Carolina*, 2: 33–40.

unlike many of his American friends, found no efficacy in the juices of various snakeroots in treating rattlesnake bites. The best Indian remedies consisted in cutting open the bite and sucking out the poison. Catesby also rejected other apocryphal items. He showed his skepticism of stories that rattlesnakes charm their prey by saying that he had never seen it happen. In this, he steered a course between Sir Hans Sloane, his old patron, who sought to disprove these tales by experiment, and many American correspondents, who repeated them uncritically. Catesby also denied that the tail of the water moccasin was a deadly as its fangs, and he refuted the persistent story that the "Coachwhip Snake" could cut a man in two by the jerk of its tail.[40]

The remaining zoological plates of the second volume, consisting mainly of lizard-like creatures, amphibians, and mammals, followed the pattern set for all except the birds; that is, they were less complete and had less artistic merit. There were exceptions. The two plates of the flying squirrel were well-posed, with one, at least, conveying the same sense of strength and motion found in Catesby's better ornithological drawings. Similarly, the great bullfrog, *Rana catesbeiana*, named for the author of *The Natural History of Carolina* by George Shaw, who borrowed much from that work for his own *General Zoology* (London, 1800–1826), displayed a great sense of power as it leaped towards the top of the page.[41]

Shaw's use of Catesby's work well into the next century was significant. For all its scientific and artistic shortcomings, *The Natural History of Carolina* was immensely important in providing English and European naturalists with a view of American species, and in giving eighteenth-century Americans a point of reference. This can be seen in the apparent profitability of these volumes for booksellers. Two more English editions using

40. Ibid., pp. 41–60; Hans Sloane, "Conjectures on the Fascinating Power Attributed to the Rattle-Snake," *Philosophical Transactions* 38 (1734): 321–31.
41. *Carolina*, 2: 76–77, 72.

Catesby's own plates were published in 1754 and again in 1771, purportedly under the editorship of Catesby's principal successor in English ornithological illustration, George Edwards. Edwards, whom Catesby had instructed in etching, made a few changes. If anything, the watercolor washes on the plates of these editions were far too strong when compared with those done by Catesby or colored under his supervision. On the Continent, copies of Catesby's birds by the Nuremberg artist Johann Michael Seligmann were alternated with those of George Edwards in *Sammlung verschiedener und seltener Vögel* (Nuremberg, 1749–1770), a plagiary which also appeared in French and Dutch editions. Similarly, the plates of the second volume of the *Natural History* were copied by Nicholaus Friedrich Eisenberger and George Lichtensteger, and appeared in Nuremberg in 1750 and again in 1777 as *Piscium, serpentum insectorum, aliorumque nunnullorum animalum.*[42]

Even with this apparent popularity, Catesby's great accomplishment might have fallen into a scientific limbo as did many pre-Linnaean writings. Modern binomial nomenclature began for botany with the second edition of Linnaeus's *Species plantarum* (Stockholm, 1753), and for zoology with the first volume of the tenth edition of his *Systema naturae* (Stockholm, 1758). In these circumstances, even the rather poor Linnaean index appended to the 1771 edition of the *Natural History* had no validity because it was merely an addition to an earlier work. *The Natural History of Carolina* bridged this nomenclatural divide because it was the major, almost the only, pictorial source for North American animals and plants available to European naturalists, from its first publication through the early nineteenth century. While English and Continental compilers and classifiers would have preferred to work from live or preserved specimens, they frequently had to use Catesby's work. This was especially true in the case of birds, where, except for occasional depictions in publications devoted

42. For these editions, see Frick and Stearns, pp. 109–10.

mainly to Old World species, Catesby had few predecessors and few successors until Alexander Wilson's *American Ornithology* (Philadelphia, 1808–1814). Linnaeus and those who followed him depended, therefore, upon the *Natural History.* Eliminating duplicates of one kind or another, Catesby illustrated a total of 109 species, 75 of which became the basis for modern designations of North American birds, and 3 more of which became the sources for names of Bahamian species. Although the "type" of a botanical or zoological classification is the actual specimen upon which it is based, many of Catesby's illustrations are, in something more than a metaphorical sense, the "types" of particular designations. It is little wonder then that Catesby has been called the "founder of American ornithology," and that his work constituted the basis of that science for the whole of North America.[43]

Catesby's contribution to other branches of natural history necessarily had less effect than his impact upon ornithology. As has been remarked, his plants lacked sufficient precision for easy inclusion in Linnaeus' highly artificial sexual system of classification; in addition, the plants of southeastern North America were treated more fully elsewhere. Catesby had himself contributed specimens to such works as the *Hortus Elthamensis* (London, 1732), the catalogue of the garden of his patron, James Sherard, prepared by J. J. Dillenius, which Linnaeus often cited. More important was the great collaboration between Catesby's friend John Clayton of Virginia and J. F. Gronovius of Leyden, which produced the *Flora Virginica* (Leyden, 1739–43), a work which utilized Linnaean classification and which included many of the mainland species of the *Natural History of Carolina.* As a result, Linnaeus usually relegated Catesby's plates to his plant synonymies, which made them useful references, since *Flora Virginica* and many other

43. See ibid., p. 56; Allen, *American Ornithology,* pp. 463, 465–467; W. L. McAtee, "The North American Birds of Mark Catesby and Eleazer Albin," *Journal of the Society for the Bibliography of Natural History* 3, pt. 4 (1957): 177–94; Witmer Stone, "Mark Catesby and the Nomenclature of North American Birds," *The Auk,* 46 (1929): 447–54.

lists of American plants lacked illustrations. Even so, the great Swedish taxonomist based twenty-two designations upon Catesby's sketches, and these include the genus *Catesbaea*, named originally by Gronovius for his English correspondent, with its type, *Catesbaea spinosa*, taken from the concluding plate of the first volume of the *Natural History*.[44]

Catesby's nonavian animals were utilized in somewhat the same way as the plants, though more often by naturalists later than Linnaeus himself. The fishes fared somewhat better than the others: twenty-six scientific names were founded in whole or in part upon Catesby's work, out of a total of forty-six illustrated there.[45] The continuing importance of the *Natural History of Carolina* can be seen in the fact that one of its fishes was published as late as 1829 by Georges Cuvier, in the second edition of his *Regne animal*.[46] Similarly, one of Catesby's crabs (out of three that support modern binomials) was copied for still another French compilation in 1818, only a few years earlier.[47] The same pattern holds for other categories. Four reptiles, four amphibians, and two mammals from the *Natural History of Carolina* provided whole or partial bases for modern designations, while Linnaeus and his late eighteenth- and early nineteenth-century successors used more of Catesby's illustrations in synonymies so as to provide visual references for species taken from other sources.[48]

Even in America, where the originals were close at hand, the *Natural History* was used and admired well beyond the time of Catesby's own circle of friends and correspondents. Except for Alexander Garden, who had only disdain for Catesby's inaccuracies, American naturalists and gentleman-amateurs continued to depend upon the two great folios. Thomas Jefferson, though he

44. J. E. Dandy, ed., *The Sloane Herbarium* (London, 1958), p. 12.
45. Frick and Stearns, pp. 77, 104.
46. (Paris, 1829–30), 2: 352.
47. Pierre André Latreille, *Tableau encyclopédique et méthodique . . . crustaces, arachnides et insectes* (Paris, 1818), vol. 2, pl. 284; Frick and Stearns, p. 78.
48. Frick and Stearns, pp. 80–83.

found the coloring of Catesby's birds too high, based the list of Virginia species in his *Notes on the State of Virginia* upon them.[49] William Bartram, who was a far better (if unpublished) scientific artist than Catesby, utilized *The Natural History of Carolina* to identify species found during his 1773 and 1774 explorations, which formed the basis of his famous *Travels in East and West Florida*.[50] Even Alexander Wilson, whose great work began publication six decades after Catesby's last section saw print, referred frequently to his precursor in his *American Ornithology* and quoted him directly and often.

For Americans, as for Europeans, the worth of *The Natural History of Carolina* lay in its uniqueness. It was the most successful attempt before the American Revolution to give the whole natural history of any mainland colony—virtually the only one. In the West Indies, the works of Sir Hans Sloane and Patric Browne on Jamaica and Griffith Hughes on Barbados accomplished that task; they combined descriptions with plates as Catesby did. In none of these, however, did the same hand produce both illustrations and text. Catesby's friend Cromwell Mortimer, secretary to the Royal Society, called the *Natural History* "the most magnificent Work I know of since the Art of Printing has been discover'd."[51] It was not that, but it was an ambitious and elegant book which provided the eighteenth century with a view of North America's natural produce.

49. William Peden, ed. (Chapel Hill, N.C., 1955), pp. 65–69.
50. (Philadelphia, 1791), pp. 284, 299–301.
51. *Philosophical Transactions* 44 (1748): 173.

3.

Cadwallader Colden's Noble Iroquois Savages

Wilbur R. Jacobs

Cadwallader Colden, colonial governor of New York, physician-scientist, and historian of the Five Nations of Iroquois had good reason to write about the confederated tribes that bordered his colony.[1] He helped plan a legislative scheme to close the profitable Indian trade between neutralist Albany merchants and French fur traders, and he agitated for Iroquois support in the British intercolonial wars against the French. Colden also had a deep-seated personal interest in New York Indian politics, for he actively speculated in land and could easily feather his nest by promoting extensions of the Indian frontier which would bring new lands under British imperial control.[2] Beyond these practical considera-

1. *The History of the Five Indian Nations Depending on the Province of New-York* (New York, 1727). This first edition, which does not have Colden's name on the title page, was dedicated to New York Governor William Burnet. A second edition, enlarged to include Part Two of Colden's *History*, was dedicated to James Oglethorpe and published in England as *The Five Indian Nations of Canada Which are dependent On the Province of New York in America* (London, 1747). The use of the word "Canada" in the title of the book, undoubtedly an error made by English publishers, has been repeated in American editions including the well-known edition of 1902 (*The History of the Five Indian Nations of Canada* . . . 2 vols. [New York, 1902], hereafter cited as Colden's *History*).

2. Stanley Nider Katz, in his perceptive study *Newcastle's New York, Anglo-American Politics, 1732–1753* (Cambridge, Mass., 1968) pp. 178, 179, stresses that although Colden was a "Presbyterian moralist," he was also "a speculator in land, and an official who profited by every acquisition of Indian territory." This judgment is borne out by examination of Colden's extensive correspondence and papers published in eleven volumes in the *Collections* of the New-York Historical Society. For example, an undated and unsigned letter in Colden's handwriting, probably written in 1722 to Archibald Kennedy, New

tions, however, Colden's letters and other writings demonstrated his sincere admiration for the most formidable native people of colonial times, the Iroquois. Roy Harvey Pearce caught the spirit of Colden's *History* when he wrote that it portrayed "the aristocratic, cruelly domineering Iroquois, natural men who are impassioned lovers of freedom and warfare, polished orators, virtually heroes out of Homer." No other provincial writer gave us such a history, a work tinged with romance as well as with an understanding appreciation of Indian character. Colden preserved for posterity a portrait of a once-powerful Indian confederacy that was soon to be completely overwhelmed by the forward moving Anglo-American frontier.[3]

York receiver-general, reveals Colden's extraordinary preoccupation with all phases of land dealings and his concern about collecting his salary as surveyor general. *Collections* of The New-York Historical Society for the year 1934, *The Letters and Papers of Cadwallader Colden*, 7 (New York, 1937): 166–170.

3. Roy Harvey Pearce, *The Savages of America, a Study of the Indian and the Idea of Civilization*, rev. ed. (Baltimore, 1965), pp. 45–46. Colden's *History* has special value because it is based upon now lost registers of New York Indian records. Although Peter Wraxall's *Abridgement* of these records has a brief account of some Indian speeches quoted by Colden, and the Robert Livingston Indian records also duplicate much of the material quoted by Colden, Colden's *History* preserves the most complete account of Iroquois seventeenth-century history embellished with long quotations from now missing manuscripts. See Charles Howard McIlwain, ed., *An Abridgement of the Indian Affairs Contained in Four Folio Volumes, Transacted in the Colony of New York, from the Year 1678 to the Year 1751* (Cambridge, Mass., 1915), pp. xcvi–xcvii, 3–29; Lawrence H. Leder, ed., *The Livingston Indian Records, 1666–1723* (Gettysburg, Pa., 1956), pp. 8–14, 29–38. Minor variations occur in documents quoted by both Colden and Livingston and a number of these same documents and related materials also appear in volumes 2, 3, and 9 of E. B. O'Callaghan, ed., *Documents Relating to the Colonial History of the State of New York*, 15 vols. (New York, 1853–1887). The complexity of transcribing Indian speeches accounts for variations in Colden and other sources. As Lawrence H. Leder wrote in his introduction to *The Livingston Indian Records*, pp. 9–10;

> The blend of nationalities in New York necessitated the employment of three languages in the conferences. The original proposition of the Governor was usually prepared in English . . . the document would then be translated into Dutch. . . . the official interpreter would verbally expound the ideas in the Indian tongue. The Indians' replies would go through the same procedure in reverse. It is because

Who was this shrewd, provincial author-physician who played such a significant role in New York Indian politics? Did Colden's career as a politician, office holder, and scientist have an indirect influence on his historical writings? Questions such as these are answered by examining the extraordinary record he left behind. His multivolumes of correspondence and his varied pamphlets on medicine, taxation, fur trading, politics, physics, botany, cartography (plus a plethora of children) revealed his determination to make a name for himself, to make a reputation that posterity would recognize as distinguished. But in order to become a man of leisure, in order to provide offices for his sons and to amass a personal fortune so that he could devote himself to literary and scientific pursuits, Colden became expert in exploiting all legal means of collecting his various fees and "sallarys" and of amassing huge land holdings at the expense of the Indians, fellow colonials, and the Crown itself.[4]

Colden virtuously defended royal government in the colonies and, at the same time, helped, as surveyor general of New York, to bring about regularized procedures in handling land purchases and sales. Moreover, he was the most eminent figure on the colonial

---

of this complex mechanism that we have so few examples of the legendary oratorical prowess of the Iroquois. Their speeches simply could not retain any lyricism after being put through the wringer of three languages by interpreters more concerned with meaning than style.

Peter Wraxall complained that some of the original records remained "in the Low Dutch language which I luckily understanding, was my own Translator." McIlwain, *Abridgement*, p. 4.

4. Colden's search for fame is the subject of a University of California, Santa Barbara, graduate paper by Raymond Geselbracht, "The Stillborn Myth: Cadwallader Colden," now being revised for publication. A similar theme is set forth in a study by the late Douglass Adair, "Fame and the Founding Fathers," *Papers and Comments Presented at the 19th Conference on Early American History* (Bethlehem, Pa., 1966), pp. 27–51. Colden's official correspondence as surveyor general contains an underlying tone of self-interest. See, for instance, Colden's account of warrants for land in Orange County, New York, *The Letters and Papers of Cadwallader Colden*, 8: 157–60.

scene (aside from Sir William Johnson, Indian superintendent and large land holder) to publicly defend Indian interests on the northern frontier. In all his public actions Colden adopted a posture of one who stood for truth, justice, honesty, integrity, and respect for the law; Colden's writings convincingly demonstrated his own belief that he stood for those things. Moreover, he even convinced his biographer, whose account of Colden's life was largely a long apologia for his policies and acts.[5]

Certainly the main events of Colden's life show him to be an energetic, ambitious man who was bound to make a name for himself in the New World. Born of Scottish parents (his father was a minister) on February 7, 1688, he completed a B.A. degree at the University of Edinburgh in 1705. After studying medicine in London, he sailed in 1710 for Philadelphia where he began a medical practice and, at the same time, showed considerable business acumen by occupying himself with mercantile projects. In Philadelphia Colden quickly associated himself with influential friends, including James Logan (1674–1751), a Scottish Quaker who enriched himself by land speculation and fur trade ventures, who served as one of the colony's political leaders, and who, as a scientist, also owned a fine library. Here, indeed, was a worthy figure that Colden could imitate as a model of enterprise. Colden also came to know Dr. John Kearsley of Philadelphia, an English-born architect and teacher of young medical students who sent colonial plant specimens and scientific papers written by provincials to Peter Collinson, the Quaker scientist in London, who in turn presented them to the Royal Society. If Colden had remained in Philadelphia, he would have undoubtedly become an active member of the city's scientific group, some of whom had an interest in Indian politics and trade. But in 1715 he returned temporarily to Scotland and married Alice Christie, who bore him

5. Alice M. Keys, *Cadwallader Colden: A Representative Eighteenth Century Official* (New York, 1906). Colden is also the subject of a recent doctoral dissertation: Alfred R. Hoermann, "A Figure of the American Enlightenment: Cadwallader Colden" (University of Toronto, 1970).

a number of children, two of whom—Jane Colden Farquhar and David Colden—became scholars in their own right.[6]

In Philadelphia, where he was a practicing physician and entrepreneur from 1710 to 1718, Colden concluded, through contacts in New York, that the latter colony offered him the chance to make his fortune. He therefore moved to New York in 1718. In the very year he moved to New York he obtained the commission as Master of the Weigh House of the Port of New York. Two years later, in 1720, he obtained a lucrative office (which became a lifetime appointment that he would pass on successfully to his son Alexander) as surveyor general of the Province of New York.[7] Appointed to the New York Governor's council in 1721, he now had a platform for political activity which allowed him, as "Senior Councilor," by the year 1736, to exert a powerful influence in the colony. For example, he sometimes took the place of the governor at Indian conferences. In politics Colden shrewdly allied himself with Governor William Burnet and then with Governor George Clinton in power struggles. The Clinton-Colden political alliance profited both men, for Colden advised the governor and wrote speeches for him, receiving in turn offices for a son and a recommendation for the governorship in 1761. Colden held the office of New York governor, except for brief periods, until 1776.[8]

---

6. Raymond Phineas Stearns, *Science in the British Colonies of America* (Urbana, Ill., 1970), pp. 494 ff., 565–67, 573–74, has a searching analysis and appraisal of Colden's scientific work and a description of the scientific circle in which he moved. Allen Johnson, ed., *Dictionary of American Biography*, 3 (New York, 1946): 286–87, 288–89 has authoritative short articles on Cadwallader Colden and Jane Colden.

7. Edmund B. O'Callaghan, *Calendar of New York Colonial Commissions, 1680–1770* (New York, 1929), p. 18; Colden's close associations with Governors Robert Hunter and William Burnet undoubtedly led to the special favors and offices he obtained when he moved to New York. See Katz, *Newcastle's New York*, p. 177. In addition to having a common interest in fur-trade politics, Colden and Burnet shared a special interest in making observations on solar eclipses in the years 1722–24; see Stearns, *Science in the British Colonies*, pp. 492–93.

8. The Huntington Library copy of *A Treaty between His Excellency the Honorable George Clinton . . . and the Six United Indian Nations . . . Held in Albany in the Months of August and September 1746* (New York,

Colden's steadfast conservatism, particularly his attempts to enforce the Stamp Act, caused him to be burned in effigy and gradually alienated him from his fellow provincials. The Stamp Act uproar in 1765 might have demonstrated to him that his almost inflexible support of royal government would end his political career. In previous years, when the political infighting had been too difficult to overcome, he had retired to his Orange County estate at Coldengham, but once in power in the 1760s he doggedly hung onto office to maintain the royal prerogative. Colden was probably a Loyalist because he felt a conscious loyalty to the Crown, because the British government had been good to him, and because he had been a faithful servant amidst the fierce rivalries of New York politics and the scrambled claims over land titles, taxes, quit rents, and Indian affairs. After the battle of Lexington, Colden, supporter of the Loyalist cause, moved to his Long Island estate at Spring Hill. Here, broken in spirit and confounded by the course of events which had taken away his authority as governor of New York, he died, on September 28, 1776, at the sturdy old age of eighty-eight.[9]

Colden's political activities clearly reflected themselves in his historical writings.[10] He had an imperial view of British self-

---

1746) has annotations in Colden's handwriting concerning French and Indian attacks. In his treaty talks Colden explained that he had substituted for the governor who was ill. Then, in a long speech to the Iroquois, Colden characterized the French as "thieves" and urged the Indians "to revenge all the injuries." The treaty is also published in Colden's *History*, 2: 205–266; Katz, *Newcastle's New York*, pp. 177–79; Keys, *Cadwallader Colden*, p. 364; Edwin R. Purple, "Notes, Biographical and Genealogical, of the Colden Family and of some of its Collateral Branches in America," *The New York Genealogical and Biographical Record*, 4 (October 1873): 161–168.

9. A favorable interpretation of Colden's influence in Indian policy is set forth in Georgiana C. Nammack's well-documented study, *Fraud, Politics, and the Dispossession of the Indians, the Iroquois Land Frontier in the Colonial Period* (Norman, Okla., 1969), pp. 16, 44, 61–64, 72–76, 96–101. See also Wilbur R. Jacobs, *Dispossessing the American Indian, Indians and Whites on the Colonial Frontier* (New York, 1972), pp. 10, 86n., 102, 112–113.

10. It is not generally known that in 1937 The New-York Historical Society published Colden's *History of Governor William Cosby's Administration and*

interest in North America which shaped his perspective of local politics and their relationship to Indian affairs and Anglo-French rivalry. Few British provincials had such breadth in their writings. In addition, Colden's interest in science and medicine broadened his intellectual horizons, linked him with foreign writers, and helped him to cultivate a sympathetic understanding of historic cultures among ancient civilizations as well as the Indians.

Colden was never a first-ranking colonial scientist. Although he made minor contributions to botany in the gathering of plant specimens, and although he mastered the Linnaean system of binomial nomenclature, Colden's speculations in physics showed his unfortunate lack of appreciation of the significance of experimental science. His brashness in attempting what he called *An Explication of the First Causes of Action in Matter and of the Cause of Gravitation* (New York, 1745) bewildered his scientific friends, especially when they read that he was probing the unknown "where the great Men in Philosophy have failed, and Sir Isaac Newton stopt short." What Colden argued, to the confusion of his readers, was that the "apparent Attraction or Gravitation, is truly and really performed by Pulsion, or more properly is the Effect of the joint Actions of the moving, resisting and elastic Powers."[11]

If this sample of Colden's scientific prose is difficult for the layman to follow, scientists of the eighteenth century found it equally difficult to comprehend, and modern scientists dismiss it as nonsense. Yet in his pamphlets on medicine, and in his letters, Colden revealed that he constantly probed for causes and occasionally touched the truth. For instance, he recognized the value of certain Indian medicines, and he saw the dangers of pollution

---

of *Lieutenant-Governor George Clarke's Administration through 1737*. This work, printed from Colden's handwritten manuscript, is a complex account of provincial New York's political factionalism, but useful for revealing the growth of colonial political parties. *The Letters and Papers of Cadwallader Colden*, 9: 283–355.

11. Quoted from pp. iv, 27. For additional commentary on this work, see Stearns, *Science in the British Colonies*, pp. 568–575.

in colonial harbors when boat slips accumulated filth. In one of his pamphlets he suggested the value of an estate tax to equalize the tax burden and to cut down on duties that slowed commercial exchange.[12]

I

Colden's audacity to take up almost any subject was undoubtedly a factor in his decision to write about the Five Nations shortly after his move to New York in the early 1720s. This factor undoubtedly motivated him, along with his natural inclination to write on significant topics which he thought might bring him recognition in his own time and perhaps real fame in posterity. Of course, Colden had immediate motives for his project: he wanted to publicize the whole Indian fur-trade business, and he wanted approval of the legislation proposed by his friend, Governor William Burnet, which would halt neutralist Indian trade between Albany and Montreal.[13]

But Colden told his own story in the Indian history he produced in 1727 and in the enlargement that appeared in a London edition twenty years later. This later edition of 1747 is the basis of almost all editions readily available in modern times.[14] Almost all reprints (exemplified by those of 1902 and 1904) set forth Colden's

12. See Colden to John Mitchell, November 7 [1747], *The Letters and Papers of Cadwallader Colden*, 8: 329. [Cadwallader Colden], *The Interest of City and Country to Lay No Duties, Or A Short Discourse Shewing that Duties on Trade Tend to the Impoverishing of City and Country, Also How the Government May be easier and better Supported than by Duties* (New York, 1726), pp. 5, 18.

13. See the preface to the second part of Colden's *History*, 1: 103–106.

14. John G. Shea in his 1866 introduction to Colden's *History* discusses alterations made by English publishers in the 1747 edition. See John G. Shea, ed., *The History of the Five Indian Nations Depending on the Province of New-York by Cadwallader Colden. Reprinted exactly from Bradford's New York edition*, (1727). (New York, 1866), pp. iii–xl. The most recent reprinting of Colden's *History* in 1958 by Cornell University Press unfortunately lacks an introduction or an index and makes no mention of the "Continuation" of his *History*.

History in two volumes, in imitation of the eighteenth-century English edition. The first volume, divided into two parts, narrates Indian affairs and details the history of the Five Nations from their first contacts with Europeans in the early 1600s through the Treaty of Ryswick in 1697. Colden concentrated his account of Indian wars and treaty making, however, on the period from the 1670s to 1697, although he does mention Iroquois treaty making in 1701, which began a period of neutrality for the confederation. The second volume consisted of various published documents, many of which had no direct relevance to the first volume. In a way, however, these formed a kind of documentary history of the Iroquois and other woodland tribes in the eighteenth century and served as a sequel to Colden's narrative. For example, Colden's long "Furr-Trade" memorial included historical background to justify his case against the Albany traders who enriched themselves by sending goods to Montreal for the Indian trade. This and other fur-trade documents in volume two of Colden's *History* were accompanied by printed Indian treaties.[15] A number of these concerned seventeenth-century Pennsylvania. These latter items had little relevance to Colden's *History*, and they may well have been inserted by Colden's British publishers or by Peter Collinson, his London correspondent, who seems to have supervised the publication of the 1747 English edition. A continuation, by Colden, covering the era 1704–1720 supplemented the original history. This "Continuation," published by The New-York Historical Society in 1937, traced Iroquois attempts at neutrality during continued fur-trade rivalry and war between the French and the English.[16]

15. The fur-trade documents begin in the year 1720 with a petition of London merchants. Colden's *History*, 2: 1–5, 33 ff. One of the most significant treaties of the colonial era, the Treaty of Lancaster of 1744, which paved the way for the dispossession of the Ohio area Indians, is on pp. 119–204.

16. "Colden's History of the Five Indian Nations, *Continuation*, 1707–1720," *The Letters and Papers of Cadwallader Colden*, 9: 359–434. By the year 1712, the Iroquois had definitely decided upon peaceful accommodation with the French. See ibid., pp. 415–16. As in his earlier writings, Colden consistently blamed French agents for the backsliding of the Iroquois in their

The historical narrative in the first volume of Colden's *History* gave him international recognition in his own day and a degree of fame in posterity. Although an eager reader might expect an appetizing feast of Indian-white relations complete with heroic adventures, plots, counterplots, and noble warriors returning from their battles with fluttering trophies of conquest, the book is disappointingly dull, at least in the beginning, although the heroism and battles are there, plus some grisly accounts of torture. Furthermore, it is difficult to read, even for an Indian buff who knows something about the woodland tribes and their history. In fact, only the most determined and persistent reader can shake the rich fruits of Indian history from this knotty tree of a book.

Why all the trouble in reading a notable work that has survived centuries of criticism? Among other things, the painstaking repetitive introductions, the literary apparatus which Colden uses to set the scene for the first chapters, fend off modern readers. He began with a strange dedication to James Oglethorpe, strange because the dedication was designed for Colden's friend Governor William Burnet and the English edition substituted Oglethorpe's name, and most modern reprintings of the *History* have repeated the change.[17] This is followed by a lengthy introduction, a table of contents, and a "Vocabulary of Some Words and Names," and a preface. If the casual reader breezes by the "Vocabulary," or glossary of names, he had better turn back, because he will get no further than the first page of the first chapter before finding mysterious tribes he never knew existed. Colden tells the story of Iroquois wars with the "Adirondacks" and the "Quatoghies." Even an old standby reference work such as Hodge's *Handbook of the Indians North of Mexico* has only occasional references to clarify the array of Indian tribal names used by Colden. Neverthe-

---

reluctance to fight the French. One of these was Chabert Joncaire, or "Jean Coeur," called "Sononjeur" by the Indians. Ibid., p. 424.

   17. See John G. Shea, ed., *The History of the Five Nations . . . by Cadwallader Colden*, pp. xii–xxxi, for a discussion of variations in eighteenth-century editions of Colden's *History*.

less, with the aid of Hodge, Colden's glossary, and other references one gradually understands that these are actually names of real Indian tribes. The Adirondacks are St. Lawrence River area Algonquians, the Quatoghies are Hurons, and so forth. However, another complication arises. Some Indian names were hopelessly garbled because the English printer of the 1747 edition carefully (or carelessly) altered names of certain tribes. Thus, the Iroquois occasionally war against the Hinois (sometimes also dubbed Chictaghicks), who were actually the Illinois Indians![18]

Compared, then, to the works of other colonial writers on the Indians, Colden's *History* falls short in readability and in general literary quality. It has little of the grace of Robert Beverley's *History and Present State of Virginia*, nor does it have the wit or tonic of originality found in William Byrd's *The History of the Dividing Line*. Even Roger Williams's *Key to the Indian Language*, written almost a century earlier, a kind of dictionary-handbook on Indians, is in some ways a much easier book to use. John Lawson's description of the southern Indians, especially his spicy details about relations between white traders and Indian women, has more vitality of personal experience. So has James Adair's *History of the American Indians* of 1776 and Edmond Atkin's report and plan for Indian management. Lawson, Adair, and Atkin all wrote in a more readable style and in some respects offered more information about the particular Indians they discussed. Of course they wrote about Indians of their own time.[19]

By contrast, Colden, an eighteenth-century figure, wrote about seventeenth-century Indians. His *History of the Five Nations* ended in the 1690s, some thirty years before Colden actually became a resident of New York. Moreover, the "Continuation" of his *History* terminated in 1720, only two years after Colden moved

18. Volume 2 of Hodge, for example, has no entry under "Quatoghies," although the name appears in the long essay on the Hurons in volume 1. Frederick Webb Hodge, ed., *Handbook of the American Indians North of Mexico* (Washington, D.C., 1907), 1: 591. Colden's *History*, 1: xlviii.

19. A discussion of the writers mentioned above appears in Jacobs, *Dispossessing the American Indian*, pp. 12, 15, 61 ff., 113 ff., 125. See also Wilcomb Washburn's essay on James Adair in the present volume, pp. 91–120.

to New York. Nevertheless, Colden did something no other writer on Indian affairs had done; he provided a window into the early history of the Iroquois.[20] He told of their wars when they were at the zenith of their power, at a time when white technology first began to alter their culture. With the use of Indian records, now lost, and the sifting of other sources, as well as his personal observations, Colden gave us one of the most significant histories of the colonial era, with sidelights on what we now call ecology, sociology, anthropology, and cultural history.

One may well ask why Colden did not complete his *History*, carrying it into his own time and utilizing his own detailed personal experience in Indian affairs. Certainly, Colden was engaged in a wide variety of activities, all of which competed for his time. However, after confronting his sometimes monotonous account of treaties, wars, atrocities, attacks, and counterattacks,

20. The bibliographical commentary in George T. Hunt, *The Wars of the Iroquois, a Study in Intertribal Relations* (Madison, Wis., 1967), p. 185, indicated that Hunt had a low opinion of Colden's *History* because it had occasional factual errors and largely omitted Iroquois history before 1678. Other scholars, however, have consistently stressed the value of Colden's *History* as a significant work in the history of Indian-white relations. See, for example, Lawrence H. Leder's comments in *Ethnohistory* 6: (Summer, 1959), 317–318. W. J. Eccles writes of Colden, "I have yet to find anything in the French documents that indicated he was abusing his evidence, and I have found a great deal that corroborated his account of events, his interpretations, and his attribution of motives." Letter to W. R. Jacobs, March 15, 1972. Allen W. Trelease points to one of Colden's weaknesses: "Colden looked at the Iroquois through 18th century glasses. He tends to romanticize them, and writes about them partially for political effect . . . to magnify their importance as a means of influencing current policy in New York and London. With these reservations, which are considerable, the *History* remains indispensable as a supplement to the documentary record." Letter to W. R. Jacobs, March 15, 1972. William N. Fenton is convinced that, considering Colden's opportunity for observation of the Indians, he gave us an accurate picture of the Iroquois genius for politics. W. N. Fenton and W. R. Jacobs conference on Indian history, Old Mission Dam, Santa Barbara, Calif., Feb. 28, 1972. As Fenton has pointed out, Colden was deeply indebted to Joseph-Francois Lafitau and Baron de Lahonton and other writers. For instance, Lafitau sets forth the "genius" theme in several places in his *Moeurs Des Sauvages Ameriquains* (Paris, 1724), 1: 2; 2: 118, 165–66, 167–68. See also Baron de Lahonton, *New Voyages to North-America*, ed. R. G. Thwaites (Chicago, 1905), 1: 77 ff. for documentary material quoted in Colden, *History*, 1: 63 ff.

almost all of it concerning the French and their desperate attempts to stave off Iroquois conquest, one can conclude that Colden, like the participants in his *History* who finally made peace in 1701, was weary. In fact, chronicling such material probably left him mentally exhausted. His "Continuation," the third part of his *History*, detailed conferences and military events up to 1720 (strangely omitting the years 1697–1706)[21] and offered an uninspired compilation of dates, names, and facts, suggesting his increasing boredom with his project. And, if he never finished writing his *History*, Colden at least had the assurance that his compilation of documents made available a great deal of eighteenth-century Indian history.

Despite its literary defects, the prefatory matter in Colden's *History* contained much of the richest Indian lore. Here Colden set forth the idea that allowing the Iroquois themselves to speak in treaty negotiations would reveal their "Genius." His "introductions" served as a theoretical scaffolding for his "Genius" theme, as he sketched an overview of Indian customs. He explained Indian ideas about ownership of personal property and theft, the significance of war dances, the role of the sachems (civilian chiefs) in government, as well as Indian methods of warmaking and peacemaking. In divorce, Iroquois children continued to live with the mother, and husband and wife separated freely "without Formality or Ignominity, unless it be occasioned by some scandalous Offence." Theft, Colden assured his readers, "is very scandalous among them." If they had one weakness, it was "Male and Female are infatuated with the Love of strong drink."[22]

Since these people had "a perfect Republican Government: Where no single Person has a Power to compel, the Arts of Persuasion alone must prevail." In making this point Colden clinched his argument for including a great deal of Iroquois speechmaking

21. There is a possibility that Colden may have composed a draft (now lost) covering these years. See editor's note, *The Letters and Paper of Cadwallader Colden*, 9: 359 n.
22. Colden, *History*, 1: xxxii.

in his *History*, for he was convinced that Iroquois orators with "a great Fluency of Words" had, by study and exercise, perfected speaking into an art.[23] Colden assured us he knew many of these things because, on occasion, he had visited the Indian country.

In short, Colden set the scene for his *History*. Although sometimes called "Barbarians," these Indians defended their country with bravery and love of liberty, even to the extent of outdoing the Romans. If such natives were guilty of barbaric cruelty, Colden asked, "But what, alas! Sir, have we Christians done to make them better?" They were, Colden argued, "a poor, generally called barbarous People, bred under the darkest Ignorance; and yet a bright and noble Genius shines through these black Clouds. None of the greatest Roman Heroes have discovered a greater Love of their Country, or a greater contempt of Death, than these People called Barbarians have done, when Liberty came in Competition."[24] Here in a nutshell was Colden's portrayal of the Iroquois, the "noble savages" of North America, a people whose faults as well as nobility of character greatly resembled those of the ancient Romans themselves.

II

Colden's narrative began with a brief account of the early seventeenth-century Iroquois wars with the Canadian Algonquians (the Adirondacks) and the Hurons (the Quatoghies), and with a description of Champlain's historic intercession on the side of the Algonquians in an encounter with an Iroquois war party. French "Fire-arms surprised the Five Nations so much, that they were immediately put into Confusion; for, before that Time, they had never seen such Weapons."[25] Following this early encounter, the Iroquois made aggressive counterattacks in far-ranging campaigns carried on by "Armies" broken up into small parties "the better to

23. Ibid., p. xxxiv.
24. Ibid., pp. x–xi.
25. Ibid., pp. 5–6.

provide for their subsistence by hunting." Colden justified wearisome war party escapades which made up much of the continuing narrative by his argument that it illustrated the Indian method of war.

He gave a scant twenty-five pages to Iroquois history before 1678 because Colden's sources, the body of Indian records he used, began at that date.[26] Thus the heart of Colden's *History* covered the wars and treaties between 1678 and the Treaty of Ryswick in 1697, scarcely a quarter of a century, although his "Continuation" dealt with Iroquois history from 1704 to 1720. In his first chapters Colden described the Dutch fur trade which set the pattern for the English of following the "Arts of peace" by persuading the Indians to trade at Albany. Such peaceful expansion of the fur trade was constantly interrupted by the French, who persisted in building forts and attacking English settlements, and who were tough and courageous adversaries. Their explorers had "Courage and Resolution," and a man like Nicholas Perrot, Colden grudgingly admitted, penetrated regions far beyond Michilimackinac; "having learned those Indians language, [he] gained them over to his Country's interest."[27] An underlying theme began to emerge in Colden's *History*: the wise, peaceful, progressive Indian policies of the English as opposed to the cruel and sometimes irrational policies of the French. Despite their bad record, however, Colden graciously acknowledged the politeness of the French, their cunning, and even the heroic qualities in such figures as Perrot and Count Frontenac.

From time to time Colden temporarily slowed his narration of seemingly never ending fighting by blending in an explanation of

26. Leder, *Livingston Indian Records*, p. 11. Leder believes that Colden, in preparing his "Furr-Trade" memorial as well as his *History*, had the advice of Robert Livingston, New York secretary of Indian Affairs, and Livingston's sons. The Livingstons, in addition to possessing the records of the commissioners of Indian Affairs, were "a tremendous fund of information." See Leder, *Robert Livingston, 1654–1728, and the Politics of Colonial New York* (Chapel Hill, N.C., 1961), p. 281 n.

27. Colden, *History*, 1: 21.

Indian customs. For instance, he described the Iroquois method of making peace by adopting prisoners as substitutes for slain loved ones. These former prisoners eventually became full-fledged tribe members adopted by Iroquois warriors "in the Place of their dead Friends." In the matter of peacemaking, Colden gave his readers a number of examples of the Iroquois chain of friendship legend, explaining how Indian orators used it to justify policy and to cement alliances. This imaginary chain needed to be kept "bright as silver." During times of stress the Five Nations and their allies had to keep the chain (often described as "a new chain" when signs of weakness occurred in alliance) "bright and clean and held fast on all sides." Iroquois peacemaking was also associated with the figurative planting of a great tree of peace (a favorite design on Iroquois wampum belts) "whose top will reach the Sun, and its Branches spread far abroad, so that it shall be seen afar off; and we shall shelter ourselves under it, and live in Peace without Molestation." Colden time and again showed us that these fierce warriors were also peacemakers. The Iroquois speeches quoted by Colden offered convincing evidence that the Iroquois would fight when their national interest was at stake, but otherwise they sincerely wanted peace. As an Iroquois orator told British delegates from the southern colonies on one occasion, the Indians wanted peace, "but ye are stupid and brutish and have no Understanding. . . . Let the new chain . . . be carefully preserved." Colden's *History* offered additional illustrations of the Iroquois desire for peace, not only with the English but with the French and their Indian allies. For instance, the Iroquois were willing to dance the Calumet peace pipe dance with Algonquian Indians. In talking with the English, they said they wanted to bury all Iroquois hatchets "in a deep pit."[28]

One of Colden's literary problems in writing his *History* was

28. Ibid., pp. 26, 41–2; Photographs of such belts are in W. N. Fenton, "The New York State Wampum Collection: the Case for the Integrity of Cultural Treasures," *Proceedings of the American Philosophical Society* 115 (December 30, 1971): 430–71; wampum diplomacy is discussed in W. R. Jacobs, *Dispossessing the American Indian*, pp. 41 ff.

apparently keeping the Iroquois posture in a fighting stance. So many times in their speeches and diplomacy they appeared to backslide, despite the constant urging of New York's governors (the most belligerent being Henry Sloughter and Benjamin Fletcher) to keep the Iroquois on the flanks of the French. Hard put to explain the Iroquois proclivity for peacemaking, Colden blamed Jesuit missionaries among the Seneca. A more sinister development, Colden stressed, was that French priests had induced a number of Iroquois to move to Montreal, where they became dangerous "Praying Indians" who were highly valued by the French because of "the Intelligence they give in Time of War, and their Knowledge of the Countries."[29]

Peace was in the Iroquois' self-interest, but not at the cost of giving up beaver-hunting territory. Oratorical speeches detailed Iroquois war policy, especially in the 1680s. Colden's *History* made it clear that beaver had been virtually exterminated in what is now New York State by the mid-seventeenth century, although the Iroquois still maintained active hunting grounds between Lake Ontario and Lake Erie. Here, as well as on other fringes of their territory, the Iroquois hunters fought off Ottawas, Illinois, Twightwees (Miamis of the Ohio area), and other Algonquian tribes. By 1684 the Iroquois were fighting for their livelihood, not necessarily as middlemen in the fur trade as George Hunt has argued, but to preserve their distant beaver-hunting territories. As the famous Onondaga orator Grangula (called by the French La Grande Gueule, the Big Mouth) told the French, "We knock'd the Twihtwies and Chictaghicks [Illinois Indians] on the Head, because they had cut down the trees of Peace, which were the Limits of our Country. They have hunted Bevers on our Lands: They have acted contrary to the Customs of all Indians; for they left none of the Bevers alive, killed Male and Female." Colden accepted such orators' arguments and their rationale for carrying on a defensive war. "The Five Nations," he wrote, "have few or no Bever in their Country, and for that Reason are obliged to hunt

29. Colden, *History*, 1: 45 n.

at a great Distance, which often occasions Disputes with their Neighbours about the Property of Bever."[30]

In their wars to preserve and expand their hunting territories, the Iroquois fought far from their traditional home, the area now the state of New York. Their enemies in the 1680s and 1690s were the Miamis, or Twightwee Indians, living in parts of the modern state of Ohio, and the Illinois tribes who lived in the general area of the state that now bears their name. Earlier, in the 1640s, the Hùrons and then the Ottawas of the northern Great Lakes had been their foes in the beaver war.[31] In other words, the beaver war by the 1680s pushed the northern outskirts of the French Empire in North America into the Midwest and the western Great Lakes. By 1688, Colden stated, this beaver war, supported by the English, actually developed into an Iroquois war of conquest to subdue Canadian Indians allied with the French and to destroy French settlements as well. Although the Five Nations at this time were an "overmatch for the French of Canada," they never administered the final blows necessary to conquer the French colony largely because the Five Nations became divided in their mission. Why were the Iroquois so lacking in resolution? Colden maintained that Jesuit diplomacy among the western Iroquois affected policy-making discussions among the sachems. Another factor in the Iroquois failure was the inability of the war chiefs to comprehend "the method of attacking Forts."[32]

At this point Colden's *History* came to a semiclimax, the end of the first part of his work, published in 1727. Whatever its shortcomings, it has parts that are surprisingly modern and relevant to today's readers. Colden gave one of the first ecological histories of

30. Ibid., 166, 69, 72.
31. Colden gives only brief attention to this war, ibid., pp. 12–15. The Huron-Iroquois wars are detailed in Hunt, *The Wars of the Iroquois*, pp. 66 ff; Allen W. Trelease, *Indian Affairs in Colonial New York: The Seventeenth Century* (Ithaca, N.Y., 1960), p. 118 ff.; Robert A. Goldstein, *French-Iroquois Diplomatic and Military Relations, 1609–1701* (The Hague, 1969), pp. 62 ff; Francis Parkman, *The Jesuits in North America in the Seventeenth Century* (Boston, 1907), 1: 230 ff.; 2: 57 ff.
32. Colden, *History*, 1: 98.

America, the story of one of the great bloodlettings in American history among Indians and whites in the wilderness. Much of the fighting grew out of an ecological disaster—the extermination of beaver—along the frontiers of Britain's northern colonies in America, which took place during the early seventeenth-century fur-trade exploitation. Colden's story, told in stark realism, in the language of the Indians themselves, gives modern readers much to ponder in the history of wasteful destruction of wildlife and its consequences.[33] Of course, other factors motivated the Iroquois wars as well as the search for beaver and other fur-bearing animals, but the widening fringes of war did follow the gradually retreating beaver frontiers of the seventeenth century.

III

The preface to the second part of Colden's *History* dwelled at length on the great benefits growing out of Governor William Burnet's "Scheme" of prohibiting trade with Canada and of erecting an English fur-trading post at Oswego, on the eastern shore of Lake Ontario (called Lake Catarackui by Colden). This English post, intercepting both Iroquois furs from the West and those of the Canadian Indians, Colden said, was so much of a success that it required three hundred men to handle the blizzard of trading activity. Some Indians came from such distant places that their names were completely unfamiliar to the British.[34]

This second part of Colden's *History* was largely an account of renewed fighting accented by fur-trade rivalry. Here we have Indian diplomacy at its best, along with a war in the forest fought between the French, led by Count Frontenac, and their Canadian Indians, and the Iroquois, with their English allies, in a period of war and diplomatic exchange of less than a decade, 1689–1697. Colden began his second part narration with a description of

33. For a discussion of the impact of the fur trade and the decimation of beaver and other wildlife in America's ecological history, see W. R. Jacobs, *Dispossessing the American Indian*, pp. 9–11, 19–40, 32–33, 126–27, 171–72.
34. Colden, *History*, 1: 105.

Count Frontenac's peace proposals, debated by "the General Council or Parliament of the Five Nations . . . at Onondaga, consisting of eighty sachems." Through a knowledge of Iroquois councils, Colden assured us, one may come to better know "the Indian Genius . . . that he may see in what Manner a People that we call Savages behave on such important Occasions." Colden, for instance, pointed out that the Iroquois sachems insisted on keeping peaceful relations with Canadian Indians of the East, "for they have done us no harm."[35]

However, the Iroquois could not accept proposals from Frontenac for peace because they lacked faith in his word, especially in the matter of returning prisoners. According to Iroquois speeches, he made halfhearted promises of prisoner exchanges "when the Strawberries shall be in blossom." Soon afterwards, Frontenac's surprise attack and stunning victory at Schenectady on February 9, 1689/90 smothered immediate hopes of peace. The Iroquois offered condolences to their English allies "with Tears in our Eyes to bemoan the Bloodshed . . . by the Perfidious French." Indeed, the Iroquois declared, "One Hundred of our bravest young men are in Pursuit of them, they are brisk Fellows, and will follow the French to their Doors."

Although Iroquois warriors closely trailed the French after the Schenectady disaster, more and more evidence appeared of defection within the cantons against an uncompromising war. The Iroquois declined to attack French tribes which had not actually been foes in war, and some Iroquois allowed French missionaries to live in their villages. Even loyal Mohawks gave evidence of making direct peace negotiations against protests by New York governors. Governor Henry Sloughter, on one occasion, "check'd the Mohawks for entering into a separate Treaty with the Enemy," and urged them to keep the French in "perpetual alarm."[36]

Colden's narrative only briefly covered English expeditions of

35. Ibid., p. 124.
36. Ibid., p. 155.

William Phips and Peter Schuyler against Quebec and Montreal, but he allotted more than adequate space to French reprisals in torturing a captured war chief of the Iroquois. Meanwhile, in 1691–92, a party of eighty Iroquois and accompanying native women, hunting beaver "on the Neck of Land between Cadarackui Lake and Lake Erie" (between Lake Ontario and Lake Erie), were decimated by a formidable party of French and Montreal praying Indians who hurried back to Canada with three women prisoners.[37] This highly valuable strip of beaver-hunting ground became, perhaps, the most fiercely contested land in Frontenac's war of survival against the Iroquois.

The remainder of the second portion of Colden's *History* dealt with Frontenac's campaigns to carry the war into the Iroquois country despite their fierce resistance. Colden described a sidelight of the war, Frontenac's "monstrous cruelty" in ordering the torment of Iroquois captives, with some relish as an atrocity story to illustrate shortcomings in the French national character. But he told us, even the prospect of having one's feet "broiled . . . between two red hot Stones" or having a scalp removed "pouring scalding hot Sand upon it" would not usually frighten brave Iroquois prisoners. In fact, it was recorded as a scandal when one Iroquois captive committed suicide rather than endure such treatment. On the other side of the coin, Colden played down the ferocity of the Iroquois when they captured Frenchmen. Colden, however, did tell the story of an English commander who "told me himself" about eating campfire broth made by Five Nations warriors. The Indians, "putting the Ladle into the Kettle to take out more, brought out a French Man's Hand, which put an End to his Appetite."[38]

If survival in the winter wilderness sometimes involved cannibalism, it also involved specialized techniques of marching and making camp in heavy snow. Enlivening his narrative with an apparently authentic explanation, Colden wrote:

37. Ibid., p. 166.
38. Ibid., p. 187.

the foremost march on Snow shoes which beat a firm track for those that follow. At Night, when they rest, they dig a Hole in the Snow, throwing the Snow up all round, but the highest toward that Side from whence the Wind blows, so large, as to contain as many Men as can lye round a Fire: they Make a Fire in the Middle, and cover the frozen Ground round it with the small branches of the Fir-Trees. Thus they tell me a Man lyes much warmer, than one imagines that never tried it.[39]

, Colden used the records of a conference between the Iroquois and Governor Benjamin Fletcher in 1693–94 to explain details of negotiating between the Iroquois and their English allies. On this occasion Fletcher, a bold and sometimes reckless negotiator, made an unexpected proposal to persuade the Iroquois to give up the Jesuit missionary, Father Pierre Millet. Fletcher astonished the Indians by producing the unique gift of "a pretty Indian Boy, in lieu of the old Priest," but no trade was made.[40]

To deal with Fletcher the Iroquois, in this and later conferences of the 1690s, called upon their most famous orator of the time, Decanesora, who lived until about 1730 when Colden actually saw him in person. Colden described him as almost a reincarnation of a Roman senator:

He was grown old when I saw him, and heard him speak; he had a great Fluency in speaking, and a graceful Elocution, that would have pleased in any Part of the World. His Person was tall and well made, and his Features, to my thinking resembled the Bust of Cicero.

Decanesora's remarkable speeches, Colden related, reflected Iroquois policy and also traced the course of events since "his narration agrees in the main with the Account the French give . . . as strong Evidences of Truth."[41] As proof of this great orator's unique persuasive powers, Colden illustrated Decanesora's "Art" in soothing ruffled English feelings and mollifying their fears, even

39. Ibid., pp. 186–87.
40. Ibid., p. 197.
41. Ibid., pp. 199–200. See also Hodge, *Handbook* 1: 384. Herein his name is spelled Dekanisora. Parkman spells his name Decanisora. Parkman, *Count Frontenac and New France Under Louis XIV* (Boston, 1907), p. 419.

when the Iroquois deliberately defied the outraged pleas of English authorities. In a carefully phrased reply to suspicious questions about the Iroquois harboring the Jesuit missionary, Father Pierre Millet, Decanesora told his listeners, "we know that the Priest favours his own Nation and deceives us in many Things," but, he added, the priest did not have the "Power to alter our Affection" for the English.

Skillfully, Decanesora changed the subject to what the English could do to improve relations with the Iroquois. He urged the English to "bury all Misunderstandings" about the Jesuit and devote their attention to better management of Indian affairs by taking them out of the hands of "Rum-carriers." Throughout his oration Decanesora urged his listeners to consider "what is most for the publick Good." Do not be disturbed by French "Mischief," he said, do not be so ready to "blame one another." Reinforcing these sage observations, he laid down huge belts of wampum, one with rows of beads "fourteen deep."[42]

Colden also gave his readers samples of Decanesora's orations, recalling meetings with Frontenac in which the Indian speaker told of French duplicity and explained the problems in making peace with an enemy the Indians did not trust. At this point, in the midst of long quotations from Indian records, Colden stopped and gave his readers some reflections on the Iroquois regard for treaties and diplomacy. "Here we see these Barbarians, these Savages, as we call them," Colden wrote, "acting with the greatest regard to the Treaties they had entered into with their Allies, and that at a Time when the Exigencies of their own Affairs . . . would . . . have been . . . sufficient Excuse for their taking Care of themselves separately."[43]

At the close of the second part of Colden's *History*, he detailed the continued struggles between the Iroquois and the French and their Indian allies on the northern shore of Lake Ontario and in beaver-hunting grounds to the south. The contest over possession

42. Colden, *History*, 1: 206–207.
43. Ibid., p. 229.

of Fort Frontenac on Lake Ontario was crucial for the French because they needed it for the security of their traders passing between Montreal and Michilimackinac in the interior Great Lakes.[44] Frontenac moved the war into the heart of Iroquois country at Onondaga by leading some five hundred Canadian Indians and troops there. Carried in a chair, directly in front of his artillery, the old governor directed the destruction; but as Colden noted, the tribesmen lost only "their corn and their Bark Cottages" as they fled into the woods, leaving Frontenac with merely "a kind of heroick Dotage."[45]

Shortly before the Treaty of Ryswick in 1697, Frontenac died, and final peace arrangements between the Iroquois and the French were made at conferences at Montreal and at Albany with an exchange of prisoners, early in 1700.[46] The Iroquois had few French prisoners to deliver because the prisoners themselves desired to live with their adopted tribesmen. So attractive was the wild freedom of Indian life to whites who had sampled it that they often refused to come back to civilization. Colden assured us that even "the English had as much Difficulty to persuade the People, that had been taken prisoners by the French Indians to leave the Indian manner of living." By ending with praise for the Indian way of life, Colden left his readers with an image of a remarkable native people whose culture and way of life attracted those who had known them intimately.

IV

Colden's *History* in one sense was a memorial to the greatest of all the woodland Indian peoples, the Iroquois. Fierce barbarians,

44. Colden refers to this fort as Cadarackui Fort. Ibid., p. 232. Compare maps in Francis Parkman, *LaSalle and the Discovery of the Great Lakes*, Frontenac edition (Boston, 1907), opposite p. 3, and frontispiece map in Colden, *History*, vol. 2, opposite title page.
45. Colden's *History*, 1: 249.
46. Ibid., pp. 256 ff. These final peace negotiations are clearly described by Allen W. Trelease, *Indian Affairs in Colonial New York*, pp. 332–63.

aggressive fighters for their own national interests, they were nevertheless vitally interested in peace if they could maintain their self-determination. Reexamination of Colden's *History* highlights the fact that American writers on Indian history have stressed Iroquois militancy, probably because they attacked seventeenth-century Canada so violently, and probably a great writer like Francis Parkman overemphasized Indian warlike characteristics. Colden's *History* provided clear evidence of the Iroquois' sincere interest in peace. They clearly saw in the seventeenth century that their best interests were not involved in a never-ending contest between European powers. As Colden showed us in his "Continuation," the Iroquois sachems attempted to move toward a neutrality which would help preserve their society relatively intact well into the eighteenth century. Even with the ecological calamity resulting from the extermination of beaver and other animals within their immediate hunting grounds, the Iroquois, with agricultural skills and a reasonably stable population, could survive amid the continued storm of war that raged around them in the eighteenth century. The Indian agent and superintendent, Sir William Johnson, with blandishments and gifts, persuaded many of them to join the British in the final years of the French and Indian War. And, when the Iroquois took sides during the American Revolution by allying themselves with the British, they found the victorious Americans in no mood to grant them protection from the onrushing frontiersmen and land speculators during the formative period of the republic.[47] For the early years of this tragic story, Cadwallader Colden gave us a unique narrative of seventeenth-century Indian-white relations unequaled by any other colonial writer.

47. W. R. Jacobs, *Wilderness Politics and Indian Gifts* (Lincoln, Neb., 1966), pp. 76 ff. Anthony F. C. Wallace, *The Death and Rebirth of the Seneca* (New York, 1970), pp. 111 ff., 149 ff.; Fred Eggan, *The American Indian, Perspectives for the Study of Social Change* (Chicago, 1966), pp. 149 ff; William N. Fenton, "The Iroquois in History" (Paper read at the Wenner-Gren Symposium, Burg Wartenstein, Austria, August 7–14, 1967), copy in possession of W. R. Jacobs.

4.

Le Page du Pratz: Memoir of the Natchez Indians

JOSEPH G. TREGLE, JR.

Antoine de Ulloa, eminent eighteenth-century Spanish scientist, announced as his considered judgment (translated into the modern idiom) that "If you have seen one American Indian, you have seen them all."[1] Had later generations substantially shared his view, Antoine Simon Le Page du Pratz would probably be largely forgotten today, remembered if at all only as the author of a somewhat amusing catalogue of the early flora and fauna of the lower Mississippi valley. His 1758 *Histoire de la Louisiane,* essentially a memoir of the French colony from 1718 through 1734, treated the political, administrative, and cultural development of the settlement too sketchily to have any real value for those aspects of colonialism.[2] Considered in that context alone it could not support any lasting claim on fame. But for eight years Le Page lived among the Natchez Indians, and his *Histoire* reported on them with such insightful and sympathetic detail that the work has remained a basic source and a provocative challenge for those fumbling with the anthropology and archaeology of the first Americans.

Ulloa, it should be said, was no fool, and current scholarship has

1. T. D. Stewart and M. T. Newman, "An Historical Résumé of the Concept of Differences in Indian Types," *American Anthropologist* 53 (1951): 19. Ironically, this same Ulloa's insensitivity as the first Spanish governor of Louisiana resulted in the expulsion of Spain from the colony in 1768.

2. Justin Winsor, for example, regarded the *Histoire*'s value as "resting upon the interest of his personal experiences." See Winsor, *Narrative and Critical History of America,* 8 vols. (Boston, 1884–89), 5: 67.

reaffirmed the scientific acuteness underlying his observation. But the complexity and richness of Indian diversity rather than its elusive unity inevitably invited more specific analysis and classification, and in this ever-broadening endeavor the work of Le Page du Pratz would win its lasting recognition.

His subjects were, in truth, of such individual distinctiveness among North American Indian populations as to almost guarantee any author an audience for his observations concerning them. In the midst of generally democratic, relatively unstratified Indian societies, the Natchez possessed a monarchical and aristocratic organization characterized as a "veritable Alice-in-Wonderland of human nature." In addition, a language long thought to be unrelated to that of their neighbors and a highly developed religion of sun worship centering around an ever-burning flame in a holy temple only deepened the mystery of their apparent uniqueness. Yet they had about them an equally forcible sense of universality. Once the most powerful tribe on the lower Mississippi River, they would pass through a series of relationships with European societies which reflected the later general American Indian experience, until finally the white man's power would destroy them as an entity, a kind of microcosm of the Indian world.[3] Le Page du Pratz has told us most of what we know about this intriguing people.

3. C. W. M. Hart, "A Reconsideration of Natchez Social Structure," *American Anthropologist* 45 (1943): 374. For the ambivalent uniqueness and universality of the Natchez experience see Wendell H. Oswalt, *This Land Was Theirs* (New York, 1966), pp. 465–467; John R. Swanton, *Indian Tribes of the Lower Mississippi Valley and Adjacent Coast of the Gulf of Mexico*, Bureau of American Ethnology Bulletin 43 (Washington, 1911), 45–260; Kingsley Davis, "Intermarriage in Caste Societies," *American Anthropologist* 43 (1941): 382; William Christie MacLeod, "Natchez Political Evolution," *American Anthropologist* 26 (1924): 201–209; William Christie MacLeod, "On Natchez Cultural Origins," *American Anthropologist* 28 (1926); Andrew C. Albrecht, "Ethical Precepts Among the Natchez Indians," *Louisiana Historical Quarterly* 31 (1948): 569–597; Andrew C. Albrecht, "Indian-French Relations at Natchez," *American Anthropologist* 48 (1946): 321–354; John R. Swanton, "Ethnological Position of the Natchez Indians," *American Anthropologist* 9 (1907): 513–528; James Mooney, "The End of the Natchez," *American Anthropologist* 1 (1899): 510–521.

About Le Page himself we know remarkably little, except for the meager revelations scattered through the pages of his *Histoire*. Nineteenth-century scholars speculated that he was a native of The Netherlands, born around 1695, but no extant evidence appears to bear on this point, and Le Page remained completely silent as to his origins. Whatever his provenance, he apparently considered himself essentially French, fought in the ranks of Louis XIV's dragoons during the "German campaigns" of the War of the Spanish Succession, and by 1718 cast his fortunes with John Law's spectacular new Company of the West in its grandiose design for French empire in Louisiana.[4]

Together with some 800 other adventurers he sailed from New Rochelle in May of that year, down along the traditional French route to the Caribbean and Saint-Domingue, past Cuba and Jamaica into the Gulf of Mexico and eventual harbor on August 25 at Ile Dauphine, athwart the entrance to Mobile Bay. As to the economic status of the rest of the 800 migrants, we have no knowledge, but Le Page, at least, had not arrived as a penniless, useless casualty of European dislocation. A graduate of the "*cours de mathématiques*," and a professional architect according to his own description, he also claimed sufficient skill as a hydraulic engineer to consider tackling the already critical problem of the silting of the mouths of the Mississippi.[5]

4. Brief entries on Le Page may be found under "Pratz" in *Michaud's Biographie Universelle, Ancienne et Moderne*. New Edition (Paris, 1811–1862), 34: 295, and *Nouvelle Biographie Generale* (Paris, 1962), 39: 986; under "Du Pratz" in the *Dictionary of American Biography* article by Lionel Durel and in *Appleton's Cyclopedia of American Biography* (New York, 1888), 2: 266. In his *Histoire de la Louisiane*, 3 vols. (Paris, 1758), I: v, Le Page calls France "ma patrie." Moreover, he spoke to native Frenchmen in a fashion which implied complete identification with them in language and cultural tradition. See [Dumont de Montigny], *Mémoires Historiques sur la Louisiane Composés sur les Mémoires de M. Dumont par M. L.L.M.* [M. L'Abbé Le Mascrier], 2 vols. (Paris, 1753), 1: 120. These few biographical data are culled from the *Histoire*, 1: 131, 134; 3: 328.

5. Le Page du Pratz, *Histoire*, 1: 37–38, 131; 2: 262, 256. The Bibliothèque Nationale possesses Le Page's *Lettre sur Quelque Nouveaux Points d'Astronomie* (Paris, 1760).

But he now committed himself to the life of a concessionaire, and so gathering up his slaves and equipment he hurried from Mobile to the outskirts of the infant New Orleans, where he established his grant on the banks of Bayou St. John, "about half a league distant from the place where the capital was to be founded." Here he remained for approximately a year, until enticing reports of the superior climate and soil of the Natchez area drew him northward, and in January of 1720 he established himself as neighbor to the Indian tribe which would command so much of his attention.[6]

The Natchez villages clustered around St. Catherine's Creek, a small stream which flowed southwesterly to join the Mississippi below the bluffs upon which Bienville in 1716 had constructed Fort Rosalie as a French bastion. On the road leading from the fort to the main Indian village, in the midst of great meadows and stands of hickory, Le Page purchased from the natives a small cabin in a clearing, together with some 400 acres of light, black-soiled land ideally suited to the growing of tobacco. With his own personal plantation thus secured, he then acquired two additional sites close to the fort and the village, one in the name of the Company, the other as the private concession of M. Marc-Antoine Hubert, commissary of the colony. Le Page's arrival, in effect, signaled a considerably expanded French attempt at economic relationships with the Natchez, a development which would, ironically, lead to eventual consequences for the natives which could hardly have pleased a man who would describe them in his *Histoire* as a "brilliant and distinguished" people marked by "greatness and the beauty of their culture."[7]

For eight years he dwelled among the Natchez, observed their customs, joined their ceremonies, and became their friend and trusted confidant, known to them, he noted, as "Chief of the Beautiful Head" because of his luxuriant locks. He listened patiently and without condescension as their chiefs explicated the

6. Le Page du Pratz, *Histoire*, 1: 83, 89–92.
7. Ibid., 1: 126–127; 2: 221, 308.

meaning of honor and manhood and as their temple guardian explained their religious convictions. Trustingly, he placed himself in the hands of their medicine men [*jongleurs*] and came away assured that many of their skills far surpassed those of the butchers he had known in France. In their company he traveled long distances through the surrounding countryside, in their community he prospered, and in their society he immersed himself in what he called its "charming solitudes, far from the tumult of the world, removed from its miseries of avarice and deceit . . . exempt from criticism, mendacity, and calumny."[8]

His dyspeptic vision of the larger universe was essentially confirmed by what he considered the totally unprovoked attack upon the Natchez by Governor Bienville in 1723. "I lost from this moment," he confessed, "all hope of remaining in this country," convinced as he was that only the friendship felt for him by the ancient Great Sun and his brother, Tattooed Serpent, war chief of the Natchez, kept that nation from falling in retribution upon the French post. The death of Tattooed Serpent in 1725, with its obvious traumatic effect upon the ninety-five-year-old Great Sun, seemed to Le Page the sure signal to take his leave. However, protestations of friends in the settlement and his own deep attachment to it slowed his steps, so that he did not make his reluctant way to New Orleans until 1728, intent upon returning to Europe. In the capital he succumbed to the importunities of the newly arrived Governor Étienne de Perier and his commissary, Jacques de la Chaise, took·over the direction of the Company of the West's plantation on the far bank of the Mississippi, and thus stretched his stay in Louisiana.[9] The shift to New Orleans doubtless saved his life by removing him from the tragic Natchez Revolt in 1729, for even his unique relationship to the Natchez probably

8. Ibid., 2: 400; 1: 129, 135, 207–208, 263–264.
9. Ibid., 1: 197–199; Paris *Journal Oeconomique*, December, 1752, p. 139; April, 1752, p. 147 (Tattooed Serpent was seventy. Le Page gives their ages in these early *Journal* articles, but not, strangely enough, in the later *Histoire*), p. 140; Le Page du Pratz, *Histoire*, 3: 226.

could not have spared him in that nation's convulsive and desperate commitment to freedom or death.

The Natchez rebellion and its aftermath so shook the colony that by July 1731 the Company of the West surrendered its charter and Louisiana became a royal province of Louis XV. Perier gave way to the returned Bienville, while Cardinal Fleury strove to effect desperate economies by abolishing the post of director of the royal plantation, thus turning Le Page once more toward France. He departed Louisiana forever on May 10, 1734.[10]

How much his American experiences affected Le Page's later life we can only guess. Not until 1751 did he begin his account of the distant French colony in which he had once played a significant part. He chose a propitious time indeed for his journalistic debut. French policy was already being directed toward recouping the staggering losses suffered in America since the Peace of Utrecht of 1713, centering on confining the British to a narrow band along the Atlantic by a wall of French fortifications from Montreal to New Orleans. Louisiana perforce loomed large in any such scheme. Yet the Mississippi Bubble of John Law, the forced deportation of thousands of hapless Manon Lescauts, and the horrors of the Natchez Massacre hardly inspired popular confidence in expanding French exploitation of a region whose very name was employed as a maternal instrument to terrify the troublesome young.[11] As each month brought growing evidence of impending clashes in America between French and British colonial designs, interest in Louisiana inevitably broadened, but to Le Page the persistence of misinformation about the colony threatened to abort French realization of its true value.

Thus in September of 1751 he began a series of articles on the colony in the *Journal Oeconomique* of Paris, which he eventually expanded into the 1758 *Histoire de la Louisiane*. Le Page admittedly designed the pieces, entitled *"Mémoire sur la Louisiane,"* to

10. Le Page du Pratz, *Histoire*, 3: 399.
11. See Georges Oudard, *Four Cents an Acre* (New York, 1931), 148–149.

correct those false impressions of the colony which he ascribed to ignorance and to occasional deliberate and malicious misrepresentation. More pointedly, however, he clearly shaped the articles as a practical handbook for those whom truth might persuade to take up new careers along the Mississippi. And he set the whole series in the matrix of a forceful philosophy of French colonial policy in which he advocated his own version of mercantilism as a counter to the supposedly more successful practices of the British, Spanish, and Portuguese. In short, Le Page's *mémoire* was no simple exercise in nostalgia by an old Louisiana hand, but rather a positive call for energetic quickening of his country's response to its opportunities abroad.[12]

This intent did not escape watchful eyes across the Channel. Introducing rather extensive extracts from Le Page's *Journal* articles, the editor of the *Gentleman's Magazine* of London wryly commented:

Upon this geographical description of Louisiana I cannot help remarking that when the French have a settlement in the corner of any uncultivated country unpossessed by any nation they never fail to reckon all that country within the limits of their settlements. "Louisiana," says my author, "extends to the unknown lands in the neighborhood of Hudson's Bay." Have not the English the same rights to say, that their settlements about Hudson's Bay (giving them a general name Georgiana for instance) extend as far as the borders of the French settlements in lower Louisiana?[13]

Though contentious, British comments on the series did not disparage it. Indeed, they were considerably more generous than those of at least two of Le Page's own compatriots, whose taunts might well have determined him to expand his articles into book

12. The Le Page articles on Louisiana may be found in the Paris *Journal Oeconomique*, September, 1751, pp. 128–156; October, 1751, pp. 134–160; December, 1751, pp. 113–147; February, 1752, pp. 116–144; March, 1752, pp. 135–160; April, 1752, pp. 117–156; July, 1752, pp. 126–168; August, 1752, pp. 123–168; September, 1752, pp. 145–160; November, 1752, pp. 145–160; December 1752, pp. 119–149; and February, 1753, pp. 94–132.
13. London *Gentleman's Magazine* 23 (1753): 265–267.

form as the most effective kind of rejoinder. The attack had come from a rather remarkable pair, a French officer once stationed in Louisiana, calling himself Louis François Dumont de Montigny, and Monsieur L'Abbé Le Mascrier, his Paris editor. Dumont de Montigny (he had invented his own aristocratic patronym by simply altering his original identification as "dumont *dit* Montigny"), a roistering scapegrace constantly in trouble with his superiors, had whiled away his sober moments in the colony by composing a bloated epic poem called "*L'Éstablissement de la Louisiane.*" Failing to receive even modest encouragement from those who had seen it, he had eventually cast it into prose form, sending the new version to the Abbé Le Mascrier, who provided extensive and imaginative editing before publishing it in 1753. Although Le Page had read the work in manuscript and had actually contributed to it by written observations acknowledged by Dumont, the treatise ridiculed his own *Journal* pieces as embracing "fantastic and imaginary descriptions" by "an inaccurate and uninformed writer." This was hardly generous, though perhaps not Dumont's fault, but in addition Dumont's basic approach did violence to one of Le Page's most cherished convictions. For to him the Natchez were a noble race, enlightened and trustworthy, first in his esteem among all the inhabitants of America, whom he carefully designated as "natives," never as "savages." To Dumont, all Indians were "treacherous people without honor, in whom we cannot place any faith," barren of "any idea of religion or cult."[14]

Whatever might have been his reaction to these barbs and perversities, Le Page did not record them, but by 1758 he published his expanded version of the *Journal* articles as the *Histoire de la Louisiane*, produced, as he noted, to satisfy various scholars whose high opinion of the original had led them to demand the perfected work. In his own work, he carefully found the proper

14. Jean Delanglez, "A Louisiana Poet-Historian: Dumont *dit* Montigny," *Mid-America* 19 (1937): 31, 32; [Dumont de Montigny], *Mémoires*, 1: ix, 118, 121, 123, 127, 129, 135, 157, 163.

place to denigrate the talents and worthiness of the "engineer," Dumont.[15]

Le Page cast the three volumes of the work squarely on the model of the *Journal* pieces, and while it represented a considerable expansion, it remained essentially a guide for those enticed to the New World. After a cursory historical sketch of French settlement of Louisiana, Le Page established his own credentials by relating his experiences in settling along Bayou St. John and eventually among the Natchez. From this base he proceeded to discuss the whole environment in which a settler might find himself, tracing the colony's geographic lineaments and setting the human element in the context of French relations with the Natchez. He rounded out his account with his findings on an extensive exploratory journey to the north and west of Fort Rosalie. Sensitive to the assumed interest of his readers, he then extensively analyzed the nature of the soil in various sectors of the colony, joining to this elaborate directions for the proper handling of those black slaves whom he deemed essential to any large-scale agricultural venture in the colony, an account based on his experience as director of the Company's plantation across from New Orleans.

Le Page devoted Volume II to a description of the crops and agricultural products of Louisiana, with detailed treatment of its plants, animals, birds, and fish. From flora and fauna he naturally turned to the region's human denizens, and thus addressed himself to the most significant area of his labors. Intensive and frequently speculative analysis of native manners and customs, emphasizing language, religion, festivals, marriage and burial practices, warfare, recreation, dress, architecture, and dietary preferences, carried him into Volume III, where he pondered the intriguing question of the Indian's origins. The ineluctable progression from birth to

15. Le Page du Pratz, *Histoire*, 1: x, 310–311. The complete title of the work was: *Histoire de la Louisiane, Contenant la Découverte de ce Vaste Pays; sa Description Géographique; un Voyage dans les Terres; l'Histoire Naturelle; les Moeurs, Coûtumes & Religion des Naturels, avec leurs Origines; deux Voyages dans le Nord du Nouveau Mexique, dont un jusqu'à la Mer du Sud; ornée de deux Cartes & de 40 Planches en Taille Douce.*

destruction led him then to his most famous pages, those recounting the death of Tattooed Serpent, the consequent deterioration of relations between the Natchez and the French, and the Rebellion of 1729. A final series of chapters on the cultivation of maize, rice, indigo, tobacco, and cotton served as a base for an evaluation of these and other factors in the economic relationship between France and Louisiana—Le Page's version, in short, of mercantilism.

A murky sense of some kind of order and continuity pervaded all of this, though the three volumes should be viewed all of a piece rather than seeking the rationale between individual sections or chapters. Approaching the work with their own set of interests, some British critics praised the Le Page volumes for their "sincerity and good sense," though admitting that the author's talents as a writer "are not very extraordinary" and that his "stile is unequal and diffuse." Moreover, in that critical year, when the British reversed the earlier disastrous course of the French and Indian War, these critics recognized that the coming months might indeed hold something new for French possessions in America and that the Le Page study of Louisiana might "serve to give us a just idea, as well of the future importance, as of the present state of the colony: a thing not altogether uninteresting to ourselves."[16]

By the year of the Peace of Paris of 1763, the British had partially realized this optimistic prospect. They had not gained all of Louisiana, but they could not ignore the heady possibilities of further expansion. Moreover, the immediate gains sufficiently justified a two-volume English translation of the Le Page *Histoire* under the title, *The History of Louisiana or of the Western Parts of Virginia and Carolina: Containing a Description of the Countries that Lie on Both Sides of the River Mississippi: With an Account of the Settlements, Inhabitants, Soil, Climate, and Products.* This reaffirmed old colonial claims to the trans-Allegheny

16. London *Monthly Review* 19 (1758): 296–300.

region and it gave obvious stress to the British designation of that area in which the late war had begun. The British editor, in addition, determined to correct more than Le Page's nomenclature, and the translation totally reordered the work's content and plan of organization. Peculiar and personal as these undoubtedly had been in Le Page's original, they represented at least some vision of regularity and pertinence, all regrettably lost upon the British publishers. The English version expunged many extended passages and severely compressed others, while it rearranged whole sections in a relationship not envisioned by their author. Perhaps an unrealized indignity was the sandwiching into the text of excerpts from Dumont de Montigny. As a consequence, the English edition proved more confusing in plan than the original. Small wonder that one despairing London reviewer questioned what that source could possibly have been like given the wretchedness of the translator's "improvement."[17]

Even worse than this mangling of Le Page's delicately articulated volumes, however, was the suppression in the English edition of a number of the most significant passages. In almost every instance these related to Natchez folkways—the fashioning of arrows, pirogues, and calumets, for example—or to anecdotes illustrating fundamental aspects of the native character, such as nobility of spirit, depth of understanding, humaneness of lifestyle, and manifestations of a growing erosion of their most ancient customs.[18] Excising Le Page's harsh observations on the perfidy of the English nation as they waged cruel war against the French and their Indian allies, it must be admitted, sacrificed little. But the

17. Le Page du Pratz, *The History of Louisiana*, 2 vols. (London, 1763), 1: 348–364; London *Monthly Review* 29 (1763): 445.

18. For examples of the compressions in the English edition, compare Le Page's conversation with the female Sun in the *Histoire*, 2: 400–404, with the version in the *History*, 2: 204; the description of the funeral of Tattooed Serpent, *Histoire*, 3: 26–57, with the *History*, 2: 218 ff.; and the discussion of pirogue manufacture, *Histoire*, 2: 188, with the *History*, 2: 229. The greater part of Le Page's account of the fashioning of the calumet and of a calumet ceremony with the Chitimachas, *Histoire*, 1: 105–109, is omitted altogether in the English editions.

loss of certain philosophical musings found in the original, as those in which Le Page posits the brotherhood of all men and the universal nature of cities, for example, denied to the reader a true appreciation of the spirit in which Le Page conceived the work.[19] Therefore, the English translation was but a poor reflection of Le Page's handiwork, hardly a satisfactory substitute for scholarly use and most certainly not a sparkling or entertaining composition. Yet, this same bowdlerized and deformed text was used in the second English version of the work in 1774 and in the American printing of 1947.[20] Thus, regrettably, no satisfactory publication of the work exists in translation.

Nonetheless, the English adaptation of Le Page, especially the editor's preface, threw into sharp relief certain British attitudes toward colonization policies in 1763. For his part, Le Page had also focused on imperial relationships, by stressing as early as the *Journal* articles his conviction that Louisiana could play a determining role in revitalizing French trade. Hewing close to fundamental mercantilistic doctrine, which emphasized colonies as sources of materials otherwise obtained only by costly purchase from a rival nation, Le Page had nevertheless disagreed with interpretations of mercantilism that overemphasized the desirability of colonies rich in rare jewels, gold, and silver. "A land fertile in population, in the fruits of the earth and in necessary metals," he had written, "is infinitely superior to those from which one extracts gold and diamonds, whose first effect is to nourish luxury and the second to excite the avarice of neighbors." Proper use of the productive soil of Louisiana must necessarily develop, he maintained, the most precious of all colonial wealth, an economically viable populace bound to the mother country by emotional and cultural as well as pragmatic considerations. Without ignoring the value to France of Lousiana's furs, timber, tobacco, maize,

19. Le Page du Pratz, *Histoire*, 2: 170–171, 210–212.
20. Published under the same title as the English editions and with the same text, in New Orleans, 1947. This American edition reprints the intriguing illustrations found in the original French version.

and indigo, Le Page projected the desirability of an imperial policy
in which profit to the homeland occurred naturally from a prior
commitment to a vigorous colonial economy shaped to its own
peculiar advantages rather than to the objectives of European
planners.[21]

Le Page had written as a onetime colonial, anxious to revive
among his countrymen a flagging interest in migration to the
Mississippi. His British translator, on the other hand, buoyed by
victory over a perennial enemy, nevertheless feared that his countrymen would misread the significance of their new posture in
America and perhaps forfeit the true spoils of conquest. Like Le
Page before him, the British translator felt constrained to urge the
central importance of the Mississippi—indeed, he employed Le
Page's volumes to do exactly that, properly prefaced by remarks
which placed history, geography, and colonial policy in proper
context. This time the view was unabashedly that from the
Thames.

The "great end of colonies," the British translator bluntly
stated, was "the making of a staple commodity for Britain." For
such efforts not only provided produce desirable in itself, but,
more important, it created trade in "gross and bulky" items which
formed the "chief and principal" source of British naval strength.
"The tobacco trade alone," he argued, "employs more seamen in
Britain, than either the fishery, or sugar trade; and brings in more
money to the nation than all the products of America put together. . . . In short, the plantation trade of North America is to
Britain, what the fishery is to France, the great nursery of seamen."[22]

In the translator's view, British North America had in 1763
come to crisis state. Its lands in the north and the far south were
"very poor and barren" and produced "little or nothing, at least
for Britain." Only Virginia, Maryland, and Carolina contributed to

21. Le Page du Pratz, *Histoire*, 3: 396–397; his argument is developed at
length in Ibid., 373–397.
22. Preface to the 1763 English edition, xxxii.

British interest, he believed, and in these the available productive acres, hemmed between mountains and sea, could no longer support the needs of a burgeoning population. "In short," his observation continued, "it would appear that our colonies in North America cannot subsist much longer, if at all, in a state of dependence for all their manufactures and other necessaries, unless they are provided with other lands that may enable them to purchase them; and where they will find any such lands, but upon the Mississippi, is more than we can tell."[23]

Was this not indeed the very purpose for which the late war had been fought? To the British editor this was patently clear, as was the equally obvious fact that the regions described by Le Page had always been the legitimate property of Great Britain and were even now only partially "acknowledged to it by the former usurpers." This substantive claim, sanctioned by the victories of the last conflict, simply supported in his view the wisdom of an immediate British push west to the Mississippi, despite the "absurdity of the popular outcry, that we have already *land enough*, and more than we can make use of in North America."

They who may be of that opinion should shew us, where that land is to be found [the comment ran], and what it will produce, that may turn to any account to the nation. These people derive their opinion from what they see in Europe, where the quantity of the land that we possess in North America, will, no doubt, maintain a greater number of people than we have there. But they should consider, that those people in Europe are not maintained by the planting of a bare raw commodity, with such immense charges upon it, but by farming, manufactures, trade, and commerce; which they will soon reduce our colonies to, who would confine them to their present settlements, between the sea coast and the mountains that surround them.

Some of our colonies perhaps may imagine they cannot subsist without these employments; which indeed would appear to be the case in their present state; but that seems to be as contrary to their true interest, as it is to their condition of British colonies.[24]

23. Ibid., xxxiii.
24. Ibid., iii, xxiv, xxxiv–xxxv.

This left the question as to how the produce of these projected new plantations along the Mississippi would find its way to market. Since the very bulk of staple commodities which promoted the multiplication of British ships also prevented any profitable shipment across the mountains to eastern ports, the answer was clear, and the preface did not shrink from it: Britain must control the navigation of the Mississippi and "a port at the mouth of it":

It is not without reason then, that we may say, whoever are possessed of this river, and of the vast tracts of fertile lands upon it, must in time command that continent, and the trade of it, as well as all the nations in it, by the supplies which this navigation will enable them to furnish those people. By those means, if the French or any others, are left in possession of the Mississippi, while we neglect it, they must command all that continent beyond the Appalachian mountains, and disturb our settlements much more than ever they did, or were able to do; the very thing they engaged in this war to accomplish, and we to prevent.[25]

To such purposes had the British translator put the observations of Le Page—to encourage British settlement of Louisiana, to promote a philosophy of mercantilism substantially at odds with his own, and to spur a rival's interest in control of the Mississippi Valley. True enough, the British translator's convincing arguments did not prevail against the more forceful realities of British domestic politics and imperial frustrations, and the Proclamation of 1763 halted the march to the West. However, the point of the argument for domination of the Mississippi and its mouth was not easily blunted. Whether because of its persuasiveness or simply because of his own strategic sense, General Thomas Gage by 1772 had also come to appreciate the Mississippi's critical value and had begun to formulate plans to seize New Orleans should outbreak of war with Spain afford the opportunity.[26] But for these actualities,

25. Ibid., xviii, xix, xxii.
26. Thomas P. Abernethy, *Western Lands and the American Revolution* (New York, 1959), 20–21; Joseph G. Tregle, Jr., "British Spy along the Mis-

or possibilities, Le Page was hardly accountable. The lasting importance of his work lay elsewhere.

II

"The principal qualities of an historian," Le Page wrote in one of his early *Journal* articles, "are truth and accuracy."[27] In most respects his *Histoire* revealed a firm commitment to these virtues, reflecting a refreshing open-mindedness and objective balance infrequently met in many of his contemporaries. But we should not be misled by the work's title or by the author's preemption of a role to which he gives attractive definition, for Le Page was essentially reporter rather than historian. The *Histoire*, indeed, must be adjudged as seriously flawed if one looks to it for even a reasonably detailed chronicle of the founding and development of French Louisiana. The letters and reports of La Salle, Tonti, Iberville and others, as well as the accounts of Charlevoix, De La Harpe, and even the confusing and suspect Penicaut, give a far richer and more comprehensive view of the colony's annals. Moreover, despite his pledge to accuracy, Le Page was often gullible and trusting when relying upon other than his own experience or observation. Thus, in his very first passage describing his new home in America, he reported that in celebration of the safe arrival of his group at Ile Massacre in 1718 the Company of the West changed its forbidding name to Ile Dauphine, "an act of prudence," as he described it, "to discontinue an appellation, so odious, of a place that was the cradle of the colony."[28] In fact, of course, the alteration had antedated the Company's creation by several years, and Le Page was probably an early victim of that organization's notorious detachment from the truth.

Equally misleading was his ascription of the origin of the name

sissippi: Thomas Hutchins and the Defenses of New Orleans, 1773," *Louisiana History* 8 (1967): 318.

27. Paris *Journal Oeconomique*, September, 1751, p. 146.

28. Le Page du Pratz, *Histoire*, 1: 37–38.

"Baton Rouge" to a giant redwood cypress, his contention that Canadian voyageurs created the Pointe-Coupée cutoff as late as 1713, and his jumbled account of the abortive search for trade routes into Mexico which figured in the romantic career of Juchereau de St. Denis.[29] Despite his own censorious judgment of Dumont and L'Abbé Le Mascrier, Le Page culpably incorporated into his own work without question a lengthy account from the *Mémoires* of those suspect collaborators detailing the destruction of the French Fort Orléans on the Missouri River and the massacre of its garrison by Indians, a tragedy conceived in the fecund imagination of Le Mascrier and without foundation in truth.[30] In each instance, he simply accepted as fact what was actually hand-me-down pseudohistory, without testing its validity against any sources available to him.

This same trusting reliance on the veracity and accuracy of others was also occasionally discernible in those sections of the *Histoire* devoted to the colony's natural history. Actually, it matters but little that trusted tellers of tall tales apparently took him in and led him to believe that the peculiar opossum had stranger habits than were actually his, or that the mere presence of an aggressive wren might bring giant eagles to a state of trembling, droopy-headed cowardice. The great mass of his data, based on his own experience, remains impressive for its comprehensiveness and accuracy.[31] Some problems, not related to gullibility, still remain

29. Andrew C. Albrecht, "The Origin and Early Settlement of Baton Rouge, Louisiana," *Louisiana Historical Quarterly* 28 (1945): 44–45; Hildegard O'Reilly Sternberg, "The Pointe Coupée Cut-Off in Historical Writings," *Louisiana Historical Quarterly* 28 (1945): 70 (Le Page's version is in the *Histoire*, 2: 269); for the persistence of historical error see Philip Pittman's *The Present State of the European Settlements on the Mississippi* (Cleveland, 1906), which repeats the Le Page account almost verbatim; P. F. X. de Charlevoix, *History and General Description of New France*, ed. J. G. Shea, 6 vols. (New York, 1900), 6: 19.

30. Le Page du Pratz, *Histoire*, 1: 325 ff. For a critical examination of the confusion surrounding Fort Orleans, see Marc de Villiers du Terrage, *The Discovery of the Missouri and the History of Fort Orléans (1673–1728)*, Survey of Federal Archives in Louisiana (New Orleans, 1939), p. 117.

31. Contemporary critics found some of Le Page's observations beyond belief. See London *Monthly Review* 29 (1763): 448. [Dumont de Montigny],

to puzzle the reader. What accounted for his total silence as to the mink and the muskrat, for example, oddly missing from this catalogue of beaver, raccoon, opossum, wildcats, skunks, "crocodiles," "tigers," and the like? Yet, despite this mystery, the *Histoire* offered, as Le Page intended, a truly valuable guide to the flora and fauna of Louisiana, and it provides even today a charming record of how our forebears perceived their own environment.

Neither Le Page's sketchy and occasionally unreliable treatment of the colony's history, nor his more secure survey of its wildlife and vegetation would have won for him more than passing notice in modern scholarship. Instead, he sustained his own identity by preserving the Natchez in his pages. He had not come to Louisiana prepared to differ with his colleagues and companions as to the nature and character of the American aborigine; French missionaries agreed to a remarkable extent that the Indian was a barbarous savage, ignorant of even the most primitive promptings of morality or civilized sensibilities.[32] Hardly settled on the Bayou St. John, Le Page found himself embroiled in controversy with a native over purchase of a gun, producing such a noise that Bienville himself demanded an explanation. He would not, Le Page

---

Mémoires, 1: 104, fiercely denounced Le Page's report that alligators attacked man only in self-defense, a question which finds modern authority solidly on the side of Le Page. One of the major attractions of the original edition of the *Histoire* is the series of prints depicting the life of the Indians and picturing the animals and plants of the region. The dean of Louisiana naturalists, Stanley C. Arthur, acknowledged Le Page's pioneer contributions in the field. See his *The Fur Animals of Louisiana* (New Orleans, 1931), p. 33.

32. Dumont de Montigny characterized the Indians as unalterably "treacherous" (fn. 14 above). Iberville, founder of Louisiana, classed the Great Sun of his day (1700), as "the most absolute savage I had seen." Pierre Margry, ed., *Découvertes et Établissements des Francais dans l'Ouest et dans le Sud de l'Amérique Septentrionale,* 6 vols. (Paris, 1879–88), 4: 412. The Jesuit Le Petit spoke of "these perfidious savages called Natchez." Mathurin Le Petit, *The Natchez Massacre* (New Orleans, 1950), p. 1. The secular priest St. Cosme characterized the Natchez as "very vicious" and as "all thieves." Swanton, *Indian Tribes of the Lower Mississippi,* p. 49. Charles E. O'Neill, *Church and State in French Colonial Louisiana* (New Haven and London, 1966), p. 52n., observes that "*Sauvage and sauvagesse* were the ordinary words used by the French to designate the Indians."

told the Governor, be duped by "a brute animal," to which the more experienced Canadian replied that Le Page did not yet know these people, and that when he did he would "render them better justice"—a prophecy well made. Sixteen years in Louisiana would convince Le Page that "one does grave injustice to call 'Savages' men who know how to make good use of their reason, who think justly, who are prudent, faithful, generous, much more than certain civilized nations, who would not choose to be compared to them, not wishing to comprehend or to give to things their true value." And of all the various tribes he would know, the Natchez impressed him the most. "Their manners," he claimed, "were . . . gentler, their way of thinking truer and fuller of feeling, their customs more rational, and their ceremonies more natural and serious, which made this nation more brilliant and distinguished it from all others."[33]

These insights may well have originated in the relationship between Le Page and a young Chitimacha girl, first his slave and eventually his ward by virtue of a formal adoption according to Indian custom. Le Page's self-assigned avuncular role was singularly unconvincing, but the connection itself was of utmost importance. Because of the girl's family ties to several highly placed members of the Natchez community, Le Page received his unique entrée into their society and their confidence. Preeminent among those accepting him as friend were the chief guardian of the Natchez temple, whose name Le Page does not give us, Tattooed Serpent, war chief of the tribe, and his brother, the Great Sun himself. Le Page assiduously cultivated the opportunity, even to the point of spending much time with the tribe's women, whose general ignorance of Mobilian, the *lingua franca* of the Gulf area, forced him to develop his own skills in the Natchez tongue.[34]

Thus equipped and sincerely attracted to the Natchez, whose ways and beliefs so piqued his curiosity, Le Page would pass long

33. Le Page du Pratz, *Histoire*, 1: 86–88; 2: 308.
34. Ibid., 1: 115–117; 2: 321–322.

hours listening to the temple guardian's account of his people's past and their beliefs, sharing observations with Tattooed Serpent as to the ways of warriors and nations, and observing closely the peculiar social system which centered in the autocratic prerogative of the "Grand Soleil." Le Page's record of all this in the *Histoire* made it the unrivaled source of modern knowledge concerning the Natchez, particularly in those areas of "esoteric lore" which in all likelihood would otherwise have been forever lost to us.[35] Others such as Dumont may give richer descriptions of material culture, but Le Page offered a view into the Natchez heart and mind.

There remains, of course, the question of how far to trust the observations of Le Page with his gullibility and lapses in historical and biological accuracy. To this there can be no absolute answer, by the very nature of his unique relationship to the matters upon which he reported. But in the preponderance of his observations on the Natchez he spoke from firsthand knowledge, not relying on the findings of others. Where it has been possible to check his accuracy in matters unrelated to the Natchez and in which he was equally independent of outside authority, he had a high order of reliability. Moreover, recent archaeological excavation has for the first time produced findings against which to check the validity of his descriptive passages, with results clearly supportive of his credibility.

At the "Fatherland Site," some three miles southeast of the present city of Natchez, workers have uncovered remains almost certainly those of the Grand Village of the Natchez on the banks of St. Catherine's Creek.[36] The precise location of this center had long been confused by the apparent impossibility of squaring eighteenth-century descriptions of the village's location with the

---

35. Swanton, *Indian Tribes of the Lower Mississippi*, p. 4.
36. George I. Quimby, Jr., "The Natchez Culture Type," *American Antiquity* 3 (1942): 255–275; Robert S. Neitzel, *Archaeology of the Fatherland Site: The Grand Village of the Natchez*. American Museum of Natural History *Anthropological Papers*, 51, Part 1 (New York, 1965): 3–7, 11, 58.

realities of twentieth-century geography.[37] Le Page's *Histoire*,
which gave specific and unambiguous measurements relating the
site to Fort Rosalie on the banks of the Mississippi and to the
mouth of St. Catherine's Creek, proved most puzzling since he
gave figures which made no sense to the modern surveyor. Everything fell into place promptly once long-time residents of the area
indicated that sometime about 1871 planters had diverted St.
Catherine's Creek to shorten its run to the Mississippi, thus
moving its mouth considerably closer to Natchez than it had been
in Le Page's time. Le Page's specifications no longer mystified;
indeed, they pointed directly to a site investigated in 1930, but
regrettably abandoned shortly thereafter despite recovery of considerable artifacts strongly suggestive of the chief Natchez settlement. In 1962 Robert S. Neitzel resumed the project for the
Mississippi Department of Archives and History, and his findings
left little doubt; he uncovered the three great mounds so central in
Le Page's descriptions of the village, almost precisely aligned as he
had indicated. While certain particulars in the archaeological
record are difficult to equate with his ethnographical data, the
consonance was remarkably fine, so much so that Neitzel seemed
convinced that certain skeletal remains he discovered were those of
persons who figure in the Le Page narrative.[38] In short, modern
archaeology, while not confirming Le Page's anthropological account, provides assurance as to his fundamental reliability, thus
adding strength to his reports of the tales of the temple guardian,
Tattooed Serpent, and the Great Sun.

Some critics cautioned against Le Page's supposed overestima-
tion of the Natchez character. While this caveat certainly deserves

37. For the conflicting evidence in the early French literature see: Isaac J.
Cox, *Journeys of La Salle* (New York, 1922), p. 24; Margry, ed., *Découvertes
et Établissements*, 4: 410; Ruth L. Butler, *Journal of Paul du Ru* (Chicago,
1934), p. 4.
38. Le Page du Pratz, *Histoire*, 2: 222; Andrew C. Albrecht, "The Location
of the Historic Natchez Villages," *Journal of Mississippi History* 6 (1944):
69–72; Pierce Butler, *The Unhurried Years* (Baton Rouge, 1948), pp. 73–74;
Neitzel, *Archaeology of the Fatherland Site*, pp. 72–73.

respect, it should not divert attention from the truly remarkable objectivity which he attempted in his evaluations of Indian culture. In them he combined a respectful sympathy and analytical detachment which set him apart from the great mass of his European contemporaries. To him the native American was neither the "dumb brute" so frequently described by his clerical and other colleagues, nor the romanticized "noble savage" of Raynal and Chateaubriand. Rather he was simply another human being, whom destiny had called to the primeval forest instead of to the chateaux of the Loire, and whose peculiar environment and distinctive way of life in no measure removed him from sharing in mankind's universal experience. For Le Page, therefore, the Indian was not some bizarre freak of nature, deserving the exploitation of his betters, requiring the ministrations of the white man's theology, or inviting study as some deviant form of sublife. He was a man properly placed in his own world, creator of a culture endowed with innate dignity and deserving the same respect as the haughtiest Frenchman. Not unaware that this conviction was generally foreign to his age, he noted:

Our French, accustomed to see their cities decorated with beautiful edifices, imagine that a city must be built of houses constructed of stone, and enfold within itself superb temples, sumptuous palaces, magnificent bridges; but those who have taken the pain to inform themselves of what really makes a city, have understood that it is nothing but a great number of dwellings clustered in the same place, and that the difference in building materials reflects only the relative richness or poverty of the people making up the city. . . . Let no one be surprised then if I call a city that which is a pile of straw huts which form the dwellings of Americans naked of arts and of the tools necessary to building. Having only wood, earth, and straw with which to build, they deserve praise more than scorn, having constructed from such materials dwellings both comfortable and secure, capable of resisting all the violence of wind and the other visitations of nature.[39]

39. Swanton, *Indian Tribes of the Lower Mississippi*, p. 50; Albrecht, "Ethical Precepts among the Natchez Indians," p. 584; Le Page du Pratz, *Histoire*, 2: 171–172.

The Natchez themselves he found to have a "gentle and humane character, so long as one gives them no occasion for mistrust." "They love to learn," he observed, "and it is primarily the fault of the Europeans rather than their own if they have not yet been civilized. . . . They are serious and prudent, so far as their limited enlightenment permits; enemies of falsehood, faithful to their promises, true to their word, speak little, are never the first to give offense, but also never forget injury done to them."[40]

Such disposition toward the people among whom he lived for eight years made Le Page particularly sensitive to those things which the Natchez themselves valued most in their culture, and appreciation of that fact seemed to account for their willingness to reveal more of themselves to him than to any other man. The questions which he put to them were fundamental indeed: From whence had they come to the banks of St. Catherine's Creek? What did they know of the creation of man and of his eternal destiny? What were their rules of conduct and why were they observed? What were the bases of their peculiar social and political organization?

From the guardian of the temple, a repository of his nation's oral traditions called the "ancient word," Le Page received the most systematic responses to his queries. The Natchez, he was told, had originated in an unknown land far to the East, from which they had eventually migrated to the southwest of the Mississippi, which Le Page took to mean Mexico. Strife with the occupants of that land had eventually led them to a final relocation on St. Catherine's Creek. Even today, anthropologists offer only tentative suggestions as to the reality behind this historico-myth, and while they generally agree that all Indian populations sprang from Asian groups migrating into America across the Bering Strait, the Natchez still do not fall into any convenient pattern of explanation. Few contemporary scientists would agree that the Natchez known to Le Page had newly come to the Missis-

40. Paris *Journal Oeconomique*, March 1752, p. 147.

sippi basin, for archaeology and language analysis clearly linked the tribe to much earlier civilizations in the area.[41] Yet the tantalizing question remains as to the source of those Natchez ways so reminiscent of Mezo-American civilizations, such as a class-stratified society, retainer sacrifice, elaborate burials, temple mounds and plazas, and effigy vessels of pottery. More than one eminent scholar has kept open the possibility that the Natchez did have ties with those faraway cultures.[42]

Considered in such a context, Le Page's theories on all this do

41. Le Page du Pratz, *Histoire*, 2: 321; 3: 62 ff. The literature on this point is extensive: Robert F. Spencer, Jesse D. Jennings et al., *The Native Americans* (New York, 1965), p. 419; Gordon R. Willey, *An Introduction to American Archaeology* (Englewood Cliffs, N.J., 1966), p. 290; William G. Haag, "The Archaic of the Lower Mississippi Valley," *American Antiquity* 26 (1960): 317–323; and Quimby, "Natchezan Culture Type," p. 275.

The proper classification of the Natchez language has been a topic of confusion over the years. Albert Gallatin thought it to be completely distinct and unrelated to any other Indian tongue. In 1867 Daniel Brinton attempted to prove that Natchez was linked to Mayan, but later switched to the theory that it was a Greek dialect. Albert S. Gatschet reinforced the idea of the separate nature of the Natchez language and won J. W. Powell and other experts at the Bureau of American Ethnology over to his position. The later Bureau expert, John R. Swanton, held to the belief that Natchez was a "widely divergent' dialect of Muskhogean, despite the absence in that language of the "r" sound which Le Page identified in the Natchez speech. Most recent scholarship tends to identify Natchez as springing from a "Proto-Gulf" language group and as related to a "Proto-Muskhogean" tongue, so that it is more appropriate to speak of a "Natchez-Muskhogean stock composed of Natchez and the Muskhogean family." This supports the long identification of the Natchez nation with the Gulf area. See Daniel G. Brinton, "The Natchez of Louisiana," *Historical Magazine*, Second Series, 1 (1867): 16–18, and his comments in *Proceedings of the American Philosophical Society*, 1873, pp. 483–499; A. S. Gatschet, "Natchez," *American Anthropologist*, Old Series, 5 (1892): 51–52; James C. Pilling, *Bibliography of the Muskhogean Languages*. Bureau of American Ethnology Report 9 (Washington, 1889): 38; John R. Swanton, "The Muskhogean Connection of the Natchez Language," *International Journal of American Linguistics* 3 (1924): 46–75; Mary R. Haas, "A New Linguistic Relationship in North America: Algonkian and the Gulf Languages," *Southwest Journal of Anthropology* 14 (1958): 231–264; Mary R. Haas, "Natchez and the Muskhogean Languages," *Language* 32 (1956): 61–72.

42. See, for example, John R. Swanton, *The Indians of the Southeastern United States* (Washington, 1946), p. 22, and MacLeod, "On Natchez Cultural Origins," pp. 409–413.

not seem outlandish. Thoroughly convinced himself that the "Red Man," by which he meant Indians other than the Natchez, had come to North America from Asia (he favored Korea or Scythia as the specific region), Le Page accepted the temple guardian's story to mean that the Natchez had most recently migrated from Mexico. Their admitted ignorance of the exact location of their earlier eastern home led him to the further speculation that they likely descended from hardy Phoenicians or Carthaginians who had swept into the New World. As proof he pointed to the worship of the eternal fire common to Phoenicians and Natchez and to the "figurative style and bold, Syriac expressions" in the latter's language. His conjectures were no stranger than many which more learned men had advanced,[43] and they further highlighted his conviction as to the uniqueness of the Natchez in the midst of the "Red Men" and of the seriousness with which he approached their traditions.

Of considerably greater interest than these speculations on eastern origins were Le Page's reports on Natchez religion, ethics, and social organization. According to his account, Natchez beliefs were considerably more complex and abstract than the simple animism characteristic of most other tribes. Totemism and shamanism, for example, seemed completely unknown among them, and while they did identify certain life forms such as the rattlesnake and the honey locust with supernatural power, these apparently had little if any part in the highly formalized religion which so distinguished them from their surrounding Muskhogean neighbors.[44] The Natchez god described by the temple guardian was remarkably akin to that known to the Judeo-Christian tradition: they called him "Coyocopchill," not "*Great* Spirit," but

43. Le Page du Pratz, *Histoire*, 3: 82–87, 79, 132, 218. For the astonishing range in these speculations, see Aubry W. Williams, Jr., "Conceptions of Time in Eastern United States Archaeology," *Southern Indian Studies*, 9 (1957): 3–19.

44. Alvin M. Josephy, Jr., *The Indian Heritage of America* (New York, 1968), pp. 25–26; Swanton, "Ethnological Position of the Natchez Indians," p. 527; Swanton, *Indian Tribes of the Lower Mississippi*, p. 177.

"*Infinite* Spirit," whose power was without limit, except, as a good Thomist would understand, in his inability to commit evil because of the essential goodness of his nature. All things in heaven and in earth were the expression of his will, and he had specially molded man from clay by his hands and vivified him by his breath of life. He had created "little spirits" to do his bidding; they were everywhere, though invisible, and some, alas, led by a fallen favorite, brought evil into the world. Both required prayer and propitiation, attempted by the Natchez through fast and sexual continence. Moreover, the Supreme Spirit had sent to forebears of the Natchez a "very great number of years ago" a man and his wife who came from the sun in order to teach them "how to live better." Community well-being, this "Sun" had preached, could spring only from individual self-knowledge and virtue, realizable by adherence to the code which he had brought from the creator: "To kill no one except in defense of one's own life; never to know another woman than one's own; to take nothing that belongs to another; never to lie or become drunk; and not to be avaricious, but to give freely and with joy that which one has, and to share food generously with those who lack it." So that the Natchez would never forget these great principles, they had built their temple, whose sacred fire from the sun they forever guarded as the visible testimony of fidelity to their preceptor's admonitions.[45]

The Natchez quite possibly shared this religious tradition with tribes adjacent to them, and temple and plaza developments were

45. Le Page du Pratz, *Histoire*, 2: 326–328, 331–333. Swanton (*Indian Tribes of the Lower Mississippi*, p. 176) believes that this story of a Lucifer-like evil spirit "is so rare in American religions that we may be sure Du Pratz's statements regarding it were founded on some misunderstood myth." As in all matters Indian, Swanton's views deserve utmost respect, but his certainty in this instance is not proof. The temple guardian may not have exhaustively outlined Natchez religious practice to Le Page. A contemporary, the priest St. Cosme, indicated that the Natchez kept a stone image in their temple, to which they accorded great honor but which they apparently did not worship, since they identified it as the calcified body of a "relative" of the "great spirit." Swanton, *Indian Tribes of the Lower Mississippi*, pp. 172–173. The Natchez may have kept this fact from Le Page because they feared he would think them idolators.

certainly common to the Houma, Bayougoula, Acolapissa, and Taensa nations. However, for no other people do we have any information concerning the integration of these factors into their personal and communal lives as we do through Le Page for the Natchez. For this reason primarily his *Histoire* is unique and precious. Indeed, it more than preserved the "ancient word" recited by the temple guardian; it recounted incidents of Natchez behavior which revealed positive application of an ethic grounded in these very concepts, transcending unexamined response to a fixed ritual and demonstrating clear analytical application of a universal morality.[46] To read him is to understand his impatience with those who saw savagery in what they had not even tried to understand.

Of all Le Page's descriptions, none has attracted more intensive study than that outlining Natchez social organization, for it presented a stratified class structure unique in the region, highly unusual for any Indian nation, and baffling in its purpose and origins. According to Le Page's temple informant, the first "Sun," transmitter of the Infinite Spirit's code to the Natchez, had commanded that they organize their society into its four distinct classes: Suns, Nobles, Honored, and Stinkards. Within the first three aristocratic groupings, they enforced a strict rule of exogamy, requiring all Suns, Nobles, and Honored men and women to choose mates from the Stinkard class. They fixed a child's class membership according to the following pattern:

Suns: children of Sun women and Stinkard men
Nobles: children of Noble women and Stinkard men or of Sun men and Stinkard women
Honored: children of Honored women and Stinkard men or of Noble men and Stinkard women
Stinkards: children of Honored men and Stinkard women or of Stinkard men and women

46. Swanton, "Ethnological Position of the Natchez Indians," p. 527; Quimby, "Natchezan Culture Type," p. 274. The most extended examination of the implications of this Natchez ethic is to be found in Albrecht, "Ethical Precepts among the Natchez Indians," p. 569 ff.

Gradation of status among the ranks was real and supported by pervasive community attitudes, so much so that "Suns" frequently refused to acknowledge lineal descendants in the Stinkard category. At the apex of this structure was the "Great Sun," eldest son of the eldest sister of the preceding title holder, and a ruler of unbridled power and despotic authority. He was, Le Page tells us, "absolute master of the goods and life of his subjects," unhesitatingly obeyed in all things, though even the Le Page narrative seemed to indicate that his council or a subordinate Sun occasionally restrained this supposed omnipotence.[47] Marks of his lofty station were a crown of white feathers, a royal litter borne by his retainers, and an ornate dwelling chamber furnished with a highly decorated bed surmounted by a mattress filled with goose down.

The most forbidding aspect of this social arrangement was the putting to death of the spouse of any deceased male or female Sun, a practice, as one scholar noted, in which the "versatile Natchez seem to afford us the only example in culture history of the *obligatory immolation of the husband at the death of the wife*." Also despatched were the servants of the expired Sun, the *allouez*, who presumably considered it an honor to accompany their departed master to the next world so as to provide there for his wants. Although shocked by this institution of human sacrifice, Le Page did not condemn his Indian friends for it. Indeed, he devoted moving and compelling pages in his narrative to the funerary ceremonies attendant upon the death of Tattooed Serpent, brother of the Great Sun and war chief of the Natchez. Here he offered some of his most incisive sketches of Indian character, while carefully noting, in the midst of his horror, the relative humaneness of the Natchez even in this grisly practice. To minimize pain and terror, they fed intoxicating tobacco pellets to those awaiting sacrifice.[48]

---

47. Le Page du Pratz, *Histoire*, 2: 393–396; Swanton, *Indian Tribes of the Lower Mississippi*, p. 107.

48. MacLeod, "Natchez Political Evolution," p. 220; Le Page du Pratz, *Histoire*, 3: 26–57.

The peculiarities of this Natchez social system have naturally attracted extensive attention from anthropologists, who have found in it demonstrations of widely divergent scholarly theories. More than anything else in Le Page's work, it has sustained a continuing scientific interest in his findings.[49] The historian, concerned with the particular, would more likely center on Le Page's account of the Natchez Rebellion of 1729, so critical to the fate of the Louisiana colony. In one respect, the rewards of such study can only be marginal; Le Page did not eyewitness the events immediately precipitating the bloody massacre of the French garrison and settlers at Fort Rosalie and its surrounding concessions. He based his version of the tragedy upon the account given to him in New Orleans by a female Sun after her capture by the French troops which had so promptly visited punishment and virtual extinction upon her unhappy people.[50]

Le Page's representation of the revolt as having sprung from the vicious cruelty and grasping avarice of the French commandant at Rosalie, Captain "Chepart," would become the foundation for all later historical accounts of the massacre. In it, Le Page gave full play to his dramatic impulse, casting the female Sun as a solitary and heroic protagonist determined to frustrate the Natchez plan to engulf the French in simultaneous uprisings by Indian tribes throughout the colony. This she accomplished by upsetting the Indian timetable, pushing the Natchez into premature attack by extracting several sticks from the bundle of *bûchettes* kept in the

49. See, for example, Davis, "Intermarriage in Caste Societies," p. 382; MacLeod, "Natchez Political Evolution," pp. 220–225. Hart, "A Reconsideration of Natchez Social Structure," pp. 374–386, challenged the reliability of Le Page's representation of Natchez social organization, because marriage of all nobility exclusively with Stinkards would have exhausted the lowest class by the fourteenth generation after inception of the system. Hart maintained (p. 374) the system described by Le Page "is actually a biological impossibility." J. L. Fischer, "Solutions for the Natchez Paradox," *Ethnology* 3 (1964): 53–65, reasserted the probable reliability of the Le Page account, maintaining that Hart and other critics have overlooked various mechanisms which might have sustained the system, such as uneven birth rates among the classes, decimation of aristocrats by war, etc.
50. Le Page du Pratz, *Histoire*, 3: 230 ff.

temple as a master calendar marking the days until the planned general assault. Even intrinsically the Le Page account was shaky and unpersuasive, since he assigned at least three different motivations to the female Sun in explanation of her treacherous behavior.[51] Suspect or not, it was too good a story to ignore. Countless writers after Le Page have centered their versions of the massacre upon this tale of *bûchettes* and an Indian princess strangely dedicated to the French. Chateaubriand almost certainly based his famous *Les Natchez* and *Atala* upon it, while the greatest of Louisiana's historians, Charles Gayarré, has spread his usual romantic glow around the story by presenting La Soleille as a lovesick maiden intent upon saving the life of her French paramour.[52]

Modern scholarship has largely rejected any widespread conspiracy of Indian tribes led by the Natchez in 1729, seeing the story of the plot as merely Governor Perier's clever invention to divert attention from his own highly culpable support of the barbarous Chepart.[53] In the absence of a conspiracy, the romantic tale of *bûchettes* becomes totally irrelevant, a fabrication intended to lend credibility to Perier's propaganda.

51. Jean Delanglez, "The Natchez Massacre and Governor Perier," *Louisiana Historical Quarterly* 17 (1934): 630–641; Le Page du Pratz, *Histoire*, 3: 253; Marc de Villiers du Terrage, "La Louisiane de Chateaubriand," *Journal de la Société des Américanistes de Paris*, New Series, 16 (1924): 140.

52. In the preface to *Celuta; or the Natchez*, 3 vols. (London, 1835), 1: v, Chateaubriand acknowledged his debt to Charlevoix as a source, though he admitted that he "has not been the only writer and traveller that I have consulted." Actually, Charlevoix made no mention of *bûchettes* in his account of the massacre (*History of New France*, 6: 81 ff.) and Chateaubriand confessed his own confusion as to the origin of this part of his tale. Chateaubriand was familiar with Le Page's work, since he mentioned him in *Le Génie de Christianisme* (Paris, 1827), p. 361. Marc de Villiers du Terrage, "La Louisiane de Chateaubriand," p. 143, maintained that Chateaubriand deliberately covered over his debt to Le Page so as to hide the extent of his own romantic distortion of the original. Charles E. A. Gayarré, *History of Louisiana*, 4 vols. (New York, 1854), 1: 400 ff. As other examples of Le Page's direct influence, see Horatio Cushman, *History of the Choctaw, Chickasaw, and Natchez Indians* (Greenville, Tex., 1899), p. 542, and J. B. Bossu, *Travels through that Part of North America Formerly Called Louisiana*, 2 vols. (London, 1771), 1: 52.

53. Delanglez, "Natchez Massacre and Governor Perier," p. 630; Villiers du Terrage, "La Louisiane de Chateaubriand," p. 139.

For these reasons Le Page's version of the Natchez Massacre might well be considered almost worthless, a regrettable source from which floods of later historical distortion would flow. But this is true only of those passages of the *Histoire* based on something other than his own immediate knowledge. After dismissing these suspect pages as unsound, Le Page remains the most reliable guide to an understanding of those forces culminating in the tragedy of 1729. For his narrative among the Natchez from 1720 to 1728 recounted his own observations of a French policy toward the Indians which angered and distressed him. In return for an open welcome to their midst by the Natchez, the French responded with unprovoked and needless attacks. Time and again the Indians appeared to forgive, affording their oppressors yet additional opportunities to join them in amity. Because of Natchez generosity and hospitality, Le Page maintained, the French "had need of nothing but a profound peace in order to establish solid foundations capable of making us forget Europe. Providence, he observed, ordained otherwise, permitting the French such follies as the totally unwarranted attack upon the Natchez by Bienville in 1723. Sick at heart, Le Page foresaw the impending tragedy and planned to depart Fort Rosalie while the old Great Sun still maintained peace. By 1729 Le Page was gone, the Great Sun was dead, and the patience of the Natchez was exhausted. The massacre required no Chepart, no conspiracy—its origins were clear in nearly every line that Le Page wrote.[54]

In light of his unquestionable good will toward the Indians and

54. Le Page du Pratz, *Histoire*, 1: 177, 188, 197–199. Various English observers traced the Natchez uprising to the encouragement of English traders, especially those influential among the Chickasaw. The evidence is not particularly persuasive. See Samuel C. Williams, ed., *Adair's History of the American Indians* (Johnson City, Tenn., 1930), p. 379; Wilbur R. Jacobs, ed., *Indians of the Southern Colonial Frontier: The Edmond Atkins Report and Plan of 1755* (Columbia, S.C., 1954). The ferocity of French retaliation against the Natchez obviously worked to the English advantage insofar as their subsequent relations with the Southern tribes were concerned. See David H. Corkran, *The Creek Frontier, 1540–1783* (Norman, Okla., 1967), p. 81; Angie Debo, *The Road to Disappearance* (Norman, Okla., 1941), p. 27.

his insight into their character, Le Page's failure to completely appreciate the depth of their despair becomes all the more surprising. Shortly after the assault upon his people by Bienville, Tattooed Serpent put to Le Page the blunt question: "Why did the French come into our country?"

We did not go to seek them [he continued], they asked for land of us, because their country was too little for all the men that were in it. We told them they might take land where they pleased, there was enough for them and for us; that it was good that the same sun should shine upon us both, and that we would walk as friends in the same path; and that we would give them of our provisions, assist them to build, and to labor in their fields. We have done so; is this not true? What occasion then had we for Frenchmen? Before they came did we not live better than we do, seeing we deprive ourselves of a part of our corn, our game, and fish, to give to them? Was it for their guns? The bows and arrows which we used, were sufficient to make us live well. Was it for their white, blue, and red blankets? We can do well enough with buffalo skins, which are warmer. . . . In fine, before the arrival of the French, we lived like men who can be satisfied with what they have; whereas now we are like slaves.[55]

To this Le Page responded with no more than a halting reply, apparently under the misconception that Tattooed Serpent complained only of the most recent French foray. But the Indian had thrust much deeper. "What do you want of us?" Tattooed Serpent had asked, and even the best friend of the Natchez could not understand the question.

55. Le Page du Pratz, *Histoire*, 1: 203–205.

5.

James Adair's "Noble Savages"

Wilcomb E. Washburn

Seldom is a man as closely identified with a book as was James Adair, and seldom does a book reveal a man as did his *History of the American Indians* (London, 1775). Although a few letters in his own hand and a few documents quoting him testify to his life among the Indian nations and on the periphery of white nations, James Adair emerges primarily from the pungent comments of his *History*.

Adair's book, with its barely concealed indictment of white society and its celebration of the virtues of the "noble savage," was not the literary conceit of a chair-bound writer; it was the honest expression of a man who lived among, negotiated with, and warred against the powerful Indian nations bordering South Carolina. Historians of ideas have customarily ridiculed the notion of the "noble savage" as a fable invented by eighteenth-century philosophers like Rousseau to attack the corruptions of European society. Without arguing the question, the error may be more in the assumptions of twentieth-century historians of ideas than in the writings of eighteenth-century philosophers or the behavior of seventeenth- and eighteenth-century Indians. The literature produced by those who knew the Indian best—whether missionary or soldier, French or English—provided legitimate evidence of a "noble savage," using that phrase, however, as a shorthand expression of a general though not uncritical admiration for Indian character and government in comparison with that of the white man.

James Adair was one of many white observers who knew Indians intimately, and who compared their ways with those of his own countrymen and found the latter wanting. Adair pointed out that the Indians, following the law of nature, felt that a king or ruler only merited the position by his bravery in battle or by his demonstrated wisdom. The Indians, Adair further noted, abhorred the actions of a ruler in "taking away at pleasure, the life or property of any who obey the good laws of their country." The Indian ruler who attempted to rule without winning the right by his actions, or who attempted to act arbitrarily against the wishes of his people, would himself be the object of their wrath.

Adair's Indian friends demanded to know how he could defend the apparently arbitrary and capricious actions of incompetent and unwise English officials, since in the Indian view "leading men are chosen only to do good to the people; and whenever they make a breach of their trust, injuring the public good, their places of course become vacant, and justly devolve to the people, who conferred them." The Indians observed that English law condemned little rogues but spared great ones. Why? "I told them, that the essential part of our laws was fixed and unalterable, and also the succession of each of our great chieftains, while they observe them faithfully, and order them to be honestly executed, but no longer." Adair cited earlier English history, referring (though not by name) to the fate of Charles I as an example that Englishmen also had principles. At the same time, for his English readers, he asserted: "May none of our present or future statesmen, by wilful misconduct, and bad principles, be ever forced to appear at the dreadful bar of an abused and enraged community! For as they mete, so it will surely be meted to them again."[1] Although Adair openly admired Indian ways and freely expressed his disgust with the actions of his own government, the *History* was not a literary

1. James Adair, *The History of the American Indians: Particularly those Nations adjoining to the Mississippi, East and West Florida, Georgia, South and North Carolina, and Virginia*, intro. by Robert F. Berkhofer, Jr. (New York and London, 1968), p. 436.

exercise directed against the corruptions of civilization, but rather a hard-nosed account of a hard life spent among the Indians.

The details of Adair's life must, to a great degree, be surmised. He was an Indian trader, not an easy or safe life in eighteenth-century Carolina, which may help to explain Adair's acerbic reactions to the slow elaboration of policy in Charles Town. Governor James Glen pointed out the traders' precarious existence when he wrote to the Board of Trade on July 15, 1750 to urge the construction of a fort among the Cherokees. Glen hoped that the Board would be convinced of the necessity of such a fort "when I inform you that within these few Months no less than nine English Traders have been killed in that Country by French Indians, and We are assured that the French give a considerable Reward for their Scalps." Yet comments in Adair's *History* suggested the attractions of the wilderness life for the scholarly Scot. "I have the pleasure of writing this," he noted, "by the side of a Chikkasah female, as great a princess as ever lived among the ancient Peruvians, or Mexicans, and she bids me be sure not to mark the paper wrong, after the manner of most of the traders; otherwise, it will spoil the making good bread, or hommony, and of course beget the ill-will of our white women." Students of Adair genealogy, even when they assumed he had a wife, have been unable to name her. He probably lived, Indian-style, with more than one dusky bedfellow.[2]

Adair's *History* gave additional evidence of his marital state in his account of a raid on his Chickasaw trading house by French Indians in 1748. The Indians, he noted, "patted with their hands a considerable time on one of the doors, as a decoy, imitating the earnest rap of the young women who go a visiting that time of night. Finding their labour in vain, one of them lifted a billet of wood, and struck the side of the house, where the women and

2. Ibid., p. 416; extract of letter from Governor Glen to Board of Trade, July 15, 1750, in Public Record Office, London, C.O. 5/385, fol. 20 (British Manuscripts Project, Library of Congress, Washington, D.C., Microfilm Reel 435); James Barnett Adair, M.D., *Adair History and Genealogy* (Los Angeles, 1924), pp. 269–71.

children lay; so as to frighten them and awake me—my mastiffs had been silenced with their venison." Adair repulsed the intruders and defended his household. Support for the supposition of Adair's informal and irregular liaisons was also suggested in a long footnote to his discussion of similarities in the punishment of adultery by the Jews and the Indians. After describing how, among the Creeks, the husband's kinsmen cut off the male offender's ears after thrashing him severely, Adair added in a footnote that among these Indians "the trading people's ears are often in danger, by the sharpness of this law, and their suborning false witnesses, or admitting foolish children as legal evidence; but generally either the tender-hearted females or friends, give them timely notice of their danger." Adair seemingly wrote from personal knowledge.[3]

Adair's joy in being with the Indians emerged in his frequent discussion of personal incidents. One of the most entertaining was his account of a horse race with some Choctaw headmen. After coming across some mounted Choctaw warriors, Adair and the Indians jested with each other about the fact that the Indians mounted from the right and the Europeans from the left. Each professed the other to be "wrong."

They carried it against me by a majority of voices, whooping and laughing but, as they were boasting highly of the swiftness of their horses, and their skill in riding and guiding them, much better with a rope than with a bridle, I resolved to convince them of their mistake; for as the horse I rode was justly named Eagle, and reckoned the swiftest of any in the Chikkasah country, I invited them to a trial by way of diversion, in so merry a season, and they gladly accepted the offer.

The Indians and Adair lined up on each side of the path through the woods and with a whoop the riders started off. Adair led them deliberately into a swampy thicket where they had difficulty controlling their horses and where their plumes and ornaments were torn from their bodies. Adair exulted in his victory. The Indians could only say, "O strange!"[4]

3. Adair, *History*, pp. 144, 357.
4. Ibid., p. 426.

Adair's *History* not only criticized European society and reminisced about personal experiences, it also tried to prove the thesis that the American Indians descended from the lost tribes of Israel. The invalidity of that thesis does not diminish Adair's accurate, firsthand observations about the Indians, or his book's value as an historical, ethnographic, or political account. To fault Adair for his thesis of Indian origins would require the denunciation of countless other writers, from the early sixteenth through the nineteenth century.

Adair, as did other observers, noted cultural parallels between the Jews and the Indians. His conclusion that these similarities implied a descent by one culture from the other, albeit along a far distant path, was an error made by many. Since he stated his assumption as a hypothesis and since the first part of the book carefully laid out twenty-three "Arguments" for his tentative belief, Adair can be faulted principally for not proving his thesis. Among other writers who drew similar conclusions from the evidence was Elias Boudinot (1740–1821), a New Jersey lawyer and statesman and president of the Continental Congress, whose adopted son of the same name (c. 1803–1839), a Cherokee, edited the *Cherokee Phoenix* (1828–1835). Boudinot's *A Star in the West; or, a Humble Attempt to Discover the Long Lost Ten Tribes of Israel, Preparatory to Their Return to Their Beloved City, Jerusalem* (Trenton, N.J., 1816) cited Adair and other scholars, as well as his own experience, to demonstrate that the aborigines of America descended from Jacob. At least, in Boudinot's words, "he thinks he may without impeachment of his integrity or prudence, or any charge of over credulity, say, that were a people to be found, with demonstrative evidence that their descent was from Jacob, it could hardly be expected, at this time, that their languages, manners, customs and habits, with their religious rites, should discover greater similarity to those of the ancient Jews and of their divine law, without supernatural revelation, or some miraculous interposition, than the present nations of

American Indians have done, and still do, to every industrious and intelligent enquirer."[5]

How does Adair's *History* rank as an ethnographic treatise? His title was, of course, overambitious. He knew the Indians of the Southeast, not those throughout North America or even those dealt with by all thirteen colonies. The standard equivalent modern study is John R. Swanton's *The Indians of the Southeastern United States* (Smithsonian Institution, Bureau of American Ethnology, Bulletin 137 [Washington, 1946]). In reviewing the sources, Swanton noted that "Chickasaw material is not so extensive [as is material on other southeastern tribes], but here we have one great advantage in that it was the tribe which James Adair knew best, and his material regarding the Chickasaw is basal to everything in the Southeast inside and outside of that tribe." Robert F. Berkhofer, Jr., noted Swanton's extensive dependence upon Adair, "which points out the utility of the *History*."[6] As an ethnohistorical document, Adair's *History* posed the problems that all such documents present to the historian or ethnologist. Adair as a participant-observer recorded customs and the changes wrought by European influences. His long stay among the Indians—nearly forty years—enabled him to detect changes that would have escaped a temporary visitor.

While Adair's book combined criticism of European society, personal reminiscences, a theory of Indian origin, and ethnography, it should be judged primarily as a history of Indian-white relations in the mid-eighteenth-century southern colonies, a history related with sarcasm and asperity. Adair's bitterness stemmed from his disappointment at the ingratitude (as he perceived it) of the South Carolina government for his efforts to win for the English the loyalty and support of the uncommitted Indian nations lying between Charleston and New Orleans. Adair's exact role has been debated ever since. The absence of documentary evidence, the complexity of the moves made by Indians, French, and English,

5. Ibid., p. 281.
6. Swanton, p. 828; Berkhofer, p. viii of introduction to Adair, *History*.

and the self-interest and the varying perceptions of Governor Glen, council member Edmond Atkin, the Commons House of Assembly of South Carolina, assorted traders and members of the Board of Trade—all of this has complicated the debate over Adair's role.

The controversy surrounding the events of the period can only be understood by first understanding the divided "face" presented by the English to the Indians. In the Indian country—the home of the powerful Chickasaw, Choctaw, Creek, Cherokee and Catawba Nations—traders, licensed and unlicensed, maintained intimate contact with the Indians. Although the Indians needed the goods brought by the traders, and the traders reaped high profits, it was a lonely and dangerous occupation. In the colonial capitals of Georgia, North Carolina, Virginia, and South Carolina, governors and councils formally attempted to regulate relations with the Indians. In South Carolina the governor frequently operated without his council and more often without coordinating with the Commons House of Assembly except, as that body occasionally complained, when he needed money for Indian gifts, forts, and the like. After Edmond Atkin's appointment as Indian superintendent for the southern colonies, a third authority—with a prestigious royal commission—entered the scene. The King's commissioner, who took his instructions from the British military commander in North America, had to obtain financial support and cooperation from several colonial governments, often a vexatious and unproductive task. In all, therefore, several different voices spoke for the British interest, and all too often this led to disagreement and confusion over policy.

Between the French of Louisiana and the English lay the powerful Creeks, Choctaws, and Chickasaws. The French and Choctaws constantly attacked and harassed the Chickasaws, a small but valiant nation, which relied heavily on English goods to support its independence. On August 17, 1742, to cite a single instance, 2,000 Choctaws in the company of ten Frenchmen attacked the Chickasaws. The two English traders present, Nicholas Chinnery and John Campbell, reported that the Chickasaws lost fifty men. The traders, who had supplied the Chickasaws with ammunition to repulse the invaders, asked the South Carolina Assembly to reimburse their expenses of £486. They pointed out that the Chickasaws were "on the French Frontiers, and a Barrier to the Creek Indians against the French and our Enemy's Indians, that if they are cut of[f], the Creek Indians must fall next and consequently the out settlements of this Province must become a Prey to the Enemy."[7]

In 1745, Adair noted, two of his fellow traders were killed by twenty Choctaw Indians, instigated by the French, "in consequence of which, I staid by myself the following summer-season, in the Chikkasah country, and when the rest of the trading people and all our horses were gone down to the English settlements, I persuaded the Choktah to take up the bloody tomohawk against those perfidious French, in revenge of a long train of crying blood: and had it not been for the self-interested policy of a certain governor, those numerous savages, with the war-like Chikkasah, would have destroyed the Mississippi settlements, root and branch, except those who kept themselves closely confined in garrison." In his *History*, Adair gave a detailed account of his actions in the summer of 1746 and of the delicate negotiations with Red Shoes—one of the principal Choctaw chiefs—prior to his break with the French. That break, which Red Shoes had insisted must be accompanied by the swift introduction of trade goods by the English, was signaled by the scalping of several "strolling French pedlars."[8] The significance of the Choctaw Revolt in the French-English rivalry of the period, and its importance as an indication of Adair's reliability as a historian, makes it necessary to consider the event in some detail.

7. South Carolina Upper House Journals, December 14, 1743 (Council Journal Upper House No. 9), pp. 148–49, in South Carolina Archives, (Columbia, S.C.). For the complex problems involved in citing South Carolina documents, see the articles by Charles E. Lee and Ruth S. Green published in the *South Carolina Historical Magazine* 67 (1966): 187–202; 68 (1967): 1–13; 68 (1967): 85–96; 68 (1967): 165–83.

8. Adair, *History*, pp. 239, 314–24.

Edmond Atkin, during this period a member of the South Carolina Council of State and later His Majesty's superintendent of Indian Affairs for the southern colonies, wrote a book-length account of the revolt in 1753 which differed greatly from Adair's version. Atkin asserted that suddenly in 1746, "without the Interposition of any Person's Skill or Endeavour whatever," Red Shoes ordered the killing of three French traders and the sending of their scalps to the Chickasaws, with the request that they be forwarded to the governor of South Carolina as satisfaction for the three English traders cut off several years before by the Choctaw at French instigation. With the scalps came a message from Red Shoes to the English expressing a wish for a peace and a desire for goods. Following this message, according to Atkin, the trader Campbell went from the Chickasaws with goods, along with several other unlicensed traders, including Adair.[9]

Whatever the true origin of the 1746 event in the interior of North America, Little King, brother of Red Shoes, with numerous Choctaw headmen, came to Charleston in April 1747 to make a treaty and to solicit English help. At the conference the Choctaws agreed to undertake certain actions against French forts and the English agreed to supply arms, ammunition, and other supplies. Governor Glen also introduced a stranger who had lately come to Carolina, Mr. Charles McNaire, as his delegate, under official license to bring trade goods and the King's present to the Choctaw Nation.

Exclusion of the long-established traders among the Chickasaws, who had materially aided in the Choctaw defection, outraged the traders. In a petition of April 14, 1747, James Adair, John Campbell, and William Newbury informed the governor and council that they had put themselves in debt to help make the peace

9. Edmond Atkin, Historical Account of the Revolt of the Chactaw Indians in the Late War from the French to the British Alliance and of Their Return since to That of the French (in the form of a letter to James West, Esquire, London, January 20, 1753), British Museum, London, Lansdowne Manuscripts, 809, fol. 1–33, especially fol. 2 verso. I have cited the typescript of the manuscript in the Henry E. Huntington Library, San Marino, California.

between the Choctaw and English; yet, other traders (McNaire and Company) were "fitting out for that Nation to build upon the Ruins of the Petitioners." The traders asked for permits to trade with the Choctaw.[10]

The inexperienced McNaire and his men failed to carry the arms and gifts quickly to the Choctaw, and that proved disastrous to the colony. Not until September 25 did McNaire arrive in the Choctaw Nation with the public present and some part of his goods. In the meantime, James Adair received a letter from Governor Glen dated April 22, 1747 (four days after the treaty at Charleston), instructing him "to Stire up the Chactaws against the French, and to take Tambekbe Fort." Adair went into the Choctaw Nation and told Little King that McNaire was bringing, "besides the Publick Present of Ammunition, all kinds of Goods that the Nation wanted, as Presents for them from the Governor; and that if he did not deliver them, he himself would come again, and do it." McNaire's arrival and announcement that he had no other presents besides the ammunition left Little King confused and disturbed. The Choctaw leader protested that his people would discredit him if he could not produce the goods promised by Adair. Without the presents, he noted, the Choctaws would probably go back to the French, and he might suffer the same fate as his brother, Red Shoes, who had been murdered at French instigation for going over to the English.[11]

McNaire reluctantly gave out some of his own trade goods to the Choctaws, but he complained bitterly to the governor that Adair's actions nearly caused "a Civil War and great confusion among these People." He asked the governor to restrict the access of such men to the Choctaw Nation by a stricter enforcement of the Indian trading law. Shortly thereafter, on February 24, 1748,

10. *The Journal of the Commons House of Assembly, Sept. 10, 1746–June 13, 1747*, vol. 7 of *The Colonial Records of South Carolina*, ser. 1, ed. J. H. Easterby and Ruth S. Green (Columbia, S.C., 1958), entry from April 14, 1747.

11. Atkin, Historical Account, fol. 5. The quotation from Adair's letter of April 22, 1747, is directly quoted by Atkin from the original. Adair also refers to this letter in his *History*, p. 324.

Adair petitioned the House of Assembly for £755 for ammunition and goods delivered to the Choctaw Nation. After first refusing, the Assembly paid the account on March 7, 1748.[12]

Governor Glen, reporting to the duke of Newcastle on February 3, 1748, with great pride, claimed credit for keeping the Choctaws from the French interest, but noted that for two years past "I have been greatly assisted in it by two Indian Traders of the Name of Campbel and Adaire Masters of that Language and very enterprizing and I promised that they should be rewarded for their Service and I hope your Grace will not think a Hundred Guineas to each of them too much."[13]

In a message of June 1, 1749 to the Commons House of Assembly, Glen tried to answer complaints that he had not adequately informed the assembly on Indian affairs. He pointed out that the "Revolution lately brought about in the Choctaw Nation, and getting them to declare war against the French, was intirely owing to the Directions given by me to Mr. Adair when he was here, and to the Letters that I afterwards wrote to Mr. Campbell and him." Glen continued, "I shall at all Times pay the greatest Regard to the Advice of the Council and Assembly; yet there are some things that are in so peculiar a Manner inherent in the Crown, and so much its undoubted Prerogative, such as making Peace and War, making Treaties and many other things, that I am sure I should be blamed for insinuating that they could not be done without the General Assembly."[14]

12. McNaire to Lt. Gov. William Bull, October 6, 1747, C.O. 5/455, fol. 92 (microfilm PRO 33/1); also in South Carolina Upper House Journals (Council Journal Upper House No. 15), pp. 58–59. Adair's petition in *The Journal of the Commons House of Assembly, Jan. 19, 1748–June 29, 1748*, vol. 8 of *The Colonial Records of South Carolina*, ser. 1, ed. J. H. Easterby and Ruth S. Green (Columbia, S.C., 1961), pp. 62, 102, 123. The printed account of March 7, 1748 contains a misprint not in the original: "the same be now allowed" should be "the same be not allowed."

13. C.O. 5/389, fol. 44 (microfilm PRO 438); same to Board of Trade, February 3, 1747/8, in manuscript Records in the British Public Record Office relative to South Carolina, South Carolina Archives Department, vol. 23, 1748–49, pp. 76–77; same in C.O. 5/371, fol. 35 (microfilm PRO 416).

14. *The Journal of the Commons House of Assembly, March 28, 1749–March 19, 1750*, vol. 9 of *The Colonial Records of South Carolina*, ser. 1,

Governor Glen on December 23, 1749, asserted that "I follow no Plantation business, I am not Concerned in Commerce." Though he claimed to dedicate his time entirely to the public weal, several contemporaries accused him of having a financial interest in McNaire's trading ventures. Atkin pointed out that the governor's brother, Dr. Thomas Glen, was McNaire's partner, a "Clue" into the "Labyrinth" of confused facts in the case. Atkin took as a sign of collusion Glen's promise to pay out of his own pocket McNaire's losses sustained in the public interest should the Assembly refuse to honor them. Adair similarly treated the governor's economic motives cynically, writing in his *History* that "one of our great men [Governor Glen] was reported to have persuaded a couple of gentlemen to join in company with his brother [Dr. Thomas Glen] (well-known by the name of the Sphynx company) in the Choktah trade, and to have supplied them very largely." Adair's anger seemed directed at Glen's refusal to permit him to participate, except briefly, in the Choctaw trade.[15]

Governor Glen's later financial transactions with the successors to the McNaire firm suggested his involvement with the McNaire expedition. Nevertheless, given the ethical notions of the time, the governor probably did not consider it improper to lend money to the firm, despite the contrary views of Adair and Atkin. The governor's call to the assembly buttressed this assumption: on March 17, 1749/50, he asked for a committee of the house to investigate the conduct and behavior of those concerned in the Choctaw trade, to bring to light any faults and offenses, and to punish the offenders, if any. (Atkin, in his report on the Choctaw matter, complained that the governor should have made the inquiry himself or called upon his council—which included Atkin— to do so.)

In a letter to the Board of Trade on October 2, 1750, Governor

ed. J. H. Easterby and Ruth S. Green (Columbia, S.C., 1962), entry for June 1, 1749, p. 271.

15. Glen to Lords of Trade, December 23, 1749, C.O. 5/372, fol. 180 (microfilm PRO 416); Atkin, Historical Account, fol. 26; Adair's license to trade with the Choctaws is mentioned by Atkin, fol. 5; Adair, *History*, p. 322.

Glen also reported McNaire's misbehavior, as relayed by information from an unnamed trader (undoubtedly Adair by the description), and indicated his decision to ask the council to prosecute the offenders.[16] Although the investigation would probably have been demanded had he not initiated it, his openness suggested that revelation of his financial involvement in the affair did not concern him.

Edmond Atkin's assurance that the Choctaw Revolt owed nothing to the English traders among the Chickasaws was belied by the letter books for 1744–46 of the Marquis de Vaudreuil, governor of the French colony with headquarters at New Orleans. On September 17, 1744, Vaudreuil wrote of his effort to form a triple alliance among the French, Choctaws, and Chickasaws. Yet he feared a possible accommodation between the Choctaws and Chickasaws in alliance against France, and he attributed it to English influence. In December, Vaudreuil recognized his inability to get the Chickasaws to drive the English from amongst them, "which he persuades himself he could if had the means of furnishing these Indians with Goods etc." On October 28, 1745, Vaudreuil mentioned the Choctaws' impatience with the French failure to supply them with Indian goods "and also their hankering desire after the English Trade. Red Slipper [Red Shoes] keeps up these discontents and desires."[17]

On January 6, 1746, Vaudreuil noted the Choctaws' efforts to reach an accommodation with the Chickasaws leading to the introduction of English among them. These efforts would have succeeded had not a party of French Indians, sent out by the commandant of the fort at Tombekbe, killed two English. A month later, Vaudreuil proudly reported that the Chickasaws now

16. Robert L. Meriwether, *The Expansion of South Carolina, 1729–1765* (Kingsport, Tenn., 1940), p. 196; Atkin, Historical Account, fol. 18; Glen to Board of Trade, October 2, 1750, C.O. 5/372, fol. 258 (microfilm PRO 416).

17. Vaudreuil's letter books, along with contemporary extracts in English, are in the Henry E. Huntington Library, San Marino, California, Loudon Papers, LO 9, vol. 1, fol. 36 (pp. 15–16 of English copy), fol. 45 (p. 18), p. 21.

wanted to end their war with the Choctaws and offered to drive
out the English if the French granted them peace. Yet on November 20, 1746, Vaudreuil had to report the defection of Red Shoes
after he killed three Frenchmen and sent their scalps to the
Chickasaws and the English with whom he was reportedly attempting to make peace. Vaudreuil immediately set out to
counteract this threat to French security. He had notable advantages. "The English who are amongst the Tchactas," he reported,
"being only private Traders, cannot make the presents, that we as
as [sic] a Nation and Government are able to do, and gain a Party
amongst the Nations."[18]

By March 15, 1747, Vaudreuil noted that Red Shoes had not
furnished his Choctaws with goods as he had hoped to do, and
that the French party now had the advantage. A year later,
Vaudreuil reported with satisfaction that Choctaws of the French
party killed Red Shoes on June 23, 1747—"at a time that he
seemed to have most Triumphed in his Measures—having introduced into his Village, 6 English, with 53 horses laden with Indian
Goods."

This stroke [noted Vaudreuil], would intirely have reestablished the
Tranquility of the Nation, had they at the same time kill'd and pillaged the English. For want of this precaution, too refined for savages,
the partizans of Red Slipper withdrew the English to their Places; who
have by their Presents, engaged that Party to make reprizals on Us, at
our Fort of the Natches and on the River of Mobile.[19]

By 1750, Vaudreuil had gained the upper hand once more and
settled a peace with the Choctaw nation after the French-inclined
tribesmen had furiously slaughtered the pro-English Choctaws.
One hundred and thirty scalps were brought to Vaudreuil by the
Choctaws, who had also attacked the Chickasaws and killed three
Englishmen to regain their credit with the French leader. Vaudreuil, in commenting on the turnabout, noted the absolute neces-

18. Ibid., pp. 25, 27, 32–33.
19. Ibid., p. 39.

sity of Indian goods, "without which, they cannot carry on their Indian Politicks."[20]

Following the collapse of the Choctaw Revolt, the English in Charleston exchanged bitter recriminations over the credit and blame for the affair. These recriminations ranged from literary satire to financial claims. In the *South Carolina Gazette* of April 9, 1750, the following notice appeared:

Shortly will be published, A TREATISE Upon the Importance and Means of securing the CHACTAW Nation of Indians to the British Interest. In which are interspersed many curious Remarks Concerning the History, Policy, and Interest of that Nation, with Several incontestable Reasons, and chronological Observations, to prove, that the Year of our Lord 1738 was several Years antecedent to the Year 1747, To which is added, A Genuine Account of the most remarkable Occurrences since that Period of Time. Concluding with Some Scenes of a FARCE, as the same was some time ago first rehearsed in private, and afterwards acted publickly; in which are contained, some comical and instructive Dialogues between the several modest Pretenders to the Merit of a certain Revolt, said by them to be lately projected and effected. The whole supported by Records, original Letters, and living Witnesses.[21]

The references to a "farce" and to its rehearsal "in private" jibed at Governor Glen's failing as an administrator, as well as his alleged self-interest in the affair. The author of the treatise (if it ever existed) or of the notice of the treatise was undoubtedly James Adair. Irreverent, frank, unawed by authority, Adair periodically outraged governor, council and assembly.

20. Ibid., p. 52. The Choctaw Revolt is briefly described by Jean-Bernard Bossu in his *Travels in the Interior of North America, 1751–1762*, trans. and ed. Seymour Feiler (Norman, Okla., 1962), pp. 172–76. Bossu's admiration for the Chickasaws ("formidable because of their fearlessness") matches Adair's. The most detailed account of the Choctaw Revolt is contained in Charles William Paape, "The Choctaw Revolt, a Chapter in the Intercolonial Rivalry in the Old Southwest" (Ph.D. dissertation, University of Illinois, Urbana, 1946). Paape discusses the confused story of the revolt's origin without drawing definite conclusions about Adair's veracity. Arrell M. Gibson, *The Chickasaws* (Norman, Okla., 1971) does not discuss Adair's role in the revolt.

21. Quoted in Hennig Cohen, *The South Carolina Gazette, 1732–1775* (Columbia, S.C., 1953), pp. 116, 171. Atkin also used the word "farce" in reference to the affair in his account, fol. 26.

Following the appearance of the *Gazette* announcement, Adair petitioned the governor, council and Commons House of Assembly on May 16, 1750, asserting that the governor had ordered him in 1744 to bring the Choctaws over to the British interest with the assurance of a reward for his services. After risking his life and spending time "and his *ALL*" to bring the event about, he noted that he had not received a reward and had been "reduced to want and unable (without Relief) further to serve the Public or support myself." Adair's petition was rejected.[22]

On May 31, 1750, Isaac Barksdale submitted a petition in behalf of John Campbell, trader in the Chickasaw Nation, asking for recompense for his services in arranging peace between the colony and the Choctaws. Having been informed of Adair's petition, Barksdale asserted that he did "not call in Question the least part of what real share of Merit the said Adair may have in that affair, yet he thinks himself obliged, as well in justice to the said Campbell who, as is well known to the Indian Traders, hath better pretensions than any man else to the services rendered in the said affair."[23] The petition recalled the joint efforts of Adair, Campbell, and Newbury to exploit the breach caused by Red Shoes's action in cutting off three French traders.

Finally, Matthew Roche submitted a petition on behalf of Charles McNaire to the Commons House of Assembly. With it went a printed pamphlet entitled *A Modest Reply to his Excellency the Governor's Written Answer to the Affidavit of Charles McNair & Mathew Roche, Concerning the Late Revolt of the Chactaw Nation of Indians from the French to the British Interest*, which included a letter and affidavit from Adair dated October 30, 1749, the contents of which are unknown. Adair's letter seemed to

22. South Carolina Commons House Journals, May 16, 1750, no. 25, pt. 2, pp. 622–23, in South Carolina Archives, Columbia, S.C.; Lawrence Henry Gipson, *The British Empire before the American Revolution*, 15 vols. (New York, 1936–71), 4: 90–91. Adair eventually received £400 from the government (*History*, p. 343).

23. South Carolina Commons House Journals, May 31, 1750, no. 25, pt. 2, p. 723.

the committee to contradict his earlier letter, written in October 1747 during the affair, which reflected adversely upon McNaire and his company. The committee concluded, because of the contradictory nature of the letters, that "Adair was a great Villain, and that not much credit ought to be given to him." The committee denounced McNaire and denied that the province had appointed him a public agent among the Choctaw or authorized him to distribute presents on the governor's account. The full House, while not agreeing wholly with the committee report, affirmed its charge that misconduct and misrepresentation of McNaire and his partners[24] had weakened His Majesty's interest among the Choctaw.

What was in Adair's letters? Unfortunately, we do not know precisely. Atkin described Adair's letter of October 1747 as "blaming McNaire and Company for leaving the Chactaw Nation when there was no Appearance of Danger, and they might have stayed with Safety." Adair's letter of October 1749 gave McNaire, according to Atkin, "the Credit of bringing over the Chactaws to the British interest." Atkin concluded his analysis of the affair by asserting that no claimant to the honor of having brought on the revolt, not even Governor Glen, "hath any just Pretension thereto," but that it was "due only to the *Honour of his Majesty's Arms*, which in the Course of the late War having disabled the French from supplying the Chactaws with Necessaries, those Indians were forced to have Recourse [to] us."[25]

Adair, in his *History*, treated his 1750 petition in the context of the Chickasaw embassy to Charleston, which he accompanied at the request of the governor and council. His beloved Chickasaws were given a "cold reception" because "as something I wrote to the two gentlemen who fitted out, and sustained the loss of the Sphynx-company, had been inserted in the 'modest reply to his Excellency the Governor,' formerly mentioned, in order to obtain

24. Ibid., May 23, 1750, pp. 684–85, 689, 697–99; Atkin, Historical Account, fol. 21. The *Modest Reply* was also announced in the *South Carolina Gazette*, February 26, 1750 (Cohen, pp. 170–71).

25. Atkin, Historical Account, fol. 22, 28, 30.

bills of exchange on Great Britain, I was now become the great object of his displeasure, and of a certain sett, who are known to patronise any persons if they chance to be born in the same corner of the world with themselves." Adair had a bitter confrontation with the governor who pointed his finger at one Chickasaw war leader at the entrance of the council chamber and accused him of recently coming from Savannah and receiving presents. Adair rejected the charge as untrue and told the governor that "I had often given more to the Choktah at one time, than he had ever given to the Chikkasah, in order to rivet their enmity against the French of Louisiana, and thereby open a lasting trade with them, from which I was unfairly excluded, on account of a friendly monopoly, granted by him for a certain end to mere strangers." Adair noted that "My words seemed to lie pretty sharp upon him, and I suppose contributed not a little to the uncourtly leave he took of our gallant, and faithful old friends."

McNaire continued his efforts for compensation in England where, on April 13, 1752, the Board of Trade sent his petition with a favorable endorsement to the Lords of the Treasury to pay him £1,000 or one quarter of what he claimed he lost on the Choctaw enterprise.[26]

The most recent student of the Choctaw Revolt, the late Eugene Sirmans, believed:

Atkin is more reliable than Adair for several reasons: Atkin wrote his account immediately after the revolt, while Adair wrote his nearly 20 years later; Atkin based his conclusions on a careful study of documents relating to the revolt, while Adair relied primarily on personal recollection; there is good reason to believe that Adair exaggerated his part in the revolt in order to claim a reward for his services, while Atkin had no such personal interest; and, most important, independent sources support Atkin, not Adair, on disputed points.

Sirmans's analysis of the event and his assumptions of the accuracy of its two historians, like the account of Atkin, placed

26. Adair, *History*, pp. 340–42; C.O. 5/385, fol. 202–204 (microfilm PRO 435).

undue emphasis on later written documents concerning an earlier event in the middle of the American forest. Moreover, the documentation which does exist seems largely to support Adair's view. On the basis of Atkin's comment that Adair was an unlicensed trader for most of the period in dispute, Sirmans speaks confusingly of Adair as "an unlicensed Chickasaw trader." Atkin meant that Adair, while licensed to trade with the Chickasaws, had no license to trade with the Choctaws. Also, Sirmans erroneously asserted that Governor Glen changed his story about the Choctaw Revolt in 1750, giving credit only then to Adair.[27]

The distinguished colonial historian, Lawrence Henry Gipson, in telling the story of the Choctaw Revolt and of James Adair's part in it, noted that some students of the subject have erroneously assumed that Adair's *History* "is quite unreliable as a source."

While Adair doubtless emphasizes too greatly the importance of his own services to South Carolina and wrote his treatise with a feeling of resentment against his enemies, it is surprising how fully many of his assertions are verified in the official records of South Carolina and of Louisiana. The burden of proof, it would therefore seem, must rest upon those who refuse to accept his statements as being quite untrustworthy.[28]

John Alden, in his *John Stuart and the Southern Colonial Frontier: A Study of Indian Relations, War, Trade, and Land Problems in the Southern Wilderness, 1754–1775* (Ann Arbor, 1944), largely supported Adair's story of his role in the rebellion, though he disagreed with Adair's negative evaluation of Atkin's successor, John Stuart.[29]

Wilbur Jacobs, in his introduction to Atkin's report and plan of 1755 on the management of Indian affairs, noted that Atkin's essay and Adair's *History* "complement each other in illuminating

27. M. Eugene Sirmans, *Colonial South Carolina: A Political History, 1663–1763* (Chapel Hill, N.C., 1966), pp. 267–68, 282–83; Atkin, Historical Account, fol. 27.
28. Gipson, *The British Empire before the American Revolution*, 4:91n.
29. Pp. 27–29, 135.

an era of no little obscurity." Although Jacobs praised Adair's *History*, he gave the palm for accuracy and objectivity to Atkin, noting that Adair colored his *History* "by glaring prejudices and personal hatreds."[30]

An historian should be judged not by his attitude, but by his factual accuracy and his logical analysis. Adair clearly stated his prejudices and hatreds as the consequences of certain facts and events. For an historian to fault Adair for these attitudes, he must first prove, not the existence of prejudices and hatreds, but their false factual basis. This, Adair's critics have not done.

Adair's feud with the South Carolina governing bureaucracy continued beyond the Choctaw Revolt. The murder of certain white men by Cherokees in May 1751 created concern and unrest on the frontier and brought Adair once again into conflict with the authorities. At this time, Adair brought back, from the Overhills Cherokee to the outlying settlements of South Carolina, reports of hostile Shawnee and Iroquois movements, as well as movements of some disaffected Cherokee warriors. While staying at the house of Captain James Francis, near Saluda, Adair directed his remarks at several individuals later examined by the Council of State. Two individuals reported that Adair and certain other traders "did no good" in the Cherokee country, but rather, as David Dowey charged against William Broadway (one of the traders), "Scared the Indians out of their Sense telling them the People of Carolina were raising an Army to cut them all to pieces and to make Slaves of their wives and children." Dowey also reported that he had showed Adair certain letters he was carrying to Charleston. Adair, after examining and returning them to Dowey, said "he would put them in the fire, and said this Examinant shou'd do so," because he (Adair) had a more accurate assessment of the situation and of the numbers of "Northward Indians come into the Cherokee Nation." Adair felt he knew how to handle the situation. Perhaps knowing that his actions and words would be reported to his dis-

30. *Indians of the Southern Colonial Frontier: The Edmond Atkin Report and Plan of 1755*, ed. Wilbur R. Jacobs (Columbia, S.C., 1954), p. xxxiiii.

credit, he also penned a letter to William Pinckney, commissioner for Indian trade. In it, Adair asserted that in the past the French had tempted him to defect with a 32,000 *livre* bribe, and that when he refused, they had threatened him with capital punishment "for all the Consequences of the Chactaw War" for which he noted, he was truly responsible. He then recounted his trip, that spring, to the Cherokees where he had seen "the most evident tokens of war," narrowly escaping from a gang of Cherokees just back from killing some white men in Georgia. Although urged by some traders to warn the government, he saw little hope because of the government's remissness in similar affairs and its refusal to credit him. "[Y]et to serve the Country I offerd to Capt. Francis to prove on Oath all I knew of the affair; if Carolina designs to stand on the offensive part and willing to give me the encouragement which I possibly might merit as well in this, as I did in the Chickasaw and Chactaw affair, with sufficient Credentials I should induce the Chickasaws at Augusta, and many brave woods men, to engage in the Public Service and if I am not mistaken in my self, with such brave Wanton fellows I should be somewhat remarkable."[31]

No question about it. This was Adair: buoyant, cocky, openly contemptuous of the statesmen at Charleston, giving his evaluation and solution and urging other letters to be thrown into the fire. Governor Glen and the council did not, at this time, enlist his aid. The reference to the attempt by "Monsieur" to bribe Adair in the summer of 1750 may have led to Edmond Atkin's slanderous comment to James West: "With respect to Adair (whose *assured Friend* the Governor used [to] subscribe himself), before I left Carolina *he went over to the French.*" Adair was philosophic about being denounced from both sides. In his letter to William Pinckney, cited above, Adair noted that "the World thinks it strange that I should be punishable both by the English and

31. Dowey's affidavit of May 23, 1751, C.O. 5/464, pp. 105–107 (microfilm PRO 37); South Carolina Council Journal, May 23, 1751 (Council Journal no. 18, pt. 1), pp. 98–100; Adair to Pinckney, May 7, 1751, C.O. 5/464, pp. 98–99.

French for that, in effect was done for the one and against the other in time of a hott War, But so it happens in our Iron Age."[32] Adair considered himself lucky to have escaped the French gallows.

Despite his repeated disappointment and disillusionment with the course of colonial policy, Adair remained ready to jump into the fray. The trader Lachlan McGillivray, in a letter of July 14, 1758 to Governor William H. Lyttelton, which Adair carried, recommended his old friend in case the governor wanted to incite the Chickasaws to attack French forts at Mobile and on the Alabama. The sight of him, McGillivray wrote, would warm the hearts of the Chickasaws. McGillivray recalled Adair's earlier role in the Choctaw Revolt: "for he, in the last french war, sett them on Monsieur." Asked if he would serve, Adair "assures me, he will throw away the goosequill, and cheerfully take his sword" without thought of reward.[33]

As ignorance and mismanagement swept the English into another Cherokee war in 1759, James Adair once more offered his services. They were accepted. The Commons House of Assembly of South Carolina voted on July 19, 1760, "To Captain James Adair for leading the Chickesaws at New Savannah, during the time he shall be in actual service . . . £200." A message from Lieutenant Governor Bull of April 19, 1760, outlined the nature of Adair's mission. Bull referred to the body of Chickasaws at New Savannah "whom Mr. Adair with a Commission not giving pay, has undertaken to lead, [which] may act as an advanced or scouting Party, to gain daily Intelligence for Colonel [Archibald] Montgomery [commanding 1,200 British regulars] when he approaches the Enemy." Adair saw the opportunity of engaging pro-English Cherokees against French-inclined tribesmen, but the opportunity was lost.

32. Atkin, Historical Account, fol. 30; Adair letter in C.O. 5/464, pp. 98–99.

33. McGillivray to Lyttelton, July 14, 1758, Lyttleton Papers, William L. Clements Library, Ann Arbor, Michigan (microfilm copies in South Carolina Archives).

Adair was "pre-engaged" for the campaign, as he put it, "but as I could not obtain orders to go a-head of the army, through the woods, with a body of the Chikkasah, and commence hostilities, I declined the affair." Adair apparently took to the field with his Indians for certain periods, despite his distrust of the campaign's character. The campaign as a whole was badly botched. Friendly Cherokee chiefs, who had attempted to avert the war by seeking a conference with Governor Lyttelton, were detained by him as hostages during a fruitless expedition against their fellows and then murdered. As Adair pointed out, hostages to the Indians

conveyed the idea of slaves, as they have no public faith to secure the lives of such—yet they were taken into custody, kept in close confinement, and afterwards shot dead: their mortal crime consisted in sounding the war-whoop, and hollowing to their countrymen, when attacking the fort in which they were imprisoned, to fight like strong-hearted warriors, and they would soon carry it, against the cowardly traitors, who deceived and inslaved their friends in their own beloved country.

Adair waxed eloquent in denouncing this violation of the laws of war, and sadly related that

In brief, we forced the Cheerake to become our bitter enemies, by a long train of wrong measures, the consequences of which were severely felt by a number of high assessed, ruined, and bleeding innocents— May this relation, be a lasting caution to our colonies against the like fatal errors![34]

Adair's disgust with the fiasco of the Cherokee War must have led him to pen the memorial which he submitted to the Commons House of Assembly of South Carolina on April 28, 1761. The House Journal recorded that "A Memorial of James Adair was presented to the House and the same containing very improper

34. South Carolina Commons House Journals, July 19, 1760, no. 33, pt. 2, p. 359; ibid., April 19, 1760, no. 33, pt. 1, p. 127; Adair, *History*, pp. 250–51; David H. Corkran, *The Cherokee Frontier: Conflict and Survival, 1740–1762* (Norman, Okla., 1962), p. 216; Samuel Cole Williams, introduction to Adair's *History of the American Indians* (Johnson City, Tenn., 1930), pp. xvi-xvii.

and indecent Language was Rejected without being read thro.' "
Adair told the story of his rejected petition at greater length in his
History. He had long since given up hope of reimbursement for
his expenses during Governor Glen's administration. When William Henry Lyttelton succeeded Glen, Adair decided to petition
for the more than one thousand pounds sterling he had expended
on the public faith. Accordingly he petitioned the Commons
House of Assembly, but found that the new governor had not yet
cleansed "the infected air which had prevailed in that house for
fourteen years." Adair asserted that they first attempted to invali-
date his petition by pointing out the claim's age. They did not,
Adair wrote, attempt to disprove anything in the petition; "they
knew they could not." After a long debate Adair's enemies "seized
on a couple of unfortunate monosyllables"—specifically, two ad-
jectives Adair used to describe the character of Governor Glen's
communications. One concerned "a great many *fine* promises"
that the governor had given to the Choctaws; the other concerned
"a very *smooth* artful letter" by which the governor dispatched
Adair on public business.

The word *smooth*, so highly ruffled the smooth tempers of those
gentlemen, that they carried a vote by a majority, and had it registered,
importing, that they objected against the indelicacy, or impropriety, of
the language in my memorial, but not against the merit of its contents.
The minute, I here in a more public manner record anew, to the lasting honour of the persons who promoted it.

Despite his contempt for the delicate sensibilities of the
Charleston legislators, Adair expressed his confidence in the honor
of South Carolina: "may she abound with firm pillars of the
constitution, according to our Magna Charta Americana, as in the
present trying aera of blessed memory, so long as the heavenly rays
shall beam upon us!"[35]

Adair frequently expressed a negative view of the capacities of
colonial officials. Their ignorance, vanity, and greed, in Adair's

35. South Carolina Commons House Journals, April 28, 1761, no. 34,
p. 52; Adair, *History*, pp. 350–51.

eyes, prevented them from protecting the traders, avoiding bloody Indian wars, or advancing England's interest. On the other hand, he singled out several colonial officials for high praise. His praise of Governor Henry Ellis of Georgia has been reiterated by contemporary scholars. Adair wrote not only as a direct participant, but as an historian: in both roles he believed in praising or condemning. As Glen and Atkin provided negative examples of statesmen, Ellis provided a positive image:

When public spirit, that divine spark, glows in the breast of any of the American leaders, it never fails to communicate its influence, all around, even to the savages in the remotest wilderness; of which Governor Ellis is an illustrious instance. He speedily reconciled a jarring colony—calmed the raging Muskohge, though set on by the mischievous Alebahma French,—pacified the Cheerake, and the rest of their confederates—sent them off well pleased, without executing their base design, and engaged them into a neutrality.[36]

However, Adair satirically etched his picture of Edmond Atkin, "the honourable gentleman" who served as His Majesty's first superintendent of Indian affairs for the southern department. On the eve of the Cherokee War, Atkin was on his way to the Creeks to reclaim them to the English interest. Though Indian messengers from friendly Creek headmen urged "the absolute necessity of his coming up soon, otherwise it would be too late," and though the Indian traders urged him to go or to appoint one of them to do it, "he trifled away near half a year there, and in places adjoining, in raising a body of men with a proud uniform dress, for the sake of parade, and to escort him from danger, with swivels, blunderbusses, and many other such sorts of blundering stuff, before he proceeded on his journey." Atkin's "stiff, haughty conduct" at the conference so enraged some Creek leaders that one of them attacked him. Fortunately, the blow failed, or else, Adair pointed out, all the whites would probably have been massacred on the spot. As it was, the disaffected party, by murdering fourteen

36. Adair, *History*, p. 256; William W. Abbot, *The Royal Governors of Georgia, 1754–1775* (Chapel Hill, N.C., 1959), pp. 73–81.

Englishmen, marred the great congress at Augusta, at which four governors and His Majesty's superintendent renewed and confirmed a treaty of peace.[37]

Atkin's account of the assault varied somewhat from Adair's. In a letter to William Lyttelton, Atkin recounted the incident, which occurred on September 28, while he delivered a speech in the town square to the greatest number of headmen, he asserted, ever gathered together from the upper and lower towns. In Atkin's account, his assailant—a head warrior of Cussita—"seized with a fit of Madness, suddenly started up on the Cabbin behind me, and with a Pipe Hatchet fell on me and by repeated Blows brought me to the Ground, before I saw him, or any one red or white did the least to prevent it."[38]

Edmond Atkin's critical tone toward Adair resulted from his officious self-esteem. Formerly a member of His Majesty's Council of State in South Carolina, Atkin became superintendent of Indian affairs in the southern colonies in 1756, a position modeled after Sir William Johnson's in the northern colonies. He finally arrived at his post in 1758. Atkin considerably overstated his authority. In negotiating with Haigler, king of the Catawbas, on May 19, 1757, Atkin showed Haigler his commission from King George and informed him: "Henceforth his Governors are to take Care of the Affairs of the Red People, that live in Friendship with them."

Atkin informed the Indians that henceforth they should not talk with the colonial governors but with only him. "I am the King's Mouth for them all." Atkin made evident his contempt for traders like McGillivray, for Governor Glen, and for his former colleagues on the South Carolina council. His sensitivity to slight and his concern for his dignity had become apparent during his tenure as a member of the South Carolina council. He always looked to the authority for an action rather than to the action itself. Adair, a mere trader, particularly offended Atkin because of

37. Adair, *History*, pp. 252–54.
38. Lyttelton Papers, Clements Library.

his flippant tone. That the governor asked Adair to perform affairs of state merely added to Atkin's irritation. Atkin, as superintendent, did not have the same authority that Johnson had in the North; he could only make treaties with the southern Indians. The Board of Trade merely ordered southern governors to cooperate with him. Indeed, the Board's secretary, John Pownall, informed Governor Lyttelton that Atkin's job was only to gather information needed for the management of Indian affairs. In sum, Atkin, despite his inflated view of his own dignity, received little of it from either the Board of Trade or the colonial governors. Certainly Adair gave him very little.[39]

Although Adair incorporated, in the final text, references to events immediately preceding the Revolution, such as the Quebec Act of 1774, his manuscript seems to have been finished by 1768, when he visited Sir William Johnson in New York. Adair wanted support for printing his book by subscription. Johnson recommended Adair to General Thomas Gage, British military commander in America, as "a man of Learning tho Rusticated by 30 years residence in a Wild Country." Johnson noted that "His appearance may not be much in his favor and his voluminous Work may rather be deemed Curious than entertaining, but he is certainly well acquainted with the Southern Indians." Although Adair found his reception by Gage cold and cruelly disappointing, he went ahead with his efforts to obtain subscriptions for the book. On September 7, 1769, the *South Carolina Gazette* announced the book. In October the *Gazette* and the *Savannah Georgia Gazette* carried his proposal for printing his book by subscription, in two octavo volumes, in London, upon obtaining enough subscriptions, at a price of two Spanish dollars:

Proposals for printing by Subscription: Essays on the Origin, History, Language, Religion, and religious Rites, Priests or Magi, Customs,

39. Minutes of the negotiation between Atkin and Haigler, contemporary copy, May 18 and 19, 1757, Indian File HM 3992, Huntington Library; Atkin to Lyttelton, May 20, 1756, Lyttelton Papers, Clements Library; Sirmans, pp. 326–27.

Civil Policy, Methods of declaring and carrying on War, and of making Peace, Military Laws, Agriculture, Buildings, Exercise, Sports, Marriage and Funeral Ceremonies, Habits, Diet, Temper, Manners, etc., of the Indians on the Continent of North America, particularly of the several Nations or Tribes of the Catawbas, Cherokees, Creeks, Chickesaws, and Choctaws, inhabiting the Western Parts of the Colonies of Virginia, North and South Carolina, and Georgia. Also some Account of the Countries, Description of Uncommon Animals, etc., interspersed with useful Observations relating to the Advantages arising to Britain from her Trade with those Indians; of the best Method of managing them, and of conciliating their Affections, and therefore extending the said Trade. Also several interesting Anecdotes Collected in a Residence of the great Part of 33 years among the Indians themselves,

By JAMES ADAIR[40]

Published in London in 1775 by a man professing attachment to king and country—"whose interests cannot be divided"—Adair's tract attempted to educate the home government to the realities of the American situation. Nowhere was he more eloquent than in his warning about the ineffectiveness of a regular army engaged in a domestic insurgency. Few Americans had as much experience as Adair in guerrilla warfare; he had ranged at the head of, or in company with, Indian warriors from the Mississippi to the Atlantic, from Florida to the mountains of Tennessee. Indeed, in equating the effectiveness of one woodsman to ten regular soldiers, he hit on the precise ratio presently deemed necessary by military authorities for effective counterinsurgency operations. Adair did not discount the bravery of the British soldier:

Though the british legions are as warlike and formidable in the field of battle, as any troops whatever, as their martial bravery has often testified; yet in some situations they would be insignificant and helpless. Regular bred soldiers, in the American woods, would be of little ser-

40. Adair's letters were partially destroyed by fire while in the New York State Archives, but not before they had been transcribed and published in vol. 4 of the *Documentary History of the State of New York*, ed. E. B. O'Callaghan (Albany, 1851), pp. 259–62. The letters are also reprinted in Samuel Cole Williams's introduction to Adair's *History*, pp. xxiii–xxvi. Adair's "Proposals for printing" are reprinted by Williams, p. xxii.

vice. The natives and old inhabitants, by being trained to arms from their infancy, in their wood-land sphere of life, could always surround them, and sweep them off entirely, with little damage to themselves.

Not only was British repression of colonial freedom impractical, in Adair's eyes, but it was also unnatural and immoral. He extended to the colonists his admiration of Indian attitudes toward government and of their natural "virtues." These would lead them, he asserted, to defend their natural liberties with the same spirit.

The friendly and warlike Indians have an intense affection to their country and people, and so have the British Americans: and whatever some may think of the colonists martial abilities, our wise statesmen may be soon convinced, that they will be able to maintain all the invaluable blessings of free men for themselves, and convey them to their posterity in their purity and lustre, according to the old English constitution, which is built on plain wholesome laws, and not on the sophisms of tyranny.[41]

Adair's close observation of nature and the Indians influenced his analysis of the relationship between England and the colonies. England was the "mother," the colonies were "her children." "Instinct moves the brutal creation to defend their young ones and property at the peril of their lives. The virtue of Britons will not allow them to do less for themselves and their children." Although other Revolutionary writers utilized such analogies, and though Adair specifically singled out for praise the arguments of John Dickinson, Adair constantly and inextricably interwove his argument for the natural liberties of the colonists with his experience in the "remote woods" of America. Adair's book may thus be viewed as a revolutionary tract; it dealt not so much with the specific acts of an oppressive government as with the nature of the American—this new man—who, like Adair, had become half Indian, half white; half savage, half *savant*; as ready to fight as to talk about the philosophy of government.

Adair's frequent references to the subject culminated in his

41. Adair, *History*, pp. 266, 427, 464.

prophetic warning about the consequences of "the present Quixote scheme" which seemed designed "to fetter the British Americans, . . . and force them to pay for their fetters."

Some statesmen have shown themselves to be no less strangers to the generous principles of the constitution, and feelings of humanity, than they are to the extraordinary martial abilities of the American provincials, especially in the woods, which are continued almost through all our colonies, and would prove a grave-yard to a great army of regular troops. Tame Frenchmen might submit to the yoke intended—But Britons, of revolution-principles, especially the Americans, contemn it and all its supporters, far beyond the power of language to express. Were they impoverished, and subjugated, their own bravery would soon set them free from tyranny. When sufferings become sharp, brave men always make desperate efforts, in proportion to their pain. And the annals of the world uniformly declare, that no enemies are so desperate and bitter, as despised, abused, and persecuted friends.[42]

Although Adair as anthropologist, as polemicist, and as essayist was perceptive and enlightened, his most significant achievement was as historian of the events of his own time, particularly as they affected the relationship between red man and white man. He had the qualities that have marked good historians from the time of Thucydides: involvement in the events discussed, a broad canvas, a strong point of view, and an engaging style. To go into the woods as a trader was one thing; to come out of them as an author was another. Adair did both and produced a book which testified to the unique qualities of his experience. He comprehended the spirit of a strange and alien people—the American Indian—and he expressed the mood of a new breed—the English American. His book effectively communicated these two fundamental elements of the New World to the Old World. That few people listened to his message did not surprise the old man. Adair had long since learned the bittersweet taste of knowledge.

42. Ibid., pp. 451, 461–64.

6.

William Stith and the Virginia Tradition

THAD W. TATE

Despite his death at the early age of forty-eight, William Stith (1707–1755), a Virginia-born Anglican cleric and third president of the College of William and Mary, had already achieved a reputation as a controversial figure in both the civil and ecclesiastical politics of his native colony. He gained more lasting fame, however, for his *History of the First Discovery and Settlement of Virginia,* even though he completed only a single volume of a proposed longer work.[1] His *History* marked him as an important precursor of the kind of scholarly history that came to dominate American historical writing with the introduction in the late nineteenth century of Germanic "scientific" methods and professional graduate study. At the beginning of the twentieth century the eminent colonial historian Herbert Levi Osgood remarked, in an entry for a major scholarly bibliography of American history, that Stith "is, and is always likely to be, one of the standard books on early Virginia history"; he also praised the work as "written in dignified style, with thorough scholarship."[2]

1. William Stith, *The History of the First Discovery and Settlement of Virginia* (Williamsburg, 1747). Later editions include: a London edition in 1753, a facsimile of the 1747 edition prepared by Joseph Sabin (New York, 1865), a Spartanburg, S.C., edition of 1965 which also reprints Morgan Poitaux Robinson, *A Complete Index to Stith's History of Virginia,* Bulletin of the Virginia State Library, Vol. 5, no. 1 (January 1912), and a New York and London edition of 1969 which contains an excellent "Introduction" by Darrett B. Rutman.
2. J. N. Larned, ed., *The Literature of American History: A Bibliographical Guide with Supplement* (Boston, 1902), no. 1164. See also Michael Kraus, *A History of American History* (New York, 1937), pp. 92–95.

In an age in which the writing of history belonged largely to annalists and compilers and in which, for that matter, many historians still traced the unfolding of God's design in human affairs, Stith chose instead to investigate a more distant past—from the founding of Jamestown colony to the dissolution of the Virginia Company in 1624—and he demonstrated perception in the use and critical evaluation of documentary sources. In the end, however, his sense of what he ought to do as a historian outran his actual performance. Stith examined perhaps half the sources on Virginia's first years that a historian today would have at his disposal—a remarkable percentage for his time—and in parts of the *History* he carefully synthesized the evidence they contained.[3] Other sections of the work, however, constituted little more than a running paraphrase of a single source. One principal source, a manuscript copy of the London Company records in its final years after it had fallen under the domination of a faction headed by Sir Edwin Sandys and the earl of Southampton, was itself biased in ways that Stith did not, indeed could not, comprehend.[4] Moreover, many of Stith's major conclusions and judgments bore an unmistakable relationship to his own political convictions as the issues of his day affected them. The long duration of Stith's reputation as a founding father of scientific history notwithstanding, he perhaps belonged in another tradition, that of the historian engagé, whose concern with the past reflected his involvement with the present.

Despite Osgood's no doubt unintentionally double-edged praise for the *History*'s "dignified style," no modern reader would be likely to regard Stith as a master of eighteenth-century prose. No less a critic than Thomas Jefferson may have had both the first and

3. The estimate of the percentage of extant sources used by Stith is that of Rutman, "Introduction," p. ix.

4. Susan Myra Kingsbury, ed., *The Records of the Virginia Company of London* (Washington, D.C., 1906–1935), 1: 78–87; Wesley Frank Craven, *Dissolution of the Virginia Company: The Failure of a Colonial Experiment* (New York, 1932), pp. 6–9.

last word on this subject when he wrote in the 1780s in his *Notes on Virginia:*

> The reverend William Stith, a native of Virginia, and president of its college, has also written the history of the same period [the first years at Jamestown], in a large octavo volume of small print. He was a man of classical learning, and very exact, but of no taste in style. He is inelegant, therefore, and his details often too minute to be tolerable, even to a native of the country, whose history he writes.[5]

In sum, although Stith comes through from the scant available evidence as a man of spirit and conviction, little of that passion appeared to filter into his writing.

The brief preface to the *History* provides something of an exception to such judgments about his scholarship and style. Here Stith admirably sets out the design and method of his work. While we may run some risk of mistaking archaic charm for felicity of style, still the language of the preface clearly has an engaging quality. Stith recounted how he began his history after his uncle, who had been attorney general of Virginia, died before he could undertake an introduction to the laws of Virginia that would also have provided a historical account of the colony's constitution and government. Like many a modern historian, he also proposed to remedy the lack of an adequate book on his subject, though more candidly than they he admitted that "I could most willingly have saved myself the Trouble, of conning over our old musty Records, and of studying, connecting, and reconciling the jarring and disjointed Writings and Relations of different Men and different Parties."[6] Stith here did more, in fact, than confess his dislike of a hard task: he offered a creditable one-sentence description of the careful historian's method. He then identified some of the major printed works he had used, conceding his heavy reliance on Captain John Smith, but also examining with care the question of

5. Thomas Jefferson, *Notes on the State of Virginia*, ed. William Peden (Chapel Hill, N. C., 1955), p. 177.
6. Stith, *History*, pp. iii–iv.

Smith's reliability. Stith believed that Smith's account suffered from the captain's attachment to the wrong side of the Virginia Company's factional quarrels and from his absence from James-town during some of the episodes he described; nonetheless, Stith concluded, "I take him to have been a very honest Man, and a strenuous Lover of Truth."[7] Stith described his manuscript sources with similar precision, in particular, relating in full what he knew of the provenance of the copy he had used of the London Company records. At this point his critical sense failed him, and the bias of that key source escaped him. Stith made no secret, also, of his "contemptible Opinion" of James I, English monarch at the time of Jamestown's founding and instigator of the dissolution of the Virginia Company's charter, but even so he set a high standard of how historians should judge the past, if not the present, when he observed:

For if more than a Century is not enough to *un-solomonise* that silly Monarch, I must give up all my Notions of things. A King's Char-acter, whilst he lives, is, and ought to be sacred, because his Authority depends upon it. But when his Authority, the Reason of it's being sacred, determines, the Inviolableness of his Character is also at an End. And I take it to be the main Part of the Duty and Office of an Historian, to paint Men and Things in their true and lively Colours; and to do that Justice to the Vices and Follies of Princes and great Men, after their Death, which it is not safe or proper to do, whilst they are alive.[8]

The three-hundred-odd pages of text that followed did not altogether fulfill the promise of the preface in either method or literary grace. He, like many another historian, may have become too enmeshed in the minutiae of his evidence. Whatever the cause, Jefferson's telling juxtaposition of "large octavo volume" and "small print" may readily suggest the sage of Monticello wearily putting Stith aside for something better able to whet his intellectual curiosity. If almost 200 years ago a bookish Thomas

---

7. Ibid., p. iv. The best available text of John Smith's writings is *Travels and Works of Captain John Smith*, ed. Edward Arber (Edinburgh, 1910).
8. Stith, *History*, pp. vi–vii.

Jefferson could find only arid erudition and little pleasure in Stith, should one read him today?

There are, in fact, at least two reasons why William Stith's *History* endures. For one thing, it is an important document of its own time, not simply as an example of historical writing of that era (although it is that too), but as a guide to the ideas and attitudes of a politically active, educated, well-connected Virginian of the mid-eighteenth century. A native-born clergyman at a time when most ministers in Virginia were English, Stith was admittedly a rarity, but on the whole he was more atypical priest and typical Virginian than the reverse. Revealing relationships clearly exist between Stith's judgments in his *History* and his own active participation in some important political controversies of the 1750s. Stith's *History* also remains important in the evolution of American historical writing, for he founded a major interpretation that long dominated the study of Virginia history and that in the process shaped the values and attitudes of Virginians.

If Stith did not in the end succeed in realizing all his intentions for his *History*, he nonetheless possessed unusual qualifications for the task he undertook, not the least among them being his family background and education.[9] His mother's family, the Randolphs, had established itself in the colony about 1673 when William Randolph of Turkey Island, grandfather of Stith the historian, had emigrated from England. The Randolphs quickly emerged as one of the wealthy and powerful families in the small circle of Virginia leaders. The uncle, whose unexecuted history William Stith had taken up, was Sir John Randolph, Speaker of the House of Bur-

9. Biographical sketches or data on Stith include Christopher Johnston, "Stith Family," *William and Mary Quarterly*, 1st Ser., 21 (1912–1913): 185; Armistead C. Gordon, Jr., "Stith Family," ibid., 22 (1913–1914): 44–45; and Armistead C. Gordon, Jr., "Stith, William," in *Dictionary of American Biography*, 28: 34–35. Richard L. Morton, *Colonial Virginia* (Chapel Hill, N.C., 1960), 2: 520–522, 622–626, 768–769, adds some important details. The fullest biographical treatment of Stith is Toshiko Tsuruta, "William Stith: Historian of Colonial Virginia" (Ph.D. diss., University of Washington, 1957), chaps. 1–2. Alden T. Vaughan, "The Evolution of Virginia History:

gesses as well as attorney general of the colony. Even though William Stith may have been something of a poor relation, the connection afforded him the use of Sir John's own collection of papers and ready access to the colony's surviving public papers. No doubt it also gained him the cooperation of William Byrd II, a close friend of his mother. Byrd owned the manuscript of the London Company records used by Stith, and he allowed Stith the run of his extensive library, which the historian not unreasonably called "the best and most copious Collection of Books in our Part of *America.*"[10] The Randolph kinship was equally important for Stith's involvement in the political controversies of the 1750s, during which he worked closely with his kinsman Peyton Randolph, a powerful legislator and, like his grandfather Sir John, attorney general and eventually Speaker of the House of Burgesses. The family tie, in other words, was central both to Stith's undertaking of the *History* and to the perspective from which he wrote.

As a youth Stith attended the grammar school of the College of William and Mary (his father had died and his mother was at the time matron of the school, the first of several women of good social position who filled the post).[11] When he was seventeen, Stith entered Queen's College, Oxford, eventually receiving his B.A. and M.A. degrees. Although his stay at Oxford probably gave him the opportunity to read the authorities who would help develop his own approach to history and his own political philosophy, Stith himself never indicated, apart from one general reference to the liberal education he had received, the precise nature of those influences. The *History* itself revealed a little more, mostly about sources of his historical method. Apart from the works that he used for specific information on English exploration and colo-

---

Early Historians of the First Colony," in Vaughan and George Athan Billias, eds., *Perspectives on Early American History: Essays in Honor of Richard B. Morris* (New York, 1973), pp. 31–36, appeared too late to be used in this essay.

10. Stith, *History*, p. v.

11. Jane Carson, "College Housekeeper" (research report, Research Department, Colonial Williamsburg Foundation, Williamsburg, Va.), pp. 7–10.

nization of Virginia, Stith mentioned only a few titles, among them William Camden's *Annals* of the reign of Elizabeth I and the early years of James I, Gilbert Burnet's history of the Reformation, and William Oldys's life of Sir Walter Ralegh. Bishop Burnet's inclusion of a documentary appendix obviously influenced him, as did Oldys's sympathy for Ralegh. One also suspects that Camden's *Annals*, which emphasized an accurate chronological narrative with scant attention to style, proved a particularly pervasive model. In general—and perhaps because of the period about which he himself wrote—Stith seemed to pay more attention to historians of the late sixteenth and seventeenth centuries than to those of his own time.[12]

After his ordination as a clergyman of the Church of England, Stith returned to Virginia in 1731, where the Visitors of the College elected him master of the grammar school, one of the regular faculty positions at William and Mary. Stith remained at the college for the next five years. Although nothing indicated that he had yet conceived the idea of writing the history—his uncle was still alive and committed to preparing it as part of the colony's law code—the time at the College and in Williamsburg presumably allowed him a chance for additional study and reading and for association with his uncle and other leaders of the colony. During these years we only know with certainty that he seemed, as grammar master, to give satisfaction to the president of the College, James Blair, a man ordinarily quicker to criticize than to praise his associates. Blair wrote in 1735, "We have been very happy to have him in that Station; and the School has thriven very much under his care."[13] These comments occurred in a letter of introduction to the bishop of London, for Stith, "having some important business to dispatch," was preparing to embark on a trip to England. When he returned a year later, he resigned from the

12. Tsuruta, "William Stith," ch. III.
13. To Edmund Gibson, Bishop of London, July 7, 1735, Fulham Papers, 13:170, Lambeth Palace Library, London (Virginia Colonial Records Project microfilm).

college to take a parish in the interior of the colony, Blair, on this occasion, reporting simply that Stith was "weary of the School."[14]

Stith's new parish, Henrico, was somewhat remote, though the original Randolph seat at Turkey Island lay within it. Within two years of moving there Stith married a cousin, Judith Randolph, further strengthening his family connections. He remained at Henrico sixteen years, and the relative isolation seemingly gave him the time to write the only volume of his *History* that he ever completed. Stith dated the preface at Varina, the location of his glebe a little east of the present city of Richmond, on December 10, 1746. In the following year William Parks, the Williamsburg printer, published the *History*.

There were apparently two printings of the Williamsburg edition, generally known as the Poor Paper Edition and the Fine Paper Edition. A London edition in 1753 may have simply been a binding of the remaining Williamsburg pages with a new title page. These "editions" present a welter of problems of typographical variations, pagination errors, and the like, of the sort that delight bibliographical scholars, but none make any substantial difference in the contents or represent substantial revisions by the author. For the nonbibliographer, there was in reality but a single edition.[15] The *History* achieved neither financial nor critical success, for Stith wrote in 1755, in response to an admiring letter from Daniel Dulany of Maryland, that he had lost about fifty pounds on the volume and "also raised myself many Enemies and Censurers, upon no other Account but for having spoke a few innocent and indisputable Truths."[16] Most of what Stith wrote, particularly his condemnation of James I and praise for the early development of a representative assembly in the colony, was completely attuned to the thinking of Virginians. His critics could

14. To Edmund Gibson, Bishop of London, June 18, 1736, Fulham Papers, 15:55.

15. Robinson, "Complete Index to Stith's History," pp. 5–18, includes a textual comparison of the editions and relevant bibliographical data.

16. June 16, 1753, Maryland Historical Society, Baltimore (microfilm, Research Department, Colonial Williamsburg Foundation).

only have objected to an aside in which he characterized the council—the upper house of the assembly, high court of the colony, and chief advisers to the governor—as too powerful, thereby antagonizing a small but influential group of his contemporaries.[17]

Stith stood, in fact, on the threshold of establishing a reputation for controversy on other grounds as well. For one thing, the charge of lack of orthodoxy in religion would rise to haunt him. Accused of having come under the influence of the anti-Trinitarian doctrines of Samuel Clarke at Oxford and of refusing to use the uncompromisingly Trinitarian Athanasian Creed in services in his parish, Stith always denied the charges, or even any familiarity with Clarke's writings. Stith clearly had a tolerant, easygoing disposition in religious matters, but in the spirit of the Virginia Anglicanism of his day, he avoided theological matters rather than actively championing heterodoxy. Therefore his reputed response to the criticism of his laxity in reciting the Athanasian Creed— that his parishioners refused to accept it or return the responses— has the ring of authenticity.[18] In a like spirit, one of his published sermons, *The Nature and Extent of Christ's Redemption*, while it avoided theological controversy, stressed reason and common sense over absolute literalness in meeting the biblical requirements for salvation.[19] And Stith's remark in one of his letters to the bishop of London—he had "always accounted it the safest and most prudent Way to acquiesce in the Church's Definition, without enquiring too nicely and critically into the Matter"—offered a classic statement of the latitudinarian approach to doctrinal matters.[20]

In reality Stith's religious credo and his Whig, libertarian political ideology were logical extensions of one another, and nowhere

17. Rutman, "Introduction," p. xvi.
18. John Blair to Thomas Sherlock, Bishop of London, August 15, 1752, Robert Dinwiddie to Sherlock, July 28, 1752, William Stith to Sherlock, August 15, 1752, April 21, 1753, Fulham Papers, 13:183, 130, 179, 43.
19. Williamsburg, 1753.
20. To Thomas Sherlock, August 15, 1752, Fulham Papers, 13:179.

did he join the two more completely than in another of his
sermons, one which he delivered before the assembly on March 2,
1745/46, at the height of the alarm over the invasion of England
by supporters of the Stuart pretender to the throne. Attacking the
Jacobite uprising as an effort to reestablish tyranny, divine right
monarchy, and Catholicism in England, Stith praised the constitutional rule and the Protestant religion that had prevailed since
1688 as both lawful and consistent with true religion.[21]

Both the *History*, with its overtones of hostility toward tyranni-
cal monarchy and authoritarian politics, and the development of
Stith's religious views provided a backdrop for his reentry into the
political and ecclesiastical scene at Williamsburg. Stith had
planned to take an even more distant parish, St. Ann's, Albemarle
County, where he had acquired large landholdings, when events
changed his objective. In April 1752 the colony's new governor,
Robert Dinwiddie, announced that he would collect on his own
authority a fee of one pistole (a Spanish coin worth about sixteen
shillings) for affixing the colony's seal on each land patent issued
by the secretary. The proceeds promised the governor an additional source of revenue for which he would not be dependent on
an increasingly powerful assembly. Beyond such political implications, the pistole fee was sufficiently large to pose an economic
burden, especially for colonists involved in land speculation.

By his own claim Stith was "among the first and freest" in
speaking out against Dinwiddie's action. When called upon for a
public toast at a gathering in the "upcountry," Stith had offered
"Liberty and Property and no Pistole," a phrase that quickly
spread throughout the colony.[22] The leaders of the Burgesses,
among them Stith's cousins Peyton Randolph and Richard Bland,

21. A *Sermon Preached before the General Assembly, March 2, 1745/6*
(Williamsburg, 1746).

22. William Stith to Thomas Sherlock, April 21, 1753, Fulham Papers,
13:43. On the pistole fee controversy, see Morton, *Colonial Virginia*, 2:621–
634; Jack P. Greene, *The Quest for Power: The Lower Houses of Assembly in
the Southern Royal Colonies, 1689–1776* (Chapel Hill, N.C., 1963), pp. 160–
165; and Glenn Curtis Smith, "The Affair of the Pistole Fee, Virginia, 1752–
1755," *Virginia Magazine of History and Biography* 48 (1940): 209–221.

had taken up the fight, although Dinwiddie always held Stith among those most responsible for instigating trouble. The people of the colony, he later complained, had always been "very easy and well satisfied till an Evil Spirit entered into a High Priest, who was supported by the Family of the Randolphs."[23]

John Blair later charged that Stith's hostility stemmed from his determination to avoid payment of the pistole fee on his lands in St. Ann's parish. Whatever the exact mixture of private and public motives—Stith and his compatriots would scarcely have understood the distinction—the dispute undoubtedly stirred in Stith the same political response that underlay his historical writing on early Virginia. Although the Crown simply approved Dinwiddie's decision at a later time and did not itself order the fee collected, Stith instinctively connected the governor's actions with those of James I and the anti-Sandys faction of the Virginia Company or, for that matter, with those of the Jacobites he denounced in his sermon on the Forty-five. Nowhere, perhaps, did Stith more clearly reflect the inseparable link between his conception of history and his political views than in a letter he later wrote to the bishop of London defending his involvement in the pistole fee dispute. In it Stith declared:

It pleased God to give me (what I shall ever esteem one of the greatest Felicities of my Life) the Opportunity of a liberal Education in England; among a People justly famous for their good Sense and Principles of Liberty. I am not quite ignorant in the Laws and constitution of our Government; have been much conversant in History; and have read most of the eminent Treatises on Government, with many other political Discourses, both of the present and past Times. From all which Light, I must have been quite blind, not to have seen the Illegality of laying Taxes upon the People without Law; and I must have been something worse than blind, My Lord, to have sat down silently, and to have seen my Country oppressed, without opening my Mouth against it.[24]

23. To Capel Hanbury, May 10 [1754], R. A. Brock, ed., *The Official Records of Robert Dinwiddie* (Richmond, Va., 1883), 1: 154.
24. To Thomas Sherlock, April 21, 1753, Fulham Papers, 13:43.

A few weeks after Stith had begun his attack on the pistole fee, a second event drew him even more deeply into the colony's politics. In July 1752 Dr. William Dawson, commissary of the Virginia clergy, president of William and Mary, and member of the governor's council, died. There ensued an intense competition to succeed him as the ranking clergyman in the colony. While the same person customarily held the three positions, each appointment came from a separate authority: the bishop of London chose his commissary, the Board of Visitors of the college elected its president, and the Crown appointed councillors, usually upon the recommendation of the governor or others within Virginia.

Stith now abandoned his idea of moving to St. Ann's and became a candidate to replace Dawson, although the governor and his allies opposed him from the outset. Before the end of the month John Blair, president of the council and nephew of Dawson's predecessor James Blair, had already written to Bishop Thomas Sherlock recommending Thomas Dawson, William's brother, for the commissary's post. John Blair specifically opposed Stith, who, he warned, lacked "that sweet engaging Temper that Mr. Dawson has; being, I think, of a too overbearing, Satirical and Domineering Temper (too incident to school-masters); of which I have known many Instances in his Conduct then and since." In another letter to Sherlock a few days later, Governor Dinwiddie added the accusation that Stith was "a very improper Person," who had opposed him by "low Insinuation, contrary to Truth" and had attempted "to make a Party of the lower Class of People" and his enemies. He had to have a commissary, Dinwiddie pleaded, in whom he could confide and with whom he could work in harmony.[25] Stith was obviously not that man.

When the governor wrote, however, he had to report that he had already lost one battle, for Stith had secured the college presidency in a closely contested election. The faculty stood behind Thomas Dawson, who was one of their number as Stith no longer

25. July 25, 1752, July 28, 1752, Fulham Papers, 13:180, 30.

was. The matter of Stith's "Turbulent Spirit" and doubtful religious views had been raised, and Dinwiddie, of course, had voted against him. On the other hand, many of Stith's former grammar school students, now members of the Board of Visitors, supported him. On the second ballot Stith won the deciding vote of the rector, Dudley Digges.[26]

At the same time Stith found that Blair and Dinwiddie effectively blocked his way to the commissary's post and to the council. Twice in the late summer Stith solicited the nomination as commissary from Sherlock, claiming the office as a customary right of the president, defending himself against the charges of heterodoxy, and protesting the *"Virulence and Fury"* of those who sought to "starve" him in the single post he held. But if the earlier letters of Blair and Dinwiddie had not already made up the bishop's mind, a second protest from Blair, in which he repeated his religious charges and for the first time related at length Stith's leadership of the pistole fee fight, must have ended Stith's chances for all time. Sherlock named Thomas Dawson instead. The bad feeling continued between Blair and Stith, as did their mutual letters of recrimination to the bishop.[27]

The general supposition has been that after so tumultuous a beginning, Stith settled down to an uneventful, if brief, tenure in the college presidency before his death on September 18, 1755. By his own report the college went on "smoothly and peaceably" in those three years, with perhaps the largest enrollment in its history.[28] Stith also gained the additional financial security he had sought by his election as rector of Yorkhampton Parish in nearby York County. He even considered resuming work on the *History*, although in the end he admitted his reluctance to pick it up again and to search old records and papers once more. In truth, these

26. July 28, 1752, Fulham Papers, 13:30.
27. Stith to Sherlock, August 15, September 1, 1752; Blair to Sherlock, August 15, 1752; Stith to Sherlock, April 21, 1753, Blair to Sherlock, January 25, 1754, Fulham Papers, 13:179, 14:144, 13:183, 13:43, 15:238.
28. Stith to Sherlock, April 21, 1753, Fulham Papers, 13:43; *William and Mary Quarterly*, 1st Ser., 6 (1897–1898): 187.

last years hardly seem to have been so bland. Taking advantage of his political ties, he won appointment as chaplain to the House of Burgesses, where, according to John Blair's complaint, he continued his "black work" of inflaming opposition to Dinwiddie.[29] Dudley Digges, although always his staunch supporter, recalled some years later his troubled administration of the college. Remarking on the continuing faculty opposition after his election, Digges observed "Mr. Smith was not only a Man of Learning, but was known to have Spirit and Resolution enough to carry him through his Duty in every Station of life; but all Matters in the College being determinable by a Majority of Voices, and the President standing single, he could do nothing."[30] Digges, however much he admired him, seemed to catch a glimpse of the extent to which Stith's life had ended in anticlimax—a man, for all his "Spirit and Resolution," cut off from his larger ambitions by the enmity of Dinwiddie and John Blair, frustrated in his exercise of the college presidency by a resentful faculty, and unable in the end to bring himself to complete his *History*.

Stith's reluctance to get back to the *History* becomes more understandable when we realize that he must have known very well how much more formidable his task would have been in writing about the years after 1624. His lament at the prospect of resuming his search of old records was not an idle complaint. Except for the rather sketchy narrative in Robert Beverley's *History and Present State of Virginia* in its 1705 or 1722 edition and John Oldmixon's *British Empire in America*, published in 1708, Stith would have lacked a guide for organizing his work; and we may assume that he had Beverley and Oldmixon particularly in mind when he complained that reading the works of previous historians of Virginia had caused him "Vexation and Disappoint-

29. Blair to Sherlock, January 25, 1754, Fulham Papers, 15:238; H. R. McIlwaine, ed., *Journals of the House of Burgesses of Virginia, 1752–1755, 1756–1758* (Richmond, Va., 1909), p. 105.
30. Dudley Digges to Richard Terrick, Bishop of London, July 15, 1767, Fulham Papers, 15:23.

ment."[31] Stith would have been very much on his own, then, driven to the documents in an even more fundamental way than was the case with much of his treatment of the period of the Virginia Company's rule.

For the years from 1607 to 1624 that he had covered in his *History*, one or another of Stith's sources provided him a detailed compilation in some kind of logical chronological order. Thus he could move in turn from Thomas Hariot's account of the Roanoke colony to John Smith's narrative of the first years at Jamestown and on to the transcript of the London Company records for the final years, filling in occasionally with other material that he had found. Although, as he moved into the period after 1619, Stith could sometimes combine evidence from several sources and reach his own conclusions in a way that would meet modern standards of historical analysis, his heavy reliance on Smith before 1619 and the Company court books thereafter largely determined what subjects would receive his attention and at what length.

Stith divided the 331 pages of the body of his work into five books, a brief first book on the English drive for exploration and colonization before Jamestown, a second that covered only the two years from 1607 to 1609 of the colony's establishment and of John Smith's actual presence in Virginia, a third that carried the story much more rapidly through 1620, and two very long final books—almost half the text—that treated in the fullest detail the struggles of opposing factions in the Virginia Company with intermittent attention to actual events in Virginia itself. He also bound with the narrative a thirty-page appendix with its own title page that included the full texts of the three company charters of 1606, 1609, and 1612, plus a company ordinance, in which the Sandys-Southampton group had reformed the governing machinery of the Company. As in the case of the preface, with its sound statement of principles of historical criticism, Stith again demonstrated, this time by his grasp of the importance of full and reliable texts of

31. Stith, *History*, p. iii.

major documents, an understanding of historical methodology that he could not always realize in his own writing.

Stith began the body of his work with a similar respect for the historian's task, dismissing the mythological, fanciful accounts of America's early discovery, and promising "to give a plain and exact History of our Country, ever regarding Truth as the first requisite and principal Virtue in an Historian, and relating nothing without a sufficient Warrant and Authority."[32] For the most part, however, in the first two books and the larger part of Book III, Stith primarily followed Hariot and John Smith and tended to do little more than paraphrase the two, retaining Smith's emphases, employing similar language except for some bowdlerization, and at times giving virtually direct quotations without so indicating. Occasionally he did interpose his own judgments, readily identified by his shift to the first person.

The themes that particularly interested Stith and invited his own comment began to emerge early in the account. He uncompromisingly advocated Sir Walter Ralegh's cause in his loss of favor with James I and his ultimate execution, thereby beginning the harsh characterization of the monarch that Stith had promised in the preface. He perhaps reflected his own problems with religious critics when he defended Ralegh and Hariot against charges of atheism or deism. A little of Stith the loyal Virginian came through when he attacked James's initial dislike of tobacco and his effort to repress its growth, which would, Stith asserted, "thereby have robbed the Crown of what has since proved one of its noblest Jewels and most considerable Revenues and the Nation of a very advantageous and important Branch of Trade." He occasionally added to the *History* a detail based on his own knowledge of the Virginia locale. For example, he described, as he had found it in the mid-eighteenth century, the site of the 1611 settlement at Henrico, which stood on land acquired by his grandfather.[33]

More important, Stith began early in the work to demonstrate

32. Ibid., p. 2.
33. Ibid., pp. 20, 21, 32, 124, 125–126, 156.

his hostility to Sir Thomas Smith and his associates, the first leaders of the Virginia Company. He had, he declared, used John Smith's history cautiously on the matter of the reinforcement of the colony with men and provisions in its first years because of the latter's attachment to Sir Thomas who "was most scandalously negligent, if not corrupt, particularly in the Matter of Supplies." Stith, on the other hand, surprisingly sympathized with the military rule of Sir Thomas Dale and Sir Thomas Gates—even though he called the code of martial law that Dale had instituted in "no ways agreeable to a free People and the *British* Constitution"—for he regarded martial law as necessary to preserving the colony and credited Dale, moreover, with having headed off Sir Thomas Smith's effort to abandon Jamestown. But near the end of Book III, when he had reached the year 1618 and the impending overturn in the Company's leadership, Stith's charges against Sir Thomas and his allies, particularly Governor Samuel Argall and the earl of Warwick, became an insistent theme of the *History*.[34]

Hostility toward the Crown and the original Company leaders was but an antecedent to Stith's central concern: to establish the new Company leaders and the Virginia settlers as conscious exponents of parliamentary government. Stith had already foreshadowed his preoccupation with this theme in his analysis of the Virginia Company's first charter at the beginning of Book II. In its retention of a strong voice for the Crown in Virginia affairs and in its concentration of the Company's governing power in a few hands, the charter was considered by Stith to violate English law and the English constitution at almost every turn. It especially did so in failing to provide a legislative power in Virginia based on popular representation—a point Stith made in language more characteristic of his own times than that of the early seventeenth century as the long English struggle began against the Stuart monarchs.[35]

Understandably, then, Stith focused on the Virginia Company's

34. Ibid., pp. 57 (see also pp. 100, 132), 122, 145–154.
35. Ibid., pp. 41–42.

decision to establish a rudimentary representative body for the colony in 1619 as the greatest event that had yet occurred in Virginia's brief history. The long paragraph in which Stith made his final estimate of the significance of the founding of the House of Burgesses was perhaps the key passage in the *History*:

HOWEVER we may be certain of this happy Effect, that by the Introduction of the *British* Form of Government, by Way of Parliament or Assembly, the people were again restored to their Birthright, the Enjoyment of *British* Liberty; and that most grievous and oppressive Custom of Trial by Martial Law was thereby, if not at once, yet by Degrees, entirely banished and abolished. It is true indeed, that before, both by the Royal Charters, and by all other Law and Reason, the *English*, transplanted hither, had a Right to all the Liberties and Privileges of *English* subjects. And certainly no Person, in his Senses, would have left the Liberty of *England*, to come hither (in order to improve the Commerce, and increase the Riches of the Nation) to a State of Slavery; when without that, it was natural to suppose, that they must undergo much Hardship and Labour. Yet by the Necessity of the Times, by the Ignorance of the People, and by the Oppression and Tyranny of Governors, they had, thus far, been deprived of that their native Right. But with the *English* Form of Government, the *English* Liberty again revived and flourished; and together with the Nation, they now transplanted and diffused into *America* their most happy Constitution. From this Time therefore, we may most properly date the Original of our present Constitution, by Governor, Council, and Burgesses; which altho' defective perhaps in some material Points, yet comes so near to the excellent Model of the *English* Government, that it must be the hearty Prayer and Desire of all true Lovers of their Country, that it may long flourish among us and improve. For this Happy Change, we are chiefly indebted to the Change of the Officers and Governors of the Company in *England*, and to the Activity and Attention of Sir *Edwin Sandys*, and many other worthy Members of the Company, to the Affairs of the Colony.[36]

For Stith the establishment of the Burgesses had marked an instant birth of liberty and the achievement of a fully developed

36. Ibid., pp. 160–161.

legislative body; not, as most historians would now see it, a tentative, uncertain beginning of an institution of limited powers and purposes that in time would grow into something far stronger. The assembly was, moveover, to Stith a creation of Sir Edwin Sandys and the Company's new, enlightened leadership; not, as it indisputably was, the fruit of a policy conceived and set in motion before the upheaval in Company affairs had produced a change in leadership. Above all, it was a model for the political values and institutions of Stith's own day—indeed, in the passage just quoted, he made the Burgesses of 1619 all but indistinguishable in power and motivation from those who fought against Dinwiddie's pistole fee.

The entire second half of the *History*, comprising Books IV and V, elaborated the struggle between liberty and tyranny in great detail, with the Sandys-Southampton group and the Virginia settlers ranged against the king and the displaced Company leadership. By this point in the *History* Stith relied heavily on the transcript of the Virginia Company courts, or business meetings, owned by William Byrd. This so-called Collingwood transcript, named for the secretary who copied it, was originally made for the use of Southampton in the battle over Company affairs and was itself a "partisan and somewhat varnished" record.[37] For all practical purposes Stith's point of view and that of his principal source so intertwined and reinforced one another that his interpretation of events became much less the kind of interpolation that occasionally occurred in the first half of the work and now became an integral part of the narrative. At the same time Stith did use a variety of other sources, weighing them carefully to establish correctness of detail, but still a sympathetic treatment of the Sandys-Southampton partisans remained the focus of the final books.

Consequently Stith somehow related virtually every event that occurred in England or America after 1619 to the contest for

37. See above, n. 4.

control of the Company. In addition to the establishment of the legislative assembly in Virginia, Stith credited Sandys and Southampton with an equivalent liberalization of the governance of the Company itself, a determined effort to secure a larger number of settlers and promote economic diversification, a desire to improve the colony's quality of life by such steps as the effort to found a college at Henrico, and a willingness to cooperate with the Crown in every possible way to insure that wealth would flow from Virginia into England. On the other hand he blamed Sir Thomas Smith and his allies for using their influence at court to weaken and destroy the Company if they could not rule it, while James himself stood accused of a determination to milk the colony's growing trade unreasonably, to sacrifice its interest to his Spanish sympathies, and to snuff out any hint of political liberty at home or in Virginia. In such terms Stith traced at length the tortured factional struggle that dragged on through the early 1620s. Finally, on May 24, 1624, came the dissolution of the Company, "one of the noblest, most illustrious, and publick-spirited Societies, that ever yet perhaps engaged in such an Undertaking." Even though Stith finally conceded that establishment of royal government had served Virginia's best interests in the long run, he nevertheless lamented that it was "brought about with all imaginable Instances of Unrighteousness and Oppression."[38] And though in the conclusion Stith did not return to the subject of the assembly, he had treated it as a stalwart defender of the Sandys interest through the difficult days of the 1620s.

If Stith lamented that the *History* had made him enemies and caused him financial loss, he made these observations in 1753, at a time when he had more immediate reasons for experiencing a sense of frustration. His negative assessment came, moreover, in response to a letter of warm praise from a neighboring colony,

38. Stith, *History*, p. 329.

which suggested that the volume had, after all, begun to win a certain reputation. That reputation continued to grow, for as the history of Virginia and of America unfolded from Stith's time through the American Revolution and on to the state and national patriotism of the nineteenth century, the events at Jamestown seemed more and more to take on the meaning that Stith had found in them. For a people whose representative legislatures had been both a central issue and principal source of leadership in the struggle for independence, the founding of the Virginia House of Burgesses, and with it the whole tradition of colonial assemblies, did seem a noble event. That the charter of the Virginia Company had guaranteed the rights and liberties of Englishmen took on heightened significance, too, and the idea that colonists and enlightened Englishmen had struggled against an oppressive Crown in the 1620s seemed to foreshadow the 1760s and 1770s.

Succeeding generations of historians followed and enlarged upon Stith's point of view. In the first major Virginia history after the revolution, the ardently patriotic John Daly Burk, an Irish expatriate who had settled in the United States, began his own work with praise for Stith, "who on all occasions, displays a manly contempt and defiance of injustice and tyranny."[39] When these later historians grappled with their own problems of research, they found Stith impressive as well for the depth of his evidence. Even Thomas Jefferson, for all his impatience with Stith's style and prolixity, found him "exact" and relied upon his documentary appendix as a source for the Virginia charters.[40] By the middle of the nineteenth century, historians almost uniformly regarded Stith as an "accurate, judicious, and faithful writer" and, although they

39. John [Daly] Burk, *The History of Virginia from Its First Settlement to the Present Day* (Petersburg, Va., 1804–1816), 1: i–ii. See also Arthur Shaffer, "John Daly Burk's *History of Virginia* and the Development of American National History," *Virginia Magazine of History and Biography* 77 (1969): esp. 343–344.
40. Jefferson, *Notes on Virginia*, ed. Peden, pp. 177, 179–180.

usually worked from additional sources or from their own reading of the Virginia Company records, they essentially restated his interpretation.[41] Stith's reputation continued high enough so that the famous bibliographer Joseph Sabin published in 1865 a facsimile of the original Williamsburg edition, the first reprint of Stith since the 1753 London edition.

Toward the end of the nineteenth century, Stith seemed perhaps a more remote and less reliable guide, although his point of view now received its strongest, most uncompromising statement in the work of Alexander Brown. Drawn to his study of history by the lengthy dispute over the veracity of Captain John Smith that went on throughout the last half of the century, Brown had concluded that Smith was not only unreliable but that the publication of his history was but another plot of the king and anti-Sandys partisans. Stith, in turn, lost some favor for his heavy reliance on John Smith; Brown dismissed Stith at the same time that he outdid him in presenting a patriotic view of Virginia's beginnings.[42] In the first years of the twentieth century some of the new scientific historians began to revise that view, particularly W. R. Scott in his treatment of the Virginia Company.[43] Nevertheless, Herbert Osgood's bibliographical note of 1902 suggested that even among trained professionals, Stith's reputation had not altogether diminished.

41. Charles Campbell, *History of the Colony and Ancient Dominion of Virginia* (Philadelphia, 1860), p. 437, is the source of the quotation. See also *Historical Magazine* 1 (1857): 27–28; review of Joseph Sabin reprint in *North American Review* 103 (1866): 604–606; "Stith's History of Virginia," *Southern Literary Messenger* 37 (1863): 554–565; Edward D. Neill, *History of the Virginia Company of London* (Albany, N.Y., 1869); and Craven, *Dissolution of the Va. Company*, pp. 9–12.

42. Brown is critical of Stith in *English Politics in Early Virginia History* (Boston and New York, 1901), ch. VI. Brown's first work, *The Genesis of the United States* (Boston and New York, 1890), was a straightforward documentary compilation, but he began his criticism of John Smith and his own patriotic interpretation of Virginia origins in a second work, *The First Republic in America* (Boston and New York, 1898). Cf. Craven, *Dissolution of the Va. Company*, pp. 12–21.

43. W. R. Scott, *The Constitution and Finance of English, Scottish and Irish Joint-Stock Companies to 1720* (Cambridge, 1910–1912), 2: 266–289.

Stith's version of Virginia's founding finally received its most definitive correction with the publication in 1932 of Wesley Frank Craven's *Dissolution of the Virginia Company*. He not only placed the founding of the assembly in a more realistic—and limited—light, but he also examined the operations of the Virginia Company in its last years more thoroughly than anyone had ever done it before. What he found differed sharply from Stith: Sandys' policy of increasing the flow of settlers and attempting so many economic experiments at one time, far from being a sensible endeavor, had unwittingly driven the Virginia Company to more certain bankruptcy and kept the mortality rate in Virginia as fearful as it had ever been. The Sandys-Southampton leadership had therefore managed affairs no better, perhaps worse, than those whom they replaced; and the factional quarrels, to which they contributed their part, were so intense and so unlikely to be resolved that the king, without any other political motivation, had ample justification for revoking the charter. Scholars have since all but unanimously followed Craven's view, and only within the past year another historian has suggested that conditions within Virginia, where a speculative, booming economy based on the first growth of the tobacco trade masked a ruthless exploitation of labor and of the company resources, were hardly better after 1619 than those that prevailed within the company in England.[44]

Even after forty years, however, historians may have successfully convinced each other rather than reached a wider audience with a corrective to Stith. Those who had perpetuated him do not often read Stith, but his authority stood for a long time and many others transmitted and built upon his views. For that matter, apart from its priority as the first permanent English settlement and the romantic appeal of the John Smith-Pocahontas story, Jamestown has perhaps operated less powerfully on the popular imagination than such themes as the mid-eighteenth-century plantation culture

44. Edmund S. Morgan: "The First American Boom: Virginia 1618 to 1630," *William and Mary Quarterly*, 3d Ser., 28 (1971): 169–198.

or the familiar episodes of the American Revolution in Virginia. But here again, Stith exerted another and more indirect influence, offering in his account of Virginia's libertarian political beginnings an explanation of the origins of much that seemed essential to the politics of the Revolutionary era. In time, an idealized view of the Virginia past, centered perhaps most closely on the tradition of an open, freely chosen aristocratic leadership dedicated to virtue, liberty, and responsibility, came to dominate popular history and also to shape the attitudes and values of Virginians of a later age. It continues to exert an attraction that neither the work of professional historians nor the realities of the twentieth century has altogether diminished. Anyone tracing the process by which so potent a myth developed and persisted would certainly turn first to others, especially the nineteenth-century historians of Virginia, but if he pursued the quest long enough, some of the trails would eventually lead to William Stith.[45]

But William Stith spoke much more directly for his own age, and that, in the last analysis, is the overriding significance of *The History of the Discovery and First Settlement of Virginia*. The correlation between Stith's understanding of the colony's beginnings and his response in the pistole fee controversy requires no further comment, except that Stith had written the *History* some years before Robert Dinwiddie conceived the pistole fee—the volume was not a crudely propagandistic work but rather a telling revelation of a frame of mind that could not tolerate the governor's act. That frame of mind contained several key ingredients. Foremost, it contained a glorification of the place in the political order of a representative assembly directly answerable to its electorate. Though circumspect and outwardly approving of the institution of monarchy, it incorporated, at least subconsciously, republican and antiroyalist sentiments—no matter how much Stith drew a line between living and dead kings, he could hardly

45. Cf. Marshall W. Fishwick, "Clio in Bondage," appendix to *Virginia: A New Look at the Old Dominion* (New York, 1959), pp. 273–281.

say what he did about James I and retain even a vestige of the belief that "divinity doth hedge a king." It included religious tolerance—in reality mild lack of concern—for while Stith was hardly the religious radical John Blair sought to make him, he was clearly no doctrinaire. In truth, the world of his *History* was a very material one, where only the nature of the New World environment and economic and political realities counted, somewhat as writing history, fighting the pistole fee battle, perhaps even acquiring his estate, touched Stith more deeply than the spiritual and theological aspects of his ecclesiastical career. In other respects, however, the world of Stith's *History* had an idealistic outlook, nowhere more so than in its suspicion that corruption was the opening wedge of political tyranny.

In a sense these attitudes marked Stith's inability to grasp the essence of the early seventeenth century—probably a more conventionally religious age in spite of the savagely material quest of the Jamestown venture and certainly a less politically conscious age in Virginia than Stith could understand. By the same token the mid-eighteenth-century outlook embedded in the *History* measured how far Virginia had evolved in a century and a half and gave an early indication of the extent to which that development produced the troubled imperial relations that followed. As a social and political intimate of the older generation of revolutionary leaders in the colony, Stith in all probability would have been one of them except for his early death. Like many another historian, William Stith may, in the last analysis, have glimpsed the reality of his own age more effectively than that of the one about which he wrote.

7.

William Smith's History of the Province of New York

ROGER J. CHAMPAGNE

William Smith, Jr., historian of colonial New York, was both a Whig and a Loyalist. His rejection of the American Revolution has made it difficult to pigeonhole him neatly, or to assess him as an historical figure. After nearly three decades of close identification with the American variant of English Whiggism, William Smith refused in 1776 to follow his earlier radicalism to the extreme of separation from Great Britain. He chose instead to remain loyal to king and empire. Whigs viewed him as a traitor to his principles; Loyalists distrusted him as a johnny-come-lately. Perhaps both groups agreed that gratification of personal ambition was his primary concern, pointing to his acceptance of a royal appointment in 1780 as Chief Justice of New York as proof of his political trimming. More recently, scholars have seen William Smith as an eighteenth-century American Whig who revered the British Empire and its constitution as the bulwark of freedom in a world of tyranny.[1] The empire, although not politically perfect in his view, contained all the basic elements which would protect the mother country's economic and military interests and would recognize colonial civil and religious liberties.

The History of the Province of New York, William Smith's major literary effort, revealed him as New York's Loyal Whig, and

1. L. F. S. Upton, *The Loyal Whig: William Smith of New York & Quebec* (Toronto, 1969) is a recent biography of Smith.

provided a link between his earlier political radicalism and his later Loyalism. Conceived and written in the 1750s, the first segment of Smith's *History*, which ended with the arrival of Governor William Cosby in 1732, was the product of an extraordinary decade of vigorous literary interest and political discord. Some twenty years later, as a major public figure attempting to straddle the political issue of independence, Smith drafted a *Continuation* that carried his historical narrative to 1762.[2] Both parts of Smith's *History* showed his attachment to the British Empire; however, in Smith's view the empire had not yet recognized the economic and political realities of American development and maturity.

William Smith, Jr., was born in New York City on June 18, 1728, the first child of William and Mary Het Smith. His grandfather, Thomas Smith, had arrived in New York City in 1715 with sufficient wealth to send William's father promptly to Yale College. After graduation and a teaching stint at Yale, the senior William quickly established himself as one of New York's leading lawyers.[3] Following the practice common in the colony's developing legal profession, the elder Smith dabbled in land and politics. Aligning himself with Chief Justice Lewis Morris, James Alexander, and Cadwallader Colden, William's father participated in the land schemes and political concerns of the Morrisites, assisting in the legal defense of that group's interests against the rival claims of Frederick Philipse and Stephen De Lancey and the avarice of Governor William Cosby.

William Smith, Jr., was an impressionable seven years old when

2. *The History of the Province of New York* has gone through several reprintings since its publicaton in 1757. The *Continuation* was first published in 1826 by the New-York Historical Society, which then reissued both volumes under the title of *The History of the Late Province of New York, from its Discovery, to the Appointment of Governor Colden in 1762* (New-York Historical Society, *Collections*, 1829, 1830). Unless otherwise noted, all references will be to the 1829–30 edition.

3. Upton, *Loyal Whig,* p. 16; Maturin L. Delafield, "William Smith: Judge of the Supreme Court of the Province of New York," *Magazine of American History* 6 (1881): 264–65, 272–73.

his father became embroiled in the political trial for seditious libel of printer Peter Zenger, whose newpaper had printed the vicious diatribes of the Morrisites and his father against Governor Cosby. Though the sense of excitement in New York City over Zenger's acquittal was short-lived, the senior Smith continued his involvement in provincial politics. Within a two-year period there were three bitterly contested elections for assembly seats, legislative sessions were marked by the older constitutional dispute over the assembly's encroachment upon royal prerogatives, and the Morrisites and James Alexander, with whom William, Sr., was closely associated, were constantly plotting. In this family atmosphere of legal and political interests William Smith, Jr., spent his boyhood, attending grammar school and developing a kind of freewheeling intellectualism which emphasized opposition to the established practices and values of society, government, and religion.

William Smith, Jr.'s generation of native New Yorkers had its place in provincial society assured at birth. His father's involvement in law and politics influenced his later interest in public affairs. He followed his father and a growing number of other New Yorkers to Yale College, graduating in 1745 at only seventeen years of age, and entering an apprenticeship in his father's law office. The period between his Yale graduation and his admission to the provincial bar in 1750 was a time of continuing political crisis. War with France, Indians, and military preparations dominated public discussions, while his father and James Alexander served as principal advisers to Governor George Clinton, and while Chief Justice James De Lancey led the antiadministration forces in the council and assembly.[4] During the late 1740s the younger William Smith joined a group of equally spirited apprentice lawyers in the city's taverns and found a release from the drudgery of his legal studies. He, along with William Livingston

4. Stanley N. Katz, *Newcastle's New York: Anglo-American Politics, 1732–1753* (Cambridge, Mass., 1968), pp. 75, 76–77, 83–90; Upton, *Loyal Whig*, pp. 11–12.

and John Morin Scott—the trio that became known as New York's "triumvirate"—took a certain arrogant pride in the group's drinking prowess and practical jokes, and in its sense of intellectual superiority.[5] The triumvirate came of political age in the 1750s. From then until their deaths they would never be far from the center of public affairs.

Their youthful enthusiasm for the cultural improvement of the provincial capital initially held Smith, Livingston, and Scott together. Weaned on the liberal writings of English Whigs, they were conscious of a new intellectual age dawning in New York and America, they were aware that they represented a new generation of colonial Americans, college educated and generally better informed than their fathers in philosophy, history, and law, and they were certain that their intellectual and professional attainments fitted them for a principal role in public affairs. Smith's clerkship in his father's law office, his night prowlings with cronies, and the beginning of the triumvirate's literary experiments prepared him for his entry into the province's political life. Licensed an attorney in 1750, Smith began a brief law partnership with William Livingston, the high point of which was their editing of the provincial laws, a task completed in 1752.[6] Though his law business was important and profitable to him, public affairs over the next few years claimed equal attention.

The triumvirate, under the leadership of William Livingston, began publication in 1752 of a magazine of critical essays which quickly became a vehicle to attack those who would defend the dogma of established religion. The *Independent Reflector* soon branched out and touched upon most of the sacred values of provincial society, but the issue which most agitated Smith and his friends was the Anglican campaign to convert King's College into a sectarian institution controlled by the Church of England. Draw-

5. Upton, *Loyal Whig,* pp. 16, 19–22.
6. Milton M. Klein, "The Rise of the New York Bar: The Legal Career of William Livingston," *William and Mary Quarterly,* 3d ser., 15 (1958): 334–58.

ing upon the polemics of the English radicals John Trenchard and William Gordon, the triumvirate used the *Reflector* and the newspapers to expose the danger to liberty of a close connection between church and state. But the narrow focus of Smith's religious battle soon broadened into a larger opposition to the dominant political figure in the colony, Lieutenant Governor James De Lancey, who sided with the churchmen on King's College. De Lancey became the symbol of all that was wrong with provincial administrations. They were self-serving, unmindful of the basic principles of English liberty, and ready to sacrifice the public's welfare in order to protect local vested interests.[7] Smith may have been influenced initially by his father's older opposition to James De Lancey, but he found in the religious controversy over King's College ample ground upon which to build his own antiadministration position.

The continuing problem of defense along New York's northern frontier and the outbreak of war with French Canada gave an added dimension to Smith's political interests. Despite its importance, the college was a local matter, but war with France concerned all the colonies, and Smith quickly proved himself militantly anti-Gallic. French power in Canada and border warfare represented real dangers to America in the same way that French power in Europe constantly menaced the mother country. If both England and its colonies were to survive in a world hostile to their free institutions, they must curb French power in Canada and Europe. Only then could New Yorkers freely and fully develop the advantages of their own colony. But local politics also conditioned Smith's support of the war effort in the 1750s. Lieutenant Governor De Lancey's indifferent attitude toward New York's role in the war merely exemplified his preference for private interests over public good. Since the Albany Indian traders wanted peace, or at least neutrality, along the northern border to protect their trade interests with Montreal, and since the De Lancey family dealt in

7. Milton M. Klein, ed., *The Independent Reflector* (Cambridge, Mass., 1963), pp. 21–44.

Indian trade goods, De Lancey was evidently promoting the self-interest of a few when he failed to lead the assembly vigorously into adequate war measures. Such had been De Lancey's course earlier under Governor George Clinton, and it did not change in 1753 when he assumed the administration of the colony on the eve of the French and Indian War. Thus he seemed to sacrifice the public interest when he opposed the Albany Congress's attempt in 1754 to unite the colonies in a coordinated offensive against Canada.[8]

New York's failure to support the war plans against Canada was not entirely the result of De Lancey's local political activities. Smith believed that British policies and imperial organization also played an inadvertent role. During King George's War, for example, the Crown's insistence that the New York Assembly establish a permanent revenue for the government unrealistically failed to take into account a half-century of colonial political developments. When the Board of Trade instructed Governor George Clinton to obtain a perpetual grant of money, it tried to turn back the clock to the beginning of the century; it also prompted a needless dispute with the assembly that impeded New York's role in the war, retarded adequate defenses along the northern frontier, and promoted partisan opposition to the governor in his own council and in the assembly.[9] Altogether the revival of the issue of a permanent fund was an unsound and impolitic policy decision.

To Smith, the mother country based its policies at best upon partial information of colonial developments, and at worst upon willful misrepresentation of provincial conditions by local leaders. Whitehall's view of New York, determined largely by half-truths or outright lies, could not possibly serve as a basis for sound instructions to New York's governors at a time when the empire's future seemed to be at stake. The dismissal in 1756 of William

8. Milton M. Klein, "William Livingston's A *Review of the Military Operations in North America*," in Lawrence H. Leder, ed., *The Colonial Legacy*, 4 vols. (New York, 1971–74), 2: 119–21; Upton, *Loyal Whig*, 35–36.
9. Smith, *History*, 2: 121–28.

Shirley from his military command simply demonstrated that British authorities were being misled by accounts from America. Shirley, governor of Massachusetts, saw more clearly than most the necessity of destroying French power in Canada if the American colonies were ever to know peace, and, as commander-in-chief during King George's War, he sought to unite the northern colonies in a vigorous campaign against the enemy. Though supported in New York by Governor Clinton, James Alexander, the senior Smith, and the powerful Livingston family, Shirley ran afoul of the Albany merchants, who desired neutrality, and aroused the political enmity of James De Lancey. This led to a halfhearted effort from New York and to bitter strife between Shirley and De Lancey.[10] When Shirley resumed his military command in 1755, he found New York's political situation even worse than before. James De Lancey, now lieutenant governor, had the year before done as much as possible to wreck the Albany Congress; not even the arrival of a new governor, Charles Hardy, lessened De Lancey's influence over provincial affairs. Shirley and his New York friends soon found that De Lancey's opposition and reports to London undermined his support from the ministry and brought on his dismissal.[11] Clearly, in Smith's view, Governor Shirley had fallen victim to the political machinations of the De Lanceys who had weakened the war effort and thereby contributed to the French victories of 1755 and 1756. It seemed likely that French power in Canada would once more escape annihilation unless the mother country more actively directed the war and managed imperial affairs.

William Smith and William Livingston rose to William Shirley's defense both at home and in London. They defended Shirley's strategy and denounced De Lancey's policy of neutralism in

10. The De Lancey-Shirley fight may be followed in John A. Schutz, *William Shirley: King's Governor of Massachusetts* (Chapel Hill, N.C., 1961).
11. Klein, "William Livingston's *A Review of the Military Operations*," pp. 127–28.

the local newspapers, but the young lawyer-politicians reserved their strongest denunciations of Lieutenant Governor De Lancey for the London public and English government officials. In 1757 Livingston published in London *A Review of the Military Operations in North America,* exposing De Lancey's obstructionist politics and praising Shirley's military leadership,[12] and Smith finished *The History of the Province of New York,* providing the essential historical background to the problems of New York's relations with French Canada. Considered together, the two books were intended to give the ministry an accurate analysis of New York's development and hopefully lead the cabinet to sounder decisions on the colony's future.

William Smith saw the need for a history of New York earlier in the decade, when he and William Livingston prepared a digest of provincial laws. As they rummaged through old records in the secretary's office in their search for legislative materials, Smith discovered that the reports sent home by the colony's governors did not square with other documents. The reports were unreliable, if not false, written by governors who were "men of mean parts, and indigent circumstances" and had little concern about the colony's problems or future. Involved in "party projects and contracted schemes," they concentrated upon reaping personal profit from their office, quarreled needlessly with the people, and falsified their official reports to London to cover their peculations. The results had been damaging to New York. Englishmen thought of the colony as a "desert wilderness," a fit place to dump society's misfits, outcasts, and criminals. Worse still, the king's ministers never fully understood the French menace in North America or New York's limited resources in facing that threat, and the common enemy still ravaged and plundered the colony's frontiers at will and retarded settlement. It was necessary, therefore, to com-

12. Milton Klein's arguments supporting Livingston's authorship of the *Review* are more convincing than those of Professor Upton in favor of Smith. Ibid., pp. 136–38; Upton, *Loyal Whig,* pp. 36–37.

pile a true account of New York's history and condition to correct the false impressions created by incompetent and corrupt governors.[13]

The first volume of Smith's *History* consisted of five chapters of political narrative and six appendices describing New York's demography, trade, religious denominations, and system of law and government. Smith developed several interrelated themes as he faithfully followed each governor's administration until Governor William Cosby's arrival in 1732. First and foremost was the existence from the beginning of tension between the English and French along New York's northern frontier of the Mohawk and upper Hudson valleys—a tension marked by brutal raids upon isolated settlements, kidnappings and torture of innocent victims, and, less frequently, large-scale military expeditions. Smith never systematically analyzed the causes of that tension and conflict, but from Thomas Dongan's administration onward he saw the French as the aggressors, tampering with Indian nations with whom the English had established peaceful relations, sending out unscrupulous and cunning Jesuit missionaries to incite and lead Canadian Indians in savage attacks upon white settlements and friendly Mohawk Indian villages, and building forts at strategic places to control the fur trade. Smith concluded:

The French in Canada have always been jealous of the increasing strength of our colonies; and a motive of fear led them naturally to concert a regular system of conduct for their defence: confining us to scant limits along the sea coast is the grand object they have long had in view; and seizing the important passes from Canada to Louisiana, seducing our Indian allies, engrossing the trade, and fortifying the routes into their country, were all proper expedients towards the execution of their plans.[14]

French aggression required New York to defend itself, and Smith devoted large portions of his narrative to the actions taken

13. William Smith, *The History of the Province of New York, from the first Discovery to the Year MDCCXXXII* (London, 1757), Preface.
14. Ibid. (1829–30 ed.), 1: 61–63, 68–71, 76–79, 245–46.

by New York's governors and assemblies as they sought to protect the colony's borders. A firm alliance of friendship with the Five Nations, construction of forts, organization of militia units, and attacks upon Canada were the main elements of New York's defense against its northern enemies. But as Smith studied the documents of New York's history, he realized that incompetence, corruption, self-interest, and shortsightedness crippled every effort to defeat the French.

In a number of ways the mother country was responsible for New York's repeated failure to ward off the blows of its enemies. First, the quality of governors sent to the colony, with the exception of William Burnet (1720–28), had been uniformly poor. Generally they were inexperienced in government and administration and low in fortune and character; men who viewed their appointment, obtained through influence, as an opportunity to plunder the colony. Smith's judgments were harsh: Andros was a sycophantic tool of the duke of York, Sloughter was guided by his bottle and other men, Fletcher was a greedy bigot with a violent temper, Bellomont, though polished in manners, was inflexible in judgment, Cornbury was without honor, a thief who liked to parade about at night in feminine dress, Hunter was too political and cautious to be effective, and Montgomerie was lazy and able to perform only the routine of his office. As a group they failed to appreciate the seriousness of New York's border problems with the French and Indians. They misapplied military appropriations and funds intended to mollify the Iroquois, proved inept in Indian diplomacy and military operations, except when land cessions were involved, and wrangled endlessly with the assembly. Only William Burnet did not fit the pattern. Smith saw in him qualities of a model ruler and statesman. Scholarly but sensible, free of personal ambition and greed, polite and sociable, Burnet more than any of his predecessors understood the importance of Indian affairs, but was obstructed by James De Lancey and the Albany traders who favored a policy of neutrality.[15]

15. Ibid., pp. 44, 96, 109, 135, 167, 181, 202, 211–13, 239, 240.

England was responsible, according to Smith, in still another way for New York's difficulties. Content to allow colonials to fight alone against the French and Indians, the mother country insisted that the assembly establish a permanent fund which the governor would use to pay military expenses. British authorities persisted in that demand even when it was demonstrated that some governors pocketed as much tax money as they spent on military operations. The consequences were unfortunate. England challenged local control of public finances, if not self-government itself, and gave rise to a spirited defense of colonial political rights. Even when the French threat was greatest, when New York should have been vigorously defending its northern frontiers, the assembly and governors fought over finances. In any case, reports sent home by governors placed the blame for their ineffectual administrations upon local politicians. Factional politics, originating in the turbulence of Jacob Leisler's time (1689–91), intensified the controversy as some men sided with the governor for the favors he could bestow or the power he could use to destroy their rivals, while others looked to the assembly to protect their interests. And all parties appealed to England for support.[16] Though the struggle over control of finances varied in intensity from governor to governor, and the composition and ascendancy of factions fluctuated, Smith's historical narrative related a political instability which prevented New York from dealing with its real enemy, French power to the north. And the mother country's appointment of incompetent, self-seeking governors and its demand for a permanent revenue played an important part in that political instability.

If England and the men it sent over to govern New York were not overwhelmed with a sense of the colony's importance to the empire, William Smith felt otherwise. In a series of appendices to the 1757 volume of the *History*, he fully discussed New York's condition and future at mid-century, leading to the conclusion that the colony—its people, land, and commerce—equaled any

16. Ibid., pp. 126–27, 130, 138–39, 142, 154, 158–59, 165–66, 181–83, 187–90, 216–17, 237.

other British possession. New York City had more business, "at least business of profit, though with less show and appearance," than Philadelphia, and New York had far cheaper costs of transporting farm products to market. Boston might have a brighter and gayer social scene, but New York did not have the Massachusetts city's extremes of poverty and riches. "Every man of industry and integrity has it in his power to live well," Smith boasted, "and many are the instances of persons who came here distressed by their poverty, who now enjoy easy and plentiful fortunes." Geographically centered on the Atlantic coast, the port of New York had a superior location and a unique connection to the continent's vast interior. The provincial assembly followed the House of Commons, and the people further benefited from the adoption of the English judicial system. Only in education did New York show a serious defect: "through our utter neglect of education," Smith pointed out, "the ancient assemblies consisted of plain, illiterate, husbandmen, whose views seldom extended farther than to the regulation of highways, the destruction of wolves, wild cats, and foxes, and the advancement of the other little interests of the particular countries, which they were chosen to represent." Considering the colony's extensive agriculture and trade and its geographic importance, New York "ought always to receive the generous aid and protection of our mother country."[17]

William Smith's *History* argued powerfully in favor of Britain taking a more active role in New York's battle with French Canada, a struggle that could not be left to colonial politicians. He had originally intended to carry his narrative well beyond 1732 to cover the administrations of William Cosby and George Clarke, which would have revealed the private ambitions and intrigues of leaders like James De Lancey. From documents and materials supplied by James Alexander, Smith had even prepared a preliminary draft on Cosby and Clarke, but the political emotions of the 1750s apparently caused him to stop.[18] Too many of the local

17. Ibid., pp. 270, 277, 279, 280, 306, 309, 320.
18. Ibid. (1757 ed.), pp. x–xi.

parties were still about, and any writer, as Smith well knew from his father's experience in the Zenger business two decades earlier, "who exposes the conduct of the living, will inevitably meet with their fury and resentment. The prudent historian of his own times will always be a coward, and never give fire till death protects him from the malice and stroke of his enemy."[19]

William Livingston's anonymously published *Review of the Military Operations* suffered from no such restraint. By merely an impartial recital of events, Livingston exposed the way De Lancey had thwarted the military operations of William Shirley; Livingston also called for a union of all the colonies, as proposed in 1754, to face the common enemy. Smith's *History* and Livingston's *Review* were tracts of the times, written in a decade of intense political factionalism and imperial crisis. Designed to convince the ministry of the need to crush French power in North America, both stressed the danger of relying, as in the past, upon New Yorkers, preoccupied with their petty political intrigues, to get the job done, and both urged a structural change in the empire to capitalize upon America's developing maturity.[20] To Smith and Livingston, New York's future depended upon a militant and triumphant British imperialism.

The war in America changed dramatically after 1757, more because of a change in ministries than because of the persuasiveness of Smith's and Livingston's writings. In June of that year William Pitt succeeded the venal Newcastle and brought to the government a determination to win the war at all costs. The new policy meant that Britain would assume a much larger military and economic role in the North American phase of its worldwide contest

19. Ibid. (1829–30 ed.), 1: 249.
20. Klein, "William Livingston's *A Review of the Military Operations,*" p. 130. Commenting on Governor Fletcher's effort in 1695 to create an inter-colonial force to invade Canada, Smith concluded, "as such an union appeared to be necessary so long ago, it is very surprising that no effectual scheme for that purpose has hitherto been carried into full execution . . . The danger to Great Britain, apprehended from our united force, is founded in a total ignorance of the true state and character of the colonies." Smith, *History* (1829–30 ed.), 1: 118.

with France. The organization of the empire would remain unchanged though much invigorated by Pitt's attention to the details of imperial administration. Energetic generals, more troops and ships, ample supplies and money evidenced Pitt's fixed decision to destroy once and for all the French menace to England's American colonies. Even if Smith and Livingston could not claim credit for the shift in the war effort, they could take comfort in the fact that Pitt's militancy vindicated their own.

Twenty years passed before William Smith resumed writing New York's political history. During that time he rose to eminence in the legal profession and became a principal actor in New York's factional politics. He served as a political adviser to a succession of governors, but unlike William Livingston and John Morin Scott of the triumvirate, he never sought elective office. He was appointed to the council in 1767, following his father's resignation from that body, and as the political confidant of Moore, Dunmore, and Tryon, he gained influence in government far beyond what he might have achieved through the electoral process and a seat in the assembly. He liked to think of himself as above partisanship, content to remain behind the scenes, employing his legal talents for his friends in the Livingston faction against the De Lanceyites.[21]

Throughout the turbulent years of imperial crisis following the French and Indian War, Smith's political views did not appreciably change. From the first crisis over taxation during 1764–66 to the eve of American independence he adhered to his belief that colonials enjoyed the same rights and privileges of Englishmen as did the people of England. As he had implied in his *History*, and in other writings of the 1750s, colonial assemblies were not merely local bodies similar to English corporations with only police

21. Smith's prerevolutionary political activities, as well as those of Livingston and Scott, are examined in Dorothy R. Dillon, *The New York Triumvirate: A Study of the Legal and Political Careers of William Livingston, John Morin Scott, and William Smith, Jr.* (New York, 1949), Chaps. 5, 6, 7.

powers; they were instead full-blown legislatures modeled after the House of Commons with an inherent right to control matters of taxation and expenditure within the framework of English law. He had opposed the British practice of instructing royal governors to secure a permanent revenue because it assumed an essential difference between the colonies and England: the assemblies had no legislative function beyond that granted by the king's commission and instructions to the governor.[22] Smith's judgment remained the same when Parliament levied taxes upon the colonies: as an unlawful action it deprived New Yorkers of their constitutional and natural right of self-taxation. The manner of defending colonial rights was another matter. Smith took a legalistic approach; he favored petitions to king and Parliament rather than the street violence and threats to life and property of extremists like the Sons of Liberty. But he did recognize the realities of English political life and supported economic sanctions against British commercial and manufacturing interests to stimulate a settlement of the Anglo-American constitutional differences.[23]

As the gulf between Britain and America widened by 1774, with each side more unyielding than ever, Smith began to lag behind the growing separatism of colonial Whigs. He thought that Joseph Galloway's plan of union offered to the First Continental Congress would provide a basis for a settlement, as he had once hoped for the Albany plan of 1754, and though Congress rejected Galloway's proposal, his faith that reason would prevail never faltered. But Lexington and Concord and the military ardor expressed everywhere led to Smith's political isolation. Loyal to the empire, to England's political and legal system, Smith refused to follow the more radical Whigs toward independence, always hoping that Britain would send over peace commissioners to settle the constitutional relationship between Parliament and the colonial assemblies. Britain had only to recognize the colonial right of self-

22. Smith, *History* (1829–30 ed.), 1: 307–09.
23. William H. W. Sabine, ed., *Historical Memoirs . . . of William Smith*, 2 vols. (New York, 1956–58), 1: 44.

taxation and thereby colonial legislative autonomy, and the rebellion would collapse.[24] Instead of negotiations to restore peace to the empire, war and independence came to New York in 1776. Smith moved into the country to try to sit out the contest, still clinging to his belief in the empire, still hoping for a settlement.

As a political exile, William Smith, in early 1777, began writing a continuation of the *History of New York.* He lived comfortably among the Livingstons of Dutchess County, kept abreast of events as best he could, and continued his habit of digesting the day's news in his diary.[25] But he was still awed by the facts of military conflict, independence, and statehood, and like other men who rejected independence he must have asked himself many times how the empire had reached this point of self-destruction. Smith never gave a full answer, but the *Continuation* offered several clues to his turn of mind on that vexing question.

Smith blamed both the mother country and New York politicians for those conditions which obscured a proper imperial relationship between the two parties. Britain's insistence upon a permanent fund, which continued a struggle between the governors and assembly dating back to the beginning of the century, was evidence of Britain's lack of understanding of the American condition. Even when the Crown finally relented in 1757, it did so as the price for energetic colonial support of the war and not because the colonials possessed, as they claimed, a constitutional right to control their own public finances. The British view of the colonies as inferior surfaced again over the tenure of judicial appointments in 1760. New York's bench and bar argued that English custom and the constitution sanctioned the colonial practice of commissions "during good behavior"; the Board of Trade replied that the principles of the Revolution of 1688 did not apply in this case because the colonies were different, less developed, and lacked men sufficiently trained in the law to follow England's

24. Upton, *Loyal Whig,* pp. 90–91; Sabine, ed., *Historical Memoirs . . . of William Smith,* 1: 249.
25. Ibid., 2: 94; Upton, *Loyal Whig,* p. 108.

example of impartial justice.[26] Smith calmly analyzed both issues, but the narrative led to an inescapable conclusion. The mother country's perception of the colonies, based on inadequate information and arrogance, relegated them to an inferior status in the empire. Colonial leaders could argue their case as often as they wished, with as much learning in law and history as they could command, but in the end England knew what was best for its colonies. Its debasement of the American colonies, whether by design or out of ignorance, received the support of a few colonials who were paid off with government positions. Smith judged two men in particular, James De Lancey and Cadwallader Colden, as guilty of selling out colonial rights to gratify their own ambitions. Both were equally culpable, but Smith reserved his severest criticisms for De Lancey, whose actions helped thwart an opportunity to settle the empire upon a new foundation.[27]

Smith sketched De Lancey in acid. A "demagogue" and "artful politician," his ambition was "pre-engaged into the service and aims of the ministry" to obtain a permanent revenue by a commission as lieutenant governor in 1753. But De Lancey proved too slippery for the British. While he scolded the assembly for failing to obey the revenue instructions, he "confederated" with his friends to defeat that instruction. By the "mock quarrel" De Lancey cultivated a popularity on both sides of the Atlantic. His friends were paid off with minor appointments, land grants, contracts, and King's College, which became an arm of the Church of

26. Smith, *History* (1829–30 ed.), 2: 159–60. Earlier Smith had concluded: "The colony politicians of early days contented themselves with general declarations owning a subordination and yet claiming English privileges; leaving it to their posterity to ascertain the boundary between the supremacy of England and the submission of her colonies." Ibid., 1: 156. His father and James Alexander were given credit for originating annual legislative appropriations. Ibid., 2: 161, 290–92.

27. Smith accused Colden of promising John Pownall, clerk to the Board of Trade and friend of Lord Halifax, that he would have the assembly name him New York's agent in England. Colden knew he could not deliver his promise, but he wished to ingratiate himself with Halifax and "soon after received the reward of his art in the commission to be Lieutenant Governor." Ibid., p. 303.

England. At the Albany Congress of 1754, though "conscious of an awkward inferiority," De Lancey alone among the deputies fought against a plan of union that would have provided the American colonies with a common constitutional basis within the empire. Smith admitted that the Albany Plan was perhaps beyond hope of approval, either by the colonial governments or the Crown, but De Lancey grounded his opposition in "an impatience for distinction, prompted by ambition." Many deputies thought his earlier politics placed him on the side of colonial interests, but they "discovered that he had his eye to the other side of the water." Britain did not want a colonial union, and De Lancey's opposition to the Albany proposal was a grandstand play for the benefit of home authorities. Like everything else in his public life, De Lancey's part in the Albany Congress revealed clearly his inability to grasp the larger aspects of government policy. "Qualified as he was rather for short altercation than copious debate" and as "he seemed to draw no advantages from meditation," he could only raise exceptions and "cavil" at the particulars in a proposal. That cast of mind, complemented by a driving ambition for power and acclaim, prevented De Lancey from seeing the true merit and advantage of an American constitution that would marshal colonial strength against the French and serve as protection against imperial officers who "do not know the state of America."[28] The empire to which Smith always remained loyal in his view would have been far different if the Albany Plan had been adopted.

William Smith's book, *The History of the Province of New York,* was the first history written on such a large scale by a New Yorker.[29] Smith modestly stated that his work was not really a history but only a political narrative.[30] Modern scholars have

28. Ibid., pp. 161–62, 172–73, 176, 178, 183, 190–92, 198–99, 203, 257, 283.

29. Jarvis M. Morse, "Colonial Historians of New York," *New York History,* 23 (1942): 395–409.

30. Smith, *History* (1757 ed.), pp. xi–xii.

accepted Smith at his word and have used the *History* as a record of the partisanship of New York politics. Though Smith liked to pose as a concerned citizen standing above party politics, he was as partisan as those whom he accused of self-interest and of abusing their public trust. And that partisanship permeated the *History*, adding color and life to what would be an otherwise dull story. But if Smith gave us insights into the peccadilloes and peculations of royal governors, and the ambitions and intrigues of colonial leaders, he also revealed his own values. Intensely anti-French in a colony where neutralism was popular among many people, opposed to established religion at a time when the Church of England was on the offensive, defender of the assembly's autonomy against Britain's much narrower view of the colonial legislative function—Smith relished the vigor and stimulation of opposition politics. His criticism of others, however, was condescending and self-righteous, a mask for his own aspirations to power. He wanted to be chief justice and nearly received the appointment in 1761 from Governor Robert Monckton, whom he assiduously cultivated, offering to pay the expenses of a lobby in England. As New York's "historian" he well knew that James De Lancey's rise to power came through opposition politics and then the chief justiceship. While other politicians were guilty of promoting their self-interest at the public's expense, Smith confidently believed in the correctness of his principles and the soundness of his judgments. He never doubted New York's future within the empire, if only the colony could be freed of government leaders and policies obstructing its development.

volume IV

Early Nationalist Historians

1.

Early Nationalist Historians: An Introduction

Lawrence H. Leder

The successful conclusion of the American Revolution quickly led Americans into a reexamination of their past so that they might capture both it and the future. They had been bred on history, particularly from a Whig viewpoint; they had used it extensively in their debates and arguments with Britain; and they understood its value, not merely to justify their past actions, but to point out the future for the generations that would follow.

The goals of these early nationalist historians included a justification of the Revolution, an explanation of the new politics to which it had given rise, and an exposition of the virtues of the United States and its citizens. Although the critical and fruitful debates over the federal Constitution seemed to them the summit of political wisdom, they had reached that peak only after a lengthy and tortuous trek, and they did not forget the time it took to get there.

The Constitutional Convention delegates, as well as the participants in the state debates over ratification, made full use of examples and analogies, drawing deeply from the histories of ancient times, of other nations, and of their own states. However, the history of their own immediate past had special relevance for Americans because ancient republics had all failed, leaving no discernible evidence as to why they had not succeeded, and modern European nations had founded their governments on force or fraud. The American experiment thus had no real model, past or contemporary, but ploughed new, and to the revolutionary generation, fertile ground. America's history differed from that of any other country, and the new nation's historians extolled its unique story of wisdom and achievement. Thus the history of the American colonies took on a pressing importance for those planning the nation's future.

A classic illustration of the new history emerged from the pen of John Marshall, who sought to unify the disparate past of the thirteen colonies by emphasizing the inevitable evolution of a nation out of its separate parts. To Marshall, the attainment of ordered liberty had been the goal of the colonists from their earliest days, and they attained it under the leadership of George Washington.

Marshall originally prepared his statement of colonial history as an extended introduction to his *Life of Washington*, but he soon separated the introductory material, since it stood on its own as a clear statement of the evolution of the colonies into a nation. The colonists' heritage of political liberty, carefully nurtured over the years, successfully rebuffed threat after threat, finally overcoming the great challenge posed by the British after 1763. Marshall found several elements in the colonial past which worked toward the preservation of political liberty—the colonial assemblies, human virtue which restrained men's passions and permitted them to attain high goals, the impact of experience as a moderating influence on dangerous schemes, and finally the kind of patriotism exemplified by George Washington. In his *History of the American Colonies*, Marshall prepared a didactic analysis of the colonial heritage as a guide into the future for the new nation. However, even Marshall had to accept the parochial beginnings of the American people and had to deal with the individual colonies, although he sought out every evidence of intercolonial activity.

Among those who dealt with the history of their own states was William Henry Drayton, a South Carolinian who converted to the revolutionary cause late in its development. One of that colony's primary grievances, at a time when its social, economic, and political systems were maturing, lay in the increasing limitation placed upon its prominent native sons as they sought higher political offices. More and more of those posts, which South Carolinians judged to be within their own competence, went instead to English placemen. For example, five of the nine councillors in South Carolina were Englishmen, strangers to the colony. The political frustration resulting from such a situation caused Drayton's conversion to the revolutionary cause, which came at the time of the Intolerable Acts of 1774.

Drayton hoped to record the progress of the Revolution in South Carolina by accumulating data from all possible sources. Although he died before he could put his memoirs in order, his son finally published them, but only after Henry Laurens had made important excisions in the record. Nonetheless, Drayton's *Memoirs* emphasized the difficulties which faced those who remained loyal to the Crown. Although the South Carolina backcountry harbored many Loyalists in the early years of the Revolution, the English obstinately failed to utilize that resource and instead gave the rebels a major advantage. The rebels used economic pressure, forced neutrality on the backcountry leaders, and took full advantage of the governor's ineffective mobilization of potential support for the Crown.

Drayton emphasized in his *Memoirs* the political causes of the Revolution, giving little or no attention to economic or social factors. British despotism, he concluded, had converted loyal colonials into rebellious Americans. He viewed the Americans as a conservative people seeking to prevent changes instituted from abroad; thus the Revolution involved no social upheaval, no economic reformation, and no leveling tendencies. Indeed, the fear that the British intended such things strongly motivated the colonials into declaring their independence.

The overthrow of British rule provided Ira Allen with both a theme for his *History of the State of Vermont* and an opportunity for personal gain. He sought to use the revolutionary moment to create the state of Vermont out of an area contested by both New Hampshire and New York. Ira and his better-known brother,

Ethan, had become deeply involved in the speculative land schemes that developed in the Lake Champlain area in the 1770s. To win recognition of their land claims was not an easy matter, but the task became simpler once the Revolution presented them with the opportunity to declare Vermont independent of both New York and New Hampshire, as well as of Britain.

The Allens merged the revolutionary cause with their own, proclaimed the necessity for Vermont's self-determination, thereby echoing the arguments of the revolutionary leadership, and announced the necessity of cultivating a special relationship between Vermont and Quebec. In accomplishing their goals, the Allens took advantage of microcosmic situations at home which duplicated the macrocosmic ones fomenting Anglo-American hostility. Having begun with a determination to make Vermont independent, they utilized every situation to bring about that result.

In the chaos of Revolution, the Allens seized the initiative and created an independent Vermont, complete with constitution, a Council of Safety, and various delegations to the Continental Congress seeking its sanction. At the same time, the Allens and their clique conducted clandestine negotiations to restore Vermont to the British Empire as a separate government—negotiations which collapsed only after the surrender of Cornwallis's army at Yorktown.

Ira Allen promulgated the view that Vermont's negotiations with the British merely neutralized the military threat while pressuring the Congress to accept the new state's independence from New Hampshire and New York as well as Great Britain. Yet Vermont needed the British Empire more than it did the United States. The new state, and particularly that area of it in which the Allens and their friends had their largest land holdings, depended for trade on the St. Lawrence River. The American victory in the Revolution circumscribed the Allens' field of play; the adoption of the federal Constitution virtually demolished the Allens' opportunity. Acceptance of statehood in the federal Union proved no blessing to Ira Allen and his friends, but they could do little to avoid it.

Ira Allen's *History* reflected the confluence of turbulent streams which made up the American Revolution. As it developed in one corner of the United States, the revolutionary movement carried with it ambitions and goals sometimes widely at variance with the mainstream of Independence.

A far different approach to history found expression in Jeremy Belknap's work on a neighboring colony—his *History of New Hampshire*. Belknap began his history before the Revolution broke out, and he started with the colony's founding, exploring all possible facets of its development. However, once the Revolution erupted, it became the focal point of his work. The *History* reflected revolutionary themes in its condemnation of religious intolerance and its criticism of the treatment given the American Indian, but the book also reflected the conservatism of the Revolution in its defense of political liberty and republicanism.

Belknap, like many of his generation, found that British officials had disrupted an otherwise tranquil people by seeking to introduce tyranny and despotism. Americans had sought to preserve their traditional liberties, but the British plotted to subvert them by usurpations of power and authority. All that Americans wanted prior to the Declaration of Independence was to preserve their ideal society; after the Declaration, they wanted to restore it and reinforce its understanding, rationality, tolerance, moderation, and republicanism. These, Belknap declared, were the virtues that New Hampshiremen had striven to develop for two centuries.

The history of North Carolina's past and its role in the Revolution came late, and it emerged from the pen of a Frenchman who had emigrated to the state at the end of the war. Francois-Xavier Martin, who served as public printer in Newbern, received a commission to compile those English statutes still in force in the new state. From this he gleaned a view of the British colonial system as it operated in North Carolina, as well as an interest in preparing a history of the state. His official position made the public colonial records of North Carolina available to him, and he gained access to private papers of prominent North Carolinians.

Martin's history was interrupted when he entered on a new career as a judge in the Mississippi and then the Orleans territories. His fascination with Louisiana's past led him to write a history of that state, which he published before completing his *North Carolina*. Indeed, Hugh Williamson beat him to the draw by publishing a *History of North Carolina* in 1812, but Martin found that Williamson had not treated the Revolution with proper thoroughness. When another author threatened to publish a history, Martin returned to his own work, and his two-volume study finally appeared in 1829.

To Martin, history had to record both the virtues and mistakes of significant figures so as to provide didactic lessons for present and future generations. Those who sought public careers could best learn the dimensions of their responsibilities from objective histories which neither flattered nor pleaded for special interests. And Martin's history did avoid overt bias, although he exhibited a sympathy for the indigenous inhabitants who suffered from constant encroachments by the Europeans, and he expressed his own admiration for the Quakers and the Moravians.

As with most other historians of this era, Martin also emphasized the rise of colonial assemblies as one of the most significant eighteenth-century developments. He viewed the colony's search for control over its internal affairs as a most important pattern in the movement toward the Revolution, although he nowhere suggested that any North Carolinians intended beforehand to break their relationship with England. In many respects, Martin foreshadowed the modern Neo-Whig historians' approach to the Revolution.

Thomas F. Gordon, another historian of the period who foreshadowed Neo-Whig interpretations, devoted himself to a variety of historical studies, particularly of the Middle Atlantic region. His most important work, however, was his *History of New Jersey,* the first comprehensive study of that colony.

Gordon took as his mission the rescuing of New Jersey's past from absorption into the nationalistic and patriotic studies that had swept historical writing between 1789 and 1812. He intended to do justice to those Jerseyites who had participated in the revolutionary movement and to trace the colony's development from its earliest settlements to its part in the adoption of the Constitution, at which time the history of the state merged with that of the nation.

The view of colonial New Jersey's history put forth by Gordon typified the histories then being written. It "was moralistic, deterministic, Messianic, and Europhobistic." He had no doubt that the colonials were the children of light, while the British imperial officials were the children of darkness. Gordon's history had a didactic purpose which he did little to hide—he sought to imbue his own and succeeding generations with nationalistic impulses. New Jersey provided ample opportunities for this task because its past was so glorious.

Gordon viewed man as the product of historical development, rather than its producer. He also believed progress to be inevitable, and looked upon colonial America as an illustration of the truism that barbarism inevitably gives way to civilization. Finally, Gordon accepted the inevitability of the Revolution, particularly as the political struggles of the eighteenth century developed.

Gordon glorified the emergence of growing nationalism and intercolonial unity as the prelude to the Revolution and the federal Constitution. He also reflected the attitudes of his own day (the 1830s) in his general avoidance of the issues of Indian-white relationships and slavery. The former he dealt with in the context of wars; the latter he passed over in a general criticism of the English slave trade and a denial that slavery had taken deep roots in the colony.

Not all early nineteenth-century historians took Neo-Whig positions as they evaluated the colonial past. Thomas Jones of New York, a decided loyalist, espoused the Tory viewpoint and often dipped his pen in acid as he examined the men and events that led to the Revolution. As a refugee living in England, Jones sought to analyze not the American victory but the British failure.

Jones had always felt an animosity to the leading Whigs in colonial New York, an attitude that developed from his and his family's long association with the De Lancey clan. Although he did not actively engage in politics prior to the Revolution, he astutely garnered offices for himself as a consequence of his De Lancey connections.

Radicalism disturbed Jones more than British policy, and the turbulence of the Sons of Liberty alienated him from the sympathy he otherwise felt for proposed limitations on British authority in the colonies. Order represented to him the highest goal of society, and mobs, mass meetings, illegal committees, and intimidation indicated the collapse of order, not a proper challenge to constitutional presumptions by the British. The actions of the First Continental Congress marked the limit of tolerance for Thomas Jones. He could accept a call for a redress of grievances; he could not accept a conclave which assumed to itself powers as illegal as those against which it contended.

When he went into exile in England in 1780, he kept alive the hope that a rebel defeat and a restoration of orderly government would still occur. That hope faded hard and left in its place a sense of bitterness which dominated his work. In retrospect, the golden years of New York's history were those of the De Lancey hegemony. The Livingstons, the Presbyterians, and the Whigs represented the epitome of evil to Thomas Jones.

Nonetheless, Jones also found fault with the British, although he accepted the monarchy, the English constitution, and the Church of England without question. The English approach to politics had led men to pursue personal ambitions, not the national interest. Parliamentary politics interfered with military decision making to the point of bringing Britain to its knees. Sir William Howe and Sir Henry Clinton both received condemnation from Jones for their failure to bring an effective force to bear against the rebels. Jones's history vigorously condemned those who supported the Revolution, as well as those who failed to suppress it, for he viewed the conflict as a civil war in which the wrong side won.

Not all of those who had lived in New York and then returned to Britain took as harsh an attitude toward the rebels and the new nation. Anne McVickar Grant certainly had a more kindly view. As a young girl she had lived in the Albany area, had consorted with the Schuyler family and leaders of that frontier community, and retained a romantic impression of her youth. Mrs. Grant, a widow, tapped an increasing market in early nineteenth-century Europe for information about the new United States when she wrote her *Memoirs*. Indeed, she even found an extensive market in America for her volume.

Memoirs of an American Lady detailed the story of the Albany frontier, the patroon aristocracy, military activity in the wilderness, and the problems of Indian life and trade. In dealing with the Iroquois Indians, Mrs. Grant emphasized the noble savage who remained faithful to his English allies and whose life had "peculiar" attractions for the European. In discussing the black population of Albany, Mrs. Grant emphasized the gentle treatment given their slaves by Albanians.

However, the bulk of the *Memoirs* dealt with the highest levels of New York society, which perfectly reflected the environment in which Mrs. Grant had lived as a youngster. She wrote of their customs, their business activities, the training of their children, and of their homes and furnishings. Indeed, she presented an incisive social history of colonial New York's aristocracy in its heyday.

From the romanticism of Anne McVickar Grant to the truculence of Thomas Jones to the patriotism of John Marshall—all of these reflected the ebullient state of American historiography in the turbulent quarter-century since the Revolution. A new nation had been founded; its historians now aided its people in finding themselves by emphasizing the special values and meanings of the past that they hoped future generations would continue to hold dear.

2.

John Marshall and the Development of
a National History

DANIEL R. GILBERT

The public career of Chief Justice John Marshall has so interested historians that they have largely ignored other parts of his life. His writings, in particular, deserve attention as a significant example of nationalistic literature developing in the new republic. Marshall wrote in the tradition of the gentleman-lawyer-historian at a time when few professional historians existed and the canons of the craft remained undefined.

Marshall brought forth his major work, an uneven five-volume *Life of George Washington*, between 1802 and 1807, the first part of which included a history of the American colonies up to 1775.[1] The *Life* was received with less than critical acclaim, and Marshall was dissatisfied with its literary quality. After a decade or more of desultory work, a new edition appeared piecemeal beginning in 1824. The introductory section had been detached and published separately under the title of the *History of the Colonies Planted by the English on the Continent of North America from their Settlement, to the Commencement of that War which terminated in their Independence* (blessedly shortened on the introductory page to the *History of the American Colonies*.)[2]

1. John Marshall, *The Life of George Washington, Commander in Chief of the American Forces, during the War which Established the Independence of his Country, and First President of the United States*, 5 vols. (Philadelphia, 1804–1807). (Hereafter referred to as the *Life of Washington*.)

2. John Marshall, *A History of the Colonies Planted by the English on the Continent of North America, from their Settlement, to the Commencement*

Marshall's *History* typified the new scholarship of the time. Whereas earlier studies of America had emphasized the settlement and growth of separate colonies, the new tradition emphasized the evolution of one nation out of many separate parts and identified the patriots and heroes who started America toward its destiny.[3]

In his writings Marshall betrayed his deficiencies as a historian. His prose is often dull and lifeless, and he cavalierly misused published sources. In spite of these weaknesses, however, he infused his work with mature political thought. From the pages of the *History of the American Colonies* emerges a defense of an ordered system of government run by virtuous men. To this extent, his ideology was clearly English in origin and conservative in character. But Marshall's preoccupation with national union and the protection of liberty reflected his concern with the attempts to return the union to a league of sovereign states and with what he saw as a threat to liberty in the democratic upheavals in his native Virginia and in the nation at large.[4] Therefore Marshall's publication of a new edition of the *Life of Washington* and of a separate history of the colonial era did more than attempt to heal his wounded pride. It tried to remind America of its heritage and its heroes.

Marshall was, from all accounts, an easygoing man who always reflected the simplicity of his frontier background. He had little formal education, and his practical, lawyer's mind did not take to

---

of that War, which terminated in their Independence (Philadelphia, 1824). (Hereafter referred to as the *History of the American Colonies*.)

3. For a more complete analysis of the new national history, see David D. Van Tassel, *Recording America's Past* (Chicago, 1960), chaps. 4–8.

4. Marshall to J. Story, July 13, 1831. (Unless otherwise noted, the dated correspondence refers to copies of letters which the author used at The Institute of Early American History and Culture, Williamsburg, Virginia.) Albert J. Beveridge, *The Life of John Marshall*, 4 vols. (Boston, 1916–1919), 4: 10. For similar comments, see John S. Adams, ed., *An Autobiographical Sketch by John Marshall* (Ann Arbor, Mich., 1937), p. 43; Jack L. Cross, "John Marshall on the French Revolution and on American Politics," *William and Mary Quarterly*, 3d series, 12 (1955): 645–646.

the study of political theory.[5] Also, the distractions of a busy public life and an apparent lack of personal discipline kept him from developing his talents as a writer or an historian. Although he has been called a spokesman for the Federalist party, he was independent in his historical writing. His belief in ordered government contains evidence of orthodox Federalist ideology, but the individualism of his economic thought suggests the expansive egalitarian outlook of the nineteenth century.[6]

Although the Jeffersonians believed that Marshall began the Washington biography in order to influence the outcome of the 1804 election, evidence suggests otherwise. His large family, convivial social habits, and heavy investments in land kept him in constant debt, and since he had given up most of his legal practice upon moving to the national scene, he could only meet these obligations by finding additional income beyond his salary as Chief Justice. He therefore concluded, in one of his more serious errors in judgment, that there "would be tens of thousands of prosperous Federalists who could be depended upon to purchase at a generous price a definitive biography of George Washington."[7]

Marshall's eagerness to solve his financial problems in this way matched the desire of Federalists for a biography of Washington which would counter Democratic-Republican efforts to make the late president one of their own. Bushrod Washington, General Washington's nephew, when solicited to write such a biography,

5. A modest man, Marshall left little record of his private life. See Adams, *An Autobiographical Sketch*, or Joseph Story, *A Discourse upon the Life, Character, and Services of the Honorable John Marshall* (Boston, 1835). An older but still useful biography, containing many letters, is Henry Flanders, *The Life of John Marshall* (Philadelphia, 1904). For more recent commentary see William W. Crosskey, "Mr. Chief Justice Marshall," in *Mr. Justice*, ed. Allison Dunham and Phillip Kurland (Chicago, 1956), pp. 17–46; Max Lerner, "John Marshall and the Campaign of History," in *The Marshall Reader*, ed. E. C. Surrency (New York, 1955), pp. 91–130. Beveridge, *Marshall*, 3: 224–225.

6. Lerner, "John Marshall and the Campaign of History," pp. 91–99; David Fischer, *The Revolution of American Conservatism* (New York, 1965), pp. 380–382.

7. Beveridge, *Marshall*, 3: 224, 225, 229.

enlisted Marshall for the project. In a flight of fancy, the Chief Justice thought he could find at least 30,000 subscribers for the work (at an estimated $5.00 for a five-volume set) which would take no more than a few years to complete.[8]

A contract was finally negotiated by the fall of 1802, but the project was in trouble from the start. Marshall had underestimated both his court responsibilities and the sheer mass of Washington papers. Then he squabbled endlessly with the publisher, Caleb Wayne of Philadelphia, who became impatient with Marshall's slow writing pace. They had assumed that local postmasters would serve as agents for the volumes, but the slowness of publication and the partisanship of some of the agents hurt the sale. That esteemed book agent, Parson Weems, busily promoted the books, but he too worried over the political charges. He noted that some people were "very fearful that (the biography) will be prostituted to party purposes," and he urged the publishers to "drop now and then a cautionary hint to John Marshall, Esq. Your all is at stake with respect to this work. If it be done in a generally acceptable manner you will make your fortune. Otherwise the work will fall an Abortion from the press."[9]

After many delays, the first volume appeared in 1804, the next two in 1805, and the remaining volumes in 1807. The format of the original biography made possible the later publication of the separate *History*. To introduce the life of Washington, Marshall wrote a history of the colonial era. As he explained in his preface:

The history of general Washington, during his military command and civil administration, is so much that of his country, that the work appeared to the author to be sensibly incomplete and unsatisfactory, while unaccompanied by such a narrative of the principle events preceding our revolutionary war, as would make the reader acquainted

8. Van Tassel, *Recording America's Past*, p. 81; Beveridge, *Marshall*, 3: 225–227.

9. Ibid., pp. 227, 230–236; Flanders, *Marshall*, p. 203; Van Tassel, *Recording America's Past*, p. 82. Beveridge notes: "In the cities most of the lawyers took Marshall's book," Beveridge, *Marshall*, 3: 236. Approximately 8,000 subscribers purchased the set.

with the genius, character, and resources of the people about to engage in that memorable contest. This appeared the more necessary as that period of our history is but little known to ourselves. Several writers have detailed very minutely the affairs of a particular colony, but the *desideratum* is a composition which shall present in one connected view, the transactions of all those colonies which now form the United States.[10]

This history, drawn from published works on individual colonies, took up the first one and one-half volumes (725 pages) and covered events from the beginning of English colonization through the appointment of Washington as Commander in Chief of the Armies in 1775. As an introduction to Washington, it was a disaster, for the first volume contained only two references to him, and the early sections of the second had only a few brief pages on his youth. Understandably, the results discouraged the subscribers, to say nothing of the publisher. However, Marshall, in keeping with the new national history, regarded this emphasis on the continuity of the American development as necessary.

The reception of the *Life of Washington* was less than enthusiastic and Marshall himself was unhappy with his own performance. About that time he wrote to his publisher: "I am just finishing a review of the first volume, and am mortified beyond measure to find that it has been so carelessly written. Its inelegancies are more numerous than I had supposed could have appeared in it." He blamed the haste to publish the entire series, as well as the press of public business, for his literary troubles and admitted that he might better "have composed the introductory volume at leisure, after the principal work was finished."[11]

The Jeffersonians had a different reaction. They were angry with what they regarded as the partisan tone of the last volume of the biography in which Marshall, writing mainly out of his own experiences, viewed the Republicans as a disorganizing influence bent on disrupting the government under the federal Constitu-

10. Marshall, *Life of Washington*, 1: xi–xii.
11. Flanders, *Marshall*, pp. 210, 214.

tion. In response, Jefferson, who preferred a more "republican-ized" American history, sought out Joel Barlow to write a history of the Washington years from the Republican perspective.[12] Jefferson's reaction was ironic, however, because the first volume of the *Life of Washington* essentially paralleled the Republican view of the American Revolution as a struggle to preserve tradi-tional liberties and emphasized the danger to the rights of man of arbitrary power in any person or agency of government.

Work on a revised edition of the biography proceeded slowly over the next decade, and Marshall apparently completed the rewriting by 1816. But not until 1824 did a revised first volume appear as the *History of the American Colonies*, apparently after protracted negotiations with potential publishers. The revised *Life of Washington*, condensed into two volumes, was published in 1832. Marshall had apparently heard the critics of his earlier, verbose style, for he had shortened Volume 1 from 725 pages to 457, and he had cut the original four volumes dealing with the Revolution and subsequent events to two.[13]

Marshall explained his plan for the new edition: "to separate the introduction from the other volumes and to publish a small edition of it at my own risk if I may be permitted to do so. . . . As it is considered rather as an incumbrance on the residue of the work I presume there will be no objection to this." A month later he wrote again, "I wish to publish a few copies and to do it first, because (excuse this vanity and keep it to yourself) I think it so

12. Thomas Jefferson, "Notes on the Fifth Volume of Marshall's Life of Washington," in *Writings of Jefferson*, ed. Paul L. Ford, 10 vols. (New York, 1892–1899), 10: 262; Van Tassel, *Recording America's Past*, pp. 82–83. Barlow apparently never undertook the assignment.

13. Beveridge, *Marshall*, 3: 272. Details of negotiations with publishers can be pieced together from the following letters: Marshall to B. Washington, December 27, 1821; May 3, 1823; May 28, 1823; June 25, 1823; July 12, 1823; August 12, 1823; October 11, 1823; October 6, 1824; April 9, 1825; April 13, 1825; Marshall to R. Small, December 3, 1829; Marshall to Caleb Wayne, September 29, 1823. For the various editions, see William A. Foran, "John Marshall as a Historian," *American Historical Review* 41 (1937–1938): 52–53. Marshall, or his publisher, compressed Washington's life into two vol-umes by using small print; thus the revision was not as complete as might be assumed; Beveridge, *Marshall*, 3: 272–273.

much improved that its publication may probably be useful to what is to follow." He then added, ". . . I am willing to incur the risk of the publication, my object being to do justice to my own reputation in this work." Judging from this and related correspondence, Marshall's main motive for the reissue of the *Life* was to salve his wounded pride. Certainly he did not expect to realize money from the project this time, although the businessman in him appears in his suggestion that publication of the one-volume *History* might somehow stimulate sales of the revised *Life*, when and if it ever appeared.[14]

The History of the American Colonies, the separate introductory volume published in 1824, covered the years from Cabot's voyage to America in 1496 through the Battle of Breed's Hill in 1775. In describing the settlers' evolution into one nation, Marshall discussed the exploration, settlement, and eventual growth of all thirteen colonies.

Chapter 1 focused on events prior to Jamestown, Chapter 2 on Virginia's settlement, and Chapters 3 and 4 on New England's settlement and early history. Passing briefly over the events of the Puritan Revolution in England, Marshall took up in Chapters 5 and 6 the renewal of colonial ventures after the Restoration of 1660, the Dominion of New England, and the events of the Glorious Revolution in America. Chapters 7 through 10 dealt mainly with colonial wars and related Indian problems, and only occasionally, as in Chapter 8, took up such domestic developments as relations between assemblies and governors. Chapters 11 and 12 covered the French and Indian War, and the two remaining chapters dealt with the growing quarrel between Great Britain and its colonies from 1763 through the middle of 1775.[15]

14. Marshall to B. Washington, July 12, 1823, August 12, 1823; Marshall to R. Small, December 3, 1829.
15. Marshall also attached an appendix, as he had in the 1804 edition. It included an account of the New England witchcraft "delusion," a copy of the Albany Plan of Union, resolutions written during the revolutionary crisis, and a list of members of the First Continental Congress. The volume had a comprehensive table of contents, but no index, maps, charts, or statistical tables.

To Marshall, history was more than past politics, but not much more. He gave military events some attention in the *History*, but he failed to give a detailed study of the people of colonial America and their institutions. In this sense, Marshal fell short of his stated goal to explain the "ideas of America, of the character of our revolution, of those who engaged in it, and of the struggles by which it was accomplished."[16] However, he did clarify his conception of the colonial heritage and its relevance to the life of the early republic.

Central to Marshall's political credo, as stated in the *History*, was what he called at various times, "political liberty" or "civil and religious liberty," which men never willingly surrendered.[17] (Unfortunately he drew no precise distinction between the people's liberties, the "choicest rights of humanity," and the natural rights of Englishmen.) These liberties, based upon the English Constitution and tradition, came to America with the first settlers; the migration did not cause the colonials to lose their liberties. The early history of the colonies was replete with threats "to the choicest rights of humanity" posed by such phenomena as Puritan intolerance. Marshall also concluded that Massachusetts' struggles in the late seventeenth century over taxation manifested those "general principles respecting the liberty of the subject, that are asserted in *Magna Charta*." Colonial Americans continued to appeal to these ancient rights through the Revolution, and Marshall underscored this by quoting at length from the various memorials of the period. To him, the guaranteed rights and liberties would have been protected in the traditional manner had not Great Britain itself begun violating them after 1763.[18]

Although Marshall at no point made it explicit, he believed that sovereignty in government lay with the people, and he repeatedly emphasized the importance of colonial legislative assemblies. For example, he concluded that the people of early Virginia suffered

16. Marshall, *History of the American Colonies*, p. vi.
17. For examples, see ibid., pp. 27–28, 54, 90, 290.
18. Ibid., pp. 90, 207, 225, 352, 359, 370, and chaps. 8 and 9.

because they "had no voice, either personally, or by their repre-
sentatives, in the government of themselves," and he also noted
that the establishment of a more representative arrangement in
early Massachusetts represented an "important improvement in
their system." Marshall felt that regular assemblies or "other
expedients," such as those developed during the revolutionary
crisis, were the best guarantee of good laws, which could only
result "from men perfectly understanding their own situation, and
legislating for themselves."[19]

But Marshall never clarified what he meant by "the people" in
this context; he made few references to voting or elections,
although he usually emphasized agencies of popular control such
as legislatures. He probably had misgivings about the mass of
people and their capacity for abusing their prerogatives. He noted,
for example, that "popular governments" were not "always the
most inclined to tolerate opinions differing from those of the
majority," and sometimes men were known to "close their eyes on
encroachments committed by that party to which they are attached, in the delusive hope that power, in such hands, will always
be wielded against their adversaries, never against themselves." He
also made some uncharitable comments about "a number of
ignorant people" in North Carolina in 1775, who supposed "themselves to be aggrieved" by a piece of legislation and therefore "rose
in arms for the purpose of shutting up the courts of justice,
destroying all officers of government, and all lawyers, and of
prostrating government itself."[20]

On the other hand, Marshall had little to say in the *History* in
defense of elite rule. While he made occasional references to men
"highly respectable in character and station," and added that
traditional British concepts of rank "had given great disgust in
America," his thinking reflected a continuing tension between
conservative, aristocratic Federalism and the more egalitarian currents of his time.[21]

19. Ibid., pp. 54, 91, 379, 63.
20. Ibid., pp. 119, 118, 395–396.
21. Ibid., pp. 362, 301.

If the sovereign people might wield power improperly, and if no particular class could provide balance and leadership, what hope was there for political stability? Marshall saw the answer in several contrasting elements. First, colonial assemblies could check the arbitrary power of the governor or the Crown. He noted with satisfaction, for example, that the Massachusetts legislature, which had lost its power to appoint the governor in the late seventeenth century, could still control that official by means of "power over salaries (which) was a source of influence . . . pertinaciously maintained."[22]

The second check to potential abuse of power was human virtue. As an eighteenth-century "enlightened" man, Marshall accepted the idea of a universe ruled by general laws, including those governing human conduct. While he feared "egoism," or unrestrained pursuit of self-interest, his copybook maxims on human conduct in the *History* make it clear that he believed men could restrain their passions and work for higher, more worthy objectives in their private and public lives.[23]

Third, he placed great faith in reasonable, evolutionary change based on experience and common sense. For example, in commenting on the inadequacies of Locke's famed constitution for Carolina, he called attention to "the great but neglected truth, that experience is that only safe school in which the science of government is to be acquired." Governments, he added, had to be adaptable to "the condition of the people."[24]

Finally, he placed his hopes in the kind of selfless patriotism demonstrated by Washington. Paradoxically, Marshall cited as the best example of this the Englishman, William Pitt, who was "Too great in his spirit, too lofty in his views, to become the instrument of faction; when placed at the head of the nation, he regarded only the interest of the nation." Only once, when discussing the

22. Ibid., p. 218.
23. Lerner, "John Marshall," p. 93. For examples of such maxims, see Marshall, *History*, pp. 34, 43, 82, 160, 213, 263.
24. Ibid., pp. 155, 159.

seventeenth-century New England Confederation, did Marshall use the term "general will." But he concluded that Americans had accepted such a concept at the time of the Revolution, when they reflected "that spirit of enthusiastic patriotism, which, for a time, elevates the mind above all considerations of individual acquisition."[25]

Marshall's concern for political stability is marked by his constant distaste for violence. He referred to Bacon's Rebellion as an event which "produced much misery, and no good, to Virginia." Leisler's Revolt, he noted, produced a factionalism which produced "much uneasiness and mischief to the province." Marshall referred to Leisler himself as a "man of low birth," an "infatuated man" who engaged in "ill-judged obstinacy" when he refused to turn over the reins of government in 1691. Likewise, the revolutionary tumult of the Stamp Act crisis brought forth a violence in which many "houses were destroyed, much property injured, and several persons, highly respectable in character and station, were grossly abused." Marshall clearly preferred the calm, deliberate actions of legislatures which took a "solemn and deliberate stand" on issues and conducted their opposition to arbitrary acts "with temperate firmness, and legitimate means."[26]

Speaking from the vantage point of the early nineteenth century, Marshall saw the great central event of his youth, the American Revolution, as essentially a constitutional struggle. He had no doubt that the English constitution extended to America, and that Anglo-Americans prided themselves on their membership in the empire. Yet he saw the seeds of the clash between the English Constitution and a developing American Constitution in the earliest settlements. He noted, for example, that by 1640 the "habit of self-government" had become confirmed in America, and that during the English Civil War the mother country's belief in the subordinate status of the colonies conflicted with the fact that

25. Ibid., pp. 314, 123, 405.
26. Ibid., pp. 162, 181, 188, 189, 362, 228, 376.

New England "had been permitted to govern itself as an independent nation."[27]

This quarrel over the constitutional status of the colonies continued over the next century and climaxed in the period after 1763. Marshall concluded that the specific bone of contention was the issue of taxation. Throughout the *History* he pointed to events, seemingly minor at the time, which anticipated the debates of the revolutionary era. For example, in discussing early eighteenth-century New York politics, he paused to summarize an assembly resolution which stated that "imposing and levying of any monies upon her majesty's subjects in this colony, under any pretence or colour whatsoever, without their consent in general assembly, is a grievance and violation of the people's property." He then added pointedly that this was a "strong assertion of a principle, which afterwards dismembered the British empire."[28]

By the 1760s this "great constitutional question of taxation" split the empire, but Marshall quickly added that there were other relevant issues. For example, he called attention to the Virginia Burgesses' statement in 1769 that, in addition to taxation, the House took exception to threats to their right to petition for redress of grievances, as well as to their right to trial by jury. In any case, he said: "The contest with America was plainly a contest of principle, and had been conducted entirely on principle by both parties."[29]

Marshall thought the bonds that united the colonies to the empire were "never stronger" than in 1763, when Americans, enthusiastic in "their admiration of British valour (in the late war) . . . were proud of the land of their ancestors, and gloried in their descent from Englishmen." But, he continued, the "system of measures" developed by Great Britain to reorganize the empire

27. Ibid., pp. 352, 113, 123.
28. For references to the constitutional issue, see such examples as ibid., pp. 123–124, 207, 217–218, 230, 352ff. For references to the taxation issue see ibid., pp. 62–63, 206–207, 225, 232, 354–359, 363, 369–371, 380, 388, 399.
29. Ibid., pp. 380, 383–384, 388.

after 1763 "tore asunder all the bonds of relationship and affection that had subsisted for ages, and planted almost inextinguishable hatred in bosoms where the warmest friendship had long been cultivated."[30]

In this uneven section of the *History*, in which he discussed only the better known measures, Marshall traced the progression of actions designed to strengthen the imperial system and raise revenue in the colonies. He also discussed various forms of colonial protest, including the Association schemes developed to resist the Townshend program. However, the written memorials and resolutions of the various revolutionary bodies held much of Marshall's attention. In these documents he saw the best evidence that the colonial Americans were fighting for principles rather than selfish ends.[31] But he frankly noted how petty jealousies and suspicions broke down the Association schemes in 1769, and he criticized the violence which sometimes accompanied colonial protests.[32]

The Tea Act was the crucial piece of legislation in Marshall's analysis of the Revolution. "The crisis was arrived," he said, "and the conduct of the colonies was now to determine whether they would submit to be taxed by parliament, or meet the consequences of a practical assertion of the opinions they had maintained." Marshall had little to say about property destruction in the Boston Tea Party; instead, he reserved his condemnation for the "high-handed system" of the Coercive Acts of 1774. He also noted with delight how the colonies thwarted Great Britain's hopes for dividing the colonies. "Never was expectation more completely disappointed. All perceived that Boston was to be punished for having resisted, only with more violence, the principles which they had all resisted."[33]

30. Ibid., pp. 350, 356.
31. Ibid., pp. 371, 379, 384–386, 388.
32. For comments on the inadequacies of the Association schemes, see ibid., pp. 389–391. Marshall's reaction to the violence of the revolutionary period can be found on pp. 362 and 376–377. For his rather moderate view of the Boston Massacre, see pp. 391–394.
33. Ibid., pp. 399–401, 404.

The closing section of the *History,* which dealt mainly with the First Continental Congress and the written protests of the period, lacked coherence. Marshall seems to have rushed this section into print, and even in the 1824 revision he made little effort to analyze the drama or the personalities of the period. He made it clear, however, that the events of 1774 marked a turning point, leading to the emergence of a national consciousness. While he noted the confusion over possible reconciliation with Great Britain, he emphasized that the people no longer thought of themselves as citizens of individual communities, but as Americans.[34]

John Marshall attempted in his *History of the American Colonies* to define a colonial heritage which would give cohesiveness and inspiration to the young nation. There was no question in his mind that the nation was one, an organic whole. Yet the colonial experience clearly dealt with individual settlements, each with its own history, traditions and cultures. Therefore, he had to tell the colonial story in such a way as to recognize the uniqueness of each settlement and to explain the colonies evolution into a nation. Marshall achieved this by emphasizing the frequent cooperative ventures of the colonial era, the developing sense of a common concern for liberty, and the recognition during the revolutionary crisis of their unity in support of one cause.

Since he relied so heavily on the traditional histories of individual colonies, Marshall's description of the early settlements had a parochial tone.[35] But he quickly applauded occasions when

34. Ibid., pp. 408, 421.
35. For a detailed analysis of Marshall's use of sources see Foran, "John Marshall as a Historian," pp. 51ff.

In the 1804 edition of the *Life of Washington,* Marshall listed the following authors as his sources: Stith, Robertson, Chalmers, Beverly, L'Escarbot, Hutchinson, Hume, Trumbull, Gordon, Ramsay, Smith, Belknap, Charlevoix, Minot, Belsham, Russel; a *History of South Carolina and Georgia;* letters of General Abercrombie, Bradstreet, and General Townshend, and the *New York Gazette.* Usually he listed the authors used for a particular section at the end of the chapter, but upon occasion he would note them at the bottom of a page. In some instances he listed no authors at all at any point in a chapter. Only on rare occasions did he cite specific pages as his source.

In the 1824 *History of the American Colonies* he cited authors at the bottom of the page, but there were no titles or page references given. For the

colonies cooperated in some common cause. For example, he called the New England Confederation the result of "good sense, and of a judicious consideration of the real interests of the colonies." Similarly, he praised joint military ventures and noted that colonial efforts in the French and Indian War suffered from "the want of one general superintending authority." Marshall deplored the occasional failure of colonies to cooperate in times of crisis. He thought Massachusetts, for example, was guilty of attempting to dominate the New England Confederation, and he noted the reluctance of the "cautious people" of Connecticut to accept the union proposals of the Albany Congress of 1754.[36]

Marshall concluded that by the mid-eighteenth century the separate colonies had come to a point where their historical cooperation, physical growth, and common attachment to the basic tradition of liberty presaged the emergence of one union and one people. In a long section he explained in detail the prior divisions of the colonies and, in particular, the regional separation of northern and southern colonies. "Neither participated in the wars or pursuits of the other," he noted, "nor were they, in any respect, actuated by common views, or united by common interest." But he added that new developments changed all this. "The conquest of the country between Connecticut and Maryland, laid a foundation, which the settlement of the middle colonies completed, for connecting these disjoined members, and forming one consolidated whole, capable of moving, and acting in concert. This gradual change, unobserved in its commencement, had now become too perceptible to be longer overlooked; and, henceforward

most part those listed were the same as cited in the early volumes of the *Life of Washington* although there are a few omissions (L'Escarbot, for example), and the spelling is different in a few cases. Thomas Hutchinson, for example, became "Hutchison" in the 1824 edition.

In only a few, rare instances did Marshall relate a title to an author's name. Consequently one can only guess at what book, or edition, he used. For a judicious attempt at such a correlation see Foran, "John Marshall as a Historian," or the excellent Van Tassel, *Recording America's Past*, particularly parts 1 and 2.

36. Ibid., pp. 115, 123, 196, 197, 202, 203, 297–298, 285.

the efforts of the colonies, were in a great measure combined, and directed to a common object."[37] The revolutionary crisis completed this process of unification.

Although Marshall was most interested in political developments and thought that social history furnished "none of these remarkable events which interest posterity," a few asides clarify the Chief Justice's conception of the people of the new nation and the spirit which activated them. He had little to say about the physical environment, other than a few references to America's fertile soil and climate, and to the west as a "delightful region which forms the magnificent vale of the Mississippi" and which could "produce and maintain an immense population."[38] But the land was apparently only a stage to him for the enactment of a greater human drama. And America's success was due, not to the natural advantages of the land, but to the energies, discipline and character of the people, and the all-pervasive freedom of enterprise.

Few individuals stand out in the pages of Marshall's *History*. Such contrasting figures as Jacob Leisler and William Pitt received a few lines, but most persons seem curiously anonymous. Yet Marshall felt great affection for the early Americans. He referred to them as "sober, industrious, and economical" people who "laboured indefatigably in opening and improving their country." Upon several occasions, Marshall singled out women for special attention. For example, Pocahontas, whom he portrayed in terms of the traditional myth, rescued John Smith "by that enthusiastic and impassioned humanity which, in every climate, and in every state of society, finds its home in the female bosom." He also commented on the civilizing influence of the arrival of "ninety girls, of humble fortune and spotless character" who came to Virginia in 1620. And he acknowledged the contribution to the Revolution of "the fair sex," who, by "laying aside the late fash-

37. Ibid., pp. 268–269.
38. Ibid., pp. 252, 278–279.

ionable ornaments of England, exulted, with patriotic pride, in appearing dressed in the produce of their own looms."[39]

While Marshall portrayed both the black and the Indian in traditional terms, he did stress their importance to the history of America. With apparent misgivings, for example, he noted that the Virginia tobacco trade provided "the immediate cause of introducing a species of population which has had vast influence on the past, and may affect the future destinies of America, to an extent which human wisdom can neither foresee nor control." He did not, however, follow up this hint of apocalypse with any detailed analysis of the black man's role in early America beyond occasional references to the repression of slave insurrections.[40]

Marshall also perceived the Indian from the viewpoint of the predominant white culture. While he admitted some were "brave and intelligent," he more frequently referred to that "barbarous fury which distinguishes Indian warfare." He noted, for example, that "wherever they [the Indians in King William's war] were victorious, [they] perpetrated their usual cruelties."[41]

Marshall specified the motivating spirit of colonial Americans in his infrequent comments on colonial economic life. From the first pages of the *History*, Marshall made evident his preference for individual enterprise, private property, and the pursuit of profit and his suspicion of communal efforts. Also, he opposed currency experimentation which, he said, was "unfavourable to morals and to industry."[42]

Americans, according to Marshall, were "a distant people" who could enjoy the opportunity afforded by America to employ themselves "in cultivating the earth, and in spreading themselves over the vast regions which were open to them." Such freedom of enterprise, however, was threatened by all communal efforts. He said of the leaders of Plymouth colony, for example: "Misguided

39. Ibid., pp. 188–189, 312–315, 106, 35, 55, 386.
40. Ibid., pp. 56, 249, 251–252.
41. Ibid., pp. 166, 191, 343.
42. Ibid., p. 233.

by their religious theories, they fell into the same error which had been committed in Virginia, and in imitation of the primitive Christians, threw all their property into a common stock, laboured jointly for the common benefit, and were fed from the common stores." Such a "pernicious policy of a community of goods and of labour," Marshall added, meant trouble for the colonizing effort. The problem was that "Industry, deprived of its due reward, exclusive property in the produce of its toil, felt no sufficient stimulus to exertion, and the public supplies were generally inadequate to the public necessities."[43]

Later, Marshall turned his scorn on the evils of currency manipulation. The use of paper currency repeatedly produced, as he saw it, depreciation and inflation which threatened both creditors and morals and led on several occasions to the "decay of trade." The evil, which Marshall termed "almost incurable," inevitably substituted "cunning and speculation, for honest and regular industry."[44]

The History of the Colonies Planted by the English on the Continent of North America has generally been criticized on three grounds. First, Marshall's treatment of the main events of the colonial era was uneven, with the result that he gave insufficient attention to some significant figures and events. Second, historians of a later day, armed with the canons of "scientific history," severely criticized Marshall's use of sources. Finally, some have criticized the quality of his writing.[45]

The History has a certain episodic quality to it, and it is sometimes hard to understand the rationale for Marshall's selections of events. Too often, it appears, he was a victim of his sources, for he relied upon detailed histories of individual colonies. Thus Marshall never created a balanced view of the colonial era, in which

43. Ibid., pp. 49, 81, 82, 252.
44. Ibid., pp. 215, 273, 274.
45. Beveridge, *Marshall*, 3: 242–244; Foran, "John Marshall as a Historian," pp. 51ff; Flanders, *Marshall*, p. 219; Allan B. Magruder, *John Marshall* (Boston, 1885), p. 236; Justin Winsor, *Narrative and Critical History of America*, 8 vols. (Boston, 1884–1889), 7: 300.

America would be seen in all of its parts, yet as more than a sum of those parts.

Marshall's limited sources also probably accounted for certain omissions from his narrative. He apparently lacked detailed studies of such events as Bacon's Rebellion, or of such important people as Roger Williams or Patrick Henry, and he therefore gave these less than satisfactory treatment. However, with his clear preference for orderly processes of government, Marshall would have had a hard time agreeing with a Roger Williams, and his abhorrence of violence would have prevented him from giving undue emphasis to such an aberration as Bacon's Rebellion.

There is less defense for Marshall's uneven analysis of events leading to the Revolution. He had lived through this period and certainly knew more of the events than he could obtain from printed sources alone. His lack of detail on the Stamp Act crisis can only be explained by his limited conception of the internal socioeconomic conflict reflected in this event. He emphasized the issue of parliamentary authority and he saw the Stamp Tax as well as other measures of that period in that context.

Marshall justified his ending of the narrative at the point when Washington took command of the American forces by explaining that he wanted to publish a volume which contained "a history of all which precedes the appointment of Gen. Washington to the command of the army."[46] Marshall did not see any particular event as a clear end to the colonial era; instead, he saw the continuity of the American experience through the Revolution and the Constitution. Thus any date chosen for the end of the *History* would have been, in a sense, arbitrary, and he picked that which best fit his larger purpose, which was the study of Washington's career after 1775.

Marshall prepared the early sections of the *Life of Washington* from secondary materials. He had no reason to do intensive research in original sources for an introduction to his major work. Indeed, he noted in the preface that he would never have written

46. Marshall to B. Washington, May 3, 1823.

a historical introduction at all if a general history of the English colonies had been available. He anticipated the more serious charge that he borrowed without acknowledgment from sources, and that his narrative often weakly paraphrased published writings. He stated in his Preface to the 1804 edition of the *Life of Washington* that the sources' "very language has sometimes been employed without distinguishing the passages especially when intermingled with others, by marks of quotation, and the author persuades himself that this public declaration will rescue him from the imputation of receiving aids he is unwilling to acknowledge, or by wishing, by a concealed plagiarism, to usher, to the world, as his own, the labours of others."[47]

This apology apparently satisfied such a critical jury as Justin Winsor and John Spencer Bassett in the nineteenth century and Herbert L. Osgood and Charles Beard in the twentieth century, all of whom praised the *Life of Washington* and failed to charge plagiarism or faulty techniques. Moreover, if Marshall did borrow heavily from other sources, at least he had the good judgment to use the best available and he footnoted the most important ones. One can, however, agree with Justice Story that Marshall should have cited specific works and pages rather than simply noting the author.[48]

The best that can be said, to use an oft-quoted phrase, is that it was "a generation of successfully plagiarized histories," and that some of the Marshall's sources were shallow copies of earlier publications.[49] Moreover, eliminating the copied sections would still leave a distillation of Marshall's judicious interpretation of the colonial heritage.

Marshall lacked the ability to develop a satisfactory prose style. Although fashions in writing change, both contemporaries and

47. Marshall, *History of the American Colonies*, p. vii; Foran, "John Marshall as a Historian," pp. 53–62; Marshall, *Life of Washington*, p. x.
48. Foran, "John Marshall as a Historian," p. 52. The review, generally credited to Joseph Story, was printed in *The North American Review* (January 1828), pp. 1–40.
49. Quoted in Foran, "John Marshall as a Historian," p. 62.

later historians took exception to his verbose style and to his lack of dramatic quality. In some places the seemingly dull prose was not Marshall's, but that of his sources; this does not excuse him for failing to improve on his borrowed material. Justice Story perhaps made the most perceptive comment when he said: "The style is in perfect keeping with the character of the author. It is perspicuous, simple, and forcible. It possesses no studied ornaments, no select phrases, no elegant turns, and no ambitious floridness. It is plain, pure, and unpretending."[50] It was, in brief, what one would have expected from a pragmatic lawyer, inexperienced as a writer and known for his rustic, simple, republican style of life.

What then is the place of Marshall's *History of the American Colonies* in our national literature? When J. Franklin Jameson called attention to the inferior quality of the culture of the early republic, he admitted the scene was "not wholly barren" and cited Marshall's *Life of Washington* as an example of the "pale and sickly product coming forth at that time."[51] Whether or not we accept Jameson's critical judgment, Marshall's work was an example of a new kind of national history designed to promote national unity. It rejected the parochialism of eighteenth-century histories of separate colonies, and it emphasized the connection of the colonial past with the emerging United States.

The patriotic historian also identified new heroes who would truly be citizens of the new republic; in the *Life of Washington* Marshall attempted to cast Washington in such a mold. The *History of the American Colonies*, as an introduction to that biography, played an important role in his effort, for it delineated the historic stage on which the new heroes would act out their roles. Marshall, in his eagerness to prepare for the central figure of Washington, wrote a colonial history regrettably devoid of other significant personalities.

Many patriotic historians, it has been said, surrendered "to the

50. Story, "Review," p. 39.
51. J. Franklin Jameson, *The History of Historical Writing in America* (New York, 1961), p. 83.

uncritical nationalistic bias of the Federalist Whig writers."[52] But these new nationalist historians of the early nineteenth century were more than mere chroniclers, for they infused their histories with differing political philosophies which illuminated both the colonial era and the new republic. As one of these writers, Marshall interpreted the American colonial experience in terms of a concern for liberty and constitutional order that had implications for the future of the republic. He saw lessons in colonial history which bore directly on the political problems of his own time.

But was Marshall writing Federalist history? To support this familiar charge would require labeling Marshall a true Federalist, and he defies such an easy generalization. While he always regarded himself as a member of that faction, he often took independent stands on public issues and eschewed partisan politics completely after he became Chief Justice. Recent scholarship has classified him as a transitional figure, standing midway between the conservative, doctrinaire Old Federalists, and the more flexible Young Federalists.[53]

Paradoxically, much in the *History of the American Colonies* seems almost Jeffersonian in character. Both men were nationalists at heart and saw the American Revolution as legally just and as symbolic of American unity. Marshall also agreed with Jefferson's passion for liberty and his concern about the perversion of power and the danger of tyranny. Both men held an essentially Whig view of the British and colonial tradition, although Jefferson understood it better because of his wider reading and more subtle, theoretical mind. In addition, Marshall shared Jefferson's belief in the usefulness of history as a guide for a nation's political conduct.[54]

The two men parted company in their differing conceptions of the people's role in government and in their sense of the future. In

52. Harvey Wish, ed., *American Historians* (New York, 1962), p. 5.
53. Fischer, *The Revolution of American Conservatism*, pp. 380–382.
54. Van Tassel, *Recording America's Past*, p. 77. For an important analysis of Jefferson's views on history see H. Trevor Colbourn, "Thomas Jefferson's Use of the Past," *William and Mary Quarterly*, 3d series, 15 (1958): 56–70.

his analysis of the colonial heritage, Marshall acknowledged the people as the ideal source of power in government, and he reflected egalitarian overtones in his praise of individual enterprise. But he rejected Jefferson's belief in democracy because he doubted the people's capacity for exercising power once they were given it. Instead, he placed his faith in institutions such as legislatures or the courts.[55] Marshall's caution was paralleled by his different view of the future. Both men drew upon the colonial and British past to support their understanding of political behavior and to perceive directions for the nation's future. But Jefferson viewed that future with hope and optimism, while Marshall reflected a sense of foreboding.

Thus Marshall emerges from his *History of the American Colonies* as an independent in his interpretation of the colonial era. In his defense of the general will, his conception of society as an organic whole composed of many parts, his belief in institutions, his skeptical view of democracy, and his commitment "to the cause of order," Marshall remained true to orthodox Federalism. But his failure to defend elitist rule or property qualifications for voting made his overview of the colonial period less conservative in tone and hardly a "classic defense of Federalism."[56]

Although John Marshall may have begun his literary career for personal, mundane motives, the reissue of his biography of Washington and the separate publication of the *History of the American Colonies* were acts of public service. Marshall doubted whether he could, in his private or public life, stem the tide and save the republic. But he tried, and in so doing contributed significantly to the national historical literature.

55. Daniel Boorstin makes this point in *The Lost World of Thomas Jefferson* (New York, 1948), pp. 240–241.

56. Charles A. Beard, *An Economic Interpretation of the Constitution* (New York, 1941), p. 181.

3.

William Henry Drayton's Memoirs

SOLOMON LUTNICK

In recent years scholars have rediscovered some of the excellent contemporary historians of the American Revolution. Page Smith, for example, has posited the thesis that "the best interpretation of the causes of the Revolution was made in the decade following the treaty of peace in 1783," and that we subsequently moved further and further from the truth about our revolutionary beginnings.[1] Smith has concluded that David Ramsay's *History of the American Revolution*, published in 1789, remains a seminal study which clearly placed him in the front rank of American historians.

Ramsay's fellow South Carolinian, William Henry Drayton, who will probably never be rescued from the dust bin of history, was a gentleman of wealth and position who kept both a running diary as well as the letters, documents and other sources that came his way between 1763 and his death in 1779. In 1821 his son, John Drayton, collected, emended, and published the writings and sources of his father. John claimed full authorship, and William Henry's name did not appear as either author or even coeditor.[2] Yet, just as in the case of Ramsay, Drayton's study provided a veritable vein of information and interpretation for mining by later scholars.

1. Page Smith, "David Ramsay and the Causes of the American Revolution," *William and Mary Quarterly*, 3d series, 17 (1960) : 51.
2. John Drayton, *Memoirs of the American Revolution, from its commencement to the year 1776, inclusive; as relating to The State of South Carolina: and occasionally refering* [sic] *to the states of North Carolina and Georgia*, 2 vols. (Charleston, S.C., 1821; reprinted New York, 1969).

The improbable career of William Henry Drayton was one of the most fascinating to emerge from the Revolution. Born in 1742, he was descended from wealthy Tidewater planter stock. His mother, Charlotte Bull, a member of a most prominent family in the province, died two years after his birth. Young Drayton continued his studies in England. Entrusted to his father's friend, Charles Pinckney, then South Carolina's agent in London, Drayton enrolled in Balliol College, Oxford, for two years. Returning to South Carolina in late 1763, he soon married Dorothy Golightly, one of the colony's wealthiest women.

Drayton's career followed the expected path of a young patrician making a mark for himself. Elected a member of the commons house, he took his seat the day the Stamp Act Congress in New York made its report. As his father was a councillor and his uncle the lieutenant governor, and since both opposed the Stamp Act resolution, Drayton's most recent biographers assumed, probably correctly, that he, too, had pro-English political proclivities after having spent more than a decade in England.[3] Obviously out of touch with the rising patriotic sentiment, Drayton was not re-elected in 1768; however, the governor dissolved the commons house of the assembly chosen in that year a few days after it convened.

Once out of the commons, Drayton was more active in politics than he had been before. On June 22, 1769, Christopher Gadsden published a letter in the *South Carolina Gazette* attacking Charleston's importers. He urged the planters and mechanics to support a nonconsumption agreement which he had duly drawn up. Drayton, using the signature "FREE-man," attacked the non-importation movement, especially the last article of the association which proscribed all persons who failed to sign within nine months. He even suggested lodging Gadsden in the madhouse at public expense. A series of rejoinders followed, but one letter, penned by the mechanics on the committee of enforcement and

3. William M. Dabney and Marion Dargan, *William Henry Drayton and the American Revolution* (Albuquerque, N.M., 1962), chap. 2.

published on September 28, 1769, so hurt Drayton that he omitted it from his collection of pertinent personal documents. In it the mechanics chided him for inheriting and marrying into great wealth without ever knowing how it felt to work for a living. This attack by his social inferiors stung Drayton, as did the effectiveness of the nonimportation agreements. Merchants refused to handle his crops for fear of boycott reprisals. Since most judges and potential jurymen signed the association, he could gain no redress in the courts, and the commons rejected his petition for compensation without reading it.[4]

On January 3, 1770, a disgusted William Henry Drayton sailed to England on a ship which carried "returned goods," items banned by the boycott from entering South Carolina. Once in England he republished his letters in book form. The proministerial arguments expressed in *The Letters of Freeman*[5] found favor at court. In February 1771, on the recommendation of Lieutenant Governor William Bull, Jr., his uncle, Drayton received a seat on the Council of South Carolina, the apogee of his career as a Crown supporter. Returning to Charleston vindicated in early 1772, Drayton could not have known that within the next year his loyalty to the Crown would be put to the test and found wanting. Thus the *Memoirs*, as edited by John Drayton, and William Henry Drayton's biographers (of whom Marion Dargan and William M. Dabney are the most recent) piece together not only a history of South Carolina during the years prior to independence, but also a history as seen through the eyes of perhaps the most influential convert to the cause of rebellion in the entire colony. And William Henry Drayton demonstrated his zeal, if not his intelligence, on almost every page of his *Memoirs*.

The seeds of Drayton's conversion to the colonial cause were planted in London even while he met and mixed with Lord Sandwich and others of the British nobility. Drayton's uncle, Lieutenant Governor Bull, had nominated him to replace Peter

4. Ibid., pp. 36, 37, passim.
5. William Henry Drayton, *The Letters of Freeman* (London, 1771).

De Lancey as postmaster general of the southern district of North America. Despite the personal intercession on his behalf by Lords Hillsborough and Sandwich, the position went elsewhere, as did the assistant judgeship in South Carolina for which Bull nominated Drayton. Thus throughout the *Memoir* the theme recurred that English appointees unjustly received the most prestigious and lucrative positions over the heads of qualified and eager South Carolina gentry.

Shortly after his return to Charleston, Drayton, with the approbation of the South Carolina Council, entered into a seemingly lucrative deal to lease a large tract of land held by the Catawba Indians. The deal soon was voided, however, after opposition by John Stuart, Superintendent of Indian Affairs for the Southern District. Drayton never forgave Stuart, whose position required him to protect the Catawba lands. Stuart, an unpopular Scotsman, helped speed Drayton's growing antagonism toward royal appointees in South Carolina.[6] Further, Drayton saw that the Council of South Carolina, with five of its nine members "strangers from England,"[7] was no longer a stronghold for patrician Carolinians. Finding himself in an American minority, Drayton soon utilized terms like "profligate placemen" to describe the Englishmen who helped to administer his colony.[8] Drayton's dislike of English placemen was not alleviated by his interim appointment in 1774 as an assistant judge, a position denied him three years earlier in London when his politics and his feelings were much closer to the Crown. But, despite his increasing alienation from the Crown, his uncle now obtained that judgeship for him. Drayton was both the only nonlawyer and the only South Carolinian on the bench. During his brief tenure as a judge—he was replaced within a few

6. Dabney and Dargan, *William Henry Drayton*, pp. 42–44.
7. William Henry Drayton, *A Letter of Freeman of South Carolina to the Deputies of North-America, Assembled in the High Court of Congress at Philadelphia* (Charleston, S.C., 1774), p. 18.
8. William Henry Drayton, *Answer to Considerations on Certain Political Transactions of the Province of South Carolina written by the profligate placeman, Sir Egerton Leigh* (Charleston, S.C., 1774).

months—he acquired a hearty disrespect for Chief Justice Thomas Gordon and his fellow judges. Drayton believed his colleagues on the bench were both ignorant of the law and cavalier in their concern for the welfare of the province.[9]

With the passage of the "Intolerable Acts," Drayton finally abandoned his earlier proadministration position. On the eve of the meeting of the First Continental Congress, he published *A Letter of Freeman of South Carolina to the Deputies of North America, Assembled in the High Court of Congress at Philadelphia,* in which he championed the cause of American rights under the British constitution. The tract seemed almost an extension of the arguments he had with his fellow judges over minor local issues. The theme of a prominent provincial family superseded by outsiders when it came to preferment ran through Drayton's writings. Political frustration mixed with honest grievances became the key to understanding his conversion to the "popular side" by late 1774 and to the all-out radical cause less than a year later. He denied Parliament's right to legislate for America, and he proposed solutions somewhere in between those proffered by Franklin at Albany in 1754 and Galloway in Philadelphia twenty years later. Besides earning the enmity of South Carolina loyalists,[10] Drayton's *Freeman* earned for him the enmity of his fellow judges. (One challenged him to a duel, which never was consummated due to technicalities arising over a further quarrel over seconds.) The judges' remonstrance asking for Drayton's removal from the bench was agreeable to Lieutenant Governor Bull, who would not remove his nephew immediately for fear of martyring him but who suggested Lord Dartmouth do it. Thus Drayton remained on the bench and on the council until the official axe fell.

Meanwhile, Drayton sat for three circuit courts in November.

9. Dabney and Dargan, *William Henry Drayton,* p. 55.
10. For a detailed attack on Drayton's *Freeman,* see "A Backsetter's" charge that Drayton was "soured by Disappointment." *Some Fugitive Thoughts on a Letter of Freeman of South Carolina* (Charleston, S.C., 1774).

His address to the grand jury, written in a style and with a vehemence and logic that none of his other writing ever attained, led some cynics to maintain that he employed a ghost writer. But no evidence to this effect was ever found. Drayton expounded upon the threat to South Carolina's civil liberties and Britain's constitution. Two grand juries, rising to the charge, challenged Parliament's right to tax them as they pledged their lives and fortunes to defend the constitution.[11] In this fashion Drayton and the grand juries still considered themselves political conservatives, defending the British constitution. To them, the radicals were in London, not Charleston. But to Chief Justice Gordon, Drayton's removal from the bench in late November was just the first step in stripping the South Carolinian of power. By March 1, 1775, Drayton was suspended from the Council as well. These two acts now placed Drayton for the first time in the good graces of the radicals.

Thus from the spring of 1775 onward Drayton's *Memoirs* reflected the South Carolina political upheaval from the point of view of a newly baptized patriot. Drayton became active on numerous patriotic committees, both public and secret, and by the summer of 1775 he joined the handful of leading activists in the colony. He participated in a successful raid upon the state house armory, he helped borrow money to finance the radicals, and he devoted time to propaganda and communications efforts within the province as chairman of a committee on correspondence. The news from Massachusetts by July 4, 1775, led Drayton to claim that peace was out of the question and a civil war was "absolutely unavoidable."[12] Soon he went off to the back country on behalf of the council of safety to convince both militia and frontiersmen of the justice and eventual triumph of the colonial cause. As a former supporter of the Crown, his arguments carried much weight. Elected president of the Second Provincial Congress in November

11. Peter Force, ed., *American Archives, 1774–1776* (Washington, D.C., 1837–1853), 4th series, vol. 1.
12. Colonial Office Papers 5, DLV, 255. Cited in Dabney and Dargan, *William Henry Drayton*, p. 87.

1775, Drayton became the acknowledged leader of the South Carolina radicals. When not engaged in politics, Drayton, with no military experience, impetuously helped equip South Carolina's navy as well as fortify Charleston. Drayton so muddled the job that even the *Gentleman's Magazine* took note:

> Self created from nought, like a mushroom we see
> Spring an able Commander by land and by sea;
> Late of Tories the Prince, and his country's great foe,
> Now the Congress's Chairman, a split shirted beau:
> All titles of honour and profit do wait on
> Judge, General, Councillor, Admiral Drayton,
> Who never smell'd powder, nor handled a rope,
> But infallible more than Lord Peter the Pope;
> Who makes flesh and blood of his bread and his wine,
> While Drayton of schooners makes ships of the line,
> Makes all laws of mechanics and nature knock under,
> Can cram in an egg-shell a twenty-four pounder;
> Can burn in an instant the whole British navy,
> And eat up an Army without salt or gravy.[13]

Drayton, indeed, was totally committed. By February 6, 1776, he told the Provincial Congress that it could only choose between independence or slavery.[14] Christopher Gadsden agreed two days later. By March South Carolina had established a new government and the general assembly had voted to give its chief judicial plum, chief justice of the state, to Drayton. Although he knew the conservatives intended to rid the Assembly of him by shunting him off to a less influential position, he found it pleasant to occupy the seat once held by his archfoe James Gordon. The state courts opened in April and Drayton's famous charge to the Charleston grand jury on the 23rd harkened back to 1688 for its defense of liberty and independence. Further, Drayton soon went to Georgia to rally—and hopefully annex—the disaffected areas away from a seemingly loyalist colony.

13. *Gentleman's Magazine*, 46: 279.
14. *Journal of the Provincial Congress of South Carolina, 1776* (Charleston, S.C., 1776), p. 3.

Drayton's aggressive confidence had a way of alienating friends as well as foes. He almost dueled General Charles Lee because the latter considered Drayton's defensive plans for batteries of the city foolish, and Lee referred to the chief justice as a "d——d bad engineer." Lee was correct—Drayton was a poor engineer, procurer of naval stores, and military liaison. But his words, either as a politician or historian, had much more effectiveness than his deeds. He continued writing competent pamphlets in defense of independence and the war.[15]

However, Drayton hoped to make his mark as an historian of the revolution in South Carolina. He lacked knowledge on colonial affairs outside the borders of his own state, and he tried to rectify this weakness as best he could. Writing to Henry Laurens, president of the Continental Congress, Drayton explained his historical project to his fellow South Carolinian, asking him to take some time from congressional business to answer several historical questions.[16] Drayton made a conscious effort to instruct posterity about South Carolina's decisive role in the revolution. His subsequent falling out with Laurens—and his swift and unexpected death two years later—left his *Memoirs* poorly organized and incomplete.

Yet Drayton's *Memoirs* still remain one of the most valuable sources for the Revolution in South Carolina. For example, Drayton thought the Articles of Confederation gave too much power to the central government and did not fully guarantee the rights of the individual states. And he understood the geography that made the new United States a sectional rather than a truly national political unit.

In March 1778 Drayton entered the Continental Congress. He continued arguing against the Articles of Confederation, but he

15. See, for example, his defense of the American position during the abortive negotiations on Staten Island, *To Their Excellencies Richard Viscount Howe, Admiral, and William Howe, Esq., General of His Britannick Majesty's Forces in America* (Charleston, S.C., 1776).

16. Drayton to Laurens, November 1, 1777, Henry Laurens Mss., Library of Congress.

eventually signed them along with the four other South Carolina delegates. Drayton served on many congressional committees and as a historian he assiduously collected as many pertinent documents as he could relative to the war in general and South Carolina in particular. He became embroiled in the Deane-Lee affair and soon he had both a private and public falling out with Henry Laurens. Their disagreements were sometimes petty— arguing over a display of fireworks for July 4th, for example. But when Drayton chose as one of his closest friends Charles Thomson, secretary of the Congress and a constant adversary of Laurens, the two South Carolinians ceased even speaking. Thomson regularly supplied Drayton with the proceedings of the early days of the Continental Congress which he used in his history of the revolution.

In August 1779, Drayton became seriously ill and, as his condition rapidly worsened, he made his deathbed peace with Henry Laurens. This may have proved doubly tragic, because the Congress appointed Laurens as one of the administrators of Drayton's affairs in Philadelphia. Laurens proceeded to destroy the "many secrets of state" that Drayton had collected during his tenure at Philadelphia. Laurens put Thomson's contributions and Drayton's notes to the torch because he thought it improper that Drayton's papers "fall into the hands of his family."[17] Laurens obviously had the last word not only in his quarrel with Drayton, but in choosing the permanent omissions from his colleague's published *Memoirs*.

Still Drayton's incomplete *Memoirs* offered many important lessons. First, the argument—all but forgotten by present-day historians—that if Governor William Campbell, who had arrived in Charleston in June 1775, had moved the royal government into the backcountry, the war in South Carolina would have had quite different results. Surely Drayton's uncle, Lieutenant Governor William Bull, had apprised Campbell that the newly formed rebel council of safety was arming and well on its way to controlling the

17. Drayton, *Memoirs*, 1: vii.

town. Further, historians have agreed, and Campbell must have known, that backcountry South Carolina had virtually no representation, and that its heavy tax burden and Scotch-Irish proclivities favoring Britain coupled with a disaffected German population made the backcountry appear a natural haven for the royal administration.[18] Drayton understood this. While his *Memoirs* passed in silence over the Reverend Charles Woodmason, leader of the upcountry protesters, Drayton estimated that Thomas Fletchall's loyalist backcountry militia consisted of about 1,500 men under arms in July 1775. Meanwhile, John Stuart, having fled to Georgia, wooed the Catawba Indians. Drayton's attempt to win the "disaffected country" back to the colonial standard admittedly failed on all counts. His arguments could not dent the armor of backcountry loyalism, and he reasoned that their intransigence resulted from the same factor that explained his own conversion: "We soon found that reasoning was in vain with those who were fixed by royal emoluments." Despite the oversimplification of this interpretation of backcountry intransigence, Drayton also offered a better analysis of the backcountry: "if Lord William Campbell had gone up among the disaffected—had collected Fletchall and his men around him—and had conducted himself with promptness and efficiency—the whole proceedings of the Provincial Congress would have been overthrown." Drayton thanked Providence for leaving the governor in Charleston "to experience the daily loss of his executive powers."[19]

Drayton and the council of safety moved swiftly to remove this option from Campbell. Economic pressures placed upon upcountry wagoners, millers, and others forced them to support the association or their goods would not be allowed into Charleston. The same type of pressure had been exerted upon Drayton a few years earlier when he was a victim of economic coercion. Further, even if the association bargained Fletchall into a stance of neutrality, the talented Robert Cunningham again rallied the back-

18. Ibid., pp. 311–313.
19. Ibid., p. 323.

country to the king's standard. Drayton thought it so obvious that Campbell would have to move to the backcountry that he pleaded with the council of safety to take the Governor into custody. It rejected his motion by twenty-three to sixteen. But William Campbell's lethargy, Drayton argued, made the rebel take-over in South Carolina much easier. By June 1776 the rebels had militarily neutralized the Highlanders, Regulators, and other loyal groups. Having received inadequate support from Britain, they soon were worn down, if not out. Ironically, South Carolina's state constitution of March 1776 still greatly underrepresented the backcountry.

The Draytons also reminded us of their belief that primarily political factors brought on the American Revolution, with almost no economic or social causation. George Bancroft could have studied William Henry Drayton or any of hundreds of his contemporaries to cull a phrase like Drayton's "The Almighty created America to be independent of Britain." American rights and British aggression were constant themes in the *Memoirs*. Drayton considered the colonials a "loyal but highly injured people" goaded into rebellion by Englishmen who "had made up their minds to enforce by the sword, measures which were untenable by any principle of law or of Justice." In the Quebec and Quartering Acts Drayton saw "the Crown now made despotic, and the Romish church established in a part of America." The Draytons utilized the simple devil theory in their political interpretation of the Revolution. The devil was one part Parliament, one part Pope, one part Lord Bute and the Scottish influence, and one part a naive George III. The Draytons placed no blame on Governor Campbell, who arrived too late either to understand or control the situation, nor on Lieutenant Governor William Bull, who ruled the colony on five separate occasions in the post-1760 era, when the devil first entered the scene. Bull, of course, was an uncle and a sincere man even if on the wrong side of the political fence. As late as April 1775 the Draytons still paid homage to their "much respected and beloved" relative.

When John Drayton saw the war as a battle between "taxation

and royalty vs. Liberty and social happiness," he used a Charleston planter's definition of social happiness. Drayton's *Memoirs* made it clear that the American Revolution in South Carolina was not a social movement, and if it ever was, the losing side had favored social change. Not only did the Draytons demonstrate little sympathy for the problems of the backcountry, their history omitted mention of one of the most important documents in William Henry Drayton's political life—that letter written by a Charleston workingman and published October 5, 1769, in the *South Carolina Gazette*. While William Henry might have failed to keep a copy of this issue at hand, John Drayton, fifty years after the occurrence, also chose to forget it. In it, the "Charleston mechanic" attacked Drayton for his insensitivity to the problems and political desires of the lower classes. Even after Drayton found himself on the same side as the mechanics, he still believed they should keep to their trades and leave the job of governing to the tidewater patricians. Except for his support of the disestablishment of the Anglican Church in order better to woo the backcountry, William Henry Drayton's independent America was a vision of the pre-1763 *status quo*, with the additional improvement of tidewater patricians substituting for royal placemen in the seats of power.

The final thread woven by Drayton into his memoirs was the obvious but real fear of the black man shared by South Carolina's revolutionary leadership. South Carolina had a higher ratio of blacks to the total population than any other province. And while Governor Campbell never followed the lead of Governor Dunmore in Virginia by suggesting freedom for slaves who took up arms in the king's cause, Carolina had a constant fear that this would happen. In May 1775 a letter arrived from Arthur Lee in London intimating that the English ministry was considering a plan for "instigating the slaves to insurrection." A committee was immediately formed "to secure the colony," and Drayton noted that the people were "greatly apprehensive of instigating insurrections of slaves, and depredations from Indians." These tightened security measures, however, only resulted in the hanging of a black ship's pilot named Jerry "for conspiracy to incite an insurrection among the slaves and to burn down Charleston." The principal charge against him was that he had reportedly said, "If the British ships come here, he would pilot them over Charleston bar." Many, though not Drayton, understood that hysteria rather than safety of the province necessitated the hanging. The Clerk of the Council of Safety, one Timothy, wrote Drayton that "more force was exerted for his being saved, than there would have been for you or me."[20] But the fear nagged on well into the war.

Drayton's *Memoirs* reminded us of an occasionally neglected theme of the American Revolution. Some of our newer, more sophisticated interpretations of the struggle never entered his mind—and modern historians have chosen to ignore some of the most salient points made by a patrician adherent of the Crown turned rebel. Although David Ramsay must be read to comprehend the era of the American Revolution in the Carolinas as well as in the other colonies, William Henry Drayton's *Memoirs* formed an important piece in the puzzle of what made the colonies independent.

20. Ibid., 2: 24.

4.

Ira Allen's Vermont

H. N. MULLER, III

History has seldom, if ever, been written in a vacuum, as a mindless chronicle of events. The broad scope of motivation for historical writing ranges from history as the metaphysics of progress or repetition to its use as a blatant tool of argument, vindication, or condemnation. Often it obscures the very past it purports to elucidate. Ira Allen's *The Natural and Political History of the State of Vermont* was not written as the sober reflection of the scholar or even with the smoldering anger of an abused participant, but instead for the rough market place in which the author sought immediate advantage from his writing.[1] Using quill and paper to win allies and to slay enemies by appealing at once to an influential elite and to a wider public had long been a tactic of Ira Allen. As the youngest of six boys and two girls, all of whom survived in an age when the weak perished quickly, he had to rely on his cunning and facile wits.[2]

---

1. Ira Allen, *The natural and political history of the state of Vermont, one of the United States of America. To which is added, an appendix, containing answers to sundry queries, addressed to the author* (London, printed by J. W. Myers, sold by W. West, 1789). Allen's *Natural and Political History of the State of Vermont* has been reprinted with minor corrections and a dated introduction in Vermont Historical Society, *Collections* (Montpelier, Vt., 1870), and more recently by the Charles E. Tuttle Co. (Rutland, Vt., 1969), which reissued the 1870 edition adding only a brief foreword. Subsequent references are to Tuttle's 1969 edition, and the work is hereafter cited as *History*.

2. The only adequate biographical treatment of Ira Allen is James Benjamin Wilbur, *Ira Allen, Founder of Vermont, 1751–1814*, 2 vols. (Boston and New York, 1928). Wilbur amassed a prodigious amount of evidence and

Ira Allen's *History of the State of Vermont* represented the expurgated version of the actions of the coterie of men who first conceived of the notion of Vermont and then guided the state into existence. Written in 1797–1798, more than two-thirds of the work concerned the highly dramatic and complex events that took place in the eight years between 1775 and 1783, during which Ira Allen more than any other man controlled the destiny of the fledgling state. Appropriately, the successes and failures (mostly successes in his version) constituted the book's main subject matter. Yet the form in which Allen portrayed these events, the evidence he selected, and the interpretation he espoused were more the product of the subsequent fifteen years (1783–1798), which he quickly disposed of in only a few disorganized pages. Writing to rescue himself from imminent ruin in 1798, Allen had the advantage of knowing how things worked out, where power lay, and to whom he must appeal. Labeling the work history, Ira Allen unabashedly pleaded his case. Unfortunately the resulting tract long served as a standard source for Vermont historians too frequently inspired more by filio-pietistic fervor than objective inquiry. Surely it is now time to sweep away the myths and legends which Allen propagated so fruitfully and to reassess the value of this seminal book. To judge its value as history or as a document, it is imperative to assess the role of the author in the creation of the state about which he later wrote.

Led out of Litchfield County, Connecticut, by Ethan, the oldest and most famous of the brothers, Heman, Levi, Zimri, Heber and Ira Allen invested much of their enormous energy and their futures

---

quoted copiously from the documents, which in itself makes the work useful, but in his overzealous and heavy-handed attempt to rehabilitate Allen's somewhat tarnished reputation, Wilbur greatly diminished the work's value. A. L. Burt in his careful study, *The United States, Great Britain and British North America* (New Haven, Conn., 1940), pp. 171–176, finds Wilbur a "hero-worshipper," who "accepts Allen's every word as gospel truth" and who had invented "hypothetical monsters" to explain some of Allen's actions. Burt thinks that Wilbur has "proved too much" and has undermined the credibility of the biography.

in the green and mountainous country defined by the Connecticut River and Lake Champlain to the east and west and the Canadian and Massachusetts boundaries to the north and south. Though part of Charles II's grant to the Duke of York in 1674 (and thus in theory British), the area long remained an unsettled buffer between the competing and hostile empires of the French in the St. Lawrence Valley and the British in the Hudson Valley. As early as 1750, brashly ignoring the 1674 grant, Benning Wentworth, the portly New Hampshire merchant-governor, began to enrich his estate along with those of his associates by granting townships in the region west of the Connecticut River. The first of these grants (which in time totalled more than 125) lay a scant forty-five miles from Albany. It was logically, if immodestly, named Bennington.

In 1760 Jeffrey Amherst's large army, which had marched north through the Champlain Valley, joined Wolfe's victorious troops on the St. Lawrence. Together they ended France's hegemony in Canada and in their success opened as well as advertised Vermont for settlement. The New York government, at last fully awakened to this rich heritage of land, immediately engaged Wentworth in both a race to grant the virgin territory and a legal battle to wrest it from the New England interlopers. The granting race, heated by the prospects of self-enrichment, ended in 1764 when the Privy Council determined the disputed territory to be New York's. But the war to establish unchallenged ownership over the acreage already granted, often by both governments, raged, officially at least, until Vermont joined the Union in 1791.[3]

In the late 1760s, Ethan Allen entered this tumultuous battle-ground of competing interests, a battleground rapidly filling with settlers often holding conflicting or dubious titles. He came fresh from the frustrating work of trying to farm the rock-strewn fields of western Connecticut, and fresh also from several unhappy business ventures. Above all a man of action, Ethan with his huge

3. The most detailed account of the disputed New Hampshire Grants is Matt Bushnell Jones, *Vermont in the Making* (Cambridge, Mass., 1939).

brawny frame, direct, profane speech, and rollicking, boisterous manner thrust himself naturally into the center of the conflict. By 1770, both in spirit and in fortune, he had thoroughly identified himself with the hardy and obstreperous minority of settlers and speculators who gambled their future on the dubious Wentworth grants. Theirs became a guerilla war with New York's government and with any of its friends who held title to vast tracts or who dared to settle and to organize the territory.[4]

In the fall of 1770 in Stephen Fay's Catamount Tavern atop the hill in Bennington, a small group of defiant men formed the Green Mountain Boys. As their commander, Ethan Allen devised the bellicose, rough and tumble tactics that angered Yorker governors and that held Yorker surveyors, settlers, sheriffs, posses, and claimants at a respectful distance. At this time, Ira Allen, a small, alert youth of nineteen, first came to the "Grants," as the area had come to be called.

Ira had spent most of his youth on the family farm in Cornwall, Connecticut, under the tutelage of his older brothers. The deceptively frail boy, derisively nicknamed "Stub," acquired a sound common school education and learned the ways of the farm and the woods. Ira was a fast learner, and he rarely forgot. At sixteen he went to Salisbury, Connecticut, to help in the diverse operations of his brother Heman's general store. For the next three years Ira devoted his energy to driving herds of his brother's hogs across Connecticut and Massachusetts to market at Albany and to helping out with their business by dressing deer hides and making leather breeches. All this time Ira cautiously invested his small

4. Ethan Allen has been the subject of many biographical and less ambitious accounts, but most of them are best categorized as folklore. John Pell in *Ethan Allen* (Boston and New York, 1929) began the task of rescuing Allen from myth and establishing his proper and important place in Vermont and revolutionary history. Charles Jellison, building on Pell and profiting greatly from his own and others' research, has written what must stand as a highly readable and the definitive biography: *Ethan Allen, Frontier Rebel* (Syracuse, N.Y., 1969).

earnings and £48 inherited from his father in the disputed New Hampshire titles, available for a few pennies an acre.[5]

By 1772, Ira made the Grants his home. As a trusted lieutenant in Ethan's Green Mountain Boys, he took an active part in the defying of the hated Yorkers, but his attention never strayed far from the land, the thousands of undeveloped acres waiting to be exploited. In the tangled thickets and mixed forest of hardwoods and fir, Ira quickly learned the crude arts of the frontier surveyor, and he would run lines for absentee speculators and for his own small holdings, all the while keeping a keen eye out for opportunity. On more than one occasion Ira combined his firsthand knowledge with precocious Yankee business acumen. He exchanged his own rocky, mountainside rights covered with useless balsam trees (billed imaginatively as "fir gum woods . . . tall Straight trees that had gum, much like the gum on cherry trees") for funds for a large fertile intervale tract well-forested with oak and pine. On other occasions he deliberately misrepresented land he had surveyed in order to purchase it himself at a depressed price.[6]

Ira's surveying furnished the material for his first book, *Containing the most Usefull Rules in Surveying Wrote with My Own Hand and Agreable to My Invention*, finished in 1773. The surveying also led to his sure decision that Burlington, situated beside a broad harbor on Lake Champlain and near the mouth and falls of the Winooski (Onion) River, would "become a place of consequent . . . both for commerce and society in the neighborhood." He lost no time in advising his brothers to "sell the whole, or any part of their holdings in southern Vermont that would command ready pay . . . to apply to the purchase of lands contiguous to Onion river, and Lake Champlain." In 1773, Ira, Heman, Ethan,

5. Ira Allen's *Autobiography* published in Wilbur, *Ira Allen*, 1: 1–59, contains useful information about his early life and first years in Vermont. Unfortunately the only extant segment of his *Autobiography* concludes in 1773.
6. Allen, *Autobiography*, pp. 37–38.

and Zimri along with their cousin Remember Baker, established the Onion River Land Company, a loose organization which ultimately controlled nearly 80,000 acres in the tenuous Wentworth titles, primarily around Burlington and in the Winooski River Valley.[7] Before long they had sold parcels to a number of Vermont's future leaders, including Thomas Chittenden, who was governor for nearly twenty-two years.

The Allens' rapid investment of their capital in the Onion River country and their commitment to Lake Champlain and the north gave added direction to their growing role in the troubled affairs of the New Hampshire Grants. From this time until Ira's financial collapse in the late 1790s their strategy was dictated first by the necessity to win recognition of their disputed New Hampshire titles, and second by the need to maintain easy commercial access from their holdings in the Champlain Valley through the Richelieu and St. Lawrence Rivers to both Canadian and European markets. Though they made tactical adjustments to the vicissitudes of the times with bewildering speed and facility, the Allens and their cohorts never lost sight of their basic strategy. Although this determined strategy, formulated largely by Ira Allen, neither favored nor appealed to all the Grants' residents, more immediate issues temporarily united the diverse interests. However, once those had been solved, the Allens would find themselves and their leadership increasingly under attack.[8]

7. Allen MSS, Wilbur Collection, Bailey Library, University of Vermont, Burlington, Vermont, photostat of *Ira Allen His Book Containing the most Usefull Rules in Surveying Wrote with my own Hand and Agreable to my Invention* (1773); Ira Allen, *Autobiography*, p. 53; Chilton Williamson, *Vermont in Quandary* (Montpelier, Vt., 1949), pp. 29–30.

8. W. A. Mackintosh in his brief article, "Canada and Vermont: A study in Historical Geography," *Canadian Historical Review*, 8 (March 1927): 9–30, suggested that the answer to the puzzling relations between Vermont and the Province of Quebec lay in the geographic relationship of Lake Champlain and its extensive drainage basin to the commercial artery of the St. Lawrence River. In his revisionist history of early Vermont, Chilton Williamson, *Vermont in Quandary*, very fully developed Mackintosh's thesis, clearly demonstrating the important role of the Allens in formulating and espousing the policy, even after it became unpopular and a political liability. For the

After years of frustration in the battle to keep out Yorker officials and to win recognition of the Wentworth titles, leaders of the Green Mountain Boys and some of their friends on the west side of the mountains which divided the strife-torn territory began to consider local independence as the best solution to their problems. They reasoned that independence would offer confirmation of their titles and a large measure of control over their own destinies. The Allens were among the first to espouse Vermont independence, and with their close associates, many of whom were linked by family ties,[9] they naturally assumed leadership of the movement. Between July 1775 and July 1777 they called a series of "conventions" at Dorset, Westminster, and Windsor, Vermont. At each session a small group of men representing the land speculators and a minority of the settlers pushed Vermont toward independence. They campaigned for wider support in the Grants, sent agents seeking approval from the newly organized Continental Congress, and desperately sought an issue to win popular support.

While Ira's skillful hand can readily be detected in the planning of this movement and in other work behind the scenes, it was Ethan who, as usual, occupied center stage. Ethan led the rag-tag band of Green Mountain Boys across Lake Champlain to capture Fort Ticonderoga in "The name of Jehovah and the Continental Congress." Again, Ethan insisted on an abortive raid on St. John, and on an audacious and ill-conceived attempt to take Montreal which led to his capture by the British. Until Ethan's period of captivity between November 1775 and 1778, Ira remained in the background. After this date, however, he rapidly emerged as the leader of the Vermont independence faction, guiding it with a deft hand, if in a less flamboyant fashion than Ethan. This faction

---

importance of the commercial relationship see H. N. Muller III, "The Commercial History of The Lake Champlain-Richelieu River Route, 1760–1815," (Ph.D. diss., University of Rochester, 1968).

9. Patricia L. Thomas, "A Study in Familial Ties in Early Vermont Government" (M.A. thesis, University of Vermont, 1972).

had already found an issue, self-determination, which could unite a majority on the Grants behind the Allens' leadership. Now their task became one of merging the wider Revolution with their own plans, of achieving a revolution within a revolution.[10]

At the urging of his brother Heman, Ira left the army encamped before the walls of Quebec in February 1776 and returned to Vermont. There along with three others, he took command of the movement. In October he penned the first of many addresses and pamphlets stating the case against the Yorkers and arguing for the recognition of Vermont independence. He argued that the special geographical relationship to the Province of Quebec and the St. Lawrence made it unlikely that Vermont could develop close ties with New York, a theme he repeated many times. In addition, arguments for Vermont's self-determination echoed those of the larger body of Americans engaged in a similar struggle with Great Britain. In these legalistic tracts, replete with frontier echoes of the Enlightenment and appeals to the natural rights of man, Ira Allen developed the style that characterized his *History*.[11]

Even with the dubious aid of Allen's inside account (or perhaps because of it), a definitive story of the political machinations surrounding the founding of Vermont has persistently eluded historians. The movement Ira Allen led was extraordinarily complex. It embraced the vacillating and frequently conflicting ambitions of a number of ill-defined, chameleon-like local factions, as well as the states of Massachusetts, New Hampshire and New York, and the larger entities of Great Britain and the United States. All of these groups operated within the swirling crosscurrents of the American Revolution.

Vermont's political make-up presented as confused a mosaic as the kaleidoscopic pattern of conflicting land claims that in part

10. Allen, *History*, p. 52; and Wilbur, *Ira Allen*, 1: 78.
11. Ira Allen, *Some Miscellaneous Remarks and Short Arguments on a Small Pamphlet. . . .* (Hartford, Conn., 1777). Wilbur, *Ira Allen*, 2: 527–531, contains a useful bibliography of Allen's published writing. Twenty-six items can be attributed to Allen and several others carrying another author's name can be reasonably attributed to Allen's pen.

created it. The Allens and the Green Mountain Boys represented settlers and speculators who had invested their future in New Hampshire titles and who formed a bellicose minority located mainly on the west side of the mountains. Though Ira's version of the story ignored the fact, they continually encountered the quiet opposition of a cowed and more conservative group in their midst who could tolerate Yorker sovereignty and even welcomed the stability it promised.[12] Across the mountains in the Connecticut River Valley, the Allens found natural allies in a few radical mavericks, but the bulk of the population did not initially find the notion of Vermont independence especially attractive. Only with the intensification of the problems that precipitated the American Revolution did the Allens find a lever sufficient to force their policy.

Vermont experienced many of the same backcountry-seaboard, debtor-creditor, royalist-republican frictions that characterized the revolutionary movement elsewhere in the country. Colonel Jacob Bayley at Newbury and Eleazor Wheelock and Bezaleeh Woodward, his conniving Dartmouth college friends across the Connecticut River in Hanover, New Hampshire, had generally favored a close relationship with New Hampshire (or even New York, in Bayley's case). However, they found the distance from their homes to the Portsmouth-Exeter aristocracy vexing, as they had little say in vital decisions that affected them. The College Party viewed Vermont independence at best as a useful threat to help them extort more power from seaboard New Hampshire and at worst as a slightly distasteful alternative to the status quo. Thoroughly dissatisfied with the failure of the New Hampshire government to respond to their grievances, they reluctantly joined forces with the Allens, a fragile alliance which would later foment trouble.[13]

---

12. Allen, *History*, p. 53.
13. Jere R. Daniell, *Experiment in Republicanism; New Hampshire Politics and the American Revolution, 1741–1794* (Cambridge, Mass., 1970), pp. 150–151; and Williamson, *Quandary*, p. 62.

The tensions created by the revolutionary movement also confronted the Connecticut Valley Yorkers in their heated struggle over the direction of their Committee of Correspondence. In March 1775 a group of angry men, fearful of legal action by creditors, took over the courthouse in Westminster. After two men had been killed and the rioters ignominiously jailed, Ethan Allen adroitly dispatched a company of Green Mountain Boys to free the protesters. While Ira Allen and others viewed the "Westminster Massacre" as an initial step against British tyranny, it was really a debtor uprising that conveniently provided an issue with which to cement an alliance between east and west sides.[14] The Allens demanded Vermont independence, and those who identified with the Westminster rioters accepted those terms as part of the price for their political and economic freedom. The promulgation of the very conservative New York constitution in April 1777 finally discredited the Yorkers who held out against local independence, producing a loose coalition supporting Vermont independence and the American Revolution (not always in that order) and leaving only the "Tories" to be dealt with at home.[15]

Left to themselves, the components of the coalition might have accommodated their various aspirations, but New York had too much invested in the territory to allow local option, and Massachusetts and New Hampshire each carefully nurtured their own ambitions. In Congress the Vermont issue became part of a larger question of land disputes that directly involved Connecticut, Pennsylvania, and Virginia. However, New York's opposition to

14. Allen, *History*, pp. 41–42. Walter Hill Crockett, *Vermont, The Green Mountain State*, 5 vols. (New York, 1921–23), often considered the standard history of the state, typifies the interpretation of the "Westminster Massacre" as an opening blow in the Revolution. See 1: 381–418. The incident might better be termed a riot. See the "State of Facts" in Vermont, *Records of the Governor and Council of The State of Vermont*, 8 vols. (Montpelier, Vt., 1873–1880), 1: 337–338.

15. Williamson, *Quandary*, pp. 61–62, 64. The records of the Convention and pertinent material relating to the constitution of 1777 are in Vermont, *Governor and Council*, 1: 62–75 and 81–103; H. N. Muller III, *Oligarchy or Democracy?*, Vermont Academy of Arts and Sciences Occasional Paper no. 5 (1970), pp. 5–10.

resolving the matter except by its own patent formula hamstrung the Congress.

The political scenario was played out on the stage of the Champlain Valley, long a classic invasion route. Ethan Allen began it at Ticonderoga in May 1775, and was followed by Schuyler and Montgomery on their way to Canada later that year. The next year witnessed the headlong American retreat, with disaster only averted by the combination of British procrastination and Benedict Arnold's valiant fight at Valcour Island. Despite the surrender of Burgoyne's army at Saratoga, the British returned for the duration in 1777, and Lt. General Frederick Haldimand maintained military hegemony in the Champlain Valley. Men from the Grants marched to Canada, and also fought at Hubbardton, Bennington, and Saratoga—perhaps as much to defend their homes as to win American independence.

From this confusing mix Ira Allen, only twenty-five years old when the United States declared its independence, forged order, an order very much the product of his personal style. That he succeeded in creating Vermont was no mean feat, but in the process he sowed seeds that would eventually grow beyond his control and destroy him.

Exercising every blandishment, Ira Allen and his associates turned their enormous energies toward achieving Vermont independence. They reached an important milestone in July 1777 when a convention assembled at Windsor to consider a constitution drafted by Allen. The members sat only long enough to approve the document and to establish a Council of Safety as a provisional government before rushing off to defend themselves against Burgoyne's advancing army. The constitution of 1777, notable for its prohibition of slavery and its establishment of universal manhood suffrage, has usually been treated as a very liberal document patterned after Pennsylvania's revolutionary model. But by putting all authority in the hands of a governor, lieutenant-governor, and twelve-member elected council, this constitution left Vermont open to government by a small oligarchy.

The Council of Safety, which included most of the leaders of the independence movement, immediately left Windsor for the west side of the mountains to begin governing the new state. Meeting in the homes of Allen, Chittenden, the Fays, Nathan Clark, Moses Robinson, or Timothy Brownson in Arlington, Sunderland, and Bennington, and formulating policy around kitchen tables, the "Arlington junto" or "private cabinet" ruled Vermont throughout the revolutionary period. Printing difficulties, plus the suspicion that the majority of the population would not support it, delayed promulgation of the constitution until early 1778. In the first elections in March 1778 the junto maintained its control with Chittenden as governor and with the backing of a majority of the powerful Council.[16]

The new government worked hard to consolidate its position and pursue its enemies. Congress received a steady stream of delegations and petitions seeking its recognition of Vermont's self-proclaimed independence. Chittenden even tried to reach a *modus vivendi* with New York, too hard pressed by the Revolution to deal with an insurrection at home. Never forgetting the importance of the St. Lawrence entry, the small state proposed in 1778, at Ira Allen's urging, to launch a campaign to drive the British from Canada, but could not get the necessary help from the beleaguered Washington. Again on Allen's inspiration, Vermont won friends at home and attracted new settlers by levying no taxes, supporting itself and the war effort instead by the sequestration and confiscation of Tory property. "Tory" became a convenient label to hang on any number of the junto's enemies, and many an American patriot, who only sinned by supporting New York's claims, found himself run out of the state. The junto also tried to win friendship and influence by confirming Vermont land titles of important persons both inside and outside the state.[17]

Yet the fate of the state hung in the balance. In 1778–1779 at

16. Vermont, *Governor and Council*, 1: 106–309.
17. Ibid., pp. 217, 219, and 225; Ira Allen, *History*, p. 65; Jellison, *Ethan Allen*, p. 199; and Williamson, *Quandary*, pp. 69–76.

the instigation of Jacob Bayley and the College Party, sixteen New Hampshire towns in the Connecticut River Valley joined Vermont. This union provoked the rage of New Hampshire and gave Vermont's enemies in Congress nearly enough support to act. At home the union provided a voting bloc that threatened the control of the junto. With customary guile, Ira Allen maneuvered the assembly into expelling the New Hampshire towns and dissolving the union, but the state's future remained precarious since it had not found solutions to many basic questions. In Vermont much of the populace remained hostile to the state and to the men who governed it, and some groups actively worked either to control the state or to dissolve it. New York and the Continental Congress steadfastly refused to recognize Vermont and, along with New Hampshire and Massachusetts, kept up a steady flow of menacing gestures. The British, firmly entrenched astride the St. Lawrence with an army of 2,500 to 3,000 men, posed a constant threat.[18] Moreover, the American Revolution no longer offered a convenient screen behind which the Allens could carry out their plans, for increasingly the Revolution's most ardent supporters opposed the Allens and their designs. Thus, they had to find a new set of tactics.

An opportunity to shift tactics presented itself in July 1780, when a letter to Ethan Allen from John Beverly Robinson, a Loyalist officer close to General Clinton, indicated British interest in Vermont's rejoining the empire as a "Separate Government." Robinson's letter was reinforced later in the summer when Justus Sherwood, a Tory and former neighbor of Allen's, clandestinely visited Ethan. The British had watched with interest the struggle over the Vermont question and correctly judged that they could woo its leadership away from the American Revolution. Ethan

18. Ibid., pp. 78–84; Daniell, *Experiment*, pp. 154–162; Vermont, *Governor and Council*, 1: appendix G. Governor Chittenden thought the British had an army of 7,000 in Canada, while Allen claimed the number to be 10,000. In reality Haldimand had 2,500 to 3,000 men. Ira Allen, *History*, p. 100; and Henry S. Wardener, "The Haldimand Negotiations," *Proceedings of the Vermont Historical Society* 2 (no. 1): 6.

Allen, who had helped to determine policy since his release by the British in 1778, took the proposal to the junto, which decided to explore the possibility with General Haldimand, the British commander in Canada and the most convenient and obvious negotiator. In the Allens' eyes such an arrangement with the British would, among other things, strengthen their own direction over the state, recognize New Hampshire and Vermont land titles, and, since Vermont would be a member of the empire, guarantee free access to the St. Lawrence. In embarking on the Haldimand Affair, the lengthy negotiations with the British, the Allens had decided on their new tactics and had taken a dangerous step that later would become a heavy liability and a source of much embarrassment. The negotiations to return Vermont to British rule ended when the news of Cornwallis's defeat at Yorktown made the attempt at reconciliation impossible. Despite the unpopularity of the scheme, the Allens continued the flirtation until the boundary provisions of the Treaty of Paris ended British pretensions to the area.[19]

The Haldimand Affair was at the heart of the action explained by Ira Allen in his *The Natural and Political History of the State of Vermont*. The negotiations occupied nearly a quarter of the text. His analysis of the importance of these negotiations was probably correct, as they marked the first of a number of miscalculations that for once neither Ira's guile nor Ethan's bluster could redeem. Henceforth the brothers increasingly moved to the

19. Most of the important documents on the Haldimand Affair from the Haldimand, Clinton, Colonial Office (series 42), Allen, Vermont, and other papers have been published in collections or secondary sources. Wilbur, *Ira Allen*, 1: chs. 6–9, presents many of the documents, despite the fact that his interpretation of them follows the standard line of Vermont historians from Samuel Williams, *The Natural and Civil History of Vermont* (Walpole, N.H., 1794) to Crockett, *Vermont*, absolving the Allens of any real attempt to put Vermont back under British rule. More balanced accounts are Wardener, "The Haldimand Negotiations" and "Journal of a Loyalist Spy Justus Sherwood," *The Vermonter* 28 (1923); Jellison, *Ethan Allen*, chap. 13; A. J. H. Richardson, "Chief Justice William Smith and the Haldimand Negotiations," *Proceedings of the Vermont Historical Society* 9 (no. 2, June 1941): 84–114; and Williamson, *Quandary*, chaps. 7 and 8 (perhaps the best short treatment).

outer limits of politically acceptable behavior, to ill-judged acts, which were frequently as chimerical as they were desperate. When he wrote of these acts, Ira defended himself from the consequences of his last grand fiasco, a plot to wrest Canada from British control. Ira believed that the interpretation of his role in the Haldimand Affair contained the key to establish his honesty and good intention toward the British and Canada, as well as to buttress his fading reputation in Vermont. One of the most notable features of the *History* was Allen's reluctance to use his own name, manifested by his frequent reference to himself in the third person. His biographer attributed this to modesty,[20] but it could also have been his desire to obscure his own leadership and to give the appearance of his being inexorably swept along by events.

While both contemporaries and subsequent observers have argued about what really happened in the negotiations, none denied that a handful of Vermont's leaders secretly flirted with the British. They only debated whether the flirtation actually became an affair. Generations of Vermont historians have defended their heroes and have praised the Allens for protecting Vermont by cleverly neutralizing the British military threat through prolonged innocent negotiations while at the same time shrewdly leaking news of the talks to force recognition of Vermont's independence from Congress. This generous interpretation stemmed directly from Ira Allen. He began to build the case for his innocence even as the negotiations proceeded by preparing several versions of the same documents to protect the conspirators whichever way the affair turned out.[21] Then in his *History*, omitting crucial details and changing others, Allen declared his honorable intentions toward both his suitors in Canada and his mistress, Vermont.

Impartial scholars, uninterested in enshrining local heroes and using Canadian and British sources not doctored to obscure the truth, have reached another verdict. They demonstrated that

20. Wilbur, *Ira Allen*, 2: 162.
21. Wardener, "Haldimand Negotiations," pp. 17–18.

British reports, which had no reason to alter fact, revealed the serious intentions of the Vermonters. In addition, these scholars noted the repeal of the statute banishing Tories and the rapid appointment of Tories to public office which caused widespread public comment. They also pointed to Ira Allen's and Joseph Fay's specific request that General Haldimand issue a proclamation with the terms for Vermont's return to the British and have a military force ready to handle opposition. Yet in his *History*, Allen changed his own request to a British demand and claimed that "the Agents of Vermont were unpleasantly situated at these proposals." Ira Allen knew full well what a dangerous business he had embarked upon. After carefully telling a story built on partial truths to the Vermont Assembly (with British agents in the gallery), Allen smugly noted the curiosity of "opposite parties perfectly satisfied with one statement, and each believing what they wished to believe, and thereby deceiving themselves."[22] As an accomplice in many incidents of gross duplicity, doubled sets of documents, deliberate half-truths, and even forgery, Ira Allen's account of the affair must be seriously questioned.

The evidence on the Haldimand Affair has been arranged and rearranged to support many theses, but one version best fits the facts: the Allens seriously attempted a reconciliation. Applying A. L. Burt's apt metaphor, "the master key of his guilt" opened the door. "Then, instead of having to pick lock after lock, we pass right through."[23] However one chooses to view Allen's behavior, either the British or the Vermont revolutionaries had to have been the intended victims of Allen's duplicity. And that realization must have perplexed Allen himself when writing the *History*, a book designed to establish at once his own good character, the innocence of his intentions toward Canada, and his credentials as a loyal Vermonter and American. That his work succeeded in becoming a major and too often relied upon source in accounts of

22. Allen, *History*, pp. 108, 115.
23. Burt, *The United States, Great Britain and British North America*, p. 172.

the affair and of early Vermont political life attested to his dexterity in concocting the story.

Unhappily for the conspirators, the veil of secrecy enshrouding the negotiations was unexpectedly lifted, revealing what their growing legion of enemies clearly regarded as treason. The stunning American victory at Yorktown, British war-weariness, and the generous peace of Paris ended Vermont's chances of rejoining the empire and discredited those who had actively pursued it. The Allens' policy could no longer be the same as Vermont's, whose independence remained officially unrecognized but tacitly conceded. Yet soon after the peace came into effect, Ira Allen and other "persons of Influence in the State of Vermont" hastened to Quebec where "They made no scruple" of telling Haldimand "that Vermont must either be annexed to Canada or become Mistress of it, as it is the only channel by Which the Produce of Their Country can be conveyed to market."[24]

With the question of independence no longer a burning issue, the commercial aspects of their plans came more clearly into the open. Having moved north to their estates in the Onion River country, the Allens and others worked to gain commercial access to the St. Lawrence. They bombarded the Quebec government with petitions for special trading permits. In 1785 Ira Allen journeyed to Quebec as an agent of the "republic" of Vermont to negotiate for free trade.[25] He tried to convince Haldimand of the efficacy of a ship canal between Lake Champlain and the St. Lawrence that would admit ocean-going vessels to Vermont ports. The British later undertook a survey of the proposal and judged the project too expensive and perhaps politically inexpedient, as it would make Quebec more vulnerable to invasion.[26]

24. Haldimand to Lord North, Quebec, 24 October 1783 (private), in *Documents Relating to the Constitutional History of Canada, 1759–1791,* 2 vols., ed. Adam Shortt and Arthur G. Doughty (Ottawa, 1918), 2: 735–736.

25. Vermont, *Governor and Council,* 1: 160; and Public Archives of Canada (hereafter PAC), Q, 24, part 2: 289–290.

26. Williamson, *Quandary,* pp. 150–151; Wilbur, *Ira Allen,* 1: 437; G. P. deT. Glazebrook, *A History of Transportation in Canada,* 2 vols. (Toronto,

The Allens gradually withdrew from public life, Ethan to his farm where he dabbled in philosophy, Ira to his business interests. In the meantime, the republic they had helped to found drew closer to the United States, and negotiations with New York to achieve statehood, which began in 1787, reached fruition when Vermont became the fourteenth state in February 1791. The Allens feared that the growing national unity institutionalized by the federal Constitution would threaten Vermont's latitude of action. In February 1788 Ethan lectured the Governor of the Province of Quebec, Lord Dorchester, "on the subject of American Politicks," reiterating the importance of the St. Lawrence route, and informing him that previously "could Great Britain have offered Vermont protection," it would have rejoined the empire. Vermont, he added, should now maintain its independence until "they can on the principle of mutual interest and advantage return to the British Government without war, or annoyance, from the United States."[27] Working with brother Levi, a Loyalist conveniently located at St. John on the Richelieu River, the Allen brothers endeavored to return Vermont to the British.[28] Ethan died in 1789, but Ira and Levi kept the scheme alive. In 1790, as Vermont grew close to statehood, Levi went on a secret mission to London to sell their "large plan."[29] Yet Ira at home could clearly tell which way the winds blew, and he wrote to Levi, advising him to forget politics

1964), 1: 84–85; and *Report of the Canadian Archives* (hereafter CAR) *1889* (Ottawa, 1890), note F.

27. Ethan Allen to Dorchester, July 16, 1788, quoted in Wilbur, *Ira Allen*, 1: 509–512.

28. See Muller, "Commercial History," pp. 92–101. "If the large plan takes place shall not begrudge the time nor cost . . . but otherwise all is lost, and I shall retire from the bussel of the world to the deserts of St. Albans, there with my Nancy, dog and gun be contented with the little simple natures requires and no longer grasp and reach beyond my strength for baubles on the other side of the Atlantic. (ah Says, the fox Sour grapes when he could not reach them.)" Allen MSS, Levi Allen to Ira Allen, 11 October 1788.

29. Ira and Levi tried to disguise the true nature of the mission, and Levi wrote to Ira using a steady stream of fictitious names such as "Bumper B," "Constantine Alonzo," "D. Alonzo," "Americanus D'Alonzo," or "Americanus D. Allen." See Allen MSS from 1787 to 1791.

and concentrate on winning a mast contract. Ira knew that to "try to convince people of the south end of the State with their prejudices is not worth the attempt," and with resignation voted along with the vast majority at the special convention at Bennington to ratify the Constitution of the United States.[30] The persistent notion of many Vermont historians that the Allens had deliberately kept Vermont out of the Union until such time as the state could extort favorable terms of entry did not match the evidence.[31] Ira Allen made no observation on the issue in his *History*.

During the first years following statehood, Ira Allen retired from public life and concentrated on his widespread business interests, which had reached a critical juncture. Most of his reputedly vast wealth lay in undeveloped land which did not yet provide cash income. In addition, he faced serious challenges to the legality of his claim to many acres acquired when he held various state offices, particularly that of surveyor-general. Near Burlington he erected a forge and an anchor shop, and he traded in various agricultural commodities, but the major commercial undertaking involved sending huge lumber rafts each spring to Canada, where he sold the wood to Quebec merchants (middlemen Levi identified as "the sharpers at Q——"). Over the years in Quebec Allen had accumulated large debts, which he secured on the promise of the following year's timber sales. A long period of depressed prices, oversupply, usurious interest rates, the high risks of transit, and the capricious and monopsonistic market frustrated his hopes of clearing a substantial profit, much less of paying his anxious creditors. Allen had far overextended his investments in relation to his ability to develop the cash flow to protect them. By the mid-1790s, unable to borrow to meet the pressing demands of his investments, his creditors and his tax load, Allen was desperate. Rather than blame his own over-

30. Ibid., Ira Allen to Levi Allen, Colchester, Vermont, 4 January 1790; and Ira Allen to Levi Allen, February 7, 1790 quoted in Williamson, *Quandary*, p. 183.
31. For example see Crockett, *Vermont*, 2: 493–496.

extension and slipshod business methods, he found a culprit in his inability to reach the St. Lawrence *entrepôts* and European markets without passing through British regulations and merchants. A ship canal to the St. Lawrence would answer his needs and get him past the greedy Quebec middlemen; were this impossible, as in 1775, the Green Mountain Boys would once again have to fall upon Canada.[32]

During the early 1790s, as the crisis in Anglo-American relations deepened, authorities in Canada expressed serious apprehensions about the hostile intentions of many of the "Vermontese," as well as about the safety of their colony. From Philadelphia the notorious Citizen Genét countenanced and encouraged much loose talk about a French-inspired filibustering expedition to "liberate" Canada with the avid support of the Green Mountain Boys. The appearance of a few French agents and rumors of blank French army commissions floating around Vermont made the British nervous. The rambunctious statements made by the anglophobe Democratic-Republican Societies in Chittenden, Addison, and Rutland counties lent credibility to Genét's flamboyant claims, but the signing of the Jay Treaty, very unpopular in Vermont, momentarily laid the French plots to rest.[33]

The Jay Treaty did not please Ira Allen. But by late 1795, using much of his land as collateral, he financed a voyage to Europe, where he hoped finally to secure his ends. If he could not sell his plans for a ship canal to the British, he would deal directly with the French. Once again, unfortunately for Ira, his ambitions ran counter to the policy of the United States, which had just made

32. Allen MSS, Levi Allen to Ira Allen, October 11, 1788. For a description of Allen's commercial operations and the climate with which they contended see Muller, "Commercial History," chap. 3, and "Floating a Lumber Raft to Quebec City, 1805: The Journal of Guy Catlin of Burlington," *Vermont History* 39 (Spring 1971): 116–124; Williamson, *Quandary*, pp. 223–225; Wilbur, *Ira Allen*, 2: chaps. 20–23; and many documents in the Allen MSS.

33. CAR, 1921, appendix B; and Eugene P. Link, *Democratic-Republican Societies, 1790–1800* (New York, 1942), pp. 142–143.

peace with the British and increasingly grew hostile to the French.[34]

Allen embarked for England in December 1795, arriving in London early the next year. He arranged an interview with the Duke of Portland, Home Secretary and twice formerly the Prime Minister. Forewarned of Allen's probable hostility to Canada, Portland treated the plans for a canal in the best noncommittal bureaucratic tradition. After several subsequent attempts to win acceptance of the scheme met frustration, Allen secretly slipped out of London for France on May 20, 1796.[35] On July 11, 1796, he concluded an agreement with the French Directory to wrest Canada from the British.

Allen's extraordinary agreement with the Directory has come to light in a document drafted by Talleyrand, a private memorandum meant only for French eyes and with no obvious reason to be falsified. The plan called for a French naval force to fall on Halifax in August 1797 and, successful or not, to proceed to Quebec to form a crushing pincer with an army of Green Mountain Boys coming north from Vermont. The Directory, realizing that despite his great stature and reputed wealth, Allen would need aid, agreed to furnish 20,000 muskets and bayonets, twenty-four field pieces, gun carriages and cannon wagons. Allen agreed to pay for the arms at the end of seven years, meanwhile paying a modest interest rate of 5 percent. To guard against the arms being seized on the seas by the British as French contraband, the Directory furnished Allen with a false invoice stating they were his and showing he had made an initial payment of over 100,000 *livres*. In addition, they granted him a loan of 200,000 *livres*. Had the deal not miscarried, Allen stood to clear at least $50,000 on selling the arms in Vermont, enough to shore up his sagging fortunes.[36]

In September, 1796, Allen hurried back to London, making one last-ditch attempt to negotiate for adoption of his canal plan. Fail-

34. Wilbur, *Ira Allen*, 2: 80–85.
35. Ibid., p. 89.
36. Ibid., pp. 191–199, 220.

ing in this, he returned to the Continent to supervise the loading of the arms at Ostend in a ship gloriously misnamed the *Olive Branch*. The whole scheme ended on November 20, 1796, when a British ship captured the *Olive Branch* in mid-channel and, charging that the arms were French and therefore contraband, took the ship and its cargo to England to wait disposition by the Admiralty Courts.[37]

Allen, of course, claimed the arms as his own, intended for the ill-equipped Vermont militia. His credibility was further diminished by news from Lower Canada that another French-inspired plot had been discovered along the Vermont-Canadian border and that one American acting as a French agent had been hanged as a result. M. Adet, a successor worthy of Genét, had revived the old plans, this time more seriously. The British could not easily accept the idea that the 20,000 muskets were not eventually meant for an attack on Canada.[38]

Ira Allen spent the next year and a half in England trying to extricate himself from this predicament, much of the time in a form of house arrest caused by the actions of his growing list of English creditors. He left no stone unturned, no avenue unexplored in his frantic attempt to have the arms released. In May 1798 he foolishly returned to France to get further evidence of his ownership of the arms. Unfortunately, the political climate in France had taken a nasty turn and perhaps because of his return to England to negotiate after his agreement with the Directory, the French had him arrested, and except for a brief period he languished in a Parisian prison until September 1799.[39]

The arms were finally released by the British at the urging of the United States Secretary of State, Timothy Pickering, who reluctantly believed some of the many affidavits Allen had had written to support his innocence. When the arms arrived in New York,

37. Ibid., pp. 93, 99–102.
38. CAR, *1891*, note D; and Burt, *United States, Great Britain, and British North America*, pp. 174–177.
39. Wilbur, *Ira Allen*, chaps. 26, 27.

the state of Vermont refused to buy them, thereby sealing Allen's financial doom. He eventually returned to Vermont a broken and discredited man, his land having been sold to satisfy creditors and tax obligations. He left Vermont for good in the fall of 1804 under the threat of a legal suit brought by the heirs of his former associates in the old Onion River Land Company, who claimed Ira had defrauded them of their rights. He passed the remainder of his life in exile in Philadelphia, unable to pay his creditors, writing tracts to redeem his good name, and dabbling in a fanciful scheme to win Mexican independence.[40] Even from a French prison cell or in Pennsylvania, he never ceased believing in the importance of canals and in the close geographical relationship of Vermont and Canada.

James B. Wilbur's evaluation that Allen's *History* "still remains the best political history of Vermont" does not reflect well on Wilbur's objectivity, nor does it flatter students of early Vermont political history. In reality the book had little to do with an accurate presentation of history. Allen began the book in mid-May 1797, shortly after he decided against returning to Vermont in order to remain in England and argue for the return of the confiscated arms. He wrote it hastily, as it represented only one of his many efforts to prove his contention (including at the same time publication of another book specifically on the *Olive Branch* affair). Allen began the brief preface of the *History* by admitting that "one reason amongst others that led to the publication of this memoir, was the proceedings of the High Court of Admiralty of England."[41] He wanted to answer questions about the character of both Vermont and himself that the proceedings following the capture of the *Olive Branch* had raised.

Allen hoped that the *History* would lend narrative support and also put into context many of the documents he was busy

40. Allen's books on the *Olive Branch* affair alone amounted to eight volumes filling over 1600 pages. See the bibliography in Ibid., 2: 528–530.
41. Ibid., 2: 121, 130. Wilbur even compares the *History* to Marco Polo's travels (p. 162). Allen, *History*, p. 9.

collecting and having manufactured. He knew the necessity of demonstrating that the Vermont militia actually needed such substantial armaments and to that end had a map of the state drawn to show the vulnerability of its frontiers.[42] The map later appeared with the *History*. In addition, he sought to establish the intimate relationship with Canada and his own long-standing friendly and honorable attitude toward the colony on the St. Lawrence. Allen also feared that his very visible role in winning ultimate recognition of the New Hampshire and Vermont land titles to the detriment of the many influential Loyalists who held New York patents would militate against him in England. The *History* paid much attention to the land controversy, the plight of the settlers, and the justice of his actions supporting them, while largely ignoring the less savory motivations of the speculators he represented. Wherever possible he avoided calling attention to or ascribing even innocuous actions to himself.

Writing to Stephen Thorn on June 9, 1797, Samuel Peters revealed the true nature of the book. The Reverend Samuel Peters, an ambitious adventurer in Anglican cleric's clothing, had been in Vermont before the Revolution and liked to take credit for naming the state. A Loyalist, he left during the war for England, where he wrote about Vermont and actively worked for its return to the empire. With the promise of a sinecure as Anglican Bishop of Vermont and President of the University of Vermont (founded, at least on paper, by Ira Allen), Peters had happily joined Allen's conspiracy and was most anxious to have the arms returned and shipped to Vermont for the attack on Canada before Britain and France could negotiate an armistice. Sharing Allen's haste to complete the *History*, Peters helped write and edit the manuscript. "Time is wanted," he wrote, "to put proper documents and quotations necessary to make a history of it." Then, thinking of their plans, "besides the object in view, of some consequence to others, will perish with Port Admiral Parker, by a

42. Colonel William Tatham to John King, Under-Secretary in the British Foreign Office, April 19, 1798, quoted in Wilbur, *Ira Allen*, 2: 169–170.

ger.eral peace—for 1797—then a fig for future sorrows and foreign coasts to I, thou [Thorn], he [Allen] and me."[43]

A third man, Stephen Thorn, also worked on the manuscript in those months of frantic activity in May and June 1797. Allen had known Thorn in Granville, New York, a town temporarily annexed to Vermont in 1781. An ardent republican, Thorn preferred not to live under a government headed by an anglophobe like George Washington and had joined a group of Americans living in France. Allen had seen him there while negotiating with the Directory, borrowed some money, and undoubtedly confided in him at least part of his scheme to remove Canada from the British Crown.[44]

Anxious to leave London and return to France, Thorn became exasperated working with Allen's "scrawl." Regarding it as repetitious, he asked for Peters's aid. "I conceive it not necessary," Thorn wrote, "to make a long story about nothing." He cautioned Peters "to follow the General Allen's ideas and language . . . as he concludes his style is superior to that of Demosthenes, or Robespierre and do not put him out of that conceit and let the history be what it will a . . . ."[45] Peters joined Thorn in lamenting the difficulty in working with Ira's text, "any thing not exactly conformable to Vermont ideas and family egotism will be rejected." Peters thought that Allen should "depart from 1,000 things in his manuscript or be damned . . . half of his sentences are imperfect and he chuses his own way, why in the name of common sense does he torment you and me with four pages about nothing? All his story about Gale [a Yorker surveyor] is in a nut shell and resembles the man who went around a copse of wood expecting to find a bear and when he got round he did not find a bear." The Gale story did appear, though probably not all four

43. Williamson, *Quandary*, pp. 233–235; Allen MSS, Peters to Thorn, June 9, 1797.
44. Ibid., Ira Allen to Thorn, London, May 24, 1797, June 20, 1797, and July 24, 1797; Wilbur, *Ira Allen*, 2: 89.
45. Allen MSS, Thorn to Peters, London, June 8, 1797.

manuscript pages of it.[46] Despite Peters's and Thorn's work, the manuscript belonged largely to Allen. Its dryness and run-on sentences, built phrase-on-phrase as evidence is introduced, reflected Allen's years of drafting political tracts and government documents. The book has little of the lighter, clever touch that marked Peters's work. "I wish you to burn all I have done after you have gutted it," Peters ordered Thorn, "for if the Genl. will print according to his own plan—I wish never to see it."[47]

The collaborators all relied heavily on Dr. Samuel Williams's *The Natural and Civil History of Vermont*, which Allen had brought to London. "I am writing from memory," Allen admitted, "but Williams has a number of matters in his history that are correct. I furnished him with many of the materials for that purpose." At the time Williams wrote his book, he asked Allen for documents on the Haldimand Affair, promising that "They shall be kept entirely secret till I have your advice on the Matter." Ironically, Allen, for much of the information in his own book, found himself at the mercy of a source he may have previously censored. Most of the natural history came from Williams, as did many of the copious quotations of documents, though Wilbur illogically attributed this to the author's having been the principal actor in the events under discussion. Even Peters and Thorn admitted the impossibility of making progress without Williams's book.[48]

By June 1, 1797, Peters thought he could have the *History* ready for printing within a week and claimed he could have been ready earlier if he "could have read the general's writting"—remarkably rapid completion for a book begun only two or three weeks before. Peters's optimism notwithstanding, January and February of the next year found Allen still at work on the *History*, and not until

46. Ibid., Peters to Thorn, June 9, 1797; Allen, *History*, p. 36.
47. Allen MSS, Peters to Thorn, June 9, 1797.
48. Williamson, *Quandary*, p. 229; Samuel Williams, *The Natural and Civil History of Vermont*; Allen MSS, Ira Allen to Thorn, June 14, 1797, Samuel Williams to Ira Allen, Rutland, Vermont, July 11, 1792, Thorn to Ira Allen, May 1797.

May 1798 did J. Myer of No. 2 Paternoster Row in London publish the volume, nearly a year after work on it commenced. However, Allen apparently circulated the manuscript to key figures in an attempt to put it to work before the actual publication date. Peters suggested that the manuscript was readable by summer of 1797, and the map drafted for the book had already been circulated. In addition, the book included an appendix, addressed to a person who had read the manuscript and posed questions about Vermont to the author, a gentleman of some stature obsequiously referred to by Allen as "one of the few that looks for nothing beyond truth and plain language."[49]

Evidently Allen thought that the *History* did much to help his case and reputation. While in France he often sent copies to officials he hoped to impress.[50] After returning to the United States, where he continued to publish prodigiously to establish the manifold wrongs he suffered, he set about a revision of the *History*.[51] In 1805 he sought to have the state of Vermont underwrite the costs of publication of a revised edition, and in return, promised to give a copy to every legally incorporated town in the state. Vermont refused the proposition, and the revised edition was never published. By 1805 even Allen had trouble finding a copy upon which to base his revision, as most of the copies had been impounded by the executors of his publisher's estate against the debt owed by Allen.[52] Because of its scarcity, the Vermont Historical Society republished the *History* in 1870.

That a reviewer of the recent reprinting of Ira Allen's *History* could seriously contend that "there is no better evidence than Ira Allen's account of the beginnings of Vermont that the best way to tell history is in the lives of those who made it," or that it should be included in a volume devoted to the classics of American his-

49. Ibid., Peters to Thorn, London, July 1, 1797; Wilbur, *Ira Allen*, 2: 175; Allen, *History*, p. 155.
50. Allen MSS, Ira Allen to Minister of the Interior, Gravelines, France, May 20, 1798; Ira Allen to the Minister of Police, Gravelines, France, May 20, 1798; and Ira Allen to Petiet, late Minister of War, September 4, 1799.
51. Allen MSS, Peters to Ira Allen, London, September 10, 1802.
52. Wilbur, *Ira Allen*, 2: 395, 422.

tory bears testimony to its continued reputation and pervasiveness.[53] The work has tyrannized Vermont historians for generations; moreover, a continuing fascination with the colorful Allens and the domination of the state's early history by their version has led to an unfortunate neglect of other important groups and their role in the founding and early development of Vermont.

Because of the reasons for which Allen wrote it, his heavy reliance on memory and the previously expurgated Williams text, and his obvious distortion of many facts, *The Natural and Political History of the State of Vermont* should be viewed as Allen's account and only that. We know, after all, that "anything not exactly conformable to Vermont ideas and family egotism" was in Peters's judgment, "rejected." Even granting this, the *History* remains doubly suspect in that it was an account written in 1797–1798 some years after the key events. Not only may a historian's memory fail him in such circumstances, but a man's perspective on a set of events will change over time. Thus we must recognize that a history of Vermont written earlier, when Allen had a different set of objectives and needed to influence a different set of people, probably would have turned out very differently.

Allen's *History*, then, must be used with extreme care. But this should not blind us to the fact that, when so used, it still offers the historian a valuable insight into early Vermont in general and a very dynamic, resourceful, and important man in particular. Ira Allen was not an ordinary mortal, even to his most hostile critics.

One speculates whether Allen's perspective was better than his *History* suggested, and one is tempted to find deliberate irony in a paraphrase of Adam Smith with which he concluded the final paragraph:

Machiavellian policy has long been celebrated, though it has been as long destroying the noblest production of nature, the rapid increase of people, the strength, prosperity, and wealth of nations.[54]

He might well have written his own epitaph!

53. Review by Ralph Nading Hill in *Vermont History*, 37 (Autumn 1969): 292–293.
54. Allen, *History*, p. 154.

5.

Jeremy Belknap and the History of New Hampshire

JERE DANIELL

No early nineteenth-century American history has had a better press than Jeremy Belknap's three-volume *History of New Hampshire*. Fellow historian David Ramsay, for example, after reading parts of the study, labeled Belknap "indefatigable, intelligent, impartial and well informed." Benjamin Rush was so impressed that he asked Belknap to write a history of the establishment of the federal government. Two generations later—after the *History* had been republished twice—Alexis de Tocqueville remarked that "the reader of Belknap will find more general ideas and more strength of thought than are to be met with in other historians, even to the present day." Twentieth-century commentators have been equally generous with their praise. John Spencer Bassett applauded Belknap's "modern spirit," as well as the "fine sense of proportion and ease of expression" which marked his writing. Michael Kraus, who has devoted much of his scholarly life to a study of American historiography, concluded that "Jeremy Belknap belongs in the very front rank of historians who wrote in the revolutionary period. So close in spirit to the modern historians was his approach," Kraus added, echoing Bassett's exact thought, "that his work has been of lasting value." Clifford Shipton's biographical sketch of Belknap included a comment that the *History* "still stands as a priceless record."[1]

1. Letter from Ramsay, August 11, 1792, Andrews-Eliot Papers no. 159, Massachusetts Historical Society, Boston (hereafter MHS); Rush to Belknap, January 5, 1791, MHS *Collections*, 6th series, vol. 4 (Boston, 1891): 473;

Like many a "priceless record," however, the *History of New Hampshire* has received much more praise than careful study. In part, this stems from New Hampshire's marginal importance in the history of colonial America: had Belknap settled in Massachusetts and written about that commonwealth, his work undoubtedly would have received greater attention. In a period dominated by politics, Belknap was a literary figure, and that also contributed to his and his *History*'s low profile. Virtually every important military and political figure of Belknap's era has his modern biography, yet its publicists, historians, and men of letters remain unexplored. Belknap has been the subject of only two biographical sketches, one by his granddaughter in the mid-nineteenth century and the other a twenty-page summary by Clifford Shipton.[2]

Indeed, one index of the low priority accorded to Belknap's work by historians is the fact that the one substantial assessment of his *History* has been written by a professor of English. In 1964 Sidney Kaplan's *"The History of New Hampshire:* Jeremy Belknap as Literary Craftsman" appeared in the *William and Mary Quarterly.* Kaplan emphasized Belknap's difficulty in finding and maintaining a strong central theme for his study, his failure to solve the problem of organizing complex sets of material, and his reliance on anecdote to give force to his narrative. Kaplan also dealt with the way in which Belknap's own perceptions affected his treatment of historical phenomena. Belknap tried hard to remain the dispassionate observer, but failed. His *History* reflected his point of view in all its parts. Sometimes he played the secular and scientific historian, sometimes the New England parson dispensing conventional morality. Above all, according to Kaplan,

---

Alexis De Tocqueville, *Democracy in America,* ed. Phillips Bradley (New York, 1945), 2:349; John S. Bassett, *Middle Group of American Historians* (New York, 1917), p. 24; Michael Kraus, *The Writing of American History* (Norman, Okla., 1953), p. 73; Clifford K. Shipton, *Biographical Sketches of Those Who Attended Harvard College* (*Sibley's Harvard Graduates,* vols. 4–15 [Boston, 1933–   ]), 15: 180.

2. [Jane B. Marcou], *Life of Jeremy Belknap* (New York, 1847); Shipton, *Biographical Sketches,* 15: 175–195.

Belknap applauded the value of rationality; so much so, in fact, that one might view man's use of his rational powers as the primary theme of the *History*. Belknap, then, was very much a man of the Enlightenment, who accepted its values and encouraged others to follow his example—his supposedly objective study of New Hampshire, as a result, reflected the "constant judgment of a conscious partisan."[3]

Kaplan's sensitive and probing analysis should be read by anyone trying to understand either Belknap or his study of New Hampshire. But the article has its limitations. Kaplan did not use the Belknap Papers in the Massachusetts and New Hampshire historical societies, and these collections—the one in Boston especially—contain unpublished correspondence about the *History*, notes that Belknap used in preparing his volumes, and a good deal of material about his personal life. More important, Kaplan's emphasis on literary analysis meant, as he half-apologetically noted, that he could not "illustrate the play of Belknap's critical intelligence at length."[4] He only explored two examples of Belknap's enlightened rationalism in detail: his liberal attitude toward American Indians, and his criticism of the religious intolerance of early New England Puritans. More can be said about the way in which Belknap's intellectual assumptions and perceptions affected his *History*. Finally, Kaplan did not spend much time discussing how and why Belknap wrote the *History of New Hampshire*. Earlier critics, John Spencer Bassett more than others, have dealt with the problem, but mostly in mechanical terms. No one has satisfactorily explained, for example, why Belknap set such high standards of scholarship for himself, or what inner resources enabled him to overcome the immense difficulties he encountered in completing his project.

This essay supplements the work begun by Professor Kaplan and

---

3. Sidney Kaplan, "*The History of New Hampshire:* Jeremy Belknap as Literary Craftsman," *William and Mary Quarterly*, 3d series, 21 (1964): 18–39. The quotation is from p. 31.

4. Ibid., p. 33.

his predecessors; it proceeds on the basic premise that the *History of New Hampshire* can best be understood as ideological biography. Quite apart from what Belknap tells us about New Hampshire, his work reflects the changing pattern of his personal concerns and values between the early 1770s, when he first drew up a plan for the *History*, and the early 1790s when he finally published the second and third volumes. As narrative history, Belknap's study has been supplanted,[5] but it remains a rich and revealing document, one which students of late eighteenth-century American culture should exploit more fully.

Jeremy Belknap's decision to write a history of New Hampshire stemmed in part from his long exposure to men fascinated by study of the past. Throughout his early life he maintained a close relationship with his uncle, Mather Byles (a grandson of Increase Mather), whose interest in New England's history undoubtedly affected the content of their discussions. Moreover, Thomas Prince, who in 1736 had published A *Chronological History of New England in the Form of Annals* and who probably owned the largest collection of historical documents in colonial America, ministered to the church attended by the Belknap family. Jeremy listened to his sermons, came under the influence of his counseling, and witnessed his mentor's passion for historical understanding. Formal education under John Lovell at the Boston Latin School further stimulated the young intellectual. By 1759, when he entered Harvard at the age of fourteen, Belknap had already developed what he later described as a "natural curiosity to enquire into the original settlement, progress, and improvement" of his native land. In fact, he may already have been thinking about writing history. The first entry in a notebook of miscellaneous quotations, which he started in 1758, was a passage from Laurence Echard's *Roman History*. "There are required so many qualifications and accomplishments in an *Historian*, and so much

5. See especially Charles E. Clark, *The Eastern Frontier* (New York, 1970) and Jere R. Daniell, *Experiment in Republicanism* (Cambridge, Mass., 1970).

care and niceness in writing *History*," Belknap copied, underlining for emphasis, "that some have reckoned it *one of the most difficult labors human nature is capable of*."[6]

Belknap's decision was also a function of personal circumstances. His interest in history had been diluted by the general intellectual excitement of his college years and by the unsettled conditions of life following his graduation in 1762. First he worked as a schoolmaster in Milton. Next he moved to Portsmouth, New Hampshire, where he taught and studied theology under a local congregational minister. A year later, in 1765, Belknap moved to neighboring Greenland, where he kept still another school and went through "many agonies of soul" trying to decide whether his failure to experience conversion disqualified him from entering the ministry. Sympathy with the plight of American natives led the anxious young man to consider joining the staff of Eleazer Wheelock's Indian Charity School. Belknap, however, had little tolerance for confusion and indecision. Convinced by his Uncle Mather that many of New England's most sensitive and effective clergymen had never been dramatically "converted," and warned by friends and relatives against becoming involved with anyone as unpredictable as Wheelock, Belknap made known his intention to enter the ministry. In January 1767, he accepted a call to the First Congregational Church in Dover. Love may have had something to do with his decisions, for the following spring he married Ruth Eliot of Boston. In any case, soon after the newlyweds settled, Belknap found time to pursue the discipline which had so excited him a decade earlier.

Location dictated the direction of his studies, since no published history existed of Belknap's adopted province. Furthermore, nearby Portsmouth contained many a cache of the old records that

6. The quotations are from Jeremy Belknap, *The History of New Hampshire*, 3 vols. (Philadelphia and Boston, 1784–1792) 1: iii, and Quotidiana Miscellanea no. 1, Belknap Papers no. 161. Ja. 3, MHS. Most of the biographical details here and in the rest of the essay are taken from Shipton, *Biographical Sketches*, 15: 175–195. For Prince's influence see David D. Van Tassel, *Recording America's Past* (Chicago, 1960), pp. 21–22.

he, like Thomas Prince, so loved to explore. Not one to hide his ambitions—in the 1790s he advised those who shared his interests not to wait "at home for things to fall into the lap" but to "prowl about like a wolf for prey"—Belknap soon parlayed his acquaintance with some of New Hampshire's leading clergymen and political officials into access to those records. As he explained in the preface to the first volume of the *History*, he soon "met with some valuable manuscripts which were but little known" and "began to extract and methodize the principle things in them"; this activity quickly became his "hobby horse." By 1772 it became something closer to an avocation. "You cannot help having observed in me an inquisitive disposition in historical matters," Belknap wrote Thomas Waldron, a provincial councillor and close friend of Governor John Wentworth. "I find it so strong and powerful . . . that it has become a question with me whether I might not freely indulge it, with a view to the benefit of my fellow man, as well as for my own improvement." He also mentioned to Waldron that as of late he had made it his "principal amusement" to read and to interview "aged and intelligent persons" about early town and provincial history.[7]

Belknap did "freely indulge" himself for the next three years. He continued with his interviews, spent much time reading and collating government documents provided by Theodore Atkinson, the provincial secretary, and Governor Wentworth himself, and even used some of the time set aside for preparing sermons to work out historical problems. He also began to write. By July 1774, when Belknap drew up perhaps the first detailed plan for his projected *History of New Hampshire*, he had already drafted several parts of the manuscript. Chapters 1 and 2, which dealt with discovery and settlement, were almost completed. Much of the religious history, which he planned to include in the third chapter, had been worked out as his Thanksgiving sermon the previous

7. Belknap to Hazard, August 21, 1795, *MHS Collections*, 5th series, 3 (Boston, 1877): 357; Belknap, *History*, 1: iii; Belknap to Waldron, quoted in Bassett, *Middle Group*, p. 29.

winter. A chapter on King Philip's war was in an advanced stage of preparation. The rest of the *History*—at this point Belknap anticipated a single volume—would deal alternately with politics and Indian affairs, and would possibly include an appendix on the "geographical state of the province, the curiosities in natural history, etc."[8]

The scholarly habits, intellectual concerns, and moral values developed in Belknap's youth appeared in what he wrote in the early 1770s. His old mentors—Thomas Prince especially—would have applauded the thoroughness of his research. He documented details of the narrative by references to Prince's own *Annals*, John Smith's *Voyages*, the writings of Neal, Douglass, Hubbard, Hutchinson, Hume, and many others, as well as papers in a number of private and public collections. Belknap had carefully checked the various sources against each other. He later explained his technique with some precision. "Mr. Hubbard, Dr. Mather and Mr. Penhallow," he noted, again in the preface to Volume 1, "have published narratives of the several Indian wars: These have been compared with the public records, with ancient manuscripts, with Charlevoix's history of New France, and with verbal traditions of the immediate sufferers or their descendants." When the logic of his conclusions seemed questionable, Belknap planned to present his evidence in appendices. Dover's young historian, in short, did everything he could to convince potential readers of the accuracy of his story. He soon learned that he had been successful. Governor Wentworth read the first chapter and reported he could find nothing wrong with it. Other "gentlemen" whose judgment Belknap sought were equally impressed.[9]

The manuscript's scholarship impressed its early readers, but so too did the quality of mind reflected in Belknap's treatment of historical events. Like other "rationalist" historians—the term is taken from Thomas Peardon's analysis of late eighteenth-century

8. Belknap Papers no. 161, D. 95, MHS.
9. Belknap, *History*, 1: preface, chaps. 1–5; Wentworth to Belknap, November 18, 1774, *MHS Collections*, 6th series, 4 (Boston, 1891): 64.

English historical writing—and unlike, for example, Thomas Prince, Belknap went beyond mere narration. He tried to explain the underlying causes of the events he described and the motives of those who took part in those events.

Thus, when dealing with the abandonment of the first settlements on New Hampshire's seacoast, Belknap dutifully summarized Fernando Gorges's account of the reasons for their failure and then he offered his own interpretation. He suggested that the migrants had been victimized by their own preoccupation with trade and fishing and by the greediness of Gorges himself who leased his land and demanded quitrents. Had Gorges, who financed the project, granted the land outright and had the settlers practiced husbandry, Belknap suggested, different results might have followed.

At another point, he noted that earlier historians of the Indian wars had "recorded many omens, predictions, and other alarming circumstances," which they somehow linked to those tragic events. Belknap felt obliged to explain their preoccupation with such phenomena. "When men's minds were rendered gloomy by the horrors of a surrounding wilderness and the continuing apprehension of danger from its savage inhabitants, when they were ignorant of the causes of many of the common appearances in nature and were disposed to resolve every unusual appearance into prodigy and miracle," he wrote, "it is not to be wondered that they should imagine they heard the noise of drums and guns in the air and saw flaming swords and spears in the heavens, and should even interpret eclipses as ominous."[10] Other passages in the manuscript reflected Belknap's assumption that he must explain what he described.

Belknap's expression of moral sentiments widely held among the intellectual elite of New England added to the manuscript's appeal. As Sidney Kaplan has emphasized, the *History* offered a brief on the value of reason; the chapters written in the 1770s

10. Thomas P. Peardon, *The Transition in English Historical Writing, 1760–1830* (New York, 1933), pp. 34–68; Belknap, *History*, 1: 31, 132–133.

made this clear. He interlarded disapproving comments into his explanation of why others, who had written about King Philip's War, seemed so concerned with portents: in "a more philosophical and less credulous age" the omens and predictions "would not have been worthy of notice"; "these things would not have been mentioned, but to give a just idea of the age"; and, "if mankind are now better enlightened, superstition is the less excusable in its remaining votaries." Observation of riotous and adulterous behavior among New Hampshire's first clergymen elicited the following remarks: "We find in this relation a striking instance of that species of false religion which, having its seat in the imagination . . . influences the passions, stupifies the reason, and produces the wildest effects. . . . The excesses of enthusiasm have often been observed to lead to sensual gratifications."[11] Belknap included other passages which indicated his dislike for superstition, enthusiasm, and other enemies of reason.

Belknap also used the manuscript to declare his agreement with the Enlightenment emphasis on religious tolerance. That that theological conflict had played almost no part in New Hampshire's early history did not inhibit him; he simply made all of New England the subject matter of the chapter on seventeenth-century religion. The discussion of Massachusetts Bay gave him the opportunity he sought. "The idea of liberty in matters of religion," Belknap wrote, "was in that day strangely understood and mysteriously expressed." Governmental and church leaders, in fact, did not believe in the idea. They thought "liberty of conscience and toleration . . . offensive terms" and considered men who used them "to be enemies of religion and government." As a result, the Bay Colony suffered by forcing able churchmen like Roger Williams and John Wheelwright to settle elsewhere. It treated dissenters who refused to leave with inexcusable cruelty: Belknap labeled, for example, the treatment of Quakers a series of "disgraceful transactions." He concluded his remarks with a general

11. Ibid., 1: 132, 133, 46.

condemnation of commonwealth magistrates and pointed with pride to Rhode Island and Pennsylvania to support his contention that toleration "conduces greatly to the settlement and increase of an infant plantation." Belknap once advised a friend that "a preacher ought to be conversant with the history of the church, where he will find indeed much to exercise his patience." He displayed his own well-exercised patience in the third chapter of the *History of New Hampshire*.[12]

Indian-white relations provided Belknap with still another chance to articulate his convictions. Like many other New England intellectuals, Belknap found it difficult to accept the prevailing assumption that native Americans deserved the miserable fate forced on them by European migration to the New World. He may, in addition, have had some lingering regrets about deciding not to join Wheelock.

Whatever the reasons, Belknap wrote at length in the early 1770s on Indians and the Indian wars. Much of his prose was straight narrative, emphasizing the courage and endurance of settlers confronted by unpredictable, marauding savages. At the same time, however, he worked hard to correct what he felt were false generalizations about Indian behavior. Some stereotypes Belknap found impossible to refute: Indians, for example, never "gave proofs of truly masculine courage" and often engaged in unspeakable acts of "cruelty." But that was not the whole story. Indian behavior had also been marked by many "instances of justice, generosity, and tenderness," several of which Belknap narrated in detail. He noted with approval that Indians did not assault captive women sexually, and sometimes manifested an almost paternal concern for the welfare of captured children. Then there was the matter of provocation. Settlers had stolen land—Belknap described a deed purchased from Indians as "more valuable in a moral view than the grants only European princes could

12. Ibid., 1: 71–78; Belknap to Peter Thatcher, quoted in [Marcou], *Belknap*, p. 41.

convey"—sold Indians into slavery, and offered as much brutality
as their enemies. Indeed, the newcomers had started most of the
trouble. "However fond we may have been of accusing the Indian
of treachery and infidelity," Belknap concluded, "it must be confessed that the example was first set them by the Europeans. Had
we always treated them with that justice and humanity our religion inculcates, and our true interest at all times required, we
might have lived in as much harmony with them, as with any
other people on the globe."[13]

The parts of the *History of New Hampshire* completed by 1774,
then, reflected Belknap's passion for accurate scholarship, his
assumption that he should explain as well as describe observed
historical phenomena, his faith in the efficacy of applied reason,
his commitment to religious tolerance, and his belief that European settlers had unjustly treated native Americans. These habits,
concerns, and values had been nurtured at home and school, had
developed in the broad context of the intellectual excitement of
what modern historians call the Enlightenment, and had been
conditioned by Belknap's personal decision to enter the ministry.
Written history served as one vehicle for his preaching.

Belknap did little or no writing for the next five years. In the fall
of 1774 he became so ill that a local physician advised him "to
abandon study" and take "to physic and exercise"; he did not
recover completely for some time. More important, the American
Revolution complicated his affairs immensely. Frequent town
meetings, endless debates over local and state responses to the
imperial crisis, and the necessity of working out his own position
on matters of public policy all took time and energy. He also faced
new financial problems, for inflation diluted the value of the
money he received from his parishioners, and his domestic responsibilities also increased. Both his parents and his sister moved from

13. Belknap, *History*, 1: 11–18, 100–130, 195–230. The quotations are
from pp. 225, 228, 18, and 11.

Boston to Dover soon after the war began. He had to care for his own three children, and his wife, Ruth, became pregnant again in early 1776. All this made for a busy life, one in which, as he put it, his duties "as a son, a husband, a father, a pastor, and a friend" made it extremely difficult to concentrate on scholarship.[14]

Not that he gave up his project completely. Quite to the contrary, as time passed Belknap began to feel even more obligated to complete his *History* than he had before, and he became more excited about its possibilities. The excitement stemmed from his growing conviction of the Revolution's momentous nature in human history and of the potential of the self-conscious experiment in republicanism entered upon by Americans to alter fundamentally patterns of governance throughout the civilized world. What better way to advertise the Revolution and explain its meaning than to write its history?

Others shared his convictions. When Belknap asked New Hampshire's wartime president, Meshech Weare, for permission to examine state papers, Weare wrote back, "The great advantages of perpetuating memoirs of the transactions and various occurrances which may have happened in any community from its first rise never appeared to me in a more striking light than since the commencement of the present disputes." Friends throughout New Hampshire offered similar encouragement. Ebenezer Hazard, a New York book seller and postal official also interested in historical studies, not only urged Belknap to keep going, but collected documents for him and promised to help get the manuscript published. Practical considerations were also important: Belknap hoped that sales of his book would produce some much needed income.[15]

14. Belknap to Wentworth, quoted in [Marcou], *Belknap*, p. 127; Belknap to Hazard, January 13, 1784, *MHS Collections*, 5th series, 2 (Boston, 1877): 294. See also Charles C. Smith, "Financial Embarrassments of the New England Ministers of the Last Century," *American Antiquarian Society Proceedings*, 7: 129–135.

15. Weare to Belknap, June 20, 1781, *MHS Collections*, 6th series, 4 (Boston, 1891):208. Most of Belknap's lengthy correspondence with Hazard during this period is in 5th series, vol. 2 (Boston, 1877).

By 1780 he was hard at work again, interviewing, collecting and copying documents, and trying to organize his accumulation of vast amounts of material. It soon became clear that he would have to change the plans made in 1774. What he then thought would be a single chapter on late seventeenth-century politics became four separate chapters. Carrying the study through the Revolution would necessitate an additional expansion of the text, perhaps even a second volume to which he could add a "pretty long chapter" on geography and natural history. The writing itself progressed steadily. In March 1782, he informed Hazard of the completion of eleven chapters, including the ones written before the Revolution. Hazard had already arranged for publication of the first volume, which appeared in 1784.[16] By then Belknap had the second well under way and expected to have it ready in two or three years.

Like most historians, Belknap underestimated. Troubles with his congregation complicated his already complex and busy personal life. Sales of Volume 1 were discouraging. The task of writing became more difficult as he uncovered more and more material. "None but those who have tried it can tell what is the trouble of writing an history out of fresh materials as I have," he wrote a friend in 1785. "'Tis like taking a piece of wilderness to convert into a field. Many a hard knock and heavy loss be requisite in the one and many headaching and brain-perplexing hours must be spent in the other."

Belknap, however, persisted and his decision to accept a ministerial post in Boston gave him more time to write. In fact, the desire to write helped trigger the move: "My principal concern," he informed Hazard, "is to be usefully employed in such a way as shall not be a hindrance to literary improvement."[17] By the end of

16. Belknap to Hazard, April 11, 1784 and March 20, 1782, *MHS Collections*, 5th series, vol. 2 (Boston, 1877): pp. 327, 119. See also Lawrence S. Mayo, "Jeremy Belknap and Ebenezer Hazard, 1782–84," *New England Quarterly*, 2: 183–198.

17. Belknap to Paine Wingate, January 20, 1785, Belknap Papers, New Hampshire Historical Society, Concord, New Hampshire; Belknap to Hazard, 1786, *MHS Collections*, 5th series, vol. 2 (Boston, 1877): p. 429.

the decade, he had the chapters covering events through the Revolutionary War almost ready for the printer.

Time and the American Revolution had a strong impact on the chapters Belknap wrote in the 1780s. Although he remained committed to accurate scholarship, rational explanation, and the general values of the Enlightenment, he changed the way in which he expressed those commitments. To begin with, he became more cautious, or at least more sensitive to the possibility he might offend his readers. Belknap's conservatism in personal matters had been reinforced by his experiences during the Revolution. Sympathetic to the problems of men like John Wentworth, and worried lest the Revolution fall victim to emotional excesses, he had spoken out both publicly and privately. His temerity had been costly. Some thought him a Tory at heart; others suspected him, not without reason, of wanting a republican government which would preserve many imperial institutions and encompass many values implicit in the imperial system. These sentiments not only led to disagreeable verbal disputes, but infected his relationships with the congregation. He decided, therefore, to avoid future conflicts. "Our good friend Lawrence Sterne," he explained to Hazard, "calls discretion an 'understrapping virtue.' It may do for such eccentric geniuses to talk so, but we middling folks can do better with it than without it."[18]

Discretion dictated, for example, an occasional alteration in the old manuscript; for instance, at the last minute, he asked Hazard to expunge a passage suggesting that Massachusetts Bay could have kept Quakers out by less severe laws, explaining that it might "cause some uneasy sensations in the minds of some of that people." Discretion also meant bridling his critique of the actions of New Hampshire people during the Revolutionary War. Belknap included none of the bitter and ridiculing remarks about

18. Evidence of Belknap's discomfort may be found in his Memoranda Books, Belknap Papers, A. 1.6, MHS and the *MHS Collections*, 5th series, 2 (Boston, 1877): passim. The quotation is from Belknap to Hazard, October 23, 1783, ibid., p. 268.

New Hampshire, its citizens, and its government which marked his correspondence with Hazard. He said little about the tarring and feathering of Loyalists and other "excesses" which so angered him. He simply limited himself to single-sentence remarks like "jealousy, hatred, and revenge were freely indulged and the tongue of slander was under no restraint," and complained in private about the difficulty of writing contemporary history.[19]

The manuscript also reflected a reordering of Belknap's intellectual concerns. The Revolution had convinced him that politics and government had a primary importance in human affairs. Description and explanation of these developments, therefore, became his central concern. Chapter 6 of Volume 1 became Chapters 6 through 9 because he found he had so much to write. Most of Volume 2 dealt directly or indirectly with politics and government. As he became more skilled in interpreting public and private documents, political analysis became a greater and greater challenge to his powers of rational observation. To be sure, he provided a full narrative of wars and Indian relations—concerns which dominated his earlier writing—but politics clearly excited him more. He knew, for example, that he had discovered an important truth when he wrote Hazard about the problems of being a colonial governor. "They were a set of dependent creatures," he noted, "dependent on the breath of a favorite, or the smile of a minister, or the avarice of a clerk. At home they kept spies in the public offices to watch the words and looks of their superiors, and the motions of their enemies, and here they were plagued with cross assemblies, their support withheld, their views obstructed, their tempers (unless like Job) always in a fret . . . to steer between Scylla and Charybdis of offending their master and the people whom they governed, was a laborious task." Moreover,

19. The quotations are from Belknap to Hazard, October 23, 1783, ibid., p. 267, and Belknap, *History*, 2: 302. On the difficulties of writing contemporary history see Belknap to Mathew Carey, May 18, 1787 and Belknap to Hazard, August 2, 1788, *MHS Collections*, 6th series, vol. 4 (Boston, 1877): p. 337, and 5th series, vol. 3 (Boston, 1877): p. 55.

application of the general truth to the specific case of New Hampshire helped him defend the reputation of his old friend Governor Wentworth. Belknap portrayed him as a victim of impossible circumstances, unable because of events beyond his control to please both his superiors and those he governed. "His intentions were pacific" and "when matters had come to the worst his faults were as few, and his conduct as temperate as would be expected from a servant of the Crown," Belknap concluded.[20] It was a sensitive observation, one which pleased both his moral and rational faculties.

Finally, the portions of the *History of New Hampshire* written in the 1780s mirrored Belknap's own commitment to the values professed by most revolutionists of political liberty in general and republicanism in particular. This commitment gained expression in several forms. He used the language and perceptions of the revolutionists to interpret past political developments. He followed his description of jurisdictional arrangements at one point in New Hampshire history by the comment, "That mutual confidence between rulers and people which springs from the genius of a republican government is observable in all their transactions." The chapter which discussed Governor Andros and the Dominion of New England began, "when an arbitrary government is determined to infringe the liberty of people," and it included such expressions as "large strides toward despotism," government in the hands of "a set of hungry harpies," and "many instances of tyranny and oppression." Belknap cast his treatment of the unpopular Governor Cranfield in the same Whiggish mold: "Cranfield and his creatures"—the phrase was used several times—attempted to strip a liberty-loving people of their property and their political rights. In a private letter Belknap made explicit the assumption of direct linkages between past and present. "It appears that the enemies of this country," he commented when

20. Belknap to Hazard, July 18, 1783, *MHS Collections*, 5th series, vol. 2: p. 233; Belknap, *History*, 2: 296.

discussing some seventeenth-century material, "have been playing at the same game from the beginning; viz., first to provoke the people to acts of violence, and then make those acts of violence a pretext for further violences upon them."[21]

Discussion of the Revolution itself smacked of outright advocacy. Belknap began to use "we" and "us," asking in a footnote that he be excused for "expressing the feelings of an American." He talked of "the 'spirit' of venality and corruption so prevalent . . . at this time in Britain" and described at length the logic of the colonists' argument against parliamentary authority without mentioning the confused manner in which the argument developed. He noted that ideological differences became so great that only "the most delicate and judicious management" by the British could have prevented "irritation," then observed that the British had been decidedly injudicious. The Continental Congress, though "not supported by any written law," was "evidentally founded on self-preservation, the first law of nature."[22] Belknap also eagerly sought to disprove the notion, widely held in England, that the colonists had been engaged in a systematic plot to overthrow the king. He used the correspondence of the Portsmouth Sons of Liberty to prove the point. The letters, he noted, were "replete with expressions of loyalty and affection to the king, his person, family and authority. Had there been any disaffection to the royal government or desire to shake off our allegiance," he added, "where would the evidence of it be more likely to be found than in the letters which passed between bodies of men, who were avowedly endeavouring to form a union to resist the usurped authority of the British Lords and Commons?" To make sure his readers got the message, Belknap added a footnote asserting his absolute conviction that "the public professions of loyalty made by

21. Belknap, *History*, 1: 86, 153–181, 185–190; Belknap to Hazard, October 5, 1779, *MHS Collections*, 5th series, vol. 2 (Boston, 1877): p. 14.
22. Belknap, *History*, 2: 246–257, 283–292. Belknap's general interpretation fits neatly with the arguments presented by Bernard Bailyn in his *Ideological Origins of the American Revolution* (Cambridge, Mass., 1967), passim.

his countrymen were sincere."[23] Eventually he went on to other matters.

The continued existence in America of the institution of slavery offered Belknap still another opportunity to express his concern for the maintenance of political liberty. He did not dwell on the problem, in part because New Hampshire contained few slaves, in part, perhaps, because of his reluctance to criticize his fellow revolutionists too openly. But Belknap did declare his sentiments. He added them to the section on early Massachusetts history, in which he had noted laws prohibiting the selling of slaves not captured in a just war. "How long after this the importation of blacks continued to be disallowed is uncertain," Belknap wrote, "but if the same resolute justice had always been observed, it would have been much to the credit and interest of the country, and our own struggles for liberty would not have carried so flagrant an appearance of inconsistency."[24] It was a logical conclusion for one deeply committed to the dual values of tolerance and liberty.

Meanwhile Belknap had begun to focus attention on the section dealing with geography and natural curiosities. His interest in such matters had increased with time, fueled by the hope that America might become, as he put it, the "Mistress of the Sciences, as well as the Asylum of Liberty." Regular correspondence with Hazard, a member of the American Philosophical Society, provided an opportunity to exchange observations on natural phenomena. Belknap behaved cautiously at first—"I am not ambitious," he announced, "of being noticed as the author or communicant of discoveries, the truth of which will depend on my observations alone"—but he gained confidence with time. The success of Hazard's efforts to have Belknap elected as an honorary member of the society stimulated him further. Although the move to Massachusetts made personal investigation more difficult, there

23. Belknap, *History,* 2: 256. See also Belknap to Hazard, March 20, 1782, *MHS Collections,* 5th series, 2 (Boston, 1877): 121.
24. Belknap, *History,* 1: 65–66.

were compensations. Boston, unlike Dover (or even Portsmouth, for that matter), was a cosmopolitan community, many of whose inhabitants shared Belknap's intellectual concerns. New friends, including Noah Webster and Jedediah Morse, encouraged him to publish the natural history of New Hampshire. Using his old notes, information gathered on occasional trips northward, and the data he accumulated by circulating a questionnaire to clergymen in every New Hampshire town, Belknap set to work.[25] The "pretty long chapter" planned in 1784 became several. Since the second volume already seemed too long, he decided on a third. The decision had the additional advantage of making space available to append chapters on a variety of philosophical topics not treated systematically in what he already had written. By the spring of 1792 it was all over. Volume 2, to which he had added two chapters on the postwar period, had appeared already. Volume 3 was in the hands of the printer.

Belknap must have enjoyed himself immensely while drafting these last portions of the *History of New Hampshire.* Occupational security, a lessening of domestic responsibilities, and the company of educated men all had helped restore his sense of personal well-being which had evaporated during the years of revolutionary turmoil. His faith in republicanism had been at least partially restored by defeat of the Shaysites and their counterparts in New Hampshire, ratification of the federal Constitution, and the apparent stabilization of state authority throughout America. He had also begun to reap the rewards of past scholarship. The subscription lists for Volumes 2 and 3 contained a flattering number of signatures, and so many orders arrived for complete sets that a reprinting of the first volume had been necessary. The legislature of New Hampshire finally provided the subsidy he sought for nearly a decade. What pleased him most, however, was

25. Belknap to Hazard, February 4, 1780 and April 30, 1783, *MHS Collections,* 5th series, 2 (Boston, 1877): 255, 208; Belknap Papers, 161, D. 60, 161, D. 81, MHS. In the early 1780s Belknap complained about the barrenness of life in Dover with increasing frequency.

the simple fact that he was about to complete a project which, had, as he explained, "struggled with many embarrassments and . . . more than once had been thrown by as impracticable."[26] Under such circumstances Belknap felt free to discuss whatever interested him, and to moralize without constraint. He did just that.

Thus the natural history became a miscellaneous collection of observations on anything about New Hampshire of interest to Belknap. Volume 3 covered geography, climate, transportion, farming techniques, plant growth, Indian relics and monuments, animal life, commerce, industry, population statistics, examples of longevity, religion, government, social habits, and much more. He copied some passages verbatim from the journals, notebooks and correspondence accumulated over the years. Others took shape as Belknap thought out problems he had long pondered. Some of his most perceptive social analysis developed out of these speculations. He explained the reluctance to engage in agricultural experimentation as follows: "So sudden is the succession of labors that upon any irregularity in the weather, they run into one another; and if help be scarce one cannot be completed before the other suffers for want of being done. . . . It is partly from this cause, partly from the ideas of equality with which the minds of husbandmen are early impressed, and partly from a want of education, that no spirit of improvement is seen among them, but everyone pursues the business of sowing, planting, mowing, and raising cattle with unremitting labor and undeviating uniformity." Among the "native and essential characteristics" of New Hampshire's inhabitants were "firmness of nerve, patience in fatigue, intrepidity in danger, and alertness in action" which he thought a function of childhood exposure to hardship and the influence of oral traditions

26. Belknap, *History*, 3: vii. The best secondary account of the problems Belknap faced in publishing the *History* is Roland L. Schoelph, "The Versatile Dr. Belknap" (M.A. thesis, University of New Hampshire, 1941). Primary material on publication and sales is scattered throughout the Belknap Papers, MHS.

emphasizing ancestral endurance and courage.[27] This kind of commentary led de Tocqueville to praise Belknap for his "general ideas" and "strength of thought."

Belknap's moralizing appeared with increasing regularity as the manuscript progressed. Some of it was political in nature. He devoted the last two chapters of Volume 2 to a sustained polemic against paper money, legal tender laws, and insurrection; both chapters contained high praise for the Constitution and the federal government. At times he became more abstract, adding comments such as: "It was . . . necessary . . . that men should be taught . . . the folly of relying on any system of politics which, however supported by popularity, is not founded on rectitude," and "government is a science, and requires education and information as well as judgment and prudence."[28] But politics was no longer Belknap's primary concern.

By the 1790s he had become far more interested in the social dimensions of liberty, or, more precisely, in defining the behavior of a republican citizenry. For one thing, he felt that the inhabitants of New Hampshire should cut down on their drinking. Life in Dover, a lumbering community whose laborers acted much as do their modern counterparts, had made Belknap such a fanatic on the subject that he spent a great deal of effort in trying to estimate the economic cost to the state from the "unnecessary consumption of spiritous liquers." For unexplained reasons, he did not include the results of his computations—£20,411 and 12 shillings annually—in the *History*, but he did present other arguments in defense of his assertion that liquor was a "bane of society" which destroyed "health, morals, and property." Lumbermen who drank heavily, Belknap stated as a fact, were unhealthy, always in debt, and frequently at law. The first European settlers in New England used nothing stronger than beer, wine, and cider, and

27. Belknap, *History*, 3: 102, 194.
28. Ibid., 2: 352, and 3: 193. Belknap's nationalism has been analyzed in Charles W. Cole, "Jeremy Belknap: Pioneer Nationalist," *New England Quarterly*, 10: 743–751.

lived long and productive lives. The slave trade stemmed in part from the dependence of Americans on liquor; therefore, "the disuse of ardent spirits would . . . tend to abolish the infamous traffic."[29]

New Hampshiremen should also concentrate on agriculture if they wanted to live virtuous lives. Belknap had earlier suggested the theme in his *History*, through passages praising Governor Benning Wentworth for granting land to Connecticut and Massachusetts residents who were "better husbandmen than the people of New Hampshire," and praising John Wentworth for entering "vigorously into the spirit of cultivation." Now Belknap developed the idea more aggressively. At one point, he wrote, "Agriculture is, and always will be, the chief business of the people of New Hampshire if they attend to their true interest." Later, after commenting that husbandry was "much preferable to the lumber business, both in point of gain, contentment, and morals," he noted with approval that New Hampshire no longer had to import grain to feed its inhabitants. The change from importer to exporter worked to everyone's advantage. Still later Belknap repeated the point: "Those persons who attend chiefly to husbandry," he wrote, "are the most thriving and substantial."[30]

A final piece of advice had to do with education, a matter of special importance to Belknap. Formal study had shaped his own life and been in part responsible for the development of his personal values. Moreover, experiences in New Hampshire had convinced him that society should place a high value on education. As a schoolmaster he had witnessed widespread indifference to his own instruction and the general avoidance of provincial laws ordering communities to support public schools. The Revolution, if anything, had made conditions worse. So many communities ignored the laws that men interested in instruction for their families had established private academies. Belknap himself had to

29. Belknap Papers no. 161. D. 143, 161. D. 144, 161. D. 175, MHS; Belknap, *History*, 3: 197, 249–250.
30. Ibid., 2: 264, 266, and 3: 105, 156–157, 197.

educate his own children—a task he engaged in only half-heartedly —because no academies existed nearby and because the citizens of Dover steadfastly refused to vote funds for even a temporary "scholar." All this he considered most unfortunate. How could an uninformed populace possibly elect wise rulers? How could America become a mistress of the sciences if it raised its youth in ignorance?

Belknap therefore pleaded for what he considered necessary in the last volume of his *History*. In a chapter on "Education, Literature, and Religion," he described developments during the Revolution and then commented, "This negligence was one among many evidences of a most unhappy prostration of morals during that period. It afforded a melancholy prospect to the friends of science and virtue." The final chapter included several long passages on the subject of education. "It is your duty and your interest to cultivate" the capacities of your children "and render them serviceable to themselves and the community," wrote Belknap. Laws requiring public education should be enforced; instructors should be supported; they should be "men of good understanding, learning and morals" who practiced what they preached; citizens should sponsor social libraries to stimulate learning among adults; and, in fact, whole communities should exchange knowledge and seek self-improvement.[31]

Given these broad societal concerns, Belknap decided to conclude his study with the following paragraph:

Were I to form a picture of happy society, it would be a town consisting of a due mixture of mills, valleys and streams of water: The land well fenced and cultivated; refreshment of travellers, and for public entertainments: the inhabitants mostly husbandmen; their wives and daughters domestic manufacturers; a suitable proportion of handicraft workmen, and two or three traders; a physician and lawyer, each of whom should have a farm for his support. A clergyman of any denomination, which should be agreeable to the majority, a man of good understanding, of a candid disposition and exemplary morals; not a

31. Ibid., 3: 217–218, 246–248.

metaphysical, nor a polemic, but a serious and practical preacher. A school master who should understand his business and teach his pupils to govern themselves. A social library, annually increasing, and under good regulation. A club of sensible men, seeking mutual improvement. A decent musical society. No intriguing politician, horse jockey, gambler or sot; but all such characters treated with contempt. Such a situation may be considered as the most favorable to social happiness of any which this world can afford.[32]

His vision provided a fitting commentary on the concerns he expressed throughout the *History*. Belknap's ideal community would breed men committed to values he had cherished since his youth, as well as those which had been shaped by his experiences as an adult. Understanding, rationality, tolerance, moderation, and republicanism all would thrive in such an environment. Many other Americans who, like Belknap, had lived through the revolutionary era, shared his vision.

32. Ibid., p. 251.

6.

Francois-Xavier Martin's History of North Carolina

R. Don Higginbotham

The forty or so years following the American Revolution witnessed the production of many state histories. In part these traced the accomplishments of individual states, but some, like Jeremy Belknap, wrote histories because such chronicles would "lay a good foundation for some future compiler in writing a general history of the country."[1] North Carolina was slower than most states in obtaining a narrative of its development. Its neighbor to the south could boast of Dr. David Ramsay's *History of the Revolution in South Carolina* as early as 1785, more than twenty-five years before the appearance of a history of the Tar Heel State. Ironically, a Frenchman, arriving in North Carolina at the end of the War of Independence, made the first serious effort to write the state's history.

Third son of a prominent Marseilles merchant, Francois-Xavier Martin was born on March 17, 1762. He received a classical education from a priest who served as his family's chaplain. A quiet, retiring, introspective young man, Martin would live a life of the mind. The bookish youth quickly mastered the major classical writers; sixty years later he still could recite long passages from memory, especially from Horace, his favorite author. Martin's family hoped he would study for the priesthood, but he rebelled at

1. *Massachusetts Historical Society Collections*, 6th series, vol. 4 (Boston, 1891), p. 139.

the idea, and at the age of seventeen or eighteen he sailed for Martinique to work for an uncle engaged in mercantile affairs.

When his uncle soon returned to France, Martin continued the business in Martinique. After two or three years he came to the United States, presumably to search for a stray cargo of molasses, and decided to cast his lot with the new nation. According to one report, he landed in Virginia and served briefly in that state's revolutionary army. In any case, he made his home in Newbern, North Carolina, by 1783 and lived there for the next twenty-six years.

Below medium height, with a large head and nose, and a thick neck, Martin was very nearsighted, which caused him to hunch slightly forward when he walked. In later life, when he resided in Louisiana, Martin was known as an eccentric, a crotchety, miserly bachelor whose shabby appearance and peculiar habits made him an object of pity and ridicule. However, his manner or appearance as a young man in Newbern was not considered especially strange, for he quickly established himself as a respected and influential citizen.

Energetic and thrifty, the twenty-one year old Martin taught French for a time before obtaining a contract to deliver mail to the surrounding rural areas. Though without prior experience, he subsequently secured a job as a typesetter and soon mastered the art. By 1785 Martin had saved enough money to open his own printing shop and published school books, almanacs, acts of the assembly, and a newspaper—the *North Carolina Gazette, or Newbern Advertiser*—which he put out under various titles until 1798. In addition, he imported books from Europe and advertised them for sale in his newspaper. By 1793, at least, the enterprising Martin was also the postmaster of Newbern. In that year he informed his newspaper readers of the possibility of receiving home mail delivery, possibly one of the earliest extensions of such service in the country:

A number of inhabitants of this town having evinced a desire that the Post-Master would cause their letters to be delivered at their own houses *immediately* on the arrival of the mail. He will in the future do so, with regard to such persons as may require it and be willing to pay therefore 50 cents per annum.[2]

The public printer occupied a unique position in eighteenth-century American society. Seldom if ever has a single individual involved himself in so many jobs as did Martin and printers like him. Storekeeper, bookseller, newspaper and book publisher, state printer and postmaster, Martin somehow also found time to study law under Abner Nash, a distinguished attorney and former governor. Admitted to the bar in 1789, he then practiced law in addition to his other enterprises. In 1802 Martin produced a translation of *Pothier on Obligations*, having allegedly set the French text on his type case and translated it directly into type. He also turned out reprints of numerous novels, including *Lord Rivers, The Female Foundling*, and *Jenny*.

But law increasingly drew most of Martin's time and interest. He wrote and published under his own imprint treatises on the duties of sheriffs, justices of the peace, and executors and administrators.[3] Martin wrote these tracts largely out of a desire to probe the areas more deeply for his own benefit as a lawyer and legal scholar; but his works were widely praised and had rather substantial sales. Several young men read law under his guidance, and one of them, William Gaston, later became a distinguished judge of the state supreme court.

Martin's growing reputation resulted in his receiving a legislative commission to prepare a compilation of British statutes still in

2. Quoted in Alonzo T. Dill, *Governor Tryon and His Palace* (Chapel Hill, N.C., 1955), p. 219.
3. Francois-Xavier Martin, *The Office and Authority of a Justice of the Peace, and of Sheriffs, Coroners, &c. According to the Laws of the State of North Carolina* (Newbern, N.C., 1791); *A Chart of the Law of Inheritance, of the State of North-Carolina, Exhibiting a Historical View of It* . . . (Newbern, N.C., 1796); *A Treatise on the Jurisdiction of Justices of the Peace, in Civil Suits According to the Laws of the State of North-Carolina* (Newbern, N.C., 1796); *Treatise on the Powers and Duties of Executors and Administrators* (Newbern, N.C., 1803); *Treatise on the Power of a Sheriff According to the Law of North Carolina* (Newbern, N.C., 1806).

force in the state.[4] Martin afterward remembered that, in preparing this work, he had "examined all the statutes from Magna
Charta to the Declaration of Independence"; "those which related
to America afforded him a complete view of the colonial system of
England." At this time, in 1791, he first turned his attention to
the idea of writing a book on the development of his adopted
state—so Martin informed his readers in the Preface to his *History
of North Carolina*.[5]

Not until 1803, when the legislature employed Martin to publish a revisal of the acts of the general assembly, did he begin to
work seriously on his history.[6] Soon after his election to the state
house of commons in 1806, the general assembly passed a resolution authorizing the secretary of state to give Martin full access to
all the state records.

Record-keeping in the colonial and revolutionary periods had
been little more than an incidental responsibility for the clerks of
the houses of assembly, the provincial secretary, and, later, the
secretary of state. Careless and inexperienced governmental em-
ployees, combined with the frequent turnover of officeholders, led
to the loss or damage of countless materials. Moreover, the
absence of a permanent capital for North Carolina before the
completion of the Governor's Palace at Newbern in 1771 led to a
further loss of official records.

The honor bestowed upon Newbern was short-lived. During the
Revolution the government moved from place to place. Between
1774 and 1781 provincial congresses and revolutionary legislatures
met at Newbern six times, Halifax five times, Hillsborough three
times, and Smithfield once. In April 1781, when British General
Cornwallis threatened the state, authorities loaded the records in
two wagons and sent them to the present state of Tennessee for

4. Francois-Xavier Martin, *A Collection of the Statutes of the Parliament
of England in Force in the State of North Carolina* (Newbern, N.C., 1792).
5. Francois-Xavier Martin, *The History of North Carolina from the Earliest Period*, 2 vols. (New Orleans, La., 1829), 1: vi–vii.
6. Francois-Xavier Martin, *The Public Acts of the General Assembly of
North Carolina . . .* (Newbern, N.C., 1804).

safety. During the Confederation era the government continued its meandering, meeting at Hillsborough, Tarborough, Newbern, Fayetteville, and elsewhere.

By the time Martin began his labors, the government and its records had found a permanent home in Raleigh. The legislature and state officials occupied the newly built capitol—"with all the Publick Papers and Records of their Several offices"—in 1794.[7]

Of the records available to Martin in the two-story state house, the most numerous and significant were the papers of the general assembly: bills, resolutions, petitions, and especially manuscript journals. Although the papers of prerevolutionary governors were scarce, Martin managed to find a number of the chief executives' speeches delivered at "the opening of the sessions" of the legislature. "There were few important events . . . which left no trace on the journals of legislature, or the proceedings of the executive."[8]

Martin seemed less interested in the surviving financial records, although his occasional statistical compilations indicate that he did not entirely ignore them. If the economic records were sparse, the land grant materials were plentiful, but Martin made relatively little use of them.

Martin did not limit his manuscript research to the State House in Raleigh. "During several journeys, which he afterwards made to several parts" of the state, "he received considerable information from individuals." George Pollock of Newbern lent him a letter book and documents left by his ancestor Thomas Pollock, a prominent Albemarle settler in the late seventeenth century who served as president of the proprietary council and acting governor. George Pollock made an exceedingly valuable contribution because of the papers' importance and also because Martin found only a smattering of information in Raleigh dealing with the period of the Carolina proprietors. Former United States Senator Samuel Johnston of Edenton gave Martin access to some papers of his

7. Quoted in H. G. Jones, *For History's Sake: The Preservation and Publication of North Carolina History, 1663–1903* (Chapel Hill, N.C., 1966), p. 75.
8. Martin, *History of North Carolina*, 1: vii.

uncle, Gabriel Johnston, governor from 1734 to 1752. Elsewhere Martin obtained materials formerly belonging to Gabriel Johnston's successor, Matthew Rowan. In the same manner he benefited from the generosity of Governor Samuel Ashe, who had played a leading part in the Revolution, as had other members of his family. And, as Martin acknowledged, "the gentlemen in possession of the records of the Quaker meetings, in Perquimans and Pasquotank counties, and the head of the *Unitas Fratrum*, or Moravian Brethren, cheerfully yielded their assistance."[9]

Between 1806 and 1809 Martin had not only collected the bulk of his source material, but he had also progressed in his writing as far as the Declaration of Independence. Since he had assembled sources covering the postrevolutionary years as well, Martin had every intention of bringing his history down to the opening years of the nineteenth century. But twenty years passed before North Carolinians could read Martin's history.

After over a quarter of a century in North Carolina, Martin, at age forty-seven, began a new career as a jurist in the Old Southwest, never returning to his adopted North Carolina. On March 7, 1809, President James Madison appointed him a judge of the superior court of the Mississippi Territory. A year later he received a commission as judge of the superior court of the Orleans Territory.

Martin, who spent all but a few months of his remaining thirty-seven years as a Louisiana judicial official, was superbly equipped for his new post. He had a great asset in his familiarity with both English and French languages in the predominantly French-speaking region. Martin and his colleagues on the bench set to work to integrate French and Spanish jurisprudence with the English common law and American statutory law. They had to offer well-reasoned decisions that could serve as precedents. In order to make the court's opinions available to lawyers and lower tribunals, Martin began to publish reports of cases heard in the

9. Ibid., p. viii.

superior court. He continued to do so until the territorial court came to an end with the admission of Louisiana to the union as a state in 1812.

Notwithstanding his fondness for North Carolina, Martin never regretted his move to Louisiana. In 1811 he wrote John Hamilton of Elizabeth City, North Carolina, that Louisiana was indeed a promised land. Farmers were getting rich, plantations were mushrooming everywhere, and lawyers were prospering in a get-rich-quick environment. Their annual incomes averaged between four and five thousand dollars, but some more enterprising attorneys made as much as ten thousand a year. As for Judge Martin, he assured his friend that the public got its money's worth from him. "For there is not a day in the year that the court does not sit somewhere in this territory."

Martin indicated that he might step down from the bench and become a practicing attorney, but he never did. In 1813, he became attorney general of Louisiana, and two years later he stepped up to the state supreme court, eventually becoming chief justice. Martin also announced his intention of completing his North Carolina history in the near future. "I still keep working at my history of N. Carolina," he reported; and he asked John Hamilton to secure him a "copy of a pamphlet and map" describing the so-called Granville District, a huge tract of land reserved by one of the North Carolina proprietors at the time the other proprietors transferred their rights to the Crown.[10]

But as the years passed, Martin all but forgot about his unfinished history, hoping to return to it when his judicial duties became less demanding. Continuing his chores as a court reporter, he published the decisions of the state supreme court, which eventually came to eighteen volumes. Meanwhile, fascinated by the linguistic and cultural diversity of Louisiana, Martin now devoted his extra energies to a history of that state, which he

10. Martin to John Hamilton, March 22, 1811, in *Plantation and Frontier Documents, 1649–1863*, ed. U. B. Phillips (Cleveland, Ohio, 1909), 2: 197–200.

published betwen 1827 and 1829.[11] Martin afforded broad treatment to French efforts to build an empire stretching from the St. Lawrence to the Great Lakes and from the upper Mississippi to the Gulf of Mexico. He also gave considerable space to English settlements in North America and to the imperial rivalry between England and France. Several chapters, stressing the role of Spanish Louisiana, covered the American Revolution, and additional sections examined the conflicting ambitions of Spain and America in the lower Mississippi Valley toward the end of the eighteenth century. The final ten chapters (nearly a third of his history) embraced the period of American rule, from the cession of Louisiana in 1803 to the termination of the War of 1812.

Martin confirmed his lack of interest in his study of North Carolina by admitting in 1829 that he had never seen a copy of Hugh Williamson's *History of North Carolina*, which had appeared seventeen years earlier.[12] Williamson, a versatile man, was a Presbyterian theologian and medical doctor. During the Revolutionary War he ministered to the souls and bodies of North Carolina's soldiers, later served as a delegate to the Constitutional Convention of 1787, and then represented the state in the First and Second Federal Congresses. Martin may have learned from his North Carolina friends that Williamson's two-volume work was not as extensive as his own unpublished manuscript, and that Williamson did little more than mention the coming of the Revolution. Like Martin, Williamson had sought to procure personal papers from "some of the most ancient and respectable citizens of the state," but he seemingly met with less success than Martin. Williamson had beaten Martin into print, and thus achieved the distinction of offering the first published history of the Tar Heel State. But Williamson's tomes were a mediocre con-

11. Francois-Xavier Martin, *The History of Louisiana from the Earliest Period*, 2 vols. (New Orleans, 1827–1829).
12. Hugh Williamson, *The History of North Carolina*, 2 vols. (Philadelphia, 1812).

tribution, even by the standards of his day.[13] There was still room for Martin's history.

The threat of yet another proposed North Carolina history finally aroused Martin to publish his long-delayed book. Martin's potential rival was Archibald Debow Murphey, "the most remarkable North Carolinian of his day."[14] An advocate of a state system of internal improvements and of public education, the energetic Murphey also had a significant impact on the writing of North Carolina history. He encouraged such men as General Joseph Graham and Colonel William Polk to write articles on their revolutionary experiences, and he eventually assembled the largest and most important collection of manuscript materials ever put together by a North Carolinian of his generation.

When Murphey requested the use of Martin's manuscripts, the elderly judge refused. His justification was hardly convincing; he claimed that his historical papers had been severely damaged in shipment from North Carolina, by way of New York, to New Orleans many years earlier. "In their circuitous way . . . the sea water found its way to them." Moreover, "since their arrival, the mice, worms, and the variety of insects of a humid and warm climate, have made great ravages among them. The ink of several documents has grown so pale, as to render them nearly illegible."[15]

In 1829, twenty years after leaving Newbern, Martin published his two-volume North Carolina history, making few if any changes in the manuscript that he had brought with him to Louisiana. He had beaten Murphey to press (the latter never completed his history), but Martin's work bore all the marks of haste. It suffered from a lack of careful proofreading and from his failure to incorporate new information that had come to light since his departure

13. Jared Sparks, perhaps the most respected historian of his time, had twice read Williamson's history, finding it "dull & meager beyond description . . . the most inane of all human compositions." Quoted in *North Carolina Historical Review*, 40 (1963): 292.

14. Jones, *For History's Sake*, p. 146.

15. Martin, *History of North Carolina*, 1: xi.

from North Carolina. As he noted in his preface, Martin abandoned his intention of producing two additional volumes on the years after 1776.

According to Martin, the purpose of his history was to acquaint North Carolinians with the sufferings, calamities, and eventual achievements of their forefathers. It told the story of a people who struggled against hostile Indians and wilderness conditions to plant a thriving colony in the New World, a people who later—experiencing "alternate vicissitudes of misfortune and success"—created an impressive society and government after "shaking off the yoke of dependence" upon Great Britain.[16] Young men who desired careers in statecraft and public service would particularly benefit from his study of the past, for it was "the duty of history to record the virtues and errors of conspicuous individuals."[17] As Martin had written years earlier in North Carolina, he believed that man became more virtuous when he saw virtue practiced. "The examples of the Dead are no less powerful than those of the Living." Indeed, Martin felt that the past was more instructive than the present because "posterity praises without flattery, as it praises without interest."[18]

History, therefore, should be objective, detached from emotionalism or special pleading. The record spoke for itself. In that spirit Martin wrote his *History of North Carolina*, a straightforward, factual, chronological narrative of events. Whatever his faults, Martin almost never exhibited bias. For example, in describing the Regulator movement of the late 1760s and early 1770s, a backcountry protest against inadequate government and excessive legal fees, Martin, unlike most other historians, revealed no sympathy for either the rural farmers or for Governor William Tryon and the eastern leaders who subdued the rebellion. Doubtless Martin's own lack of involvement influenced his adequate if

16. Ibid., p. vi.
17. Martin, *History of Louisiana*, 2: 411.
18. Francois-Xavier Martin, *A Funeral Oration on the Most Worshipful and Honorable Major-General Caswell* . . . (Newbern, N.C., 1789).

uninspiring prose style. Furthermore, his preoccupation with political and constitutional history did not lend itself to literary brilliance.

Martin is usually clear and easy to follow, but he had the annoying habit at times of separating subject and predicate by a comma, and he often made abrupt transitions from one paragraph to another. This last difficulty came about because the jurist-historian constantly endeavored to treat developments in North Carolina in the perspective of events transpiring elsewhere in the New World. Thus a discussion of one governor's administration was suddenly interrupted by a few sentences about events in New England or an Anglo-French confrontation in the Ohio Valley. The idea' of an integrated history was admirable, but the author did not weave the added material smoothly into his narrative. On the other hand, some information, which would have enriched his account, he relegated to appendices, including documents on the famous pirate Edward Teach (Blackbeard), the Moravians, and Governor Tryon's handling of the Regulators.

Martin undoubtedly afforded too much space to matters unrelated to North Carolina. The criticism is especially valid for Volume 1, the first two-thirds of which traced voyages of discovery along the Atlantic coast, Spanish explorations in the Southwest, and Virginia's initial settlement and development, along with other topics that he might have condensed or eliminated.

One can also criticize Martin for plagiarizing paragraphs and even whole pages from earlier histories, such as William Stith's *History of the First Discovery and Settlement of Virginia* and Alexander Hewat's *An Historical Account of . . . South Carolina and Georgia.* Yet plagiarism was a common practice of the time. Reputable historians like David Ramsay, William Gordon, and John Marshall also took materials verbatim without giving credit to the original author. In Martin's case, he certainly plagiarized with discrimination—he borrowed excellent sections that he could hardly have improved upon.

Once he reached the period of North Carolina's settlement and expansion under the lords proprietors, Martin relied almost entirely upon manuscripts he had collected and notes based on his use of family papers and the public documents in Raleigh. Consequently, he stayed closer to his main subject. One reads of patents, treaties, land grants, and a procession of governors and their administrations; of new precincts, counties, and towns; of population growth, of exports and imports, and other vital statistics. On occasion, however, he effectively brought in material from the travel accounts of John Lawson, William Byrd, and John Brickell. Although Martin did not use footnotes, he usually listed his main references at the end of each chapter. Now and then he also mentioned information gleaned from tombstones, and he referred to the state of preservation of places of historical interest that he had visited, such as Fort Barnwell (dating from the Tuscarora Indian War) and Tryon's Palace at Newbern.

In general, Martin was at his best when writing of the Indians and of religious developments. He took pains to describe the redmen's cultural habits and their relations with white visitors and the colonial government; and he wrote with feeling and perception of the origins and course of the Tuscarora War, which had resulted from "the successive and regular encroachments" of whites upon the Indians' "plantations and hunting grounds," pushing them "from the neighborhood of the bones of their ancestors."[19] Although he referred to the Anglican church, established by law in all the southern colonies, Martin expressed his greatest admiration for the Quakers and the Moravians as solid, God-fearing people who came to build farms and villages, and who added to the stability and economic health of the colony. But such occasions, when the author's own sentiments emerged, were few and far between.

Although Martin made some factual errors, they did not for the most part detract significantly from his work. Perhaps his most serious mistake was to accept the myth of the so-called Mecklen-

19. Martin, *History of North Carolina*, 1: 242.

burg Declaration of Independence. According to a statement by John McKnitt Alexander in 1800, a group of patriots met in Charlotte (Mecklenburg County) on May 20, 1775, and announced that the citizens of the county were "a free and independent people." To be sure, the spirit of freedom was strong there. A June 1775 newspaper account revealed that a meeting held on the last day of May denounced the mother country in harsh language; but recent scholarship has found no sound evidence for the county's breaking the ties of empire at that early date. (However, Martin was scarcely alone in his error, for the state flag carries the date May 20, 1775, in honor of the Mecklenburg Declaration of Independence.) Martin frequently exercised caution when he felt the evidence was insufficient. He avoided any direct statement on the effect of Britain's Navigation Laws on the colonial economy, although he did give a good picture of the workings of the old colonial system, and he acknowledged the prosperity of the colonists.

Volume 2, covering North Carolina as a royal colony (1729–1776), emphasized the relations between Crown-appointed governors and the lower houses of the legislature. In the eighteenth century, colonial representative assemblies increased their authority at the expense of the governors and, to a lesser degree, the government in London. Assemblies in each colony became miniature replicas of the British House of Commons. The rise of assemblies was perhaps the most significant political and constitutional development in Britain's overseas empire before the American Revolution, and that fact did not escape Francois-Xavier Martin, although his recognition of it was more implicit than explicit in his *History of North Carolina.*

The lower house of North Carolina, advancing more slowly than its counterpart in South Carolina, finally came into its own during and after the mid-1750s—during the governorships of Arthur Dobbs, William Tryon, and Josiah Martin. Meeting more regularly, the lower house asserted its primacy under the leadership of Speakers Samuel Swann, John Ashe, and John Harvey, and

Treasurers John Starkey and Thomas Barker. (In 1755, the lower house denied the right of the governor's council to amend tax bills because it was "contrary to custom and Usage of Parliament.")[20]

Martin allocated more than half his second volume to the two decades from the beginning of the Dobbs administration in the French and Indian War to the Declaration of Independence. If Martin in his dry, factual manner did not spell out the long-term importance to North Carolina of executive-legislative controversies over salaries, taxes, courts, and other matters, the reader can nonetheless see North Carolina's quest for control over its own internal affairs.

Most present-day historians would agree with Martin that, while the colonists sought home rule, they did not want to sever their ties with the mother country. Only in the 1760s, in the aftermath of the Seven Years' War, did Martin find serious Anglo-American discord, which began over the question of Parliament's right to tax the colonies. Martin did not deny that Britain "groaned under the weight" of a heavy debt from the wars with France; neither did he disagree that, "as members of the empire, it was just that they [the colonists] should contribute to its defence and splendor."[21] But he indirectly questioned Britain's method of obtaining an American revenue. Whereas twentieth-century scholarship has stressed a number of factors contributing to the Revolution, Martin saw the causes almost entirely as the colonists' objections to taxes. But by noting the American concern over constitutional principles and basic rights, Martin sounded a theme developed more fully by the so-called Neo-Whig historians in the 1950s and 1960s.

Almost no information exists as to the public response to Martin's *History of North Carolina*; nearly all contemporary literary journals failed to review it. Although Martin announced his plan to bring out two additional volumes on the years between

20. William L. Saunders, ed., *The Colonial Records of North Carolina*, 10 vols. (Raleigh, N.C., 1886–1890), 5: 287.
21. Martin, *History of North Carolina*, 2: 185.

1776 and 1800 or so, he never returned to the subject. He was sixty-seven years old, in poor health, and strenuously involved on the bench, where he had earned something of a national reputation. In 1817 he had been elected to membership in the Academy of Marseilles; in 1841 Harvard College conferred on him the degree of Doctor of Laws. Concerned over his failing vision, he took a trip to France in 1844 to see a famous eye specialist, but did not benefit from treatment.

Martin was perhaps as well known in Louisiana for his eccentricities as for his legal brilliance. He was so nearsighted that a spot of ink often adorned the end of his nose. During his last years he felt his way along the street, touching houses, gates, and other familiar landmarks as he tottered toward his shabby little house. Small boys would sometimes run up behind him, jerk on the back of his patched and dirty coat, and run away laughing. More than once Tom, a faithful Negro slave, rescued the helpless old man and shrieked at his master's assailant, "You little imp o' Satan, don' you do dat to my massa. He kin put you in de calaboose fur a whole year. You don' know who you's monkeyin' wid. Dat's Jedge Francois-Xavier Martin."[22] Martin died in 1846 at the age of eighty-four, leaving an estate valued at more than $400,000.

Death did not end the story of Martin and his *History of North Carolina*. David Swain, a founder of the North Carolina Historical Society and president of the University of North Carolina, had succeeded the deceased Archibald Debow Murphey as the state's most active historical collector and publicist. Swain believed that the so-called records mentioned by Martin in his preface and throughout his history were actually public documents that Martin had taken illegally from the state in 1809. At Swain's instigation, Governor William A. Graham wrote the aging jurist, asking him to return all official papers in his possession. Martin replied evasively as to the nature and extent of his material, and ended by

22. Quoted in Edward Larocque Tinker, "Jurist and Japier: Francois-Xavier Martin and Jean Leclerc," New York Public Library *Bulletin*, 39 (1935): 676.

saying he could not "sadisfy [*sic*] you, as I would have been desirious to do."[23]

Graham persisted: after Martin's death, the governor wrote Robert N. Ogden, Martin's executor, that the old judge had probably removed from the state "a large mass of material for the History, and that a considerable portion consists of public documents."[24] When Ogden denied any knowledge of North Carolina documents in the judge's files, the matter was dropped for more than a decade. In 1858 Swain learned from Bishop William Mercer Green that Colonel John F. H. Claiborne of Shieldsboro, Mississippi, possessed Martin's manuscripts. Swain, enlisting the aid of Secretary of the Interior Jacob Thompson, sought to purchase the papers provided he could first examine them to determine their value. Claiborne agreed to sell them, and in 1860 the manuscripts arrived in Chapel Hill.

Their contents extremely disappointed Swain. Instead of finding many "ancient documents," the collection consisted of a rough draft of part of Martin's Volume 2 and notes for a history of the years 1776–1780. Had Martin or his executor destroyed or sold his original sources? Had he falsified the tale of having taken manuscripts with him to Louisiana? At any rate, Bishop Green had maintained that Martin's papers contained other materials for the late seventeenth and early eighteenth centuries. But we do not know whether or not they were original sources, nor can we now determine why Claiborne failed to send them to Swain.

Still, Swain informed the Reverend Francis L. Hawks that the Claiborne materials were "indispensable . . . and I have purchased them for the State."[25] Almost as soon as the Martin papers made their appearance, they again disappeared from sight. Swain mistakenly believed they had been carried off by Union authorities

23. J. G. de Roulhac Hamilton, ed., *The Papers of William Alexander Graham*, 4 vols. (Raleigh, N.C., 1957–1961), 3: 35.

24. Ibid., p. 199.

25. Swain to Hawks, September 13, 1860, David Swain Papers, Southern Historical Collection, University of North Carolina (Chapel Hill, N.C.).

at the end of the Civil War. In 1964 most of the Martin manuscripts were discovered in the William L. Saunders Papers in the University of North Carolina Library. At long last, the mystery of the Claiborne portion of the Martin documents was laid to rest.[26]

26. Jones, *For History's Sake*, p. 145. There is no real biography of Martin, though one is much needed. The following are useful: B. P. French, *Historical Collections of Louisiana* (Philadelphia, 1850), pp. 17–40; Holland M. Thompson, "Francis-Xavier Martin," *North Carolina University Magazine*, 12 (1893): 203–209; William Wirt Howe, *Studies in the Civil Law* (Boston, 1905), pp. 346–371; W. B. Yearns, "Francois X. Martin and His History of North Carolina," *North Carolina Historical Review*, 36 (1959): 17–27.

7.

Thomas F. Gordon's The History of New Jersey

Larry R. Gerlach

The half century between the War of 1812 and the Civil War, marked by the rise of pervasive historical consciousness in the young republic, witnessed the initial major preservation and publication of Americana.[1] It was the golden age of the amateur historian who, imbued with a strong sense of social responsibility and attuned to contemporary intellectual currents, endeavored not only to inform and entertain but also to instruct and admonish a sophisticated readership.

Unfortunately, many modern professional scholars, unduly impressed by the chauvinism, antiquarianism, archaic bias, and literary license of these pioneer craftsmen, generally regard early-nineteenth-century historiography with condescension, if not contempt; works of that vintage are often collected and discussed as quaint period pieces but only infrequently consulted and appreciated as substantive contributions to historical knowledge. Indeed, the preprofessional era is remembered, if at all, as the classic era of the literary historian and the compiler of multivolume series; as the period dominated by patrician authors such as Francis Park-

1. See George H. Callcott, *History in the United States, 1800–1860; Its Practice and Purpose* (Baltimore, Md., 1970); David W. Van Tassel, *Recording America's Past: An Interpretation of Historical Studies in America, 1607–1884* (Chicago, 1960); Leslie W. Dunlap, *American Historical Societies, 1790–1860* (Madison, Wis., 1944); Hermann E. Ludewig, *The Literature of American Local History: A Bibliographical Essay* (New York, 1846). For background consult Russel B. Nye, *The Cultural Life of the New Nation, 1776–1830* (New York, 1960).

man, Jared Sparks, and George Bancroft. As a result, a host of lesser writers whose works are neither magisterial nor monumental have been consigned by neglect to historiographic oblivion. Such has been the fate of Thomas F. Gordon.

I

There exists a paucity of information concerning the life of Thomas Francis Gordon, notwithstanding the fact that he achieved prominence in his chosen profession and was one of the most productive amateur historians of his generation.[2] He was born in Philadelphia in 1787, the first child of Elisha and Elizabeth Francis Gordon, members of the First Baptist Church. He entered the University of Pennsylvania in 1805 at the age of eighteen and matriculated a member of the class of 1808. He chose not to become an ironmonger like his father and, after brief employment as a brewer, determined to pursue a legal career. Applying himself diligently to the study of the law, he gained admission to the Philadelphia Bar on September 16, 1806, two years prior to graduation from college. (The date of his marriage to Constance, daughter of Jean Baptist Clement Rousseau of Philadelphia, is not known; they raised eight children.)[3] Gordon soon became one of the most promising young lawyers in the city. Both his reputation and his practice grew apace. In December of

2. Seemingly an ideal candidate for inclusion in the memorial and biographical encyclopedias so characteristic of the nineteenth century, Gordon appears in surprisingly few of these compendiums. A brief sketch may be found in James G. Wilson and John Fiske, eds., *Appleton's Cyclopaedia of American Biography*, 7 vols. (New York, 1888–1891), 2: 686–687; and Hiram H. Shenk, ed., *Encyclopedia of Pennsylvania* (Harrisburg, 1932), p. 225. Obituaries (supplying no additional biographical information) appeared in the *Philadelphia Evening Bulletin*, January 20, 1860; and the Philadelphia *Public Ledger*, January 21, 1860; and the *New York Times*, January 23, 1860.

3. University of Pennsylvania, *Biographical Catalogue of the Matriculates of the College, 1749–1893* (Philadelphia, 1894), p. 44; John Hill Martin, *Bench and Bar of Philadelphia* (Philadelphia, 1883), p. 272; Thomas F. Gordon, Last Will and Testament, January 16, 1860, Archives and History Bureau, New Jersey State Library, Trenton.

1818 he was appointed Clerk of the Orphan's Court of Philadelphia; at an undetermined point in his career he declined an appointment as justice of the Pennsylvania Supreme Court because of deafness. The infirmity was apparently serious enough to force Gordon into premature retirement at the peak of his career in the late 1830s. At about that time he moved to Beverly, New Jersey, where he resided until his death on January 17, 1860, at the age of seventy-three.[4] There is no evidence that he practiced law or actively pursued historical studies in that Burlington County community.

Thomas F. Gordon is known to posterity solely because of his scholarship, but he was well-known to contemporaries in the mid-Atlantic region as a compiler of legal reference works, an articulate advocate of Whig philosophy, and, most importantly, an indefatigable student of history and historical geography.[5] Gordon attained maturity at a time when interest in history reached unparalleled intensity in the United States (historical works comprised approximately 60 percent of the best sellers written from 1810 to 1839) and like many compeers in the legal profession displayed a penchant for the past.[6] A long-time interest in scholarly research and writing eventually became an obsession, and he

4. James Robinson, *The Philadelphia Directory for 1816* (Philadelphia, 1816), n.p.; Martin, *Bench and Bar*, p. 71; *Biographical Catalogue*, p. 44. I have found confirmation of neither the proffer nor the rejection of the justiceship. Thompson Wescott, comp., *Biographies of Philadelphians* (Historical Society of Pennsylvania), 2, pt. 1: 138. Gordon's funeral and burial took place in Beverly on January 20. It is not known when he moved to New Jersey, but there is every reason to believe he was still living in Philadelphia in 1836.

5. A convenient listing of Gordon's publications may be found in Joseph Sabin et al., eds., *Bibliotheca Americana. A Dictionary of Books Relating to America from its Discovery to the Present Time*, 29 vols. (New York, 1868–1936), 7: 343–345. The citations therein are not always complete or accurate; I have endeavored to provide exact references in this essay.

6. The proportion of best sellers which fall into the category of history are as follows: 1810–1819, 66 percent; 1820–1829, 88 percent; 1830–1839, 40 percent. Lawyers comprised about 30 percent of the major historians writing during the first half of the nineteenth century and were conspicuous in the activities of historical societies. See Callcott, *History in the United States*, pp. 25, 31–34, 37, 69.

produced between 1827 and 1836 eleven substantial publications on a wide variety of subjects.

Except for owning one share of stock in the Library Company of Philadelphia and being a subscriber member of the Athenaeum of Philadelphia for the year 1828–1829, Gordon, unlike most history devotees of the time, was not formally associated with institutions dedicated to the promotion of historical studies. He was deeply interested in the activities of the American Philosophical Society and on one occasion actively assisted a young scholar in submitting a manuscript on mathematics to that learned society.[7] Nonetheless, he utilized extensively the resources of such institutions, especially the historical societies of New Jersey and Pennsylvania, in preparing his historical works.

Gordon's talents and reputation as a student of the law are clearly evident in the compilation of two valuable legal digests. In 1827 he published A *Digest of the Laws of the United States, including an Abstract of the Judicial Decisions relating to Constitutional and Statutory Law,* replete with historical and explanatory notes. Undergoing three subsequent editions, this massive compendium remained the basic work of its genre until the Civil War. His proposal to launch a similar project for Pennsylvania statutes produced no tangible results. However, in 1830 he compiled at the behest of the secretary of the treasury another enduring reference work, A *Digest of the Treaties and Statutes of the United States, relating to Commerce, Navigation, and Revenue.*[8]

---

7. Gordon, "Last Will and Testament." Mr. Nicholas B. Wainwright of the Historical Society of Pennsylvania, Mr. Roger W. Moss of the Athenaeum of Philadelphia, and Mr. Whitfield J. Bell, Jr., of the American Philosophical Society graciously provided information concerning Gordon's relationship with their respective institutions.

8. Thomas F. Gordon, A *Digest of the Laws of the United States, including an Abstract of the Judicial Decisions relating to Constitutional and Statutory Law. With Notes explanatory and historical.* (Philadelphia, 1827), p. 884; 2d ed. (1837), p. 822; 3d ed. (1844), p. 998; 4th ed. (1851), p. 998; *An Inquiry into the Propriety and Means of Consolidating and Digesting the Laws of Pennsylvania* (Philadelphia, 1827); A *Digest of the Treaties and Statutes of the United States, relating to Commerce, Navigation, and Revenue,*

As far as can be ascertained Gordon held neither political office nor position of influence in the Whig Party. Nonetheless, his histories of Pennsylvania, New Jersey, and New York reveal a decidedly Whiggish orientation toward the great issues of the day. His conservatism came to the fore during the national bank controversy, when, greatly angered by President Andrew Jackson's concerted opposition to rechartering the Second Bank of the United States, he penned in 1834, at the height of the contest over the charter, an impressive contribution to the pamphlet warfare of the Jacksonian Era, *The War on the Bank of the United States*.[9]

Gordon wrote on the bank issue as a private citizen, not a partisan publicist. As he declared in announcing the pamphlet, when "interest, so important to the country as a sound and uniform currency and the legitimate construction of the Constitution, are endangered, it is not less the duty, than the priviledge, of the citizen, to participate in the discussion." For him, the issue involved political and constitutional issues as well as economic prosperity and fiscal stability. His avowed purpose in publishing the essay was to provide the public with "a concise account of the war on the Bank, with an inquiry into its causes and effects." He succeeded admirably. Albeit modest in pagination and argumentative in tone, the comprehensive account of the bank war was no sudden creation. Rather, as the numerous extensive quotations from a variety of sources indicate, it was a thoughtful exposition based upon a careful, detailed investigation of the issue both within and without the halls of Congress. Be that as it may, scholars have generally slighted this important publication, possibly because Gordon was neither an official Whig propagandist, a

---

compiled at the insistance of the Secretary of the Treasury (Philadelphia, 1830), pp. xix, 302, 319. It is not known whether the work was commissioned by Secretary of the Treasury Richard Rush (1825–1829) or Samuel D. Ingham (1829–1831).

9. Thomas F. Gordon, *The War on the Bank of the United States; or, a Review of the Measures of the Administration against that Institution and the Prosperity of the Country* (Philadelphia, 1834), p. 155.

spokesman for the Philadelphia banking establishment, nor a prominent pamphleteer.[10]

For all his varied enterprises, Thomas F. Gordon was first and foremost a historian. His interest in and enthusiasm for the past knew no bounds, and, judging from the quality and quantity of publications, his vocation must often have been subordinated to his avocation. Perhaps buoyed by that initial optimism which sometimes infects the novice, Gordon originally envisioned writing a comprehensive, multivolume "Cabinet of American History." However, he produced only the first two installments of the series: the ambitiously titled *The History of America. Containing the History of the Spanish Discoveries prior to 1520*[11] and the largely archaeological *History of Ancient Mexico; from the Foundation of that Empire to its Destruction by the Spaniards.*[12] Publishers were apparently unwilling to commit themselves to this open-ended scheme, for both studies were first privately printed by the author.

No doubt despairing of the enormity of the project, Gordon soon shifted his attention to the early history and historical geography of the Middle Atlantic states. He turned first to his native Pennsylvania, publishing in 1829 *A History of Pennsylvania*

10. Ibid., p. iii. None of the standard studies of Pennsylvania politics during the Age of Jackson mention Gordon or his pamphlet. See, for example, Marguerite G. Bartlett, *The Chief Phases of Pennsylvania Politics in the Jackson Period* (Allentown, Pa., 1919); Henry R. Mueller, *The Whig Party in Pennsylvania* (New York, 1922); and Charles M. Snyder, *The Jacksonian Heritage: Pennsylvania Politics, 1833–1848* (Harrisburg, Pa., 1958). Arthur M. Schlesinger, Jr., *The Age of Jackson* (Boston, 1945), cites Gordon's publication in the bibliography but makes no reference to it in the text. More surprising is the neglect of the essay in works dealing specifically with the bank controversy such as Jean Alexander Wilburn's excellent *Biddle's Bank: The Crucial Years* (New York, 1967) and Bray Hammond's *Banks and Politics in America, from the Revolution to the Civil War* (Princeton, N.J., 1957). Only Ralph C. H. Catterall, in his classic *The Second Bank of the United States* (Chicago, 1903) made effective use of Gordon's work.

11. Thomas F. Gordon, *The History of America. Containing the History of the Spanish Discoveries prior to 1520*, 2 vols. (Philadelphia, n.d.), pp. xx, 297, 252; reprint (Philadelphia, Carey & Lea, 1831 and 1832).

12. Thomas F. Gordon, *History of Ancient Mexico; from the Foundation of that Empire to its Destruction by the Spaniards*, 2 vols. (Philadelphia, 1832), pp. xiv, 363; xi, 265.

and a companion *Gazetteer of the State of Pennsylvania* three years later. In 1834 there appeared simultaneously *The History of New Jersey* and *A Gazetteer of the State of New Jersey*. Gordon completed the trilogy in 1836 by fashioning a *Gazetteer of the State of New York*, a considerable portion of which was devoted to colonial history.[13]

Aside from obvious differences in factual content, his works on Pennsylvania, New Jersey, and New York are strikingly similar in essential characteristics: they are virtually identical in terms of purpose, scope, and interpretation and share the same qualities of craftsmanship and design. And it is here, in the preparation of state histories and gazetteers, that Thomas F. Gordon made his chief legacy to scholarship. Of these, his study of New Jersey provides the best illustration of his strengths and weaknesses as a historian and constitutes his most important contribution to historical literature.[14]

Compared to other members of the original thirteen in general and neighboring states in particular, New Jersey traditionally has

13. Thomas F. Gordon, *The History of Pennsylvania, from Its Discovery by Europeans, to the Declaration of Independence in 1776* (Philadelphia: 1829), pp. vii, 628; *Gazetteer of the State of Pennsylvania. Part First, contains a general Description of the State, its Situation and Extent, General Geological Construction, Canals and Railroads, Bridges, Revenue, Expenditures, Public Debt, &c. &c. Part Second, embraces ample Descriptions of its Counties, Towns, Cities, Villages, Mountains, Lakes, Rivers, Creeks, &c., alphabetically arranged* (Philadelphia, 1832), pp. 65, 508; reprinted in 1833; *The History of New Jersey, from its Discovery by Europeans, to the Adoption of the Federal Constitution* (Trenton, N.J., 1834), pp. xii, 339; *A Gazetteer of the State of New Jersey. Comprehending A General View of its Physical and Moral Condition, together with a Topographical and Statistical Account of its Counties, Towns, Villages, Canals, Rail Roads, &c.* (Trenton, N.J., 1834), pp. iv, 266; *Gazetteer of the State of New York. Comprehending its Colonial History; General Geography, Geology, and Internal Improvements; Its Political State; A Minute Description of its several Counties, Towns, and Villages; Statistical Tables, exhibiting the Area, Improved Lands, Population, Stock, Taxes, Manufactures, Schools, and the Cost of Public Instruction in each Town* (Philadelphia, 1836), pp. xii, 102, 801.

14. *The History of New Jersey* is the only work by Gordon to be cited in Oscar Handlin et al., comps., *Harvard Guide to American History* (Cambridge, Mass., 1963), p. 229.

not been served well by Clio's servants.[15] Gordon's *History of New Jersey* (1834) was the first comprehensive study of the colonial history of the state; the companion *Gazetteer* was likewise a pioneering effort. This much needed brace of books both supplemented and supplanted Samuel Smith's valuable but long outdated *History of the Colony of Nova-Caesaria* (1765), a narrative history of the province to 1721 to which was appended a description of the geography and contemporary state of the colony.[16] Moreover, Gordon's work greatly influenced subsequent writings on New Jersey history produced during the nineteenth century. For example, in preparing their immensely popular and highly anecdotal *Historical Collections of the State of New Jersey* (1844), John W. Barber and Henry Howe borrowed heavily from Gordon —a debt not sufficiently acknowledged.[17] And, writing as late as 1877, John O. Raum, like others before him, drew much from Gordon (and Smith) for his two-volume *History of New Jersey* without giving credit to either authority. In fact, Gordon remained the standard work on colonial New Jersey until the publication early in the twentieth century of Edwin P. Tanner's *The Province of New Jersey* and Edgar J. Fisher's *New Jersey as a Royal Province*; it persisted as the best one-volume treatment of the

15. Ludewig's bibliographical compilation, *Literature of American Local History* (1846) contains 116 entries for New York, 76 for Pennsylvania, and 19 for New Jersey. Of the original states only North Carolina (18) and Delaware (16) ranked quantitatively behind New Jersey. Massachusetts predictably had the most citations, 346.

16. Samuel Smith, *The History of Nova-Caesaria, or New Jersey: Containing an Account . . . to the Year 1721 with Some Particulars since and a Short View of Its Present State* (Burlington, N.J., 1765). For an old, but perceptive essay on the historiography of colonial New Jersey, see Justin Winsor, ed., *Narrative and Critical History of America*, 8 vols. (Boston, 1884–1889), 3: 449–456.

17. John W. Barber and Henry Howe, *Historical Collections of the State of New Jersey: Containing a General Collection of the Most Interesting Facts, traditions, biographical sketches, anecdotes, Etc. Relating to its History and Antiquities, with Geographical Descriptions of Every Township in the State* (New York, 1844) (rev. ed., New Haven, 1868). The duo had previously published similar volumes on New York (1841) and Pennsylvania (1844); Barber alone had written comparable works on Connecticut (1836) and Massachusetts (1839).

period until the appearance in 1964 of Richard P. McCormick's
New Jersey from Colony to State.[18] Little wonder that the fore-
most student of the history of printing in New Jersey considered
Gordon's *History* and *Gazetteer* to be "possibly the most impor-
tant book" ever produced by the prominent Trenton publisher,
Daniel Fenton.[19]

Cognizant of the potential value of a gazetteer to future generations, Gordon took great pains to fashion "a full and correct
portraiture" of New Jersey in the year 1833. To this end he personally visited "almost every portion" of the state, gathering data
by observation, conversation with the citizenry, and examination
of germane records.[20] The result was an alphabetically arranged
gazetteer with extensive prefatory chapter devoted to a "Physical
View" (geography and demography) and a "Moral View" (governmental and social institutions) of the state. Notwithstanding
sundry errors and imprecisions which invariably flaw early gazetteers, Gordon's compilation, because it contains a wealth of
information not readily obtainable elsewhere, is an enduring contribution to the literature of the Garden State.

II

It has almost become axiomatic that each generation writes its
own history. Historians often find it difficult to avoid the snare of

18. John O. Raum, *The History of New Jersey, From Its Earliest Settle-
ment to the Present Time . . .* , 2 vols. (Philadelphia, 1877); Edwin P.
Tanner, *The Province of New Jersey, 1664–1783* (New York, 1908); Edgar J.
Fisher, *New Jersey as a Royal Province, 1738–1776* (New York, 1911); Rich-
ard P. McCormick, *New Jersey from Colony to State, 1609–1789* (Princeton,
N.J., 1964). Earlier volumes by Isaac S. Mulford, *A Civil and Political History of New Jersey . . .* (Camden, 1848; Philadelphia, 1851) and Edward
Sylvester Ellis and Henry Snyder, *A Brief History of New Jersey* (New York,
1910), are undistinguished. Donald L. Kemmerer, *Path to Freedom: The
Struggles for Self-Government in Colonial New Jersey, 1703–1776* (Princeton,
N.J., 1940), is a solid contribution restricted to the eighteenth century.
19. Elmer T. Hutchinson, comp., "Biographical and Bibliographical Notes
on New Jersey Printers and Publishers Active through 1850," Box 5, Collection of New Jersey Printers and Publishers, Rutgers University Library.
20. Gordon, "Advertisement," *Gazetteer of New Jersey*, p. iii.

presentism and to prevent personal prejudices from coloring their perspective of the past; to a far greater degree than scholars care to admit, certain themes, issues, and problems dominate the historiography of a given period. The historical writings of Thomas F. Gordon constitute a collective case in point, for they embody many concerns and currents of the time.

The most pervasive dichotomy to appear in the first century of historical writing in the United States was national versus local history—the former predominating predictably during the intensely nationalistic-patriotic years immediately following the American Revolution, the latter gaining ascendancy after the War of 1812 "in reaction to the rapid growth of nationalism and as a reflection of competition between the states."[21]

Most early-nineteenth-century historians deemed themselves charged with a mission of resurrection—rescuing state and local history from the domination of national studies and restoring it to a proper place among the annals of the nation's past. Gordon's histories of New Jersey, New York, and Pennsylvania can be fully appreciated only from the perspective of this provincial trend of historiography. They share a common *raison d'être*. The author was explicit about his purpose in writing about Pennsylvania:

Full justice has never been done to the magnamity and ability of the Pennsylvania statesmen and warriors during the revolutionary contest. The quiet and unpretending character of her population, has caused the historian, in a measure, to overlook their merit in the council and the field. So far as the scope of this volume permitted, an attempt has been made to remedy this injustice. . . . And a chief object of the author's labours, should they be continued, will be to exhibit in full and just relief, the great and efficient part which the people of Pennsylvania had in every stage of the revolution.[22]

This revealing declaration of intent cannot be dismissed as native chauvinism, for it also found expression in his writings on New Jersey and New York.

21. Van Tassel, *Recording America's Past*, p. 55.
22. Gordon, *History of Pennsylvania*, p. iv. Gordon never wrote the sequential volume to which he referred.

The three histories are virtually identical in terms of conception, scope, and execution. Gordon traced each colony from the arrival of Europeans to the outbreak of the Revolution, taking care to delineate their distinctive colonial origins and historic development. He intended to discuss the role of Pennsylvania (and perhaps New York) in the War of Independence in a subsequent volume, but carried the story of New Jersey forward to the adoption of the Constitution. This deviation is attributable to Gordon's concept of historical writing. Considering the historian to be a narrator, a storyteller as it were, he strove to fashion a structurally integrated tale. And, contrary to the views of later students of New Jersey, he opined that with the adoption of the Constitution "the individuality of the State, as a historical subject, is merged in the history of the nation; and the subsequent period of unvaried political prosperity, within her borders, presents few matters for the historian."[23] Gordon's attempt to write a unified, logically complete narrative was common to most of his fellow historians.

One of the most salient features of the early writings on colonial history—indeed much of American historiography produced between 1790 and the 1880s—is its homogeneity, its fundamental consensus on events, trends, and interpretations. At no other time have studies of the past been so utterly devoid of historical controversy. It is not surprising, therefore, that save for local peculiarities there is little to distinguish the theses and themes proffered in *The History of New Jersey* from those promulgated in countless other contemporary histories. Like his compeers, Gordon put forth a pervasive and all-encompassing, albeit simplistic, interpretation of American colonial history which was moralistic, patriotic, deterministic, Messianic, and Europhobistic.

To Gordon, the colonial period took the form of a contest between the children of light and the children of darkness, another phase of the eternal struggle between the forces of good

23. Gordon, *The History of New Jersey*, p. iii.

and evil. Moralisms were deliberately injected into his writing; value judgments abound. Time and again the moral is juxtaposed with the immoral, virtue with decadence, good with evil, liberty and democracy with tyranny and oppression. The so-called Protestant ethic looms as the foundation of the "good" society. Note, for example, his discussion of the initial settlement of Burlington: "In this, as in other, infant settlements of America, the success of the colonists was commonly proportioned to the original humility of his condition; and he, who emigrated as a servant, was frequently more prosperous than his master. Persevering industry, temperance, and self-reliance, always reaped a full reward, whilst self-indulgence, and dependence upon hirelings, terminated in poverty."[24] In the same vein, Edward, Lord Cornbury, and Edmund Andros, didactic symbols of political and spiritual atavism, are portrayed as miscreants with no redeeming qualities, while such personages as William Livingston and George Washington, paragons of public and private virtue, assume a heroic pose. Thomas F. Gordon wrote history to instruct as well as to inform and entertain.

As a corollary, he often engaged in the glorification (and distortion) of the past and the exaltation of historical personages in order to imbue the reader with a proper appreciation of nationalism and patriotism. He agreed with James Grahame that Americans should "feel grateful exultation" in avowing themselves of "a land which has yielded as great an increase of glory to God, and happiness to man, as any other portion of the world" and that a "nobler model of human character" could hardly be proposed to them than "that which their own early history supplies." It was, then, "their interest and their honour, to preserve with sacred care, a model so richly fraught, with the instructions of wisdom and the incitements of duty." The charge to New Jerseyans was especially great because of their unusually pristine past. Of their state, "founded by deeds of peace," he observed that "none can boast of

24. Ibid., p. 40.

greater purity in its origins—none more wisdom, more happiness in its growth."[25]

Historical determinism looms large in Gordon's work at three levels. First, he viewed inanimate force, not man, as the dynamic of history: men, being products of circumstance, could abet or hinder but not alter historical development. Thus, because the period in which "the foundations of the Anglo-American colonies were laid" was "rife with events, which sowed the indestructible seeds, and reared into strength the scions of human liberty," advances in religious and political liberty in America are depicted as "results of improvement in the moral conditions of our species, which individuals might promote, but could scarce retard." Warning against "the worst species of idolatry—of man-worship" by bestowing upon individuals "the praise of creating measures, of which they could only be servants," he nonetheless justified "plaudits for their concurrence in the good work" as a "just incentive to virtuous activities." At another level, Gordon's deterministic bent is evidenced by the assumption of the inevitability of progress. Colonial America is represented as a microcosm of the process whereby barbarism invariably yields to civilization, aristocracy to democracy, monarchy to republicanism, privilege to equality, bigotry to toleration, and so on. To a considerable extent he envisioned an organic progression: the history of colonial New Jersey is at base the transition of society from youth to maturity. Lastly, Gordon's histories are deterministic in the sense that various political and constitutional struggles of the colonial period are interpreted as foreshadowing the Revolution. For example, the challenge in 1680–1682 of New Jersey Quakers to a tax imposed by Edmund Andros on behalf of James, Duke of York, is viewed as a conflict between "the advocates of liberty, and the abettors of arbitrary power"; the Jersey protestation against the tax is seen to contain "traces of those principles, which . . . led the colonies to full emancipation"; and the ultimate Quaker victory is viewed as the initial vindication of the principle of no taxation without

25. Ibid., p. 3.

representation which eventually "triumphed more signally, in the independence of the United States."[26]

The Messianic and Europhobistic themes are less well-developed and more subtly presented than the others, but they constitute for Gordon and the public at large the essential preconceptions for viewing the American experience. The Messianic or Hebraic interpretation of American history subsumes the concepts of chosenness and mission. That is to say, Americans (especially those of Anglo-Saxon derivation) are considered to have been singled out by God as His chosen people and charged with performing, among others, the special missions of first religious, then political regeneration (i.e., Puritanism and democracy). Hence the Hand of Providence to a considerable degree shaped events in New Jersey and its sister colonies. But divine intervention was not overt or direct. Rather, the grandeur and greatness of America is seen as ample testimony of divine sanction. The concept of Europhobia in general and anti-British sentiment in particular is intimately related to rising American nationalism. Primarily a legacy of the War of Independence, it finds early expression in the story of emigrants departing the Old World to escape various forms of persecution, decadence, and stagnation and establishing a truly New World characterized by unprecedented freedom, equality, and opportunity. Implicit in this analysis is the rejection or marked alteration of European institutions, ideologies, customs, and traditions by colonials and the emergence of a "new man," the American. Almost every history written prior to the twentieth century develops these two themes to some degree.

In addition to general historiographical themes, contemporary issues and assumptions as well as the author's personal attitudes permeate *The History of New Jersey*. Convention, vocational training, and prior editing of legal digests led to a narrow focus on political history and preoccupation with such matters as constitutional development, the rise of representative institutions, the

26. Ibid., pp. 2–3, 40–42.

qualities of statesmanship, and the structure and operation of government. But Whig ideology was also a crucial factor, for it caused Gordon to emphasize the legislative branch instead of the executive or judicial, to stress the republican rather than the democratic nature of American government, and to advocate a "loose" rather than a "strict" construction of the Constitution. Typically Whiggish is his assertion that "the principal arena of public action [is] the legislative hall; and that in such details alone are to be found the sources of public measures of the province, and the character of her most distinguished citizens."[27] His Whiggism is also revealed by a covert class-consciousness (class defined as social status determined by talent), subtle elitism, and preference for deferential politics. Yet Gordon was a political historian, not a partisan polemicist. Consequently, his political views, while readily discernible, were not blatantly or even always intentionally incorporated into the book.

However, on one occasion he deliberately utilized a historical event to deliver a bold, even audacious, attack upon the patronage practices of President Andrew Jackson. The six-year row between governor and assembly over the dismissal of the treasurer of East New Jersey (at base a contest for control of patronage) stemming from the robbery of the Eastern treasury in 1768 provided the opportunity to assault the "spoils system." In a lengthy "footnote" to the affair, Gordon railed at length against the removal of public officials *"without good and sufficient reason"* as an expression of an "arbitrary and despotic temper" and the "capricious disposition, and proscriptive spirit of party," and he decried the concept of *"rotation in office"* as having "a demoralizing effect, tending to discourage industry, and to create numerous anxious, idle, venal, expectants of office." "No prudent man discharges a competent, experienced, and faithful servant," he observed, "to receive others in quick succession, who enter his service with a view solely to the

27. Gordon, *History of Pennsylvania*, p. iii.

wages, and whose capacity for service is to be acquired at his expense."[28] Certainly the implications of this and other aspects of his political message were not lost upon a generation which had experienced a "corrupt bargain" followed by "Jacksonian Democracy" with its "spoils system," "Kitchen Cabinet," exaltation of the "common man," and assertion of executive authority.

Gordon's political philosophy was an integral part of his concept of the nature of the American union—no mean issue during an era of increased sectional tensions as expressed by the Missouri Compromise, the tariff debates, and the nullification controversy. Once again the lessons of history were clear: growing nationalism and intercolonial unity presaged and made possible both independence and the federal union. Significantly, Gordon concluded both *The History of New Jersey* and the account of that state's adoption of the Constitution with the following: "The fondest wish of the patriot heart, must be, that the Union, the Federal Constitution, and the weal of the State, which are inseparable, may, also, be perpetual."[29]

Since Gordon paid scant attention to economic history, the fiscal conservatism so evident in *The War on the Bank* is not manifest in the study of New Jersey. Nor are there any obvious analogies to such contemporary economic controversies as the tariff or the bank. Nevertheless, he argued that "sound policy" entailed keeping emissions of paper "within narrow bounds," warned against the evils of wildcat speculation, and blamed inflated currency for much of the pecuniary problems of the Confederation period. Ironically, he censured Great Britain for its "pertinacious refusals" to sanction several New Jersey legal tender acts, contending that the requests made by the colony were modest and that its record of maintaining a stable medium of

28. Gordon, *The History of New Jersey*, p. 151. The same argument, much of it verbatim, appeared in *The War on the Bank*, pp. 151–152.
29. Gordon, *The History of New Jersey*, p. 332.

exchange and exercising discretion in issuing paper was exemplary.[30]

Gordon wrote at a time when considerable attention was being focused anew upon the problem of race in America, specifically the issues of African slavery and the territorial integrity of Indian tribes east of the Mississippi River. The irrepressible conflict over slavery was seemingly approaching a climax in the early thirties with the eruption of a major slave insurrection and the appearance of a militant antislavery movement of national dimension. The Indian quandary initially involved systematic encroachment by southern states upon tribal lands (especially those held by the Cherokee) and eventually the removal of the aboriginal population to the trans-Mississippi West.[31] Gordon's discussion of the "peculiar institution" and Indian-white relations is instructive, for it embodies the ambivalence if not equivocation, the insensitivity if not callousness, of the nation at large on these two volatile issues. (Actually, it can be said that Gordon and most other historians of his day wrote racist history in that implicit in their alleged superiority and virtuousness of Americans is the assumption that national character is a racial trait.)

Significantly, aside from a few perfunctory remarks Gordon avoided a substantive discussion of Jersey slavery. As could be expected from a Pennsylvania Whig, he condemned the "accursed slave trade" and involuntary servitude. Although acknowledging

30. Ibid., pp. 94–96, 297–301. On currency in colonial Jersey, see Donald Kemmerer, "A History of Paper Money in Colonial New Jersey, 1668–1775," *Proceedings of the New Jersey Historical Society*, 74 (April 1956): 107–144.

31. The Missouri Compromise (1820) and Denmark Vesey's Plot (1822) foreshadowed the tensions which occurred in the early thirties as a result of Nat Turner's Rebellion (1831), the Virginia Convention (1831–1832), the appearance of William Lloyd Garrison's strident *The Liberator* (1831), and the founding of the American Antislavery Society (1833). The Indian-white confrontation found concrete expression in congressional acts providing for removal (1830) and the establishment of a special Indian territory in Arkansas (1834); Supreme Court decisions such as *Cherokee Nation v. Georgia* (1831) and *Worcester v. Georgia* (1832); some ninety-four treaties negotiated during the Jackson administration; and sporadic warfare such as the Black Hawk War (1832) and the Second Seminole War (1835–1843).

that the enslavement of blacks had "unhappily" been established in New Jersey, he implied that primary blame resided with the "royal patronage" which the "baneful system" received from the mother country rather than with the avariciousness of colonials. Similarly, while quick to note the inherent hypocrisy of the many Quakers who owned slaves, he suggests that Friends "always treated them with humanity." Moreover, he failed to present even a cursory history of slavery in colonial New Jersey let alone an analysis of the slave system, efforts to regulate and restrict the importation of Africans, early antislavery activities, and the obvious contradiction between the rhetoric of independence and the reality of domestic slavery. Indeed, he speciously contends that slavery "did not become inextricably rooted" in New Jersey despite the fact that the province had the second largest slave population of any colony north of Maryland (10–12 percent of the populace) and that slavery persisted in the state well into the nineteenth century (indeed existed when he wrote).[32] Gordon, like his generation, was content to admit to and apologize for slavery and to avoid extended discussion of the institution, the free Negro, and the pervasive question of racial prejudice.

Compared to blacks, considerable attention is accorded the Lenni Lenape, the native population of New Jersey. Unfortunately, it is almost exclusively in the context of war. As if to rationalize future events, Gordon cites the killing of a member of a reconnaissance party sent ashore at Sandy Hook in 1609 by Henry Hudson to support the charge that in encountering Europeans "the Indians committed the first homicide." His condescending, paternalistic attitude toward the Indian is attributable to the tenets of Realpolitik and racism. As he baldly declared, "The strong are every where master of the weak. In all ages, and with all

32. Gordon, *The History of New Jersey*, pp. 56–57. As yet there is no satisfactory general study of slavery in New Jersey. But see Henry S. Cooley, *A Study of Slavery in New Jersey* (Baltimore, Md., 1896); Marion T. Wright, "New Jersey Laws and the Negro," *Journal of Negro History*, 28 (April, 1943): 156–199; and Arthur Zilversmit, *The First Emancipation: The Abolition of Slavery in the North* (Chicago, 1967).

people, the power to subdue has been accompanied with the pretension of right. The European, eminently endowed with this power, mentally and physically, over the untutored savage of America, unhesitatingly, appropriated to himself, all that the latter possessed, comprehending his labour and his life." It was, then, only natural for Europeans to displace a "simple people" who had "advanced little beyond the rudest state of nature." And if Indian lands had been purchased for "generally inconsiderable" sums and goods of "destructive luxury" which served to "debase and destroy" the recipient, it was due to the "ignorance and vanity of the native." The assumption of Indian inferiority is underscored by repeated reference to the "cupidity," the "evil passions," the "whetted appetite for plunder," the "fierce, warlike, and indomitable character," and the "unbounded lust for rapine" which motivated those "savage monsters," those "barbarous wretches." For the plight of the Indian one might feel sympathy, even pity, but never remorse or regret. Thus Gordon could fail to appreciate the irony of designating the reservation established in 1758 on infertile swamp land in Burlington County "Brotherton," and could assert that the purchase of all outstanding Indian land titles for paltry sums by the state of New Jersey early in the nineteenth century was based upon "principles of justice, humanity, and sound policy." Characteristically, humanitarian activities such as those of David and John Brainerd and the New Jersey Association for Helping the Indians are not mentioned.[33]

Then too, the dual, mutually antagonistic currents of American life during the second quarter of the century were reflected in the writings of Gordon and others. On the one hand, these historians were writing at a time when the United States was aggressively asserting its place in the international community and enjoying

33. Gordon, *The History of New Jersey*, pp. 5–6, 39, 58–65, 122, 133, 278–280; see also *History of Pennsylvania*, pp. 43–52, 614–620. For information concerning the aboriginal population of New Jersey, consult Dorothy Cross, *The Indians of New Jersey* (Trenton, N.J., 1955), supplemented by Daniel G. Brinton, *The Lenape and their Legends* (Philadelphia, 1885).

unprecedented expansion on the domestic front: buoyant optimism, audacious self-confidence, and spread-eagle nationalism were orders of the day. On the other hand, there existed clear signs that all was not well with America to a generation which had witnessed the Panic of 1819, heightened sectional animosities, bitter economic division over the tariff and the bank, unsettling political phenomena like the Missouri Compromise, the "corrupt bargain" of 1824, the rise of the "common man," and the overt appearance of racial strife relating to Negroes and Indians. Both consciously and unconsciously, writers of national as well as local histories began to assume the role of latter-day Jeremiahs, calling the attention of the public to those traditional values and assumptions which formed the historic pillars of American society. In order to be truly meaningful, history had to reinforce societal values.

Examples of how personal convictions, contemporary events, and historiographical trends colored the writing of *The History of New Jersey* could be multiplied considerably. Often subtle and unintentional, these characteristics admittedly may have been far less meaningful to early readers than to modern scholars who, in attempting to impose intellectual order upon the writings of the past, inevitably magnify and distort them. Yet the readership of the time was surely aware of the relevance of Gordon's historical message to the contemporary scene. In short, the author and his works must be viewed from the perspective of a special milieu. But ultimately Gordon's *History of New Jersey* must be appraised as a work of history, not genre.

III

Like his other histories, Gordon's study of New Jersey is the product of exhaustive research and careful craftsmanship. However, because the book is devoid of scholarly apparatus—it contains few footnotes and no bibliography—one can easily underestimate the wide range of primary and secondary materials consulted by the author. Yet a careful reading of the text supports his claim to have consulted "all the known histories of the Anglo-American colonies" and "the best writers on the American revolution" in preparing the manuscript; it also reveals undue reliance upon certain authorities. For example, Gordon based his account of proprietary New Jersey (1664–1702) largely upon Smith's *History of Nova-Caesaria*, drew heavily from William Smith's *History of the Province of New York* for the period in which New Jersey and New York shared royal governors (1702–1738), and extracted considerable information about other colonies from James Grahame. His general treatment of revolutionary America rests chiefly upon the work of William Gordon, David Ramsay, and, especially for military matters, John Marshall. Theodore Sedgwick's *Memoir of William Livingston* supplied the basic perspective for viewing the political events which transpired in Jersey during the war.[34] No mere synthesizer and popularizer of published works, Gordon also perused legislative journals, provincial statutes, newspapers, manuscripts preserved in New York and Pennsylvania as well as New Jersey archives, and printed document collections. Few, if any, nineteenth-century historians were as familiar with the materials relating to the history of New Jersey as was Thomas F. Gordon; without question his was the most comprehensive and reliable account of the colonial history of the state written during the century.

However, when Gordon shifts from narration to interpretation of the past, his craftsmanship becomes uneven. At times he reveals

34. William Smith, *The History of the Province of New York from the First Discovery to the Year MDCCXXXII: To Which is Annexed a Description of the Country* (London, 1757; 2d ed., Philadelphia, 1792); James Grahame, *The History of the United States of North America: From the Plantation of the British Colonies till Their Assumption of National Independence* (London, 1827–1829); William Gordon, *The History of the Rise, Progress, and Establishment of the Independence of the United States of America . . .* , 4 vols. (London, 1788); David Ramsay, *The History of the American Revolution* (Philadelphia, 1789); John Marshall, *The Life of George Washington*, 5 vols. (Philadelphia, 1804–1807); Theodore Sedgwick, *A Memoir of the Life of William Livingston . . .* (New York, 1833).

the discerning, critical eye of the lawyer in amassing and evaluating evidence; on other occasions he is uncritical of and seemingly oblivious to evidence, and is given to argumentation and special pleading. But his performance ceases to be erratic when it is remembered that Gordon wrote to a considerable degree as an advocate: he wrote as if he were preparing a case, a historical brief as it were. He consistently accepted at face value the testimony of his clients (assemblymen, popular leaders, Whigs) but questioned or dismissed the view of the opposition (royal officials, British ministers, and Tories). As a result, *The History of New Jersey*, a factually reliable narrative of events, must be used with caution as an interpretive study.

Although an imposing piece of scholarship, Gordon's *History* is less distinguished as literature. He made little effort at embellishment save for occasional stilted, often hyperbolic, rhetorical flourishes designed to impart to the reader a vicarious feeling for the past. For example, after noting that the early settlers of Burlington arrived in December and found a partially iced-over river, he remarks that they were "compelled to endure the hardships inseparable from the occupation of a desert land."[35] His pedestrian syntax, interspersed liberally with lengthy quotations and paraphrases, combined with a penchant for pedantry, result in a rather uninspired narrative. When discussing the revolutionary era the plodding narrative dissipates, but then in favor of the purple prose of the patriot. Finally, the tone is laudatory, even congratulatory, and argumentative; annoying platitudes and homilies further mar the work. However, to dwell on matters of style is unfair and largely irrelevant because Gordon wrote in a clear, straightforward, if somewhat strained manner. More important considerations are focus, content, and analysis.

Prior to the twentieth century, history was generally conceived of in terms of political and military events. (The pervasiveness of the belief that the drama of history was staged in the halls of

35. Gordon, *History of New Jersey*, p. 40.

government and on the battlefield is indicated by the fact that 82 percent of the space in textbooks written in the United States from 1800 to 1860 was devoted to political [46 percent] and martial [36 percent] affairs.)[36] Gordon certainly would have endorsed the dictum that history is past politics; *The History of New Jersey* is first and foremost a chronicle of the political life of colonial Jersey. Concerned only incidentally with social and economic factors, he dealt almost exclusively with the nature of the constitutional and legal environment, the structure and function of government, gubernatorial administrations, and legislative transactions. Specifically, he fashioned "official" or "public" history: an analysis of charters and constitutions, petitions and addresses, statutes and conveyances. Left unanswered or, more precisely, unasked by this institutional approach are such crucial questions as the distinction between the formal and informal dimensions of government and politics, the identification of factions or cliques, political practices and behavior, and collective and individual motivation.[37] Similarly, in offering a concise account of the part played by New Jersey in the intercolonial wars and an extensive description of the military action which transpired in the "Cockpit of the Revolution" during the War for Independence, Gordon confined himself to the traditional saber-rattling, drum-and-bugle variety of military history, with little effort to relate martial affairs to larger social, political, and economic issues.[38]

36. Callcott, *History in the United States,* pp. 102–104.
37. Much work remains to be done on colonial politics in New Jersey. But one must begin with Richard P. McCormick, *The History of Voting in New Jersey: A Study of the Development of Election Machinery, 1664–1911* (New Brunswick, N.J., 1953).
38. The standard general treatment of the war years is Leonard Lundin, *The Cockpit of the Revolution: the War for Independence in New Jersey* (Princeton, N.J., 1940); for civil matters, see David A. Bernstein, "New Jersey in the American Revolution: the Establishment of a Government Amid Civil and Military Disorder, 1770–1781" (Ph.D. diss., Rutgers University, 1969). A wealth of material relating to the war in Jersey is to be found in Douglas Southall Freeman et al., *George Washington, a Biography,* 7 vols. (New York, 1948–1957), 4 and 5. Alfred Hoyt Bill's brief *New Jersey and the Revolutionary War* (Princeton, N.J., 1964), is limited to military campaigns.

The History of New Jersey clearly shows the primacy Gordon accorded the Revolution as the culmination of the colonial epoch. But seventy pages are allotted to Jersey's formative years (from the arrival of Henry Hudson in 1609 to the royal merger of East and West Jersey in 1702), while some two hundred are devoted to the revolutionary era (1763–1789). Indeed, the latter period comprises more than one-half of the book with fully three-fifths of that coverage allocated to the war years (1776–1783). The Confederation period (1783–1789) is treated in a mere twelve pages. Many of the weaknesses of the work are directly attributable to the format, with its imbalance in coverage and improper emphasis.

To accentuate the part played by New Jersey in the pageant of American history, Gordon decided "to treat the general colonial and revolutionary history . . . no further than was indispensable to exhibit the action of New Jersey." Correspondingly, his portrait of the Revolutionary War was predetermined by a desire "to place in full relief, those events, in which the State of New Jersey bore a distinguished part, or claimed a peculiar interest."[39] This narrow, provincial focus inevitably distorted the history of both Jersey and colonial America. An inadequate discussion of developments elsewhere in the colonies makes it impossible to ascertain the role of New Jersey in intercolonial affairs; without this comparative dimension there is no perspective for viewing the events which transpired in the province. What obtains is a chronicle of external events interspersed with proceedings in Jersey which appear in a vacuum.

Similarly, the book lacks an imperial dimension. New Jersey and her sister colonies scarcely appear as an integral part of the First British Empire; there is no appreciation for the Anglo-American dimension of colonial government and politics; little attention is directed toward Whitehall and Westminster save to discuss sundry pernicious acts of Parliament and the machinations of ministerial minions and myrmidons.

39. Gordon, *History of New Jersey*, pp. iii, 320.

The History of New Jersey meets the exacting standards of precision and factual accuracy set for early-nineteenth-century historiography; the few errors of fact that appear are more a source of irritation than a serious detraction.[40] Also annoying are obvious printing errors, and there are occasional glaring inconsistencies, such as the name of Gawen Lawrie appearing also as Gawn Lawrie and Gawn Lawry.[41]

More important than occasional inaccuracies are faulty interpretations. It is no longer possible, for example, to view the so-called French and Indian War from a narrow American perspective, to attribute the conflict simply to French aggression, or to blame Braddock's defeat upon misconduct and ignorance. Neither can one portray Pontiac's Rebellion as a "secret coalition" among the "Shawanese" to attack simultaneously frontier outposts and settlements, or explain the repeal of the Stamp Act in terms of a "paralysis of trade" caused by the colonial boycott. Further, it is not possible to contend that the Massachusetts Acts of 1774 were designed exclusively to punish residents of the Bay Colony; to state that the Quartering Act of 1774 was "passed for quartering soldiers upon the inhabitants"; or to blame the deficiencies of the New Jersey State Constitution of 1776 upon the "extraordinary and unprofitable haste" with which it was drafted and ratified.[42]

40. Ibid., pp. 148, 152, 154, 201; *Gazetteer*, p. 86.
41. Ibid., pp. 35, 39, 42, 133, 334.
42. Ibid., pp. 113ff, 60, 141–142, 155, 182. The most comprehensive study of the war is Lawrence Henry Gipson, *The British Empire before the American Revolution. The Great War for the Empire*, 15 vols. (Caldwell, Idaho, and New York, 1936–1970), 6–8. There is as yet no satisfactory account of New Jersey's role in the conflict. The standard account of the uprising is Howard H. Peckham, *Pontiac and the Indian Uprising* (Chicago, 1947). The political motivation behind repeal of the Stamp Act and the dual nature of the Massachusetts Acts is discussed by Jack M. Sosin in *Agents and Merchants: British Colonial Policy and the Origins of the American Revolution, 1763–1775* (Lincoln, Nebr., 1965), pp. 66–89, and "The Massachusetts Acts of 1774: Coercive or Preventive?," *Huntington Library Quarterly*, 26 (May 1963): 235–252. On misinterpretation of the Quartering Act, see Don R. Gerlach, "A Note on the Quartering Act of 1774," *New England Quarterly*, 34 (March 1966): 80–88. The definitive study of the constitution is Charles R. Erdman, *The New Jersey Constitution of 1776* (Princeton, N.J., 1929).

Unwarranted are statements that "independence . . . was a fore-
gone conclusion" to the members of the First Continental Congress; that the Quebec Act "bore strong indications of the
resolution of the ministry to take from the colonies, generally, the
right of self-government"; that Parliamentary taxation of Americans was "unnecessary, cruel, and unjust" because they had "always made liberal grants" upon requisition; that the Anglo-Dutch
war of 1672 was "most wantonly and unjustly provoked" by a
"dissolute" Charles II "in subservency to the ambitions of Louis
XIV"; or that James II was "inexorable" in pursuing his "arbitrary
purpose" of "annulling all the charters and constitutions of the
American colonies."[43] In most cases such incorrect analyses are
attributable to the preconceptions and prejudices Gordon brought
to his subject rather than defective research.

If Gordon improperly interpreted or exaggerated some occurrences, he failed to appreciate the complexity or significance of
others. Especially cursory treatment is accorded the tangled history
of New Jersey in the seventeenth century (early colonization, the
proprietary period, and the events leading to unification and
royalization) and the Confederation period.[44] Nor is there an
attempt to discuss substantively important phenomena like loyalism.[45] Moreover, Gordon failed to discern the political ramifica-

43. Gordon, *The History of New Jersey*, pp. 29, 52–53, 136, 155, 157.
44. For further information on the seventeenth century see Wesley Frank
Craven, *New Jersey and the English Colonization of North America* (Prince-
ton, N.J., 1964); Adrian C. Leiby, *The Early Dutch and Swedish Settlers of
New Jersey* (Princeton, N.J., 1964); Amandus Johnson, *The Swedish Settlements on the Delaware* . . . *1638–1664*, 2 vols. (New York, 1911); C. A.
Weslager and A. R. Dunlap, *Dutch Explorers, Traders, and Settlers in the
Delaware Valley, 1609–1664* (Philadelphia, 1961); C. A. Weslager, *The
English on the Delaware, 1610–1682* (New Brunswick, N.J., 1967); and
three works by John E. Pomfret: *The Province of West New Jersey, 1609–
1702, A History of the Origins of an American Colony* (Princeton, N.J.,
1956); *The Province of East New Jersey, 1609–1702, The Rebellious Proprietary* (Princeton, N.J., 1962); *The New Jersey Proprietors and their Lands,
1664–1776* (Princeton, N.J., 1964). For the Confederation period, see
Richard P. McCormick, *Experiment in Independence: New Jersey in the
Critical Period, 1781–1789* (New Brunswick, N.J., 1950).
45. On Jersey loyalism, see Paul H. Smith, "New Jersey Loyalists and the
British 'Provincial' Corps in the War for Independence," *New Jersey History*,

tions of the controversy over the status of Treasurer Stephen Skinner after the robbery of the Eastern Treasury in 1768 and the political maneuvering behind the election of William Livingston as the first governor of the State of New Jersey. And he failed to appreciate the influence of events transpiring in neighboring colonies upon the revolutionary movement in Jersey; the development of a sophisticated, extralegal political structure from 1765 to 1776; the signal importance of the Continental Association of 1774 as the capstone of the protest and independence movement.[46] In short, Gordon's treatment of certain aspects of New Jersey history suffers from a failure to ask proper questions of the material.

It is this failure that is perhaps the most serious shortcoming of the work. To Gordon's mind, social and economic phenomena did not properly fall within the province of the historian; hence they received no systematic exposition. Because he was concerned with description rather than explanation, essence rather than causation, inspiration rather than motivation, the text consists mainly of a series of sequentially arranged events unified by an implied or assumed cause-and-effect relationship. And he frequently confused sequence and consequence. Finally, there is no appreciation for the complexity of either human motivation or the historical process, no sensitivity to subtleties or nuances. Personalities fall neatly into virtuous and villainous categories; thoughts and deeds are uniform and clear-cut. This is not to suggest that Gordon was an inferior scholar. Rather, like many other historians, then as now, he was blinded by personal preconceptions as to the nature of history and the purpose of historical writing.

---

87 (Summer 1969): 69–78; the dated, but still useful, E. Alfred Jones, *The Loyalists of New Jersey*, New Jersey Historical Society *Collections*, 10 (Newark, N.J., 1947); Wallace Brown, *The King's Friends: The Composition and Motives of the American Loyalist Claimants* (Providence, R.I., 1965), pp. 111–126.

46. See Larry R. Gerlach, "Revolution or Independence? New Jersey, 1760–1776" (Ph.D. diss., Rutgers University, 1968), passim; Richard P. McCormick, "The First Election of Governor William Livingston," *Proceedings of the New Jersey Historical Society*, 65 (April 1947): 92–100.

Notwithstanding dated assumptions and analyses, *The History of New Jersey* at times has a decidedly modern ring. Gordon's interpretation of the coming of the Revolution, for example, is but a less sophisticated version of the current Neo-Whig position; the argument that Americans maintained a consistent constitutional position on parliamentary taxation during the decade of imperial discord is not unlike the controversial thesis expounded by a modern student; the view that the Congressional resolution of May 15, 1776, constitutes the actual declaration of independence is supported by recent scholarship; the critique of the Constitution of 1776 squares with the definitive study of that document; the assessment of the conduct of General Charles Lee during the Battle of Monmouth is in agreement with that of Lee's biographer; the contention that New Jersey enthusiastically supported the federal Constitution primarily to alleviate fiscal distress coincides with the standard analysis of ratification.[47]

Gordon's history was markedly superior to earlier studies in three basic respects. First, in carrying the story of New Jersey forward from initial settlement to the Constitution, it was far more comprehensive than any other study. Second, based upon an extensive investigation of primary materials, it was easily the most factually reliable account available. Third, it incorporated the findings of numerous secondary authorities. To these must be added an objective treatment of Quakers, especially in the proprietary period. (Coincidentally, the standard histories of New Jersey and Pennsylvania prior to Gordon were written by Friends who viewed uncritically the actions of their coreligionists.)[48] No debunker, Gordon "endeavoured to do full justice" to members of the Society by pointing out their positive contributions as well as "some inconsistencies between their principles and their practices."[49]

47. Gordon, *History of New Jersey*, pp. 145, 179, 181–189, 270–275, 332.
48. Smith, *History of Nova-Caesaria*; Robert Proud, *The History of Pennsylvania*, 2 vols. (Philadelphia, 1797–1798).
49. Gordon, *A History of New Jersey*, pp. 32–37, 57, 320–321, 333–334; *History of Pennsylvania*, pp. v–vi.

IV

Neither Thomas F. Gordon nor his writings have received proper recognition. While he was not a first-rate scholar and his histories are not of the highest order, lesser historians and lesser works are better known. Perhaps, ironically, his cosmopolitan interests and lack of affiliation with established historical agencies contributed to his obscurity. For he was a local historian without a locale, a student of state history who owed scholarly allegiance to no one state. His death evoked surprisingly little comment in the press, and the Historical Society of Pennsylvania cryptically noted on February 13, 1860, the passing of "the Historian of Pennsylvania . . . whose talents and research were also industriously given to the illustration of the history of other States."[50] And some forty years later, in the only extant printed evaluation, *The History of New Jersey* was damned by faint praise—to the reviewer it was "merely a compilation, with little effort at originality, and none at literary embellishment, but with all its deficiencies is a meritorious work."[51] Author and writings deserve better.

A modest contribution to historical literature, *The History of New Jersey* is important principally as a pioneering achievement. As the first general history of New Jersey from 1609 to 1789 it enjoys a prominent place in the historiography of the state and early America. The product of a careful synthesis of secondary works and an exhaustive examination of primary materials, it influenced subsequent writing on the Garden State for several generations. It remains today the most comprehensive single volume political history of colonial New Jersey.

Gordon hoped his assiduous research would result in "a faithful and ample narrative" of New Jersey history from the arrival of

50. Hampton L. Carson, *A History of the Historical Society of Pennsylvania*, 2 vols. (Philadelphia, 1940), 1: 277.
51. William Nelson, "Fifty Years of Historical Work in New Jersey," New Jersey Historical Society *Collections*, VIII (1900): 21–22.

Europeans to the ratification of the Constitution of the United States. He executed that formidable task with precision and accuracy. *The History of New Jersey* is a reliable account of the period covered, excellent for official or public political history, but with no pretense of dealing substantively with social or economic matters. It is a classic of early American historiography—one which all students of New Jersey history should consult.

8.

Thomas Jones of New York, a Loyalist Historian of the American Revolution

ROGER J. CHAMPAGNE

Those men and women who committed themselves, for whatever reason, to the Tory side of the American Revolution found themselves bitterly disappointed by England's failure to crush the rebellion. To those who remained loyal to king and country, the madness of the rebel cause seemed self-evident and the prospects of a rebel victory seemed unbelievable. What chance, Loyalists asked themselves, did thirteen jealous colonies, without a regular army and navy, industry, or money, have against one of Europe's leading military powers? Despite British tactical setbacks in Massachusetts and South Carolina, their easy victories over Washington's rag-tail army in New York and New Jersey strengthened the Loyalist belief in England's invincibility. But after 1777 the war seemed to go sour, and earlier Loyalist optimism about a speedy restoration of royal control turned to frustration and impatience. Although frequently critical of the failure of British strategy and leadership, Loyalists never lost hope that the next campaign would end the war. Yorktown did just that, but not in the expected way. The Treaty of Paris, recognizing American independence, was the final act in the Loyalist tragedy.

As Loyalist refugees scattered to face an uncertain future in England, Canada, and the West Indies, they sought to understand why they had become a dispossessed class in a once mighty but now humbled empire. How was it possible, they asked, that the powerful armies of Howe and Clinton, protected by an unmatched navy and supplied with a full war chest, could not overwhelm George Washington's farmer-soldiers? Considering the heavy property and human losses of Loyalists, and considering the disparity between the two sides, that question would haunt many of them for the rest of their lives. And historians ever since have pondered the problem.[1]

Thomas Jones of New York, as a Loyalist refugee living in England, attempted a historical analysis of Britain's failure to put down the American rebellion. Writing sometime between 1781 and 1792, Jones recorded his observations of men and events before and during the British occupation of New York.[2] His observations first appeared in print in 1879 under the title of *History of New York During the Revolutionary War and of The Leading Events in the Other Colonies at That Period.*

His family background and place in New York society provided Thomas Jones with a vantage point from which he could view the start and course of the American Revolution. Born in 1731 into an established family of Long Island, young Jones had all the advantages which New York's aristocratic society could offer. His father, David Jones, lawyer and politician, possessed 6,000 acres of farm land on Long Island and maintained at Fort Neck, Oyster Bay, one of the Island's finest family seats. As befitted a local patrician, the senior Jones served Queens County in the General Assembly for twenty-one years, thirteen as speaker of the house. In 1758, David Jones was named to the provincial supreme court, an appointment he held until 1773 when he relinquished his place to his son Thomas. Like other young men of his age, Thomas Jones went to Yale College, graduating in 1750, and decided upon a law career. After serving several years in his father's New York City

1. John R. Alden, *A History of the American Revolution* (New York, 1969), pp. 245–261.
2. Thomas Jones, *History of New York during the Revolutionary War, and of the Leading Events in the Other Colonies at that Period,* ed. Edward Floyd de Lancey, 2 vols, (New York, 1879), 1: xi.

office, shared with Joseph Murray, Thomas Jones was admitted to the bar in 1755.[3]

The years ahead proved easy and exciting for the young lawyer. Although New York City was a provincial town by European standards, it was urbane and sophisticated compared to the roughness and quiet of the country. In the late 1750s, as the French and Indian War developed into Britain's greatest contest with France for empire, the city became a garrison town and military entrepôt and experienced unusual prosperity. Opportunities abounded for the ambitious and energetic, whether in commerce, privateering, or military service, and many of the city's future revolutionary leaders established modest fortunes and reputations during the war years.[4]

Local politics also interested the young lawyer and son of a prominent provincial politician. The 1750s were the years of ascendancy for the De Lancey family, and from his position as chief justice and lieutenant governor, James De Lancey dominated the politics of the decade. David Jones, as assembly speaker, allied himself with the chief justice and received his reward in his appointment to the supreme court in 1758. Even young Jones benefited from De Lancey's patronage by being named, in 1757, Clerk of the Queens County Court of Common Pleas.[5]

Although Chief Justice De Lancey's political power remained intact until 1759, it was challenged on several points during the decade. The primary issue arose over the funding and management of the new Kings College and the efforts of Anglican churchmen to make the school denominational, a program identified with De Lancey. *The Independent Reflector*, a weekly magazine started in

3. Thomas Jones's life is best followed in Edward de Lancey's Introduction to the *History of New York*, 1: iiii–lix; Peter Ross, *A History of Long Island From Its Earliest Settlement To the Present Time*, 2 vols. (New York, 1902), 1: 91, 127; B. F. Thompson, *History of Long Island*, 3 vols. (New York, 1918), 2: 328.

4. Alexander C. Flick, ed., *History of the State of New York*, 10 vols. (New York, 1962 edition), 2: 241–242.

5. Stanley N. Katz, *Newcastle's New York: Anglo-American Politics, 1732–1753* (Cambridge, Mass., 1968), 174; Jones, *History of New York*, 1: lix.

late 1752 by William Livingston, William Smith, Jr., and John Morin Scott, all Yalemen and lawyers, launched a newspaper war against Anglican attempts to control the college. Lasting several years, the war of words sent political shock waves throughout the province. As Thomas Jones remembered years later, "The whole province was put into a ferment, meetings in all the towns and districts were called, inflammatory speeches in such meetings made; the Counties were canvassed, the presbyterian pulpits thundered sedition, and every engine was set at work to gain petitioners, addressers, and remonstrants."[6] No record exists of Jones's active participation in the political quarrel, but as an Anglican and a rising member of a family closely linked with Chief Justice De Lancey, he would naturally stand in opposition to the "triumvirate." Indeed, the long enmity that Jones felt toward William Livingston, William Smith, and John Morin Scott undoubtedly dated from that time.

The political association of the Jones and De Lancey families was placed on a more personal basis in 1762 when Thomas married Anne De Lancey, daughter of the chief justice. As a wedding gift and part of his wife's patrimony, Thomas Jones received from his brother-in-law, Captain James De Lancey, several acres of land on Manhattan Island. Located along the East River about two miles northeast from the city's center, Jones built a distinctive country house on a rise described as the island's highest elevation. The house, situated less than a mile from the De Lancey family seat, was finished in 1765 and in keeping with the political temper of the times was known as "Mount Pitt."[7]

Thomas Jones was not a political activist; at least the record does not show him to be. Yet he was clearly identified as part of the De Lancey political network. His own family background, religion, marriage, residence, and, in the prerevolutionary decade,

6. Milton M. Klein, ed., *The Independent Reflector* . . . (Cambridge, Mass., 1963), pp. 30–44; Jones, *History of New York*, 1: 13.
7. Ibid., 1: lxi; Harry B. Yoshpe, *The Disposition of Loyalist Estates in the Southern District of the State of New York* (New York, 1939), p. 38 n.

office holding marked him politically. Jones apparently never sought an elective office as had his father, but took a safer and probably more prestigious and profitable political route through crown appointments. Jones, however, had to wait during the 1760s until the Livingstons lost power. Following the De Lancey assembly election victories in 1768 and 1769, and the coming to power of Lieutenant Governor Cadwallader Colden, preferment came Jones's way.[8] Out of recognition for his De Lancey connections and his stature in the legal profession, he received the post of Recorder of New York City, served as attorney for Kings College and New York City, and in 1773 claimed a place on the supreme court bench when his father retired because of old age.[9] Jones's rise in government was hardly spectacular or one likely to leave his mark in the colony's history. Bred and reared in the law, he prepared himself for the judiciary rather than the legislative or administrative branches of government. The War for Independence and the shifts of imperial politics conspired to frustrate Thomas Jones's ambition to become chief justice.

Thomas Jones's position remains enigmatic concerning Britain's imperial administration following the French and Indian War. However, his eventual Loyalist sympathies did not mean that he supported parliamentary authority at this time, especially its superior right to tax the colonies. More likely, he supported the New York Assembly's petitions against the Sugar Act and Stamp Act, and later the adoption of nonimportation by New York City's merchants. At the heart of the issue between New York and Great Britain, as with other colonies, was the exercise of local autonomy by the provincial legislature. The problem had earlier been settled in favor of the New York Assembly to the satisfaction of provin-

---

8. The issues and results of the assembly elections of 1768 and 1769 are analyzed in Roger J. Champagne, "Family Politics versus Constitutional Principles: the New York Assembly Elections of 1768 and 1769," *William and Mary Quarterly*, 3d series, 20 (1963): 57–79; see also Lawrence H. Leder, "The New York Elections of 1769: An Assault on Privilege," *Mississippi Valley Historical Review*, 49 (1963): 675–682.

9. Jones, *History of New York*, 1: lx.

cial political leaders in the 1740s and 1750s. Those leaders were Thomas's father and the De Lancey connections on his wife's side. It seems improbable, therefore, that Jones would reject his own family's political achievements, thereby also rejecting the New York Assembly's constitutional position in the 1760s and early 1770s.[10]

However, the turbulence and violence of the more radical elements in New York City shocked Jones and other men of a conservative temper. The behavior of the leaders of the Sons of Liberty, Isaac Sears, John Lamb, and Alexander McDougall, particularly outraged the conservatives, and Jones portrayed all three as dishonest men who craftily used imperial issues to plunge the city into turmoil for their own personal gain. Jones asserted in his *History* that McDougall "was a principal promoter and encourager of the unhappy disputes which raged with such violence in the colony for many years, terminated in a rebellion, in a dismemberment of the empire, in almost a total destruction of thirteen valuable provinces, and in the loss of not less than 100,000 men." A gathering of men was a mob to Jones, and a New York City mob consisted either of "presbyterian republicans" or rabble, and in his mind there probably was not much difference between the two. As he put it frequently, the "presbyterians, republicans, and rebels" had as their avowed objective "the destruction of monarchy, episcopacy, and the established church."[11] The milling in the streets, mass meetings, parades, illegal committees, intimidation of persons not of the same views, and violence against property and individuals—all challenged the colonial order, not the constitutional presumptions of the ministry seeking to tax the American provinces. If unchecked, civil war would result.

The meeting of the First Continental Congress marked a turning point for Thomas Jones. He agreed with others on the need to oppose British policy which would undermine the hard-won autonomy of colonial assemblies; he accepted the need to

10. Katz, *Newcastle's New York*, pp. 173–176, 184–187.
11. Jones, *History of New York*, 1: 26, 59.

place the relations between America and the mother country on more satisfactory grounds. For that purpose, he supported an intercolonial meeting, and he looked forward to its work with rising hope. Jones stated the optimism of New York conservatives: "*A redress of grievances, and a firm union between Great Britain and America upon constitutional principles was their only aim. This they hoped for, this they wished for, this they expected. To this purport they also verbally instructed their delegates.*" But his expectations were "blasted by a hasty, ill-judged and precipitate" congressional endorsement of the Suffolk Resolves, which "contained in almost express terms a declaration of war against Great Britain."[12] The adoption of the Association, unleashing an army of local committeemen to harass and intimidate respectable citizens, ended all hope of internal peace.

Although Jones could support an intercolonial meeting because it served his purposes, he opposed implementation of the Association, which in his mind became illegal and a threat to the fabric of society. Jones was particularly upset by the method of establishing local committees, the decisions of their membership, and their activities, all of which resulted, in his view, in a steady deterioration of governmental authority. By the spring of 1775, following news of Lexington and Concord, he urged Governor William Tryon to call out the militia to clear New York's streets and to arrest those who defied legal authority. Although overruled, Jones's attitude remained firm. When Governor Tryon in November 1775 sent him to Westchester County to hold court for a number of capital offenders, Jones took the opportunity to urge the grand jury to indict local committeemen, who were seizing arms and ammunition, for trespass and riot. He also released four persons whom the county committee had jailed for Toryism.[13]

No question existed by 1776 as to which side of the controversy Jones supported. Events since the First Continental Congress had clearly headed the colonies toward war with Britain and toward a

12. Ibid., 1: 35 (Jones's italics), 36.
13. Ibid., 1: lxii, 41; 2: 282–283.

civil conflict. The earlier hope of a reconciliation with the mother country had become wishful thinking by 1776 for men like Jones, and he could not escape the fact that many of his relatives and friends judged him an enemy of America. Unwilling to take refuge on a British warship in New York harbor, Jones remained on his country estate at Oyster Bay, Long Island, dodging raiding parties sent into Queens County by revolutionary leaders to hunt down Tories and collect arms and ammunition. When he ignored an order of the New York Congress to appear before an investigating committee, he was arrested on June 27, 1776. He obtained a parole, but not for long. As Washington's army prepared to battle the British on Long Island, Jones was seized and on August 12 ordered to Connecticut and placed under the jurisdiction of Governor Jonathan Trumbull; several days later Jones found himself in a Norwich, Connecticut, jail. Four months later he was back on Long Island on parole.[14]

The British campaign victories over George Washington liberated areas of New York in which Thomas Jones lived and worked. Unlike many other New York Loyalists who had to move, Jones lived comfortably in his country house at Fort Neck and divided his time between managing his Queens County lands and tending to legal business in New York City. He was well off compared to others, but refugees and soldiers crowded British occupied areas; everything was scarce and high priced; and military regulations were strange and irritating.[15] Despite the difficult circumstances, the expectation of a complete British victory over the American rebels made the problems tolerable. To Loyalist frustrations, that victory never came, but Jones did not have to wait until the bitter end to leave New York. On November 6, 1779, he fell victim to a Connecticut raiding party sent to seize a Loyalist in order to effect an exchange for the captured Connecticut general, Gold S. Silli-

14. Ibid., 1: lxii–lxiii, 68–70; 2: 297–299.
15. The best account of wartime conditions in New York City is Oscar T. Barck, Jr., *History of New York City during the War for Independence* (New York, 1931).

man. Although treated moderately well, Jones suffered from the cold weather and an accidental injury.[16] When he was finally exchanged in February 1780 for General Silliman, his former classmate at Yale, Jones failed to respond to treatment and rest at Fort Neck. The next year he decided to try the famous waters at Bath, England, fully intending to return to New York when he recovered. He could never come back to America. Yorktown, the fall of the North ministry, and peace negotiations meant an end to the war; and an end to the war meant that the New York Act of Attainder of 1779, banishing Thomas Jones and others forever from the state, would become effective. Jones remained at Bath until 1785 and then moved to Hoddesdon (Hertfordshire) near London where he died in 1792.[17]

Before his death, Thomas Jones entered a claim with the Royal Commission investigating Loyalist losses in America. Jones forfeited to state authorities his property at Mount Pitt and farm lands in Queens, Westchester, Ulster, and Tryon counties, which he estimated at £9,479. Losses of salary and personal property came to £3,152, for a total claim of £12,631 sterling. The Claims Commission awarded him £5,522. The only property saved from New York authorities was the family estate at Fort Neck in Queens County. David Jones entailed the estate to his eldest son, Thomas, and his male line, but as Thomas was legally dead and without male issue, Fort Neck passed to Thomas' oldest sister, Arabella, and her male line, David Richard Floyd-Jones.[18]

When Thomas Jones sailed out of New York harbor on June 14, 1781, the Revolutionary War was already six years old. He left the military situation in New York about the same as it had been when Washington's army retreated from the colony in 1776, with

16. Jones, *History of New York*, 2: 277–278; Ross, *History of Long Island*, 1: 927–930.

17. Jones, *History of New York*, 1: lxv, lxvii, lxxv.

18. Ibid., 1: lxviii; Yoshpe, *Disposition of Loyalist Estates*, p. 46 n.

the British confined to Long Island, Staten Island, and Manhattan Island, and holding outposts in the southern part of Westchester County. Too strongly fortified and defended for easy dislodging, the British in New York thought themselves too weak to mount the offensive against the main American army up the Hudson River that would bring them closer to final victory. Even their hope of success for Lord Cornwallis's southern campaign faded by the early summer of 1781. If at the time of his sailing Jones still had hopes of a speedy British victory, he failed to reveal them, but he was probably still confident that the American rebellion would die. Within a year of his departure, Jones, like other Loyalists who left America, found himself sorely disappointed by Britain's ultimate failure.

Thomas Jones always hoped that someday he would return to America. At first he thought that he could do so in the summer of 1783, but peace and recognition of American independence meant a delay, for he first wanted to see if New York would repeal its anti-Tory legislation as stipulated by the Articles of Peace. As he wrote to his sister, "I shall return to America as soon as I receive authentic intelligence of such an event having taken place, but not before, as I will not run the risk of being hanged while I can keep my neck out of the halter."[19] What he wanted never took place. As that fact became more apparent to him, with months passing into years without a change in New York policy, his disappointment over the war turned to a bitterness which he scattered across the pages of his manuscript history of the Revolutionary War.

Just when Thomas Jones started writing a history of the war and his reasons for doing so remain clouded. He did not need self-justification, for he had an unimportant role before and during the war. Nor did he apparently set out to villify his old political enemies, though the finished product at times had that appearance. Jones probably sought answers to questions which must have

19. Jones, 1: lxvii.

nagged every Loyalist exile: why did the war start, and once begun, how could Great Britain have lost when it should have won?[20]

As Jones analyzed the coming of independence and the war, the legislative and administrative relationship between Great Britain and its colonies after 1763 had less significance than the conspiratorial nature of New York politics. The issues of parliamentary taxation and metropolitan control had importance to the colonial governmental structure, but the use made of those imperial crises by self-serving politicians had far greater impact. A network of ambitious families and church affiliations dominated New York politics, according to Jones, and this reduced itself to the Livingstons against the De Lanceys, to the Presbyterians against the Anglicans. De Lancey and Anglican control in 1752, Jones believed, meant a "golden age" of harmony and tranquility in the colony.[21]

That year also marked the beginning of the *Independent Reflector*, controlled by Livingston, Smith, and Scott. The three young men "being all of the law, nearly of an age, and linked together in friendship, in principles, in politics, and religion, they formed themselves into a triumvirate, and determined, if possible, to pull down Church and State, to raise their own government and religion upon its ruins, or to throw the whole province into anarchy and confusion." Livingston, Smith, and Scott also founded the Whig Club in 1752, where they devised plans, formed schemes and plots, and made decisions "for carrying the great project into execution, of pulling down the church, ruining the Constitution, or heaving the whole province into confusion."[22] Thus, Jones saw a political conspiracy in existence long before the British ministries and Parliament attempted to tax the colonies. Indeed, he viewed the triumvirate's activities as a far greater threat to New York than ministerial and parliamentary measures.

20. William H. Nelson, *The American Tory* (Oxford, 1961), pp. 134–152, discusses at length the Loyalist disillusionment.
21. Jones, *History of New York*, 1: 2.
22. Ibid., 1: 5, 6.

Differences over the latter, hopefully, could be reconciled, but how could one come to terms with a local cabal intent upon exploiting every opportunity to destroy the state? The "friends of government," the De Lancey party, had expected the 1774 Continental Congress to resolve the constitutional problems of empire, which would then allow them time to deal with the internal conspiracy. But the power of that conspiracy turned efforts toward conciliation into revolution and war. The republican-presbyterian conspiracy finally triumphed over monarchy, constitution, and church in New York.

The rebel victory of 1776, however, was only political. The battlefield would determine success or failure, for Great Britain did not intend to abandon its American colonies without a fight. As Thomas Jones narrated and analyzed the military campaigns, from Long Island to Yorktown, an inescapable conclusion emerged in his writing: the British possessed a clear military superiority. Both the British army and navy consisted of professional fighting men, disciplined, properly equipped, under experienced officers, and the equal of any military establishment in Europe. By contrast, the American army consisted of farmers and city mechanics, resembling an armed mob more than an obedient and responsive fighting force. And according to Jones, no gentlemen served among the American officers. The marked differences between the two armies meant that the British had no concern about the size of Washington's force, which they only had to seek out and destroy. Although defeated many times, the American army remained intact, while the main British force under Howe and Clinton was never in jeopardy. The next campaign always held out the hope of a final triumph over the Americans.[23] Yet the British lost the war, and that fact amazed and depressed Thomas Jones. It led him to the quite logical conclusion that the British lost the war away from the scenes of combat.

23. Throughout his *History*, Jones discussed each military campaign and gave an estimation of the opposing armies. The conclusion is inescapable that he expected a British victory in every battle.

Although Thomas Jones never applied systematic analysis to the problem, five factors emerge from his history of the war as important determinants of Britain's failure. First, the nature and rules of British politics emphasized, as it had in New York, the pursuit of personal ambitions rather than the national interest. Consequently, a parliamentary faction opposed Lord North's ministry and the king's intention to prosecute the war vigorously. Instead of patriotic support of the war effort, politicians challenged policies and measures to embarrass their opponents or to gain patronage for themselves and friends as the price of their acquiescence. As Jones complained at one point in his *History*, "America was lost in the British parliament."[24]

Jones saw parliamentary politics as an obstacle that a vigorous, dedicated, and wise military leadership in America could have overcome. However, the highest command levels in the British army and navy lacked that quality of leadership, according to Jones, and this represented a second factor in Britain's failure. He characterized the first commander in chief, Sir William Howe, as a cautious, slow-moving general, a member of the parliamentary faction opposing Lord North's ministry, and a military man interested in pomp and circumstance and the charms of Mrs. Joshua Loring. Jones thought his title should be "Baron Delay Warr."[25] Although Jones conceded that Howe won a few big battles, he argued that Howe failed to see his opportunities to crush Washington and end the rebellion. Military leadership sank to its lowest depths with the appointment of Sir Henry Clinton as Howe's successor.

Jones could not write of Clinton without dipping his pen in acid. After discussing, for example, Clinton's defeat in South Carolina in 1776, Jones asked, "Was there ever a more stupid piece of business, except indeed when the Ministry, after this, intrusted this man with the supreme command in North America,

24. Jones, *History of New York*, 2: 349. See also 1: 251–252 for Jones's strictures upon Howe's politics.
25. Ibid., 1: 197.

and the numberless stupid acts he did in that command?" General Clinton's record as commanding officer did not improve as the years passed. As Jones surveyed each year's campaigning, British battlefield successes were the work of competent field commanders, not Clinton, who wasted the advantages gained by his subordinate officers. A weak yet obstinate man, jealous of rivals, the general was unpopular with his own men as well as New York Loyalists: "Clinton was in general disliked; he was haughty, morose, churlish, stupid, and scarcely ever to be spoken with." While other men may have disliked Clinton, Jones clearly hated him and at times heaped the entire blame for Britain's defeat on his shoulders. "To the pusillanimity in all his action," Jones indicted Clinton, "To his want of that resolution, spirit, and abilities, which should ever attend the general of a large army. To the stupidity of his head, his enmity to Lord Cornwallis, and his implicit confidence in the advice of a few designing wretches, may be attributed the loss of America, the dismemberment of the British empire, the disgrace of the nation, and an inglorious peace."[26]

Inefficient, wasteful, and arbitrary methods of operations in the entire military establishment provided the third factor in Britain's defeat. Jones held Clinton responsible, for within the framework of traditional British military administration, the commanding general established working policies covering logistics and the rule of the civilian population living within British-controlled territory. The army behind the lines was larger and costlier than troops in the field and thus drained away the vitality and will to win of the British war effort. Considering the war as a defense of the ideals of monarchy, constitution, and church, Jones was outraged at Clinton's failure to see to it that his own household always remained clean, thereby allowing the American rebels to stand guilty of personal profit-taking and injustice. But everywhere he looked, Jones saw commissaries and quartermasters and their own army of

26. Ibid., 1: 100, 319, 2: 185.

subordinates and workers siphoning off the resources of loyal subjects and British taxpayers. "In short," Jones concluded, "from the whole conduct of the Army during the course of the war, it seemed as if the suppression of a dangerous rebellion was but a secondary consideration. The war in fact, was not levied at rebellion, but at the treasury of Great Britain; at his Majesty's loyal subjects within the lines; indiscriminately against all persons wherever the army moved; against erudition, religion, and literature in general."[27]

The conduct of the army behind the lines, no less than in the field, helped cause Britain to lose the war. In this, Sir Henry Clinton played a decisive role by his refusal to permit an immediate restoration of civil government in areas under royal control. Of all Clinton's blunders, the suppression of New York's regular government struck Jones hardest. From the beginning of the military occupation, neither Howe nor Clinton intended to relinquish their control to a civilian government. They simply pushed Governor William Tryon aside, gave him a military assignment, and promptly forgot him. Only when the administration of occupied New York became a burden to the military authorities did Clinton turn to civilians, but only in ways which largely ignored the old forms of colonial government. Courts of police controlled country areas; a military commandant, assisted by the mayor, administered New York City; and a titular royal governor headed the provincial government from 1776 to 1782. The judiciary and legislature, as Jones knew them, simply did not function, though he insisted that either could have been easily revived. Court martial trials of civilians and the arbitrary judicial and administrative proceedings of the courts of police outraged Jones's regard for the law. The suspension of regular government suited the military's purposes, giving commanding generals a free hand and

27. Ibid., 1: 139–140. Jones detailed how the various commissaries looted the public treasury. One quartermaster made off with £150,000 from his dealings in wagons and horses and retired to England; his three successors made even greater profits. Ibid., 1: 330–352.

keeping army personnel out of the clutches of a pesty civilian officialdom. It also provided a golden opportunity, as far as Jones was concerned, for "interested, selfish, peculating individuals" to build fortunes out of the country's misfortunes. If only Great Britain had convened the assembly, reinstated the regular magistrates, and opened the courts, the war would have ended differently, for loyal Americans knew how to deal with rebellious Americans.[28]

That was the situation in New York as Jones recalled it several years later while writing his *History*. Its memory must have galled him, especially as he observed the caliber of men who had been influential in Clinton's inner circle of political friends. The principals then active in office were Major General James Robertson, city commandant and governor; Andrew Elliot, customs collector, head of the Department of Police, and lieutenant governor; David Mathews, mayor of New York. Each had his flock of subordinates, each violated the public trust, and each had no interest in promoting the war effort. Two men, in Jones's view, had a particularly detrimental influence on General Clinton: Joseph Galloway, a refugee from Pennsylvania, and William Smith, Jr., a sometime New York Whig. To both men Jones attributed a good measure of New York's misery and Britain's loss of the war. After Galloway worked his way into the inner circle, he argued that the 1775 Prohibitory Act suspended the operation of government and law in the American colonies until the rebellion ended. General Clinton seized upon Galloway's interpretation to justify military over civilian rule.[29] Although the results of Galloway's interpretation of the Prohibitory Act had tragic consequences for New York Loyalists, permitting incompetents like Robertson, Elliot, and Mathews to attain place and power, the Pennsylvanian only misread the law; he did not commit treachery.

The case of William Smith, Jr., was quite different. His self-

28. Ibid., 2: 22–23, 120–124. Chapter 3 offers specific cases of seizures of property by action of the Courts of Police.
29. Ibid., 2: 108–112.

proclaimed Loyalism, his political intimacy with General Clinton, his royal appointment as chief justice, and his omission from the rebel legislature's Act of Attainder—all were achievements of a political trimmer whose only guiding principle was to serve himself. Thomas Jones choked with rage every time he thought of how Smith rose in the Crown's favor and simultaneously stayed on the good side of the rebels; how Smith, a johnny-come-lately to the Loyalist cause, got the choice appointment to the New York bench, for which Jones yearned; how Smith, because he transmitted secret British plans to the rebel Governor George Clinton, kept his property safe from rebel hands, while Jones lost so much because of his loyal principles. Little wonder, in Jones's estimation, that the British lost, with the villainous Smith daily advising General Clinton on the conduct of the war.[30]

Twentieth-century historians have characterized Thomas Jones as a "partisan," and his history of New York as a "partisan history of the state."[31] They have judged his writing as the unreliable work of a fierce Loyalist. Thomas Jones's history of the Revolutionary War was neither a sophisticated analysis nor a full narrative of the issues and personalities involved in the drama of American independence. As he wrote his history, Jones made no effort to conceal his strong loyalism, which meant to him an unquestioned acceptance of monarchy, the English constitution, and the Anglican Church. He wore the label without apology, as a badge of pride. The result was a history openly hostile toward those Ameri-

30. Jones described William Smith as possessing "all that art, cunning, chicanery, dissimulation, hypocrisy, and adulation . . . which were, was, and ever will be, the true characteristic of a person professing the religion of a New England dissenter, and the politics of an English republican." Ibid., 1: 168, 234–235; 2: 206.

31. For examples, see Wallace Brown, *The King's Friends: The Composition and Motives of the American Loyalist Claimants* (Providence, R.I., 1965), p. 89; Dorothy R. Dillon, *The New York Triumvirate: A Study of the Legal and Political Careers of William Livingston, John Morin Scott, and William Smith, Jr.* (New York, 1949), pp. 16–17; Alexander C. Flick, *Loyalism in New York during the American Revolution* (New York, 1901), p. 280.

cans who fought and died for independence. If it occurred to him at all, Jones rejected the notion that American Whigs were men of integrity and sincerity equal to himself. Thus Jones became intemperate when writing of Whigs generally, but especially when dealing with his old political enemies in New York. His intemperance toward his adversaries, however, only reaffirmed the fact that American participants, Whigs as well as Loyalists, regarded the conflict as a civil war as well as an imperial contest between England and its colonies. Jones's partisanship was a product of the passionate hatreds generated by civil war, an emotional outburst which, with equal intensity, Whig authors like William Gordon, David Ramsay, and Mercy Otis Warren directed toward their adversaries, the American Loyalists.[32]

Jones was equally hard on those Loyalists and Englishmen who, by their wartime pursuit of personal power and profit, contributed to Britain's defeat. Some of the best and most important portions of his *History* dealt with the British military administration of occupied New York. Indeed, nowhere else is there a fuller contemporary account of the operations and practices of the courts of police, the extent of plural office holding, and the degree of graft common to all levels of the occupation force.[33] An attempt to check the accuracy of Jones's facts revealed that modern historians have readily accepted as authoritative Jones's revelations of incompetence, injustice, and corruption.[34] But Jones did not stop with a mere recitation of details; he also characterized the actors, presenting a vicious portrait of Clinton, Smith, and Robertson, equaling

32. William Gordon, *The History of the Rise, Progress, and Establishment, of the Independence of the United States of America* . . . 4 vols. (London, 1778); David Ramsay, *The History of the American Revolution*, 2 vols. (Philadelphia, 1789); Mercy Otis Warren, *History of the Rise, Progress and Termination of the American Revolution: Interspersed with Biographical, Political and Moral Observations*, 3 vols. (Boston, 1805).

33. Jones, *History of New York*, 1: 330–352; 2: 1–76.

34. For example, Thomas Jefferson Wertenbaker, *Father Knickerbocker Rebels: New York City during the Revolution* (New York, 1948), pp. 158–161.

if not exceeding those he drew of New York Whigs. He was indeed a fierce Loyalist.

Great Britain should have won a complete victory over the rebellious American colonies, thereby restoring the crown and constitution to their former place in the empire. But it did not, and as Thomas Jones tried to understand that traumatic defeat and his own personal loss he concluded that human ambition, selfishness, and corruption were at the bottom of Britain's failure to subdue the American rebellion. He was struck by the horrible fact that the English nation gained nothing but dishonor from the thousands of lives lost and the huge sums of money spent; a dishonor that eroded the very human fiber of the English people as a nation. This theme runs throughout Jones's history of the war. Instead of a war over constitutional principles, national self-determination, or economic systems, as modern historians would view it, it was a war for men to satisfy their personal ambitions out of the wreckage of empire. Seen in terms of men in positions of power, whether colonials or Britons, Whigs or Loyalists, the American Revolution was a sordid affair from start to finish. It should have never begun, but once started it should have ended quickly. Thomas Jones's *History of New York During the Revolutionary War* is thus an indictment of the corrupting influence of the human spirit upon the course of public affairs.

9.

Anne Grant's Memoirs

Robert G. Wheeler

Early nineteenth-century Americans and Europeans had little knowledge of the full extent of the United States and its resources. Yet they eagerly sought such information. European commentators met the demand for some indication of the country's variety and found a good market for travel volumes in the Old World and the New.

Writers and artists were fascinated by the exploration of the New World, and their interest ran high regarding this strange, remote, wilderness country, with its fabled natural features, its red-skinned inhabitants, its settlements and accommodations, its flora and fauna.[1] Albany and the Hudson Valley became a focal point

---

1. For example: Thomas Cooper, *Some Information Respecting America* (London, 1794); J. Hector St. John de Crevecoeur, *Letters from an American Farmer* (London, 1783); Marquis de Chastellux, *Travels in North-America in the Years 1780, 1781 and 1782* (London, 1787); Isaac Weld, Jr., *Travels in North America and the Provinces of Upper and Lower Canada, during the Years 1795, 1796, and 1797* (London, 1799); Richard Parkinson, *A Tour of America in 1798, 1799, and 1800* (London, 1805); Captain Basil Hall, *Travels in North America in the Years 1827 and 1828* (Edinburgh, 1829); Frances Trollope, *Domestic Manners of the Americans* (London, 1832). Of the many European-born artists who recorded America, there were Charles Balthazer Julien Fevret du Saint Memin (1770–1852), who did portraits in crayon and topographic views in aquatint, beginning in 1793; Archibald (1765–1835) and Alexander Robertson (1772–1841), two Scots who did pencil drawings and watercolor topographic views after 1791–1792; John Hill (1770–1850), a London-trained aquatinter who engraved Joshua Shaw's *Picturesque Views of American Scenery* (1820) and W. G. Wall's *The Hudson River Portfolio* (1828); Jacques Gerard Milbert (1766–1840), who printed a *Series of Picturesque Views of North America* (Paris, 1825), and *Itineraire*

of interest as a frontier region in which Europeans and Indians touched one another and as a microcosm of the interaction between settlers of different nations, between Dutch and English. Two major mid-eighteenth century writers had chronicled Albany in the Upper Hudson Valley. Dr. Alexander Hamilton, a Baltimore physician, had sailed up the Hudson River on a sloop in 1744; Peter Kalm, the eminent Swedish naturalist, arrived in Albany five years later. Both penned their impressions of a provincial, Dutch-oriented community—Hamilton in his *Itinerarium* (New England and New York, 1744), and Kalm in his *Travels in North America* (Stockholm, 1753; London, 1770).

Anne McVickar Grant offered a third impression of the Albany region when she published her *Memoirs of an American Lady* in 1808 and offered the public a tale of a major mid-eighteenth century community and a great American family—the Schuylers. She touched on the story of the English military frontier in New York and encompassed, in a degree, the social changes in a well-established town as its living habits and attitudes were transformed from those of the founding Dutch to those of the governing English.

Mrs. Grant (1755–1838) was born in Glasgow on February 21, 1755, the daughter of Duncan McVickar, a farmer who obtained a commission in a Highland regiment. He sailed for America in 1757 during the French and Indian War, and one year later his wife and daughter followed him. They first settled in Claverack, but soon moved some thirty miles northward to Albany. In 1760 Captain McVickar led his company through the wilderness to the important fur-trading post of Oswego. His wife and Anne went with him.

However, the rigors of frontier life during wartime probably led the McVickars to make safer arrangements for their daughter. At any rate, Mrs. Philip Pietersz Schuyler (Madam Margaretta

---

Pittoresque du Fleuve Hudson (Paris, 1828–1829); and John James Audubon (1785–1851).

Schuyler) took young Anne into her Albany home, "The Flatts," and here she lived for several years. The widowed Madame Schuyler was the American lady of the book title. Through this mentor, young Anne became a short-time intimate of the Schuylers' home and their family friends.

After the conquest of Canada in 1763, Captain McVickar resigned his commission and took up a land grant in present Vermont. By 1768 he returned to Scotland with his wife and child. Anne, aged thirteen, left the New World, never to see it again. In 1799, she married the Rev. James Grant and moved with him to the Parish of Laggan, Scotland. Left a widow in 1801, Mrs. Grant turned to writing to support her children.

Her poems were collected into an octavo volume in 1802 for three thousand subscribers. She followed this work in 1806 by *Letters from the Mountains,* a book which found wide acceptance among the followers of Rousseau, who saw the Highlanders as a race uncorrupted by the vices of civilization. *Memoirs of an American Lady* (1808) gained admiration from Sir Walter Scott and Robert Southey. By 1810 Mrs. Grant returned to Edinburgh where she published *Essays on the Superstitions of the Highlanders* (1810), *Eighteen Hundred and Thirteen* (1814), a metrical poem, and *Popular Models and Impressive Warnings for the Sons and Daughters of Industry* (1815). Her house in Edinburgh, where she was known as Mrs. Grant of Laggan, was frequented by such luminaries as Scott, Francis Jeffrey, and Henry Mackenzie. She particularly welcomed American visitors.

Memoirs of an American Lady, perhaps Mrs. Grant's most popular work, went through some three English editions and at least five American printings. She wrote the *Memoirs* as an American travel book for a European market, but she found a strong American sale as well. Her selection of the Schuylers, one of New York's outstanding families, and her choice of the exotic scene of Albany and upstate New York made her work attractive to Americans as well as Europeans, for she encompassed the patroon families, wilderness military actions, the fur trade, and Indian life.

An examination of the *Memoirs* contents can perhaps indicate the reasons for its popularity, and suggest its worth as a research tool.

Mrs. Grant, in writing the *Memoirs*, was at least a gentle opportunist. She took full advantage of the public interest in the philosophy of Jean Jacques Rousseau, borrowing the concept that all is good as God made it and all degenerates in man's hand. Her Indians of the New York wilderness were noble savages until the white fur-traders demeaned them through drink and tawdry trade goods. Her headings on this subject included the "Fidelity of the Mohawks" to the English, the "Peculiar Attractions of the Indian mode of Life," and the "Management of the Mohawks by the influence of Christian Indians." The Negro slaves of Albany area families also affected simple virtues, at least until civilization and ignoble man, on occasion, corrupted them. She stressed the "Gentle Treatment of Slaves among the Albanians," "Consequent Attachment of Domestics," and "Reflections on Servitude." The last condition Mrs. Grant found to be good.[2] Nature, as God formed it, and innocent man, uninfluenced and unformed by European values and tastes, were Mrs. Grant's ideal. Indeed, the simple American-Dutch Albanians, as represented by the Schuylers with their rustic way of life, won her warm approval.

Aunt Schuyler or Madam Schuyler, the American lady of the *Memoirs*, was born in 1701, the daughter of John Schuyler, and was christened Margaretta. In 1719, she married her first cousin, Colonel Philip Pietersz (1691–1758), son of Pieter Philipse Schuyler (1657–1724). They inherited "The Flatts" (de Vlackte), a farm or bouwerie which received its name as early as 1642 from the low land of the Hudson River frontage which it occupied to the north of Albany. Mrs. Grant described this particular site as a fertile and beautiful plain about two miles in length.

Mrs. Grant had moved in the highest society of colonial New York. Her remembered Albany world was that of a family con-

2. Anne Grant, *Memoirs of an American Lady* (New York, 1846), table of contents, pp. 9–10.

nected by blood and marriage to the Hudson Valley Cuylers, Van Rensselaers, Van Cortlandts, De Lanceys, DePeysters, Livingstons, Philipses, Douws, and Beekmans. These were the wealthy merchants, the great landowners who dominated the colony's economic, social, and political life. Her Albany was a small fortified village, approximately six city blocks in length and five city blocks in width. It served as a busy shipping center for wheat, produce, and timber, and as the focus of the Indian trade in furs. It was a community still predominantly Dutch in character.

Peter Kalm had written in 1749, "The inhabitants of Albany and its environs are almost all Dutchmen. They speak Dutch, have Dutch preachers, and the divine service is performed in that language. Their manners are likewise quite Dutch."[3] Of the twenty-six mayors of the town from 1686 to 1778, twenty-four were of Dutch origin or descent, one was of English background, and one was Scotch. Almost all followed the traditional Dutch occupation of trade. Twenty-one were merchants, one was a brewer, one a military man, and one an interpreter to the Indians.[4]

Dr. Hamilton criticized Albany in 1744, "I now begin to be quite tired of this place, where there was no variety or choice, either of company or conversation, and one's ears perpetually invaded and molested with volleys of rough-sounding Dutch, which is the language most in use here." Commencing a return voyage by sloop from Albany to New York, this Baltimore physician complained, "I heard nothing but Dutch spoke all the way. My fellow passenger Volkert Douw could speak some English, but had as little in him to enliven conversation as any young fellow ever I knew that looked like a gentleman."[5]

Next to New York City, Albany was the principal town, or at least the most wealthy, in the province of New York. It had two

3. Peter Kalm, *Peter Kalm's Travels in North America*, ed. Adolph B. Benson, 2 vols. (New York, 1966), 1: 343.
4. Cuyler Reynolds, *Albany Chronicles* (Albany, N.Y., 1906), passim.
5. Alexander Hamilton, *Hamilton's Itinerarium*, ed. A. B. Hart (St. Louis, Mo., 1907), pp. 84, 85, 86. Douw later became Albany's twenty-fifth mayor, serving from 1761 to 1770.

stone churches, one Dutch, the other English. The Dutch church stood a short distance from the river on the east side of the market. The English church, situated on the hill to the west of the market, lay directly below the fort. To the south of the Dutch church, close by the riverside, was the fine town hall or *Stadt Huis*, three stories high, with a small tower or steeple with a bell and a gilt ball and a vane at its top.

Kalm wrote, "The houses in this town are very neat, and partly built of stones covered with shingles of white pine. Some are slated with tile from Holland. . . . Most of the houses are built in the old Frankish way, with the gable-ends towards the street. . . . The streets are broad and some of them are paved. In some parts they are lined with trees. The long streets are almost parallel to the river, and the others intersect them at right angles. The street which goes between the two churches is five times broader than the others and serves as a market place. . . . There are no city gates here but for the most part just open holes through which people pass in and out of the town."[6]

As to the fort which the McVickars knew well, Kalm noted, "It is a great building of stone surrounded with high and thick walls. Its location is very bad. . . . There are numerous high hills to the west of the fort, which command it, and from which one may see all that is done within it. There is commonly an officer and a number of soldiers quartered in it. . . ."[7]

Peter Kalm had described the basic topographical features of the community in which Anne Grant would live more than a decade later. She saw this town with other eyes. To her it was "a kind of semi-rural establishment; every house had its garden, well, and a little green behind; before every door a tree was planted. . . . At one end of the town . . . was a common pasture where all the cattle belonging to the inhabitants grazed together. . . . At the other end of the town was a fertile plain along the river, three miles in length, and near a mile broad. This was all divided into

6. Kalm, *Travels*, 1: 340–342.
7. Ibid., pp. 340–342.

lots, where every inhabitant raised Indian corn sufficient for the food of two or three slaves (the greatest number that each family ever possessed), and for his horses, pigs, and poultry."[8]

The main occupations of Albany were agriculture and trade. Wheat, the major crop, was ground into flour or baked into bread-stuffs for export. Again, Kalm noted the local patterns. "Albany carries on a considerable commerce with New York, chiefly in furs, boards, wheat, flour, peas, and several kinds of timber, etc. There is not a place in all the British colonies, the Hudson's Bay settlements excepted, where such quantities of furs and skins are bought of the Indians as at Albany. Most of the merchants in this town send a clerk or agent to Oswego, an English trading town on Lake Ontario, to which the Indians come with their furs. . . . The merchants from Albany spend the whole summer at Oswego, and trade with many tribes of Indians who come with their goods. Many people have assured me that the Indians are frequently cheated in disposing of their goods, especially when they are drunk, and that sometimes they do not get one-half or even one-tenth of the value of their goods."[9]

The Oswego experience was a necessary part of the education of the Albany youth. Mrs. Grant complained that all Albany boys carried guns and that they were apt "to range the whole day in search of game, to the neglect of all intellectual improvement."[10] This early training was invaluable to a lad living on the edge of the northern and western wilderness. He began his business life by securing a canoe and loading it with those goods necessary for the Indian fur trade. Favorite supplies were muskets, powder, shot and balls, white cloth with blue or red stripes on the edge, blue or red cloth for skirts, shirts and shifts of linen, hatchets, knives, scissors, needles, flint, kettles of copper or brass, earrings, cinnabar and verdigris for painting the face and body, looking glasses, burning glasses, tobacco, wampum, glass beads, brass and steel wire, and

8. Grant, *Memoirs*, pp. 32–34.
9. Kalm, *Travels*, 1: 342.
10. Grant, *Memoirs*, pp. 41–42.

brandy and rum. His canoe loaded, he set out into the woods, following waterways insofar as possible.

The young trader then invested the profits of such a trip on his return to Albany in flour and provisions for shipment via New York City to the West Indies, where they were sold or exchanged for rum, sugar, and molasses. Such a two-pronged venture put a young man well into a career of trade and commerce. If such employment was not to his liking, however, he might purchase European goods with his furs and set up a retail store. "Otherwise he settled in the country and became as diligent in his agricultural pursuits as if he had never known any other."[11] Thus a young man found his life's work.

Mrs. Grant, writing at length on this subject, omitted the major area of education and learning. To carry on a successful business of any sort, a man required a basic knowledge of reading, writing and arithmetic. General education in the Albany area may not have been of the highest standards by the 1760s, but it would appear probable as early as 1664, based on signatures to documents, petitions, and other legal papers, that the majority of New Netherlanders could at least write their own names. Albany's first schoolmaster, Evert Nolden, was at work by 1648. By 1760, the Dutch of the province had been cognizant for more than a century of the practical values of the written word and figure.

The Hudson Valley Dutch were always a lusty, vital, and independent people. Not surprisingly, Mrs. Grant did not see this whole body of beings. She restricted her Albany world to one fortunate and ruling social group. But by supplying details of the Schuylers' life at "The Flatts" in the decade after 1758, Mrs. Grant has provided "not only a knowledge of that particular household but a guage by which to measure the ways of other homes in Albany at the same time. Manners and customs at "The Flatts" were the maximum of elegance and of comfort in that vicinity at the date of Mrs. Grant's sojourn there, and to form a

11. Ibid., p. 52.

general idea of the standard of living where the standard was the highest within a given area makes it possible to estimate gradations in detail in smaller houses and among people of lesser wealth."[12] This standard of comparison is perhaps the lasting value of Mrs. Grant's work.

In the year of Colonel Schuyler's death (1758), the house at "The Flatts" caught fire and its roof and interior were destroyed. General John Bradstreet himself helped to extinguish the blaze. Madam Schuyler rebuilt the wing, or west portion, that same year. Later she restored the main portion, with a gambrel roof rather than its original steep pitched one. This renewed house, obviously, was the structure known by Mrs. Grant in her brief Albany childhood. She described it in great detail:

> The house . . . had no pretension to grandeur and very little to elegance. It was a large brick house of two, or rather three, stories (for there were excellent attics), besides a sunk story finished with the exactest neatness. The lower floor had two spacious rooms, with large closets; on the first there were three rooms, and in the upper one four. Through the middle of the house was a very wide passage, with opposite front and back doors, which in summer admitted a stream of air. . . . It was furnished with chairs and pictures like a summer parlor. Here the family usually sat in hot weather, when there were no ceremonious strangers.[13]

Fine furniture was a favorite luxury of Albanians, and the Schuylers were no exception. "The Flatts" housed mirrors, paintings, and china. They kept rooms closed so that the flies in summer would not soil the furniture and so that the temperature might be pleasantly cool when they were opened. They opened one room only, a sitting room or parlor, for the reception of company. All the rest were bedchambers for guests. The best bedroom was hung with paintings, "and in the eating room, which, by the by, was rarely used for that purpose, were some fine scripture-

12. Helen Wilkinson Reynolds, *Dutch Houses in the Hudson Valley before 1776* (New York, 1965), pp. 57–58.
13. Grant, *Memoirs*, p. 83.

paintings," including "one of Esau coming to demand the anticipated blessing."[14]

"At the back of the large house was a smaller and lower one.
There one or two lower and smaller rooms below, and the same
number above, afforded a refuge to the family during the rigors of
winter, when the spacious summer-rooms would have been intoler-
ably cold, and the smoke of prodigious wood-fires would have
sullied the elegantly clean furniture. Here, too, was a sunk story,
where the kitchen was immediately below the eating parlor, and
increased the general warmth of the house. In summer the negroes
inhabited slight outer kitchens, in which food was dressed for the
family." These winter-rooms had carpets. The lobby had an oil-
cloth or floor cloth painted in lozenges to imitate blue and white
marble.[15]

A second appendage to the main house was a portico at the
front door. Open at the sides, it had seats all around, while above a
roof of latticework supported a wild grapevine. A small shelf, built
high within this portico or porch, provided a safe nesting place for
birds, mainly wrens, to keep down the insect population. Additional bird nests were provided. Horse and cow skulls were
mounted high on the top of wood poles sunk into the ground, and
wrens lived safely within the craniums. Old hats, having small
round holes in their crowns, were nailed by their brims along the
kitchen walls as further nesting places.[16]

This rebuilt Schuyler house, "The Flatts," as described by Mrs.
Grant, was quite typical of its period in the upper Hudson Valley,
indicating as it did a gradual architectural development. An architectural description such as this, for the mid-eighteenth century, is
rare and has great interest for the social historian.

Seventeenth- and early eighteenth-century Hudson Valley farm-
houses and cottages were basically simple structures, quite similar
to their European counterparts. Two different floor plans were in

14. Ibid., pp. 83, 86.
15. Ibid., pp. 85, 86.
16. Ibid., pp. 83, 86, 87.

common use. The first was the square or rectangular one-room house, with a cellar below and a storage or sleeping area above, under the roof. The lower and upper rooms were reached from the main floor by ladders rather than by stairs. The second basic floor form consisted of two rooms on the ground floor, with two cellar rooms below and a storage or sleeping area under the roof. Infinite variations of each house type occurred owing to site demands and local needs and because of inevitable expansion to meet the needs of the occupying family.

By the middle of the eighteenth century, well-to-do families began to build or remodel existing houses in a simple English Georgian manner. They then based their homes on a central stair-hall with balanced rooms opening off each side of this center axis. Based on increasingly Anglicized architectural tastes in the eighteenth-century Hudson Valley, "The Flatts" probably followed fashion in its reconstruction. The rear or winter wing of this structure, with its one or two rooms below and the same number above, was unquestionably the earliest house at this location. The broad center-halled main section, with its portico, was definitely a later addition in the new mid-century style. It must always be remembered that Anne McVickar Grant could not have known this building before the fire of 1758, when she was brought to America at the age of three.

Anne Grant lived in Albany for approximately three years, for the period between her seventh and tenth birthdays. She quit America in 1768 and published her *Memoirs of an American Lady* some forty years later. How accurate were her memories, her observations? Many of them, describing her childhood surroundings, were reasonably bright and clear. Other memories may well have become clouded by time. Some came perhaps from other eyes and minds. It has been suggested, indeed, that certain of her statements depended on facts supplied through stories told her by her parents in later years, comments she had heard in the Schuyler household, and facts she gleaned from reading other authors.

For example, the first theatrical performance given in Albany, the *Beaux Stratagem,* had as its actors the British officers stationed in that city. Mrs. Grant criticized this play and its performers as the "very ultimate of degeneracy" in the opinions of the "simple good people" of the community.[17] Yet, this play was presented during the winter of 1757, and Mrs. Grant, then two years of age, had not yet arrived in New York from Scotland.

Grant Thorburn of New York City interviewed Mrs. Grant at Edinburgh in 1834, finding her still a woman of sound mind and body. On the basis of that conversation, Thorburn termed her *Memoirs* "not a romance; nor a novel, nor a fiction, nor a tale partly founded on reality—but . . . an authentic detail of facts."[18] Mrs. Grant herself, however, noted the dim distance of forty years' time between her living in Albany and her writing about it, unassisted by notes. Her main tools in re-creating that past were, she claimed, "a warm heart, a vivid imagination, and a tenacious memory."[19]

The authenticity of Mrs. Grant's facts as claimed by Thorburn poses interesting questions in evaluating the *Memoirs.* Many simple household details concerning Madam Schuyler and "The Flatts" could only have been known to an observant person living in that family circle. While Peter Kalm claimed that the Albany Dutch were stingy with their food, Mrs. Grant found in her social circle a more varied and festive selection of food.

Mrs. Grant recalled that her benefactress, Madam Schuyler, carefully divided a typical day into activity periods. She noted that "Aunt was a great manager of her time, and always managed to create leisure hours for reading." Madam Schuyler began her morning by reading the Scriptures. Breakfast was served at an early hour so that she might have a longer forenoon. After breakfast she gave the instructions for the day to her assistants and servants. She then retired to her closet to read until eleven o'clock. Emerging, she sought, in summer, a shaded part of her garden for conversation

17. Ibid., p. 156.
18. Ibid., Introduction, p. 3.
19. Ibid., Introduction, p. 15.

with her husband and close friends on religion and morality, subjects considered too weighty for casual tabletalk. This, too, was a time for planning future activities. Before the two o'clock dinner hour, Mrs. Schuyler moved to the front portico at "The Flatts." Here she could best meet anyone who cared to call, though personal friends were generally received in the afternoon before the hour for early tea. After tea, she scheduled a period for light reading or for knitting on the portico. Madam Schuyler's light reading consisted of essays, biography, and poetry. Next came a light supper. It must be presumed that there were evening prayers before the lady retired.[20]

This is an interesting account of a typical summer day in the life of a pious lady on the northern frontier. One cannot help but wonder how much Mrs. Grant transferred the daily pattern of the upper-class lady in Edinburgh to Madam Schuyler in Albany.

As to reading, Mrs. Grant recalled few specific books in her Albany years. she had had the use of Bailey's *Dictionary*, Milton, and Shakespeare. She had found comfort in the *Old Testament*, and in "Welwood's memoirs of the history of England." Surprisingly, in a society which appears to have read daily, she mentioned little else by title. Her references are all general, as was her description of Major Duncan McVickar's select and soldier-like library at Oswego, which consisted of volumes on military art, history, biography, various sciences, geography, and mathematics.[21]

Libraries had existed, and did exist. As early as 1642 a small private library was recorded in Albany. The inventory of Nicholas van Rensselaer's estate in 1678–1679 listed two hundred books, for the most part in foreign languages. Two notable New York libraries of the eighteenth century were those of the Rev. Mr. John Sharpe (inventoried in 1712–1713) and of Governor Montgomery (sold in 1732). The latter notably contained Cicero, Horace, Ovid, Seneca, Addison, Dryden, Defoe, Milton, Pope, Shakespeare, Spenser, and Bacon.

20. Ibid., pp. 136, 138.
21. Ibid., pp. 198–200.

Mrs. Grant, in preparing her first edition, could have known the works of Peter Kalm and Dr. Alexander Hamilton and could have used them for guidance and recall. While appearances seem to be against her acquaintance with Hamilton, a comparison of subject matter indicates she could well have read Kalm. Certainly much of Kalm's Albany material is present in some form, however abbreviated or enlarged, in Mrs. Grant's writings, though she changed the order of facts and the wordings. Perhaps Kalm's words spurred her "tenacious memory." However, the Albany-related remarks of Hamilton and Kalm were minor parts of their travel volumes. Mrs. Grant, by comparison, devoted the greater portions of her *Memoirs* to the city, its inhabitants, and its local customs.

All three writers agreed on certain points. The plan of the city, religion, trade, food, architecture, and social patterns caught the interests of each commentator, and each revealed his or her personal prejudices. The two men were obviously more objective than the lady in their viewpoints. They found as much to ridicule and dislike in the local character as they found to admire. Mrs. Grant, however, recalled an idyllic and pastoral town, where almost everything was good and kind. She could disregard, or not recall, the unpleasant and the coarse. To her, all aspects of Albany life had a basic native nobility. However the *Memoirs* were inspired and created, they have a real soundness. This is certified by a full comparison with the words of Hamilton and Kalm. If Mrs. Grant embroidered fact, it must be recalled that in Albany she knew little else than the Schuyler world; in her home country of Scotland, she moved in the better circles. If Mrs. Grant re-created, even in part, a world she would have liked to have lived in, she can be forgiven. Her warmness of heart produced an unusual narrative for the study of a town and its people in transition from a Dutch past to an English present.